A DESCRIPTIVE AND HISTORICAL ACCOUNT OF THE GODAVERY DISTRICT IN THE PRESIDENCY OF MADRAS

A DESCRIPTIVE AND HISTORICAL ACCOUNT OF THE GODAVERY DISTRICT IN THE PRESIDENCY OF MADRAS

BY

HENRY MORRIS,
FORMERLY OF MADRAS CIVIL SERVICES,
AUTHOR OF "A HISTORY OF INDIA FOR USE IN SCHOOLS,"
AND OTHER WORKS

GYAN

Published by

Gyan Publishing House
5, Ansari Road
Daryaganj, New Delhi-110002
Phone: 011-47034999, 9811692060
E-mail: books@gyanbooks.com

Distribution Network
gyanbooks.com
India, USA, Canada, UK, Australia, France

ISBN : 978-81-212-3311-8 (PB)
First Published, London, 1878

2nd Impression 2020

Printed at: Gyan Press, Delhi.

A Descriptive
and Historical Account of the Godavery District
in
The Presidency of Madras
Author: Henry Morris

A DESCRIPTIVE AND HISTORICAL ACCOUNT

OF THE

GODAVERY DISTRICT

IN

THE PRESIDENCY OF MADRAS.

BY

HENRY MORRIS,

Formerly of the Madras Civil Service,

AUTHOR OF "A HISTORY OF INDIA FOR USE IN SCHOOLS,"
AND OTHER WORKS.

LONDON:
TRÜBNER & CO., LUDGATE HILL.
1878.

PREFACE.

The following monograph is one of a series of descriptive memoirs of all the Districts in the Madras Presidency, which is being prepared under the direction of the Government. It is, however, in one respect unique. It is the history of a District which owes its prosperity to the benefits derived from judicious irrigation; and it is, therefore, of special interest at the present time. The attention of the people of England has been attracted to this subject by the terrible famine which has recently desolated Southern India. The immediate effects of this sad visitation are happily passing away; but the recollection of it cannot easily be effaced, and remedies against similar calamities are being diligently sought. The Godavery District is a proof of the incalculable advantages of irrigation, which, when carefully planned and energetically carried out, is an effectual remedy against famine, wherever it can be applied with any hope of success.

This volume has not only received the imprimatur of the Board of Revenue at Madras, to whom it was officially submitted, but those portions of it which relate to their own labours were submitted to Sir Arthur Cotton, by whose genius principally the District has been rendered prosperous; to Sir Henry C. Montgomery, whose wise suggestions tended to remove many of the evils by which it was once impoverished;

to Sir Walter Elliot, formerly Commissioner of the Northern Circars, to whose researches in antiquarian lore Southern India is deeply indebted; to Mr. George Noble Taylor, whose efforts have done so much to encourage the growth of elementary education; and to Mr. R. E. Master, under whose careful supervision the new Settlement has recently been introduced. They have all kindly expressed their entire approval.

My special thanks are due to the Collector, Mr. W. S. Foster, to Mr. J. Hope, who for a time acted as Collector, and to their native subordinates for their assistance, more particularly in preparing the statistics, which must have entailed on them very considerable labour. The authorities in the Record, the Statistical, and the Geographical Departments of the India Office have most courteously afforded me every help in their power, for which I cordially thank them.

H. MORRIS.

CONTENTS.

CHAPTER I.

GENERAL DESCRIPTION OF THE DISTRICT.

CHAPTER II.

DESCRIPTION OF THE PRINCIPAL TOWNS AND OTHER PLACES OF IMPORTANCE.

CHAPTER III.

THE PORTS OF COCANADA AND CORINGA.

PAGE

CHAPTER VIII.

ANCIENT HISTORY.

CHAPTER IX.

EARLY ENGLISH SETTLEMENTS.

CHAPTER X.

THE DUTCH AND FRENCH SETTLEMENTS.

CHAPTER XI.

THE MOHAMMEDAN PERIOD.

PAGE

CHAPTER XII.

EXPULSION OF THE FRENCH.

CHAPTER XIII.

EARLY ENGLISH ADMINISTRATION.

CHAPTER XIV.

THE FIRST COLLECTORATES.

CHAPTER XV.

THE PERMANENT SETTLEMENT.

PAGE

CHAPTER XVI.

RECENT HISTORY.

CHAPTER XVII.

THE REVENUE SURVEY AND SETTLEMENT.

THE GODAVERY DISTRICT.

CHAPTER I.

GENERAL DESCRIPTION OF THE DISTRICT.

BOUNDARIES AND AREA — DESCRIPTION OF THE RIVER GODAVERY — GENERAL SURVEY OF THE DELTA—STATISTICAL DESCRIPTION OF THE VARIOUS DIVISIONS OF THE DISTRICT.

THE Godavery District is one of the five Northern Circars, which form the most northern province of the Presidency of Madras. It is of a rather irregular shape, but compact and accessible, its length being not very much greater than its breadth, and Rajahmundry, the principal town, being situated almost in the centre. It is divided into nearly equal parts by the river Godavery. It lies between 16° 18′ and 17° 56′ 35″ N. lat., and 80° 56′ and 82° 40′ E. long. It is bounded on the north by the territory of His Highness the Nizam, and the Central Provinces; on the north-east by the District of Vizagapatam; on the east and south by the Bay of Bengal; and on the west by the Kistna District. Its area is 6224 square miles.

The District forms a portion of the rich belt of land which fringes the Bay of Bengal, and extends to the sea from the mountains that gird the peninsula on the eastern coast. The southern part of the District is flat, and exceedingly fertile, especially where it is irrigated by the innumerable canals and channels which branch from the river. Green fields of paddy extend in every direction, diversified by gardens of plantains, betel-nut, and cocoa-nut, and innumerable palmyras are dotted over the surface of the country, particularly near the coast. The north is mountainous. The hills, which commence near the coast in the north-east, and extend along the whole northern frontier of the District proper, are very unhealthy. The highest point is to the west of the magnificent gorge through which the Godavery enters the District. It is called Pápi-konda by the natives, and the Bison Range by the English. Its elevation is 4200 feet. The scenery of these mountains, particularly in the neighbourhood of the river, where the charm of water is added to the beauty of mountain and forest, is exceedingly picturesque. The sides of the mountains are clothed with luxuriant forests of teak, interspersed with bamboo and a thick undergrowth of forest shrubs.

The river Godavery rises at Trimbak, a village about sixteen miles west of Násik, and about fifty miles from the sea. The place which is traditionally regarded as the source of the river is on a hill behind the village. It is approached by a flight of 690 stone steps, flanked by a low stone wall. At the top of these steps is a stone platform built at the foot of the rock, out of which, drop by drop, issues the water of the stream, and an image under a canopy has been so placed that the water trickles through its mouth into a reservoir.*

After leaving Násik, the Godavery flows in an easterly direction, slightly declining towards the south, until, after it has completed a course of 650 miles, it receives, at Sironcha, the noble affluents, the Wardhá, the Painganga, and the Wainganga, united in the single stream called the Pranhíta. The remaining course of the Godavery to the sea is 200 miles, and before it enters this District it receives on the left two more considerable affluents, namely, the Indrávati and the Sabari. The following account of the course of the river from the Falls of the Wardhá to the gorge is taken from a description by Sir Richard Temple, who was formerly Chief Commissioner of the Central Provinces:—

"Starting from the Falls of the Wardhá near Hinganghát, the voyager would see on the right hand the wild hilly country of the Nizam's dominions, and on the left, or British side, a broad level valley covered with cultivation. Further down the river, past the junction of the Painganga, as the third or upper barrier is approached, the rich valley on the left becomes narrower and narrower, more

* Madras Church Missionary Record for March 1873.

and more trenched upon by hill and forest, till it is restricted to a fringe of cultivation along the river's bank, while, on the right, the country somewhat improves, and, though still hilly, is more open. The junction of the Wainganga is hidden from view by the hills. The barrier itself lies closed in by rocky hills and dense forests, a narrow strip being left on the right bank. Below the barrier the river is called the Pranhíta. On the left the hills at first arrange themselves in picturesque groups, one of which has been compared to the group of the Seven Mountains on the Rhine, and after that continue for many miles almost to overhang the river, sometimes displaying the fine foliage and blossoms of the teak-tree down to the water's edge. On the opposite side the next noticeable feature is the mouth of the Bibriá stream, justly noted for its beauty. Further down, on the left side, the only point of note is Sironcha, with its old fort overlooking the water; the country continuing to be hilly or jungly with patches of cultivation. But, on the other side, the junction of the Godavery proper causes great tongues of land and broad basins to be formed, all which are partially cultivated, and are dotted over by several towns. Then hills of some variety and beauty cluster thick round the second or middle barrier. The junction of the Indrávati also is concealed by the hills. Below this, on the left side, long ranges of hills, rising one above the other, run almost parallel with the river, till the junction of the Tál is reached. On the opposite side the country is more cultivated and open, and marked by the towns of Nagaram and Mangampet. Below the latter place, again, the sacred hill of Rutab Guttá rises into view, immediately opposite to Dumagúdem, where the headquarters of the navigation department are established. Proceeding downwards, at the first or lower barrier the country is comparatively level on both sides, and this barrier is far less formidable than the two preceding ones. Below the barrier, down to the junction of the Sabari, the prominent object on the British side consists of the small hills of Bhadráchalam, crowned with the cupolas, cones, and spires of Hindu temples. On the opposite side is the Tank region, which extending inland some 250 miles to beyond Warangole, the capital of the ancient Telingana, is marked by the remains of countless works of agricultural improvement, attesting a wisdom in the past not known to the native dynasties of the present. Near the junction of the Sabari the river scenery begins to assume an imposing appearance. Hitherto, as it passed each barrier and gained successive steps in its course, the river has been increasing in width, generally being a mile broad, and sometimes even two and a half miles. Here also the whole range of the Eastern Ghauts comes fully into view, some 2500 feet high, bounding the whole horizon, and towering over all the lesser and detached hills that flank the river. Passing the Sabari junction, the Godavery becomes more and more contracted and pressed on either side by spurs of the main range, till at length it forces a passage between them, penetrating by an almost precipitous gorge through the heart of the mountains that mark the frontier of the Central Provinces." *

The gorge through which the Godavery enters the plains forms one of the most beautiful pieces of scenery in Southern India. The best time to see it in all its grandeur is, unfortunately, the most dangerous to the health. During the rainy, and, consequently, the feverish, season the forest trees put on their most luxuriant foliage, whereas later in the season, the underwood, especially the bamboos, and the grass, are parched by the continual glare of the sun; and the river itself is not at its full height. I have seen the gorge at both seasons; I have looked down on the river from the mountains which overhang it; and I have passed through the winding stream, as the early morning sun gradually lighted up hill after hill, leaving the water in shade, and as the setting sun has gradually left the valley in gloom; and I can confidently assert that I have never witnessed more exquisite scenery even on the Neilgherries or the Shevaroys. As the steamer glides into the gorge, the low, broken hills which had previously adorned the banks of the river disappear, and the mountains close up to the water's edge, in one place the two sides approaching as near each other as 200 yards, and the precipitous banks appearing near enough even to be touched. They then open out, and again approach each other, forming successively beautiful little lakes, resembling Highland lochs, from which there is apparently no outlet. Sir Charles Trevelyan compares the scenery to that of the Rhine between Coblentz and Bingen; but it lacks the signs of human life which adorn, and the historical antiquities which beautify, the European stream. Here and there a faint line of smoke indicates the existence of a Koi village; but the hills are very sparsely inhabited, and there are very few villages near the river-banks.

* Grant's Gazetteer of the Central Provinces, 2d edition, p. 198.

When it enters the plain, the river widens. It passes the large villages of Dévipatnam and Purushottapatnam on the left bank, and Pólavaram and Gútála on the right. Before reaching Gútala, it passes round the picturesque island of Páta-Patesham, on which there is a Hindu temple situated on a craggy hill, whither hundreds of pilgrims flock at the annual festival in the month of February. Here, and in the whole of its future downward course, the rapid stream continually forms new islands or modifies old ones; and these constant changes are the fruitful source of litigation between the riparian proprietors. The friction of the water, which every year, during the freshes, brings down in its course the most fertilising alluvial soil, renders these islands exceedingly fruitful, the tobacco for which this District is noted being the crop most commonly grown. It has received the name of "Lanka tobacco," from the word *lanka*, which signifies "an island." Many of these islands are covered in December and January with the *rellu* or flowering reed, which, when its wavy white flowers bend before the breeze, is as beautiful as a field of ripened wheat. As the river draws near Rajahmundry, it presses against the right bank, which is, in many places, cut down precipitously by the action of the stream, and Tálapúdi, and other villages, which used to be a little distance from the river, are now on the very verge of the bank. Passing Rajahmundry on the left bank—where the court-house, the judge's residence, the great pagoda, and the houses in the western part of the town, with the hills in the distance, form a charming scene—it is barred at Dowlaishweram by the celebrated Annicut, by which the water is kept back during the dry season, and distributed in every direction throughout the delta by innumerable watercourses and canals.

At Dowlaishweram the Godavery is divided into two large streams—the eastern, flowing past Yanam and Nílapalli, and falling into the Bay of Bengal near Cape Gordeware or Godavery; and the western, flowing nearly due south, and entering the bay at Point Nursapore. A few miles above this mouth another large branch separates from the river, and falls into the bay near Bendamúrlanka, forming the island of Nagaram. The three early English factories, Injaram, Bendamúrlanka, and Madapollam, were situated near these three principal mouths of the Godavery. The rich delta was formerly known by the name of Kóna Shíma. The Hindus say that there are seven branches by which the river debouches into the sea, the principal of which are the Gautami, the Vriddha or the Old Gautami, the Vainatéyam, the Kausika, and the Vasishta.

The Godavery is regarded by the Hindus as a peculiarly sacred stream. It is considered to flow from the same source as the Ganges, but underground, and it is frequently called by the same name. The eastern branch, after its division into several streams at Dowlaishweram, is called the Gautami, and, if possible, is looked on as more holy than the rest of the river. Once every twelve years a feast called *Pushkaram* is held on the banks of the Godavery, in turn with the eleven other sacred streams of India, and pilgrims come from all parts of the land to bathe in its waters. At its source, near Trimbak; in every part of its downward course, especially at the pagoda a little north of Rajahmundry, and at Kótiphali on the left bank of the eastern stream; it is considered to be peculiarly sacred at these times, and every sin is considered to be washed away by those who bathe in it. Crowds gather on the river-bank morning, noon, and night, and convert the most favoured resorts into huge standing camps for the twelve days during which the festival lasts.

The District consists of nine Taluks and of four Divisions, as mentioned below. The former include Government villages, and small Zemindári and Proprietary estates. The latter comprise only Zemindári and Proprietary villages.

TALUKS.	DIVISIONS.
1. Rámachandrapuram 2. Narasápuram 3. Amalápuram	1. Cocanada.
4. Tanuku 5. Bhímavaram	2. Pittápuram.
6. Rajahmundry 7. Peddápuram	3. Coringa.
8. Ellore 9. Yarnagúdem	4. Tuni.

The Taluks of Bhadráchalam and Rékapalli have recently been transferred to this District from the Central Provinces, and have been placed under the provisions of the Scheduled Districts Act (No. xiv. of 1874).

1. RÁMACHANDRAPURAM TALUK.

The Taluk of Rámachandrapuram is the largest and most important of all. It is of the first class. It contains 131 Government villages, and 28 Zemindári villages, and 4 Agrahárams and Mokhásás. It is situated in the centre of the District, being bounded on the south by the Gautami branch of the Godavery, on the north by the Taluk of Peddápuram and the Division of Cocanada, on the east by the Gautami branch of the Godavery, and on the west by the Taluk of Rajahmundry.

The area of the Taluk is 507 square miles. The population is 203,583. According to the quinquennial returns of 1866–67 it was 184,110, so that the increase since then has been 19,473. Of the present population 200,345 are Hindus, 3205 Mohammedans, and 5 Christians. There are 44,000 houses in the Taluk, of which 42,981 are inhabited. The cultivable area is 89,963 acres, assessed by the Settlement Department at 269,283 rupees.

The revenue of the Taluk for Fasli 1282, including the assessment of the lands under occupation, water cess, the permanently-settled Bériz, or fixed revenues from Zemindáris, and other miscellaneous items, amounts to 833,968 rupees. The following are the details :—

	Rupees.
Land assessment	325,513
Water cess	417,354
Permanently-settled Bériz and Shrótriyam Jódi.	22,968
Other miscellaneous items . . .	68,133
	833,968

The rates of the land assessment, both for dry and wet cultivation, according to the new Survey and Settlement, which were introduced into this Taluk in Fasli 1276, vary from 6 annas to 20 rupees an acre.

The rates are consolidated when the water is received from tanks and mountain streams. When lands assessed at dry rates are irrigated from the Annicut channels, water cess is levied separately, according to the rates prescribed for each crop raised, namely, 4 rupees an acre for wet crops, 2 rupees for dry crops, 4 rupees for garden crops, and 8 rupees when they require water throughout the whole year.

This Taluk is amply supplied with the means of irrigation. There are six Annicut main canals running through it in various directions, namely, the Cocanada canal, the Samulcotta canal, the Coringa canal, the Yanam canal, the Mandapéta canal, and the Injaram canal. These are used both for irrigation and navigation. There are numerous minor irrigation channels, which are branches of the above main canals.

The products of the Taluk are chiefly paddy, Bengal gram, horse gram, green gram, black gram, red gram, gingelly and lamp oil seeds, hemp, coriander, fenugreek, mustard, jonna, cumboo, raggy, tobacco, sugar-cane, chillies, onions, garlic, turmeric, yams, country yams, and sweet potatoes.

The soil is of ten different sorts and classes, as follows:—Alluvial, permanently improved, regur pure (*régadi* in Telugu, usually called the black cotton soil), regur loamy, regur sandy, red clay, red loamy, red sandy, arenaceous loamy, and arenaceous sandy.

Most of the Taluk is flat, only a few villages being on high rocky ground.

There are swamps in a few villages. The Gautami branch of the Godavery flows to the south and east of the Taluk, and falls into the sea near a village called Tírtálamondi in the Taluk of Amalápuram.

In the Gautami Godavery there are several islands, usually called in this District *lankas*, which have been formed by the accumulation of sand and alluvium brought down by the freshes. These lankas are continually changing, some years being fertilised anew by the Godavery freshes; but sometimes they are completely washed away or covered with sand, and thus rendered unfit for cultivation.

The Taluk is productive and healthy; but in the cold season it is feverish, because almost all the ground lying round the villages is under water. The principal towns of the Taluk, together with their population, according to the last census, are entered below.

Towns.	Population.
Mandapéta	5440
Dráksháráma	2845
Álamúru	2395
Rámachandrapuram	2075

There is no special industry in this Taluk. The trade is chiefly in paddy, grain, oil seeds, &c., as well as in cloths manufactured in the

Taluk. These are bought by merchants residing in the Taluk, who transmit them to Cocanada and to other places, where they are freely sold for exportation.

The approximate average out-turn of the harvest in the Taluk in each grain, with its corresponding value, is as follows :—

	Out-turn in Garces.	Value in Rupees.
Paddy . . .	31,500	1,575,000
Raggy . . .	1,670	67,000
Jonna . . .	1,000	50,000
Other food grains . .	1,670	67,000
Oil seeds . . .	1,670	200,000
Other crops . .	430	21,000
	37,940	1,980,000
Tobacco (in puttis) .	3,000	150,000
		2,130,000

Nearly half of the above products is consumed in the Taluk, and the rest is exported. There are no imports.

2. Narasápuram Taluk.

This Taluk is of the second class, and therefore ranks in size and in importance next to Rámachandrapuram. It is composed of 139 villages, 120 being Government villages, 13 Zemindári and Proprietary villages, and 6 Agrahárams. It is situated in the south of the District, being bounded on the north by the Taluks of Tanuku and Bhímavaram, on the east by the Vainatéyam branch of the Godavery and the Taluk of Amalápuram, on the west by the Taluk of Bhímavaram, and on the south by the sea.

The area of the Taluk is 450 square miles. The population, according to the last census, was 177,876. According to the quinquennial returns of 1866–67 it was 161,537, so that the increase since that time has been 16,339. The number of Hindus is 174,253; of the Mohammedans, 3447; and of Christians, 147. There are 38,789 houses in the Taluk, of which 36,131 are inhabited. The assessed area is 105,210 acres, bearing an assessment of 234,837 rupees. The revenue of the Taluk for Fasli 1282, including land tax, water cess, quit-rent on Inams, Péshkash, &c., amounts to 578,953 rupees, as particularised below.

	Rupees.
Assessment	213,891
Water cess	301,985
Péshkash	13,865
Other miscellaneous items . .	49,212
	578,953

The new Settlement rates were brought into operation in this Taluk in Fasli 1272.

In regard to the Government lands under the Annicut channels, dry rates have been imposed, subject to a separate cess for water according to the rates prescribed for each crop. They are as described in the Rámachandrapuram Taluk. The rates of water cess are the same for the whole district in regard to Government, Zemindári, and Inam lands.

This Taluk is well supplied with the means of irrigation by three main canals, which are also used for navigation, namely, the Narasápuram canal, the Gannavaram canal, and the Mukkámala canal. There are also numerous minor irrigation channels branching off from the above.

The products of this Taluk are chiefly paddy, Bengal gram, horse gram, cow gram, green gram, black gram, red gram, gingelly and lamp oil seeds, hemp, coriander, fenugreek, mustard, jonna, cumboo, raggy, tobacco, sugar-cane, chillies, onions, garlic, turmeric, yams, country yams, limes, sweet oranges, pumple-noses, ginger, cocoa-nuts, areca-nuts, betel-leaves, and plantains.

The soil of the Taluk is of eight different sorts, namely, permanently improved, regur pure, regur loamy, regur sandy, red loamy, red sandy, arenaceous loamy, arenaceous sandy. The Taluk is flat. Narasápuram, or, as it is usually spelt, Nursapore, is a considerable seaport town. It is the headquarters of the Deputy Collector on General Duties, of the Tahsildar of the Taluk, of the Executive Engineer, and of the Assistant Superintendent of Police. The District Munsiff's Court and office of the Superintendent of Sea Customs are also situated in this town.

Some parts of the Taluk are very swampy. The branch of the Godavery called Vasishta flows through the centre of the Taluk, and falls into the sea near Antravédi. There are some islands in the

Vasishta Godavery, which are fertilised every year by the freshes. The Narasápuram canal is connected with the Godavery by a lock. This affords excellent facilities for the carriage of goods from the interior of the district for exportation. The Taluk is productive and healthy. The principal towns, together with their population according to the census of 1871, are shown below.

Narasápuram	6819
Mogalturru	4860
Pálakollu	4711
Átsanta	5846

The special industry of this Taluk is the manufacture of toys at Narasápuram. Pálakollu is noted for its orchards. The trade of this Taluk is chiefly in paddy, pulses, jaggery, oil seeds, cloths, and cotton twist. These articles are bought by native merchants residing in the Taluk, and exported in considerable quantities. Cotton twist is also imported from England for sale to the weavers, who form a large proportion of the population. Their handiwork formerly enjoyed a world-wide celebrity.

The approximate average out-turn of this Taluk in each grain, with its corresponding value, is mentioned below.

	Out-turn in Garces.	Value in Rupees.
Paddy	15,456	777,300
Jonna	2,660	133,000
Other food grains	1,600	64,000
Oil seeds	1,600	192,000

Nearly half of this quantity is consumed in the Taluk, and the rest is exported.

3. Amalápuram Taluk.

This Taluk ranks among the third class of Taluks, estimated according to the pay of their respective Tahsildars. It contains 172 villages, namely, 114 Government villages, 11 Mokhásás and Agraháramas, and 47 Zemindári and Proprietary villages.

It is bounded on the north by the Gautami branch of the Godavery, and the Rámachandrapuram Taluk, on the south by the sea, on the east by the Coringa Division and the sea, and on the west by the Vasishta branch of the Godavery and by the Narasápuram and Tanuku Taluks.

The area of the Taluk is 437 square miles. The population is 206,885, being nearly the same as that of Rámachandrapuram, according to the census taken in November 1871. According to the quinquennial returns of 1866–67, it was 189,233, so that the subsequent increase has been 17,652. The number of Hindus is 203,668, and of Mohammedans, 3215. This Taluk is the stronghold of Brahminism in the District. It contains 44,378 houses, of which 41,565 are inhabited. The area assessed by the Settlement Department is 68,962 acres, bearing an annual assessment of 203,301 rupees. The land revenue of the Taluk, including water cess, Péshkash, and all the sundry items, is 559,226 rupees.

This Taluk is irrigated by three main canals from the Annicut, namely, the Lolla canal, the Gannavaram canal, and the Amalápuram canal. These supply water to all the various branch irrigation channels. The main canals are navigable.

The principal products of the Taluk are paddy, Bengal gram, horse gram, cow gram, green gram, black gram, red gram, gingelly and lamp oil seeds, coriander, fenugreek, mustard, jonna, cumboo, raggy, tobacco, chillies, onions, garlic, turmeric, cocoa-nuts, areca-nuts, and sweet plantains.

The central part of the Taluk is noted for its cocoa-nut, areca-nut, and plantain plantations.

The soil is of the following descriptions :—Alluvial, permanently improved, regur pure, regur loamy, regur sandy, arenaceous loamy, arenaceous sandy, arenaceous heavy sandy.

This Taluk is flat. Some of the villages are swampy. The Vasishta, the Gautami, the Old Gautami, the Vainatéyam, and the Kausika branches of the Godavery flow through portions of this Taluk, or along its border, in their course to the sea. In the bed of the Vasishta Godavery there are valuable islands formed by accumulated deposits of silt. This Taluk is very rich and productive; and it is generally healthy, but in the cold season it is somewhat feverish.

The principal towns, with their population, according to the census of 1871, are—

Amalápuram	7083
Palivela	5315
Ambájipéta	3657
Ráli	3470

There is no special industry in the Taluk. A good deal of cocoa-nut oil is manufactured. The principal trade is in cocoa-nuts, areca-nuts, cocoa-nut oil, paddy, grains, and oil seeds, cloths, and cotton twist. This Taluk is noted for its luscious plantains and its various vegetable productions. These are exported by sea or by the navigable canals to Cocanada, Rajahmundry, Ellore, and other parts of the District for local consumption.

The out-turn of the harvest and the value of the same can be approximately stated as follows:—

	Out-turn in Garces.	Value in Rupees.
Paddy . . .	9186	459,300
Dry grains . . .	2660	106,400
Cocoa-nuts . . .	1000	60,000
Betel-nuts . . .	1000	36,000

Nearly half of the paddy and grain, and one-third of the vegetables grown, is consumed within the Taluk, and the rest is exported to the other towns in the District. This Taluk imports no articles from other localities, salt excepted.

4. Tanuku Taluk.

The Taluk of Tanuku is composed of 180 villages, both Government and Zemindári, 88 being Government villages, 65 Zemindári villages, and 27 Shrótriyam Agrahárams.

It is situated in the south of the District, and is bounded on the north by the Ellore and Yarnagúdem Taluks, on the south by the Narasápuram and the Bhímavaram Taluks, on the east by the Vasishta branch of the Godavery and the Amalápuram Taluk, and on the west by the Koléru (Colair) lake and the Taluk of Ellore.

The estimated area of this Taluk is 866 square miles. The population is 167,491 souls, of whom 164,705 are Hindus, 2637 Mohammedans, and 100 Christians. According to the quinquennial returns of 1866–67 the population was 152,052, so that the subsequent increase has been 15,439. There are 33,719 houses in the Taluk, of which 33,655 are inhabited. The revenue of the Taluk for Fasli 1282, including assessment, water tax, the permanently-settled Bériz, and other miscellaneous items, is 614,234 rupees, as particularised below.

	Rupees.
Land assessment	155,802
Water cess	292,192
Permanently-settled Bériz and Shrótriyam Jódi	127,810
Other miscellaneous items . . .	38,430
	614,234

The rates of assessment are the same as those of the Rámachandrapuram Taluk. This Taluk has a perfect supply of Annicut irrigation. The following are the chief canals which traverse it in various directions :—The Kákaraparru canal, the Venkayya canal, part of the Ellore canal, and the Attili canal. These are available both for irrigation and navigation. From these, several branch channels have been cut for the supply of water.

The products of the Taluk are chiefly paddy, Bengal gram, horse gram, green gram, black gram, and red gram, gingelly and lamp oil seeds, hemp, coriander, fenugreek, mustard, jonna, cumboo, raggy, tobacco, chillies, onions, garlic, turmeric, and cotton.

The soil is of eight different sorts, namely, alluvial, permanently improved, regur pure, regur loamy, regur sandy, red clay, red loamy, red sandy.

The Taluk is generally flat, but productive and healthy. The principal towns, with their respective populations, are—

Tanuku	2192
Rélangi	4554
Penugonda	3094
Attili	5878

Tanuku is the headquarter station of the Tahsildar. There is no special industry in this Taluk; the chief trade being in paddy, grain, and cotton.

The approximate average out-turn of the harvest in each of the above-named articles and its corresponding value are as undermentioned.

	Out-turn in Garces.	Value in Rupees.
Paddy	14,220	853,200
Grain	1,360	54,400
Cotton (in puttis)	2,334	280,080

Nearly half of the two articles first named are consumed in the Taluk, as is also about one-third of the cotton produced. The remainder is exported. There are no imports.

5. Bhímavaram Taluk.

The Taluk of Bhímavaram consists of 148 villages, namely, 88 Government villages, 57 Zemindári and Proprietary villages, and 3 Mokhásás and Agrahárams. It is bounded on the north by the Taluk of Tanuku, on the south and east by the Taluk of Narasápuram, and on the west by the Koléru lake and villages in the Kistna District.

The area of the Taluk is 416 square miles. The population, according to the last census, is 92,457, which is 5631 more than in 1866-67. Of these, 91,229 are Hindus, 1134 Mohammedans, and 92 Christians. There are 21,269 houses in the Taluk, of which 19,285 are said to be inhabited. The assessed area of the Taluk is 81,814 acres, being an annual assessment of 171,812 rupees. The revenue of the Taluk, including land tax, water cess, quit-rent on Inams, the Péshkash of the estates, &c., amounts to 376,565 rupees.

The new Settlement rates were brought into operation in this Taluk from Fasli 1272.

This Taluk is well supplied with means of irrigation. The principal canals are the Undi canal, the Chinna Káparam canal, the Gósta Nadi, the Akuvídu canal.

The principal product is white paddy. Gingelly-oil seed, horse gram, and raggy are cultivated in a very few of the villages.

The soil is of five different kinds, namely, permanently improved, regur pure, regur loamy, regur sandy, and alluvial.

The whole surface of the Taluk is flat. Numerous channels intersect it on all directions.

The principal towns with their population are shown below.

Undi	1758
Akuvídu	1916
Gunupúdi	1150
Víravásaram	4145

There is no special industry in this Taluk. The trade consists chiefly in paddy, which is taken in large quantities to Nursapore, Masulipatam, Rajahmundry, and Cocanada for sale. The traders are principally the agriculturists themselves.

The approximate average out-turn of the harvest of this Taluk, with the value, is mentioned below.

	Out-turn in Garces.	Value in Rupees.
Paddy	10,070	503,500
Grains	695	27,800

Nearly half of the produce is consumed in the Taluk itself, and the rest is exported.

6. Rajahmundry Taluk.

This Taluk consists of 469 villages, namely, 94 Government villages, 369 Zemindári and Proprietary villages, and 6 Agrahárams. The 369 villages entered as Zemindári and Proprietary include some very insignificant hill villages.

It is bounded on the north by the villages of the Bastar country, on the south by the Taluk of Rámachandrapuram, on the east by the Taluk of Peddápuram, and on the west by the river Godavery.

The area of the Taluk is 2058 square miles, and the population, according to the last census, is 128,901. The quinquennial returns of 1866–67 stated the population as 100,924, so that the subsequent increase has been 27,977. 124,899 of the inhabitants are Hindus, 3562 Mohammedans, 15 Buddhists, and 324 Christians. There are 34,534 houses in the Taluk, of which 32,715 are reported to be inhabited. The area assessed by the Settlement Department is 76,962 acres, bearing an annual assessment of 129,676 rupees.

The revenue of the Taluk for Fasli 1282, including the land tax, the permanently-settled Péshkash of the estates, and other miscellaneous items, amounts to 155,832 rupees, as particularised below.

	Rupees.
Land assessment	107,275
Permanently-settled Péshkash and Shrótriyam Jódi	14,092
Other miscellaneous items . . .	28,787
Water cess, including Tírvajásti . .	5,678
	155,832

There are many large tanks in the Taluk, of which the Kótapalli tank, the Gummalladoddi tank, and the Gókavaram tank are among the principal.

There is also a channel called the "Burada Kálava," which rises in the hills, and falls into the river Godavery.

The principal products are paddy, jonna, raggy, cotton, tobacco, and dry grains, such as cow gram, black gram, green gram, red gram, and oil seeds.

The soil is of eight different kinds, according to the following classification:—Alluvial, permanently improved, regur pure, regur loamy, regur sandy, red clay, red loamy, red sandy.

The Taluk is partly hilly and partly flat. In some places it is very rocky.

The principal towns, together with their respective populations, are shown below :—

Rajahmundry	19,738
Dowlaishweram . . .	7,252

Rajahmundry is the headquarter station of the Session and District Judge, of the Sub-Collector, of the Superintendent of Police, of the Executive Engineer, and of the Subordinate Judge. The District Munsiff also has his court here. A central jail has been established in Rajahmundry, to which prisoners from different Districts are sent up for confinement. There is also a Government Provincial School.

The special industry of the Taluk is the manufacture of cotton carpets. A considerable trade is also carried on in tobacco and in dry grains. These products are brought in large quantities to Rajahmundry for sale.

The approximate average out-turn of the harvest in each grain, with the corresponding values, are shown below :—

	Out-turn in Garces.	Value in Rupees.
Paddy . . .	5,026	31,560
Jonna . . .	1,226	61,300
Raggy . . .	934	32,690
Grains . . .	2,134	85,360
Cotton (in puttis) . .	1,228	147,360

Nearly half the amount produced is consumed in the Taluk, the remainder being exported. There are no imports.

7. Peddápuram Taluk.

This Taluk consists of 213 villages, namely, 156 Government villages, 54 Zemindári and Proprietary villages, 3 Agrahárams and Mokhásá villages. It is bounded on the north by the Vizagapatam District; on the south by the Rajahmundry and Rámachandrapuram Taluks; on the east by the Cocanada, Pittápuram, and Tuni Divisions; and on the west by the Taluk of Rajahmundry.

The area of the Taluk is 506 square miles, and the population, according to the last census, is 111,489. Of these 109,586 are Hindus, 1901 Mohammedans, and 2 Christians. The number of inhabited houses is 31,156. In 1866-67 the population was reported to be 101,539, the subsequent increase being 9950. The area assessed by the Settlement Department is 71,083 acres, bearing an annual assessment of 128,082 rupees.

The revenue of the Taluk for Fasli 1282, including land tax, permanently-settled Péshkash, and other miscellaneous items, amounted to 229,640 rupees, as particularised below :—

	Rupees.
Land assessment	123,953
Permanently-settled Péshkash and Shrótriyam Jódi	88,749
Other miscellaneous items . . .	15,963
Tírwajasti and Fasaljasti . . .	975
	229,640

This Taluk is irrigated from the Yéléru river and the channels branching from it, and from various tanks.

The principal products of the Taluk are paddy, sugar-cane, cotton, and dry grains—such as Bengal-gram, green-gram, red-gram, cow-gram—timber, bees'-wax, chillies, turmeric, and soap-nuts.

The soil is of eight kinds, namely, alluvial, permanently improved, regur pure, regur loamy, regur sandy, red clay, red loamy, red sandy.

The greater part of the Taluk is hilly and jungly. A small portion is flat. The tanks and channels are very numerous. Peddápuram is the headquarter station of the Tahsildar, and contains, besides, the District Munsiff's Court.

The principal towns, together with their respective populations, are shown below :—

Peddápuram	9,202
Jaggampéta	3,759
Yéléshwaram . . .	3,050

The Taluk has no special manufacture, but its trade consists chiefly in jaggery, chillies, turmeric, tamarinds, cotton, gingelly-oil seed, and soap-nuts, of which it produces large quantities. These are carried to Cocanada both for consumption and exportation.

The approximate average out-turn of the harvest in each grain, together with its corresponding value, is given below :—

	Out-turn in Garces.	Value in Rupees.
Paddy . . .	6,058	363,480
Grains . . .	3,274	130,960
Sugar-cane (in puttis) .	750	11,250
Cotton (do.) .	2,012	241,440

About one-fourth of the above quantity is consumed in the Taluk itself, the rest being exported. There are no imports.

8. Ellore Taluk.

This Taluk consists of 250 villages, namely—

Government villages	92
Zemindári, Proprietary, and Agrahárams, &c. .	100
Shrótriyam villages	58
	250

The following are the boundaries of this Taluk :—the Nizam's territory on the north, the Colair lake and the Tanuku Taluk on the south, the Yarnagúdem Taluk on the east, and the Kistna District on the west.

The area of the Taluk is 729 square miles, and the population is 136,875. Of these 128,606 are Hindus, 7996 Mohammedans, and 269 Christians. There are double the number of Mussulmans in this Taluk than in any other. In 1866–67 the total population was reported as 118,735, the subsequent increase being 18,140. There are 36,518 inhabited houses in the Taluk.

The arable land assessed by the Settlement Department is 91,877 acres, paying revenue amounting to 82,138 rupees.

The revenue of the Taluk for Fasli 1282, including land tax, water cess, quit-rent on Inâms, and the Péshkash of the estates, amounts to 200,540 rupees.

The high-level canal from Vijéshwaram to Ellore passes through the Taluk, and it is joined by the Bezwáda canal at Ellore, where the waters of the Godavery and the Kistna unite. Both canals are navigable, and there is thus through communication by water between Rajahmundry and Ellore. Several branch channels from these canals supply the villages about Ellore. A few villages are irrigated by the two mountain streams called the Tammiléru and the Rámiléru.

The principal products of the Taluk are paddy, jonna, and grains, such as Bengal-gram, horse-gram, green-grain, black-gram, &c.

The soil is of seven different kinds, namely, alluvial, permanently improved, regur pure, regur loamy, regur sandy, red clay, red loamy, red sandy.

The greater part of the Taluk is rough and jungly; the southern part, especially in the neighbourhood of the Colair lake, being flat. There are numerous tanks, large and small, in the upland villages.

The principal town is Ellore, with a population of 25,487. It is the headquarters of the Head Assistant Collector. The offices of the Tahsildar and of the Executive Engineer, and the court of the District Munsiff, are also in Ellore.

The special industry characterising this Taluk is the manufacture of fine woollen carpets and saltpetre, Ellore being particularly noted for both.

The trade is principally in paddy and other dry grains, as well as in carpets, in saltpetre, and in timber from the Nizam's territories.

The approximate average out-turn of the harvest of the Taluk in each grain, with its corresponding value, is mentioned below:—

	Out-turn in Garces.	Value in Rupees.
Paddy . . .	6,500	325,000
Jonna . . .	3,686	184,300
Grains . . .	1,496	59,840

Nearly half of the produce is consumed in the Taluk itself, and the rest is sent for sale to Masulipatam. There are no imports.

9. YARNAGÚDEM TALUK.

This Taluk consists of 203 villages, namely—

Government villages	94
Zemindári and Proprietary villages . .	92
Agraháramis do. . .	17
	203

It is bounded on the north by the Nizam's territory, on the south by the Taluk of Tanuku, on the east by the river Godavery, and on the west by the Taluk of Ellore.

The area of the Taluk is 1249 square miles, and the population, according to the last census, is 145.715, being 15,332 more than in

1866-67. Of these, 142,049 are Hindus, 3656 Mohammedans, and 10 Christians. There are 40,139 inhabited houses in the Taluk. The assessed area of the Taluk is 82,490 acres, bearing an annual assessment of 95,517 rupees.

The revenue of the Taluk for Fasli 1282, including land revenue, water cess, the permanently-settled Bériz, and other miscellaneous items, amounts to 193,232 rupees, as particularised below:—

	Rupees.
Land revenue	89,283
Water cess	4,566
Permanently-settled Péshkash and Shrótriyam Jódi	72,658
Miscellaneous items	26,725
	193,232

The new Settlement rates have been in operation in the Taluk since Fasli 1276.

A few villages towards the southern part of the Taluk are watered by the Ellore canal, and other parts of the Taluk are irrigated by means of tanks and mountain streams.

The principal products of the Taluk are paddy, Bengal-gram, red-gram, horse-gram, and cow-gram, gingelly and lamp-oil seeds, cumboo, jonna, raggy, cotton, timber, and bamboos.

The soil is of eight different kinds, according to the following classification:—Alluvial, permanently improved, regur pure, regur loamy, regur sandy, red clay, red loamy, red sandy.

The surface of the Taluk is rocky and jungly in most parts, but level towards the south, and near the Godavery.

The upper portions of the Taluk are very unhealthy and feverish in the rainy and cold seasons.

The principal towns, with their respective population, are mentioned below:—

Yarnagúdem	2,084
Pólavaram	2,734
Mádhavaram	2,240
Tállapúdi	1,405

Yarnagúdem is the headquarter station of the Tahsildar.

There is no special industry in this Taluk, if we except the manufacture of coarse blankets made of sheep's wool. The trade is chiefly in dry grains, cotton, oil-seeds, and timber, as well as jungle products, such as honey, bees'-wax, &c.

The approximate average out-turn of the Taluk harvest in the different grains, with their corresponding values, are mentioned below :—

	Out-turn in Garces.	Value in Rupees.
Paddy . . .	1,881	112,860
Jonna . . .	6,340	253,600
Other grains . .	2,606	104,240

Nearly half the produce is consumed in the Taluk, the remainder being exported. There are no imports.

BHADRÁCHALAM AND RÉKAPALLI.

The Taluks of Bhadráchalam and Rékapalli were transferred from the Central Provinces and annexed to this District on April 1, 1874. Together with the Rampa country, which had hitherto been in the Taluk of Rajahmundry, they have been constituted by the Scheduled Districts Act an agency under the Collector of this District as Agent. The Upper Godavery District, of which these Taluks lately formed a part, was transferred to the British Government by the Nizam in 1860. They are part of a large estate, the greater portion of which is in the Nizam's territories, on the south of the river. The District was at that time settled. The inferior proprietors hold their lands under the superior proprietor, who pays the Government dues. The amount collected in 1872-73 was as follows :—

	BHADRÁCHALAM. Rupees.	RÉKAPALLI. Rupees.
Collected by the inferior proprietors .	7,551	6,421
Out of this had to be paid—		
Government demand . .	4,862	4,728
Road fund . . .	115	96
School fund . . .	115	96
Dawk fund . . .	32	25
Superior proprietor's share .	657	435
Village servants . . .	1,862	551
	7,643	5,931

The population of Bhadráchalam is estimated at 22,837, and that of Rékapalli at 8896.

CHAPTER II.

DESCRIPTION OF THE PRINCIPAL TOWNS AND OTHER PLACES OF IMPORTANCE.

RAJAHMUNDRY—DESCRIPTION OF THE TOWN—THE CHURCH AND MISSION—THE COURTS—THE JAILS AND SCHOOL—COCANADA—DOWLAISHWERAM—SAMULCOTTA—ELLORE—NURSAPORE—CORINGA—KÓTIPHALI—HINDU PAGODAS—BHADRÁCHALAM.

THE town of RAJAHMUNDRY (Rájamahéndravaram) is situated in latitude 17° N., and in longitude 81° 45′ 49″ E.* It is 365 miles from Madras. It is built on elevated ground, on the left bank of the Godavery, 30 miles from the sea. It consists of one principal street, about half a mile in length, which is rather narrow and confined where it passes through the bazaar, but is wider and more airy as it passes through the southern suburb, and of several narrow lanes which branch from the chief street on either side, those on the west sloping down to the river. The great northern trunk road enters the town at the north-east. Another road branches from it, and skirting the town on the east, and passing through the eastern suburbs, joins the main street at the entrance of Innespet, whence it is continued as the road to Dowlaishweram. Innespet is the southern suburb. It was called after Mr. Innes, formerly Civil and Session Judge of Rajahmundry, and afterwards one of the Judges of the High Court of Judicature at Madras, who planned and laid it out. It is arranged on a systematic and regular plan, the roads intersecting each other at right angles. These are broad and airy. The land was given to those who desired to build houses there on most

* On the Indian Atlas the longitude is given as 81° 50′. Mr. Trelawny Saunders, of the Geographical Department of the India Office, who has kindly given me the correct latitude and longitude of each place, informs me that the longitude of the Indian Atlas is based on the adoption of 80° 18′ 30″ for the longitude of the Madras Observatory, following the observations of Goldingham and Lambton. The longitude now adopted by the Great Trigonometrical Survey of India, consequent on Colonel Tennant's investigations, is 80° 14′ 19″ east of Greenwich.

reasonable terms, and many of the wealthiest and most influential inhabitants of the town reside there. Most of the houses in this quarter are situated a little apart from the streets, and have a little ground in front of them, in which cocoa-nut and other trees are planted. The Sub-Collector's Office, the Tahsildar's Cutcherry, the Telegraph Office, and the Provincial School are situated in this part of the town.

The District and Session Judge's Court is on a portion of the old rampart overhanging the river to the north of the town. It is an old building, but situated on a most picturesque site. The Subordinate Judge's Court is not very far from it on the left of the road which runs into the great northern highway. The District Munsiff's Court is at the angle of the road at the foot of the hill on which the District Court is built. The houses of the European residents are to the north and north-east of the town. Two are on the river-bank, and the others further inland.

The Church is built on a green plain which was formerly used as a parade-ground, and is now employed for a similar purpose by the police. It is a pretty structure, very much the same as other ecclesiastical buildings in up-country stations in India. It is surrounded by a verandah, and there is a tower at the west end. It was finished in 1864, and was consecrated by the Bishop of Madras in 1867.

There is a Protestant Mission at Rajahmundry connected with the American Evangelical Lutheran Church. Three houses at the north-east corner of the town are the property of the Mission; two are used as the dwelling-places of the missionaries, and one as the place of worship, which is attended by all the native converts in Rajahmundry itself, and by all the native converts in Marumonda and the other outlying villages, who come in thither on special occasions. The number of native Christians connected with the Lutheran Mission is about 400, including upwards of 100 communicants. They belong to twelve villages. The majority of them belonged, before their conversion, to the Mála caste. Not one of them is wealthy; but, on the other hand, not one is poor enough to need support out of the mission funds. The catechists are supported out of these funds, but the teachers are paid by local subscriptions. The expense of the Society, including building expenses, amount to about £600 a year. The principal mode of work is itinerating preaching. There are elementary schools, in which the children of the native Christians receive free instruction; but those who are being educated with a view to their becoming mission agents, attend the Government schools for their secular education, and receive religious instruction from the missionaries.

The Mission was commenced by the North German Missionary Society, and the Rev. L. M. Valett took up his residence for this purpose at Rajahmundry in 1840. In 1845 the Rev. C. W. Grönning and the Rev. F. A. Heise came out to the Telugu country, the former going to Ellore and the latter remaining at Rajahmundry. In consequence of financial embarrassments in Germany, the North German Missionary Society were obliged to give up their Indian Mission, and transferred their property to the American Lutheran Mission in 1851. Messrs. Grönning and Heise joined that Mission; and Mr. Valett having gone to the London Mission at Chicacole, Mr. Heise carried on the work at Rajahmundry, and Mr. Grönning proceeded to Guntoor. In 1856 the whole charge of the missions in Guntoor, the Palnaud, and Rajahmundry, devolved on Mr. Grönning, owing to his fellow-labourers having to leave the country on account of their health. In 1858 Rev. A. Long came out from America, and established a new mission at Samulcotta, and Mr. Heise returned for a short time to Rajahmundry. On his leaving, Mr. Grönning returned, and remained at Rajahmundry, labouring with much zeal and success till 1865, when sickness and bereavement compelled him and his family to return to Europe. Mr. Long then took up his residence at Rajahmundry, but died of smallpox in the following year. Owing to difficulties, both in respect to men and money, occasioned by the American Civil War, it was found impossible to carry on the mission-work at all the Society's stations, and for a time the charge of the Mission at Rajahmundry was undertaken by the agents of the English Church Missionary Society. Meanwhile arrangements had been made in America to transfer the Mission to the General Council of the Lutheran Church, and the late Rev. Dr. Heyer, a venerable missionary, nearly eighty years of age, volunteered to go out and superintend the missions at Rajahmundry and Samulcotta until others could be sent. He remained there about eighteen months, having the satisfaction on leaving of handing over the native Christian Church to two Danish missionaries, the Rev. H. C. Schmidt and the Rev. J. K. Poulsen, who are now labouring with earnest zeal and devotion in their great Master's service.*

* For the details of the above sketch, I am indebted to the kindness of the Rev. H. C. Schmidt.

Between the Church and the Subordinate Judge's Court there is a bright and pleasant garden, which is open to all classes of the community. It is a People's Park on a miniature scale. It is kept up by the funds of the Museum, which is situated within it. This building is a plain and simple structure, consisting of a large hall, in which are arranged several cases containing various geological and zoological specimens, with two small rooms at the end, one of which was for some years used as a reading-room for the natives and Eurasians, and the other for an office. It is surrounded on three sides by a spacious verandah.

The Museum was occupied as the Zillah School from May 1862 to February 1865. There was, of necessity, very little done during that time to forward the legitimate objects of the institution itself. On the removal of the school, however, to the house built expressly for it in Innespet, the Museum was repaired, and several additions were made to the collection of specimens.* A strenuous effort was made in 1866 and 1867 to make it more attractive, and also to make it useful and instructive by converting it into an industrial exhibition of the products and manufactures of this District and of the adjoining Districts. A microscope, a telescope, some models of steam-engines, and other articles, were ordered from England. A coloured picture of Her Most Gracious Majesty the Queen was procured at the same time, and it proved a great source of attraction to the people. Crowds from the country round, especially on the occasion of a native festival, came to see the picture of the great Queen.

The number of visitors for a period of ten years is appended :—

1865–66	7,070	1870–71	15,500
1866–67	11,386	1871–72	18,860
1867–68	11,237	1872–73	30,028
1868–69	13,447	1873–74	25,447
1869–70	8,808	1874–75	20,588

There are two jails at Rajahmundry—the District Jail and the Central Jail. The former is now used only for the accommodation of short-sentenced prisoners, and of those under trial. It was built in 1806, and enlarged in 1838. It was very strongly built, but at one time it was terribly overcrowded, and the mortality in it was very great. It has recently been thoroughly cleansed, and, the overcrowding having also been stopped, it has been rendered quite healthy.

* Administration Report of the Madras Presidency for 1865–66, p. 119.

The Central Jail was begun in 1864, and was gradually completed. It receives prisoners from all the Telugu Districts from Cuddapah to Ganjam. It is constructed on the radiating principle, a tower containing the Superintendent's office and other rooms being in the centre, and the various wards branching from it like the spokes of a a wheel. Everything going on in the large yards which divide the several wards can be seen from this tower. The hospital is situated in the south-west angle of the building. The various wards are divided into large and well-ventilated cells containing from four to six prisoners in each. There is also a separate ward for women superintended by a matron. Manufactures of various kinds were early commenced in the Central Jail. The principal are the manufacture of carpets, mat and basket-making, spinning, carpentering, besides tent-making, paper-making, and pottery.*

The scheme for ensuring good conduct among the convicts, by enabling them to earn a remission of a portion of their sentences by steady and orderly behaviour, was introduced in the year 1868.† Convict servants were also employed, such employment being made a reward for good conduct. Several of the convicts were appointed warders, and were found, on the whole, to be zealous and efficient in their new duties, and deprivation of such employment was looked on as a disgrace. The best behaved prisoners were also appointed overseers of the working gangs and parties. The convict-warders, as a body, work well. Their chief failing is in their not sufficiently asserting their authority; but this is attributable in a great measure, if not entirely, to the fear of interference on behalf of the paid warders.

The Central Jail has been a great success from a sanitary point of view. Abundance of room and fresh air, a most healthy situation, regular employment for the convicts, and a good and wholesome system of diet, all contributed to this desirable end. The old diet of rice has been done away with, and the new system of feeding the prisoners on millet, raggy, and the other dry grains of the country has been adopted. At the same time a regulated allowance of animal food, fresh vegetables, oil, condiments, and salt has been substituted for the uncertain and irregular distribution of such articles which formerly prevailed. It has been proved that the health of the

* Administration Report for 1868–69, p. 36.

† A description of this system is given in the Administration Report for 1869–70, p. 42.

prisoners improved after the introduction of this new system. Patients admitted in a scorbutic condition rapidly recovered, and the frequency of other diseases considerably decreased. "It must be remembered," as it was pertinently remarked at the time, "that by the introduction of the system of feeding prisoners mainly with the staple grains of the country in lieu of rice, and supplementing these by a due proportion of animal and vegetable food, the people are provided with the kind of food which nine-tenths of them have been accustomed to use as free labourers, for, in Southern India, except on the sea-board and amongst the wealthy, rice has never been the ordinary food of the people." *

The headquarters of the police are at the entrance of the town on the north-east. The Superintendent of Police usually resides at Rajahmundry, and the Assistant-Superintendent at Nursapore, various inspectors being stationed at the large towns throughout the District.

The houses in the town are chiefly constructed of mud, many of them now being tiled. The thatched roofs were the frequent cause of fires, and they have very generally been superseded by tiles. Almost all the houses are of only one story, two or three only on the river-bank and near the main street being of two stories. Some of the shops in the bazaar are built entirely of wood. The town is interspersed with trees, principally tamarind and cocoa-nut. It looks most picturesque from the Godavery, and its sloping streets, its leafy surroundings, and the towers of its principal pagoda have a most pleasing effect as they are viewed by those who approach the town by water. The pagoda just mentioned is an ancient building situated on the western slope leading to the river. The principal mosque was built in the reign of the Emperor Mahomed Toghluk. There is a Persian inscription over the entrance door, of which the following is a translation:—"This mosque was erected by Sherif Salar Ulvi, in the reign of the Emperor Mahomed Toghluk and in the time of Humayun Gajjar, on the 20th day of Ramzan, Hijri 724," or A.D. 1324.

The population of Rajahmundry, according to the last census, is 19,738. Of these 17,970 are Hindus, 1629 Mohammedans, and 132 Christians. In 1854 it was stated to be 14,700. The country in the neighbourhood of the town is low, and is chiefly composed of

* Administration Report for 1870–71, p. 196

black cotton soil. Paddy is principally grown to the north and south. To the east there is a rise in the ground, which is covered with stunted jungle, interspersed with palmyras. The prevailing winds in January and February are from the north, but there is occasionally a sea-breeze in the afternoon. During March the wind usually blows from the south or south-east, and in April and May it is generally west or south-west. This land-wind is very hot and fiery. The south-west monsoon commences from the 8th to the 15th of June, and the wind blows continuously from the south or south-west, sometimes with great violence, till October, when the north-east monsoon commences. The freshes in the river commence soon after the first rains, but are generally highest in July and August. A high fresh in the Godavery is a magnificent and exhilarating sight. Swollen and turbid with the innumerable streams from the mountain torrents in Central India, it rushes down in its full strength, bearing everything before it, and carrying on its tumultuous surface drift-wood, the carcases of animals overtaken by the rising waters, and the *débris* collected on the banks of the river itself and of its confluent streams. The whole town is astir on these occasions. The inhabitants collect on the bank to draw in the drift-wood, as it passes, to be dried and used as firewood for the ensuing year, while scores of boys and men swim out into the stream for the same purpose, supported by a log, which serves them as a kind of catamaran. The river is not much affected by the north-east monsoon. It subsides in November, and continues to fall till March, when it generally continues about the same height during the hot weather. It is kept to a tolerable height by the barrier at Dowlaishweram, and, of course, falls according to the quantity drained off from that structure for agricultural purposes; but, before the Annicut was built, it was reduced in the hot weather to a mere narrow stream, passing through the centre of a wide expanse of sand, and the inhabitants of the town had sometimes to go daily a mile or more for water.

The Government School at Rajahmundry was established in 1854. It was originally one of the four Provincial Schools sanctioned by the Government of India for the Presidency of Madras. As it was opened before the appointment of educational inspectors, it was placed under the management of a committee composed of the principal European and native inhabitants. The first headmaster, Mr. Black, opened the school with eighty boys. In consequence of its diminished numbers, and of the low degree of proficiency attained by the pupils, it was subsequently reduced to the grade of a Zillah school; but the standard of instruction was improved, and the numbers again increased, so that when the school was removed to the new buildings specially erected for it in Innespéta, the number on the roll was 155. Mr. Black was succeeded by K. Kuppaswámi Shástri Gáru, the second master, who, for some time, kept up the tone of the school with great efficiency and vigour.

Mr. Barrow, a graduate of the University of Oxford, took charge of the school in 1868, and in the following year it was again constituted a Provincial School. It was intended to educate up to the standard of the First Arts Examination; but a class for this purpose was not properly formed until the arrival of the present head-master in December 1872. Mr. Metcalfe, a graduate of Cambridge, is now head-master. The present number of the pupils on the roll is 220, and the average attendance 169. At the commencement of 1873 a small collegiate class was formed.

The most recent report of this school is very favourable. In 1874-75 three out of five candidates passed the First Examination in Arts, and twenty out of twenty-one pupils succeeded in the Matriculation examination. On March 31, 1875, there were twenty-three pupils in the F. A. classes, which number has since increased to thirty, so that in this respect Rajahmundry now stands second among the Provincial Schools.

A school for caste girls was established a few years ago, and has since been principally supported by the liberality of the Maharajah of Vizayanagaram.

COCANADA (Kákináda), which is the headquarters of the Collector of the District, is situated on the coast in 16° 57′ N. lat., and 82° 13′ 49″ E. long. At the last census the population was 17,839. Of these 16,750 were Hindus, 595 were Mohammedans, and 455 Christians. It really forms one continuous town with Jagannádhapuram, formerly a Dutch settlement, from which it is separated by a small tidal river. The handsome bridge which now connects the united towns was completed in 1865. It is an iron-girder bridge. Sixteen out of the eighteen girders were manufactured at Dowlaishweram, but the cast-iron cylinders for the piers were procured from England by contract. The entire cost of the bridge was 16,000 rupees.

Cocanada has been gradually growing in importance on account of its increasing trade. A great impetus to its trade was given during the American Civil War, when large quantities of cotton from Guntoor and the surrounding cotton-growing country were shipped from Cocanada, which was found to be a more commodious and convenient harbour for trans-shipment than Masulipatam. The shipping in the Roads of Cocanada has much increased of late years, and constant communication is kept up with Calcutta, Madras, and Rangoon. In consequence of the increase of trade, the number of merchants residing at Cocanada has greatly increased, and many mercantile houses have been established by English, French, and German merchants. A branch of the Bank of Madras has been opened there, and has flourished in a most satisfactory manner. There are 2957 houses in the town, and its prosperity may be estimated by the fact of 55 of these being terraced, while there are only two terraced houses in the larger town of Rajahmundry. Only 459 houses are tiled, while 2439 are thatched.

The chief exports from Cocanada are cotton, gingelly oil seed, sugar, and rice; and the principal imports are iron, copper, gunny bags, and various liquors. Statements showing the value of both the exports and imports at this port during the eight years, commencing from 1864-65 and ending with 1871-72, are appended. These statements have been copied from those kept in the office of the Superintendent of Sea Customs.

STATEMENT SHOWING THE EXPORTS AT THE PORT OF COCANADA FOR EIGHT YEARS.

ARTICLES.	1864-65.	1865-66.	1866-67.	1867-68.	1868-69.	1869-70.	1870-71.	1871-72.
	VALUE.	VALUE.	VALUE.	VALUE.	VALUE.	VALUE.	VALUE.	VALUE.
	Rupees.	Rupees.	Rupees.	Rupees.	Rupees.	Rupees.	Rupees.	Rupees.
Rice . .	26,635	247,591	1,037,730	358,213	539,354	186,552	685,707	489,633
Paddy .	26,685	178,456	426,675	156,774	378,448	268,253	77,212	58, 613
Cotton Goods	79,521	264,419	332,412	290,033	195,326	276,775	253,205	227,714
Jaggery & Sugar	957,654	408,267	841,920	46,982	567,609	326,425	199,852	107,342
Bhoot-gram	46,136	145,827	79,249	98,708	179,065	171,215	10,125	109,104
Horse-gram	17,719	50,937	66,206	38,697	42,947	7,519	3,473	2,975
Gingelly oil seeds	463,160	524,190	70,787	1,066,962	926,800	2,256,132	1,469,015	834,218
Castor oil seeds	25,820	21,303	90,910	133,966	330,106	34,218	47,483	878,442
Tobacco .	145,504	59,895	74,867	68,749	93,615	240,965	108,163	219,160
Chillies .	4,590	19,374	132,366	68,845	64,713	16,384	10,035	2,529
Cotton .	2,918,515	5,583,139	1,364,933	1,206,692	2,826,426	3,580,924	1,645,454	4,202,106
Sundries	225,134	509,974	915,988	698,208	791,977	810,582	797,210	1,121,036
Total .	4,910,478	8,013,377	5,434,043	4,151,829	6,936,386	8,175,949	5,306,939	8,252,876

STATEMENT SHOWING THE IMPORTS AT THE PORT OF COCANADA FOR EIGHT YEARS.

Articles.	1864-65.	1865-66.	1866-67.	1867-68.	1868-69.	1869-70.	1870-71.	1871-72.
	Value.	Value.	Value.	Value.	Value.	Value.	Value.	Value.
	Rupees.	Rupees.	Rupees.	Rupees.	Rupees.	Rupees.	Rupees.	Rupees.
Paddy .	7,264	5,705	21,735	468	8,398	...	17,434	475
Rice . .	203,037	27,857	8,442	354	5,201	4,693	68,318	66
Iron . .	11,122	7,755	8,609	13,347	27,819	36,753	49,240	31,575
Copper .	2,379	3,630	7,582	3,978	13,400	7,112	8,075	11,071
Twist .	4,406	65,537	912,981	268,269	364,501	462,813	561,762	491,552
Wood .	8,160	4,551	5,721	27,117	10,015	561	2,216	1,359
Gunny Bags	7,619	16,216	75,679	65,344	159,739	176,233	132,609	141,281
Paper .	231	1,420	4,174	7,154	2,946	6,243	7,109	9,570
Liquors	25,779	47,067	59,400	57,819	81,546	106,717	108,263	103,672
Cotton .	32,634	198,948	26,085	2,741	...	...	647	...
Sundries	142,768	321,039	456,422	578,148	808,609	1,056,830	729,484	695,956
Total .	445,404	699,722	1,586,830	1,024,739	1,482,174	1,857,958	1,685,16[illegible]	1,486,580

The Lighthouse at the entrance of the river at Cocanada was completed in 1865. The total outlay on it, including the flag-staff, groynes, &c., was 73,011 rupees. Unfortunately, owing to the extension of the Delta northward, and to the shoals off the north-east end of Hope Island, it has been found that both this lighthouse and that on Hope Island are out of position, and, consequently, of little value to ships bound for Cocanada.

The Protestant Church is situated on the open plain at Jagannádhapuram adjoining the houses of some of the European residents. The hospital for seamen is a pleasant, airy building, near the church. It was completed in 1856 at a cost of 3437 rupees, and was subsequently improved at a further cost of 1996 rupees. A portion of the amount originally spent on it was raised by public subscription.

There are three printing presses in Cocanada, namely, that connected with the Printing Press Company, one belonging to Messrs. Abel, Will, & Co., and the Collector's official press. The only newspapers are the "Cocanada Advertiser," which is a purely mercantile organ, though the news of the District sometimes appears in it; the "Suddhiranjani," a Telugu weekly paper, containing various extracts and translations; and the official "District Gazette," published in diglott.

The line of steamers between the Northern ports and Madras commenced running in 1858–59. This was the nucleus from which the present frequent communication afforded by the British

India Steam Navigation Company started, but it was only gradually developed. There had been a fitful communication for some time, but it was so intermittent that no dependence could be placed on the movements of the steamers. A Government steamer now and then touched at the ports, but at rare intervals, and without any semblance of regularity. The Government of Madras had long advocated a periodical communication with Burmah, principally as a means of enabling the sepoys to return to their own country when sick; but the first practical proposal emanated from the Supreme Government to establish a bi-monthly line between Madras and Rangoon, including Masulipatam, Cocanada, and Vizagapatam. The advantage thus obtained was not only that of a regular communication with those ports which gave easy access to the Nizam's dominions and the Northern Circars; but it enabled the steamers to make the voyage during the stormy seasons with greater facility, as they would cross the Bay at a point where it is 160 miles narrower than at Madras, and on a course which brings the wind in both monsoons to a more favourable quarter. As the number of steamers at the disposal of the Government was not very great, and the number of troops to be transported was large, they entered into negotiations with Messrs. Mackinnon, Mackenzie, & Company, agents of the Bengal Steam Navigation Company, to take the line off their hands; but these negotiations failed. The line was worked by the Government from May to October 1859; but the steamers were run with great irregularity, and the Government, feeling persuaded that private enterprise was more likely to ensure the successful working of a line of mail steamers than they, invited tenders from private companies or individuals for undertaking this useful and important work.

The only persons who made offers in answer to these tenders were the agents of the Bay of Bengal Steam Navigation Company. A contract was entered into with them. The principal points in this contract were, that they should despatch one steamer a month from Madras to Rangoon, touching at Masulipatam, Cocanada, Vizagapatam, and Bimlipatam both ways; that they should receive a subsidy of 4500 rupees each voyage for carrying the mails; and that they should be guaranteed 7500 rupees for each voyage as Government freight and passage-money. The steamers commenced running on this line on January 11, 1861. This arrangement was continued until March 1862, when it ceased. With the reduced number of regiments in Burmah, it was found that the advantages of the line were not commensurate with the expense incurred; and, moreover, the arrangements were not of a character to merit confidence. Complaints were constant, and they were generally neglected. On one occasion it was found necessary to fine the contractors, because one of the vessels left Cocanada without waiting the specified time, and before the mails could be put on board. Mr. J. Mackinnon, the managing partner of the Company, went out to India with the object of organising a comprehensive system of steam communication along all the Indian shores. The project included a line between Calcutta and Bombay, calling at Madras and the other intermediate ports. This was the origin of the British India Steam Navigation Company, which has since attained gigantic proportions, and now vies, even on other ground than that originally occupied, with the great Peninsular and Oriental Steam Navigation Company.*

DOWLAISHWERAM (Dauléshwaram), about five miles to the south of Rajahmundry, was formerly a place of greater importance than it is at present, in consequence of its being the headquarters of the corps of Sappers and Miners, and the very centre of the life and activity occasioned by the construction of the Annicut. It is still the headquarters of the District Engineer. There is a Government workshop, where a good deal of work is done for the Department of Public Works. The value of the work turned out is about 170,000 rupees a year. Most of the houses of the former European residents have fallen down or are in thorough disrepair, the only habitable houses being near the river. The old houses were on the rocky hills in the neighbourhood. The population of Dowlaishweram is 7252. There are good stone quarries in the neighbourhood, the quantity annually worked out from them being on the increase. The average quantity despatched from them during the last three years was 30,000 cubic yards.

SAMULCOTTA (Tsámarlakóta), situated 28½ miles from Rajahmundry, was formerly a military station; but the troops have been removed, and the cantonment has been abandoned. There are still the remains of the barracks, which were erected in 1786, and the officers' houses. Before the cession of the Northern Circars it was the residence of the Rajah of Peddapore. It was originally intended to

* Administration Reports for 1858–59, p. 303; 1859–60, p. 103; 1860–61, p. 87; 1864–65, p. 63. Lindsay's History of Merchant Shipping, vol. iv. p. 455.

have a regiment of sepoys stationed at Peddapore itself, which is only two miles distant; but the site of the late cantonment was considered to be more advisable. There was formerly a fort, but it was pulled down, and the moat filled up in 1838, in consequence of the offensive state of the ditch and the rank vegetation, which produced disease. The village is insignificant; but, in case it should be considered advisable to place a regiment there again, it may be recorded that it is very healthy, and the inhabitants remarkably long-lived. There is a small river to the south-east. Its bed is usually sandy, except during the monsoons. There are but few tanks in the neighbourhood, but there are two wells in the old cantonment, which furnish good and drinkable water. The soil is alluvial, and the surrounding country cultivated. The site of the cantonment is 70 to 80 feet above the level of the sea, which is eight miles distant.* It is connected with Rajahmundry and Cocanada by canal. It is situated in a central spot, and affords an excellent strategical position for the command of this portion of the Northern Circars.

The town of ELLORE (Yélúru) is situated in latitude 16° 43′ N., and in longitude 81° 5′ 49″ E. It is 315 miles from Madras, and is 50 miles north of Masulipatam. It is called by the natives Uppu Yélúru, or Salt Ellore, to distinguish it from Vellore, which generally goes by the name of Rái Yélúru. It was formerly the capital of the Circar of Ellore, which, together with the Circar of Condapilly, occupied the whole of the country between the rivers Godavery and Kistna. When the Northern Circars were divided into districts, it belonged to the District of Masulipatam, and was connected with it till 1859, when it was transferred to the Godavery District on the redistribution of the Districts of Guntoor, Masulipatam, and Rajahmundry.

Ellore is the largest town in the District, and contains 25,487 inhabitants. Of these 5046 are Mussulmans, who chiefly reside in the Lines, 20,253 are Hindus, and 188 Christians. There are a great number of Mussulman inhabitants, and the manufacture of carpets is carried on by them. In the northern part of the town there are the remains of an old fort, which was built by the Mohammedans in the thirteenth or fourteenth century, from the materials of the pagodas in the neighbouring city of Vengi, which

* Report on the Medical Topography of the Northern Division.

were then captured and rifled. The little river Tamaléru, which rises in the neighbouring hills, divides the town into two portions. Several suburbs surround the town. The country round is flat, with hills in the distance. The soil is chiefly black cotton, and the cultivation paddy. The climate is very similar to that of Masulipatam; but, being further inland, it is hotter, and there is less sea-breeze. The land-wind during April and May is very violent and hot; and, on the whole, the climate is not so agreeable as that of Masulipatam or Rajahmundry. A regiment, or a detachment from a regiment, was stationed at Ellore for many years, but it has now ceased to be a military station. The cantonment was situated to the south of the town on the Tamaléru.* Ellore is now the head-quarters of the Head-Assistant Collector.

The town of Ellore has of late years greatly increased in population and improved in cleanliness. The first is due to the opening of the canals from Bezwada and Rajahmundry, which has brought a great deal of traffic to it, and drawn to it a considerable amount of the surplus produce from the surrounding country. It was always regarded as a cheap place to live in, and, though the canal has had a great effect in equalising prices, the necessaries of life can still be procured at a cheaper rate in the bazaars of Ellore than in any of the neighbouring towns. The improvement in its sanitary condition is due to the municipality established a few years ago. The supply-channels from the great tank near the town used formerly to send the water over the mainroad, and, during the cultivating season, the mud and water used to be ankle-deep in some of the principal thoroughfares. The different channels of the river Tamaléru were very filthy. This state of things has now been changed. Good metalled roads have been made through the town. Public latrines have been built at convenient places. A band of sweepers, superintended by East Indian overseers, clean the town daily, and the appointment of the town police, both for the preservation of the peace and for the supervision of all necessary improvements, has had the most beneficial influence on the well-being of the people. A European inspector generally has charge of the police, but it is sometimes left in charge of a Mussulman inspector. There are about fifty policemen employed in preserving order in the town. Besides the Head Assistant Collector, the Tahsildar, and the Inspec-

* Medical Topography of the Northern Division, p. 36. Pharoah's Gazetteer, p. 55.

tor of Police, who are *ex officio* members of the municipality, one of the European residents and five or six members of the native community are on the board. The revenue and magisterial charge of the town and Taluk was entrusted at first to a Deputy-Collector for general duty, and was transferred to the Head Assistant Collector in 1867. It was considered advisable that a covenanted officer, exercising the full powers of a magistrate, should be stationed at a town which, owing to its being situated on the high road, was of considerable importance, and over which the Magistrate of the District could, in consequence of its distance from headquarters, exercise no adequate control. A portion of the old barracks was converted into an office for the Head Assistant Collector.

Ellore is well off as regards both elementary and higher education. In the fort the Church Missionary Society has an Anglo-Vernacular School, which was established in 1854, on the principle of the Rev. Robert Noble's school at Masulipatam, Scriptural knowledge being a prominent part of the instruction imparted. The education afforded in it is equal to that of a Government Zillah school, the pupils being brought up to the matriculation standard; and in connection with it there are two branch schools, one in the town and the other in the Lines, where instruction is given in English, Telugu, Hindustani, and Persian, up to the fourth Government standard. The High School receives grants in aid on the "certificate system," and the branches on the "results system." In the High School there were 120 pupils according to the latest returns; in the town branch, 80; and 130 in the branch at the Lines.

A striking peculiarity in these schools is the number of Mussulman pupils under instruction. There are from 130 to 150 Mohammedan youths in the three schools, and certainly so many boys of that persuasion cannot be found in any other school, or group of schools, in the Northern Circars. From the first there has been a separate staff of Mussulmans to give instruction in English with the assistance of their own vernacular, and the Mohammedans of the place have not been slow to avail themselves of the benefit thus afforded them. At least half the pupils have belonged to that faith. On leaving school they have not entered the service of the English Government; but have generally gone to Hyderabad, and entered the service of the Nizam.

At the close of November 1854, the Rev. George English was sent from Masulipatam to open a mission at Ellore. Finding among the inhabitants of the place who visited him on his arrival a very great desire for education, he was induced to open the High School. It was at first held, by permission of the commander-in-chief, in the old hospital and guard-room of the fort. Soon after its establishment so many as forty Mohammedan students attended. Mr. English left for England in 1857, and was succeeded by Mr. Howley; and, subsequently, the Rev. C. Tanner, Mr. Goodall, the Rev. A. H. Arden, the Rev. J. Padfield, and J. Thornton, Esq., have been successively in charge of the school. Up to 1868 the attendance was limited to 80 or 90. There was then a Government Taluk School in the town, which was, in reality, an opposition institution. There were from 30 to 40 boys in this school at one time; but it created an "unhealthy rivalry," the pupils going from one school to the other at will, which was manifestly subversive of all discipline. In 1868 Mr. Arden, then Principal of the High School, had brought it into such a prosperous condition that the Taluk School was reduced in number to only nine pupils, and it was, consequently, closed by order of Government. Since then the High School has continued to prosper. An elementary school was established by Mr. Arden in 1870, and these two schools together gave instruction to about 300 boys. The numbers subsequently decreased on account of the fees having been raised by order of Government. In 1868, the highest fee was four annas, one-half of the school paid only two annas, and many of the pupils were free. Now the highest class pay 1 rupee 4 annas each, the second twelve annas, and so on, diminishing gradually to six annas, the lowest fee.

A second elementary school was established in the Lines by the Rev. F. W. N. Alexander. It was intended for the Málas, and for Christians of Mála origin, who, according to the rules of the High School, could not be admitted to study there. It hardly answers the purpose for which it was founded. There is a large Mála population around it, and yet scarcely one independent Mála has sent his children there. Subsequently Mussulmans came to it, and then a few Sudras, until in 1870, when elementary instruction in English was established, and a reasonable fee charged, some Brahmins and more Sudras joined, and received instruction with the others. This is accounted for by the lowness of the fee. The fee is four annas for the highest class, and one for the lowest. There are now about 130 boys in this school.

Besides these three schools for boys, there is a caste girls' school in the town connected with the High School, containing about twenty-five girls. There is also a boarding-school for Christian girls in the mission grounds near the Old Parade Ground. About forty pupils receive instruction in Telugu up to the fourth standard of the "results system."

Two European missionaries are stationed at Ellore—one for the school, and the other for evangelistic work in the surrounding country and in the town. The Rev. C. W. Grönning of the Lutheran Evangelical Mission first settled at Ellore in 1850 for the purpose of preaching the Gospel there. When he left, Captain Taylor, who is now in charge of the Pension Department at Rajahmundry, presented his house and grounds at Ellore to the Church Missionary Society with a view to induce them to commence work. As already stated, the Rev. George English was the first resident missionary. The Rev. F. W. N. Alexander was appointed in 1857, and has been labouring there diligently ever since. In several villages in the neighbouring Taluk of Gollapalli and in the Taluk of Ellore, there are Christian congregations, principally gathered from the Mála converts. There are about twenty village schools, in which about 400 Mála children are instructed by means of the vernacular.*

NURSAPORE (Narasápuram) is situated in latitude 16° 26′ N., and in longitude 81° 41′ 49″ E., on the western bank of the Vasishta or the most southern branch of the Godavery. It is about six miles from the sea. Its northern suburb is Madapollam, or Mádhaváyapálem, which is celebrated as one of the earliest places where the English established a factory, and was famous for its trade in cloth. The trade of the town has steadily declined since the abolition of the Company's factory in 1827, and the abandonment of the Company's "investments." The sites of the old buildings have been carried away by successive encroachments of the river, which makes a very considerable bend opposite the town. Nursapore used to be the Sub-Collector's headquarters; but, since their removal to Rajahmundry, a Deputy-Collector, employed on general revenue and magisterial duty, has been stationed there. The old public bungalow is used as his office. The Central School is near the Deputy-Collector's office. On the west of the town near the canal which communicates with Rajahmundry, is a pleasant, well-laid out suburb named

* I have been favoured with the above information by the Rev. F. W. N. Alexander, C.M.S.

after a former Sub-Collector, Taylorpet. The large and airy market-place is close to the landing-place from the canal. The canal has been carried on to join the river above the town, so that there is in reality through communication between it and the sea. The shipbuilders and boatbuilders of Nursapore are very expert. Many native craft are built and repaired there. The chief trade is with Moulmein and Rangoon, and there is a basin in the river opposite the town, in which all the ships in the British Navy might be moored; but the shifting, sandy bar at the mouth of the river renders access impossible, except for vessels of superficial draft. Formerly, however, larger vessels used to cross the bar.* A handsome and conspicuous obelisk, 75 feet high, has been erected near Nursapore Point to the east of the bar. The value of the exports amounted to a lac of rupees in 1854:† they amount now to 107,619 rupees. The population was then 8000; it is now 6819.

There is a Protestant Mission at Nursapore and Palcole. It was commenced in 1836 by Messrs. Beer and Bowden, and is now kept up by the sons of the former, and by the Rev. T. Heelis, who has diligently and faithfully laboured there for many years. The converts are chiefly from the chuckler or Mádiga class.

CORINGA (Kórangi) is situated nine miles south-west of Cocanada. It is situated in 16° 49′ N. lat., and 82° 19′ E. long. It used to be a place of very great importance, but it has very much fallen off during the present century. It was the only place between Calcutta and Trincomalee where large vessels used to be docked; but the river is now so shallow, and the approaches to it so difficult, that only small craft are now built or repaired there. In the description of the harbours of the District there is an account of the manner in which ships of the Royal Navy have been brought into Coringa, and in which large vessels were docked and repaired. There is still a considerable trade with Moulmein and Rangoon; but the glory of Coringa has departed. Being situated on a low site near the coast, it has frequently been subjected to inundations of the sea, and to the effects of hurricanes and storms. It is stated that the rising of the sea in 1784 was so high that vessels were actually drifted so far inland as Rajahmundry.‡ Coringa suffered very severely in the hurricane of 1839.

* Selections from the Records of the Madras Government, No. xix. p. 11.

† Pharoah's Gazetteer, p. 42.

‡ Hamilton's Gazetteer, 1828, p. 446.

Five miles to the south of Coringa are NEELAPILLY (Nílapalli) and INJARAM. At the latter place was one of our early settlements and a flourishing factory. GEORGEPET adjoins Nílapalli, and a little nearer Coringa is TÁLLARÉVU, which was formerly a very populous place. The prosperity of all these places declined from the date of the abolition of the Company's manufactories and monopoly. There used to be a Commercial Resident and his staff at Injaram so late as 1827, when the factory was discontinued.

The village of KÓTIPHALI, on the left bank of the Gautami Godavery, belongs to the Mahárajah of Vizayanagaram. It is the only portion of the district which belongs to him, with the exception of a few yards of land at Rajahmundry near the landing-place, behind the Judge's usual residence, on which there is a small *Bairagis'* shed. Kótiphali is considered by the Hindus to be a very sacred place; and the name—from *kóti*, "a crore," and *phalam*, "fruit"—is derived from the notion that every act of devotion performed there will be repaid ten million-fold.

Near the pagoda the river is looked upon as peculiarly sanctifying. The waters there are regarded as sufficient to wash away even the guilt of incest with a mother, and are consequently called *Mátrugamandpahári*. The Mahárajah of Vizayanagaram considers the honour of being the possessor of the village which contains this pagoda as of the highest value, although the pecuniary returns from it are small. The collections at Kótiphali at the Permanent Settlement, deducting 3000 rupees for the pagoda, were only 3953 rupees.*

The principal Hindu temples are at Kótiphali; at Dwáraká Tirumala, not very far from Ellore, which is regarded as similar to the shrine at Tirupati in the District of Cuddapah, though of inferior sanctity and importance; at Antravédi, on the coast near Nursapore; at Pattesham, on a rocky island in the Godavery, opposite Gútála; and on the hill of Kórukonda, about ten miles north of Rajahmundry. There are large pagodas in several other villages and towns; but they are not celebrated as places of pilgrimage or remarkable from an architectural point of view. The temples at Dwáraká Tirumala and at Kórukonda are continually resorted to throughout the year by those who have vows to make or penances to perform. Some ten or twenty thousand people of the Shivaite sect

* Carmichael's Manual of the Vizagapatam District, p. 283.

annually flock to Páta Pattesham and to Kótiphali at the feast of Shivarátri in February, or, according to the Hindu date, on the 14th of Mágha Bahula. The former place is regarded as a most excellent shrine at which to perform penance or to undertake vows. Multitudes go on pilgrimage to Antravédi for five days in January during the festival called Kalyánam. Upwards of twenty thousand, perhaps, attend on each occasion. But the most curious and the most characteristic description of pilgrimage is that called Saptaságana-yátra, or bathing in the river near the entrance of each of its seven mouths. This is especially resorted to by childless persons who are anxious for issue. The actual pilgrimage usually commences at Chollangi, near the most eastern, and ends at Antravédi, near the western branch of the river.

The estate of BHADRÁCHALAM is situated on the left bank of the river. It consists of 137 villages. The Ráni traces her pedigree from Anapa Aswa Row, who is said to have received the grant of the estate from the Emperor of Delhi in 1324.

The town of Bhadráchalam, or rather the long straggling village, for it is little more, is the chief place in the estate. It contains about two thousand inhabitants, who are mostly Brahmins. It is built on the bank of the Godavery, which is here very deep and rapid, and is about one hundred miles from Rajahmundry, and fifteen from Dumagúdem. It consists of one long and narrow street. It receives its name from being near the rock on which Bhadradu performed his devotions.

Bhadráchalam is celebrated for the temple of Rámachendradu, and for the annual festival which is held here in his honour, as he is said to have crossed the Godavery at this spot on his famous expedition to the island of Ceylon. The temple is built on the top of a small hill, and is surrounded by twenty-four lesser pagodas, and surmounted by a lofty *góparam* or tower, which is out of all due proportion to the edifices it surmounts. The main building is said to have been constructed four hundred years ago by Rishi Pratishta, and has been added to by successive Rajahs. The space in the centre is paved. The *mandapam* or porch, an open flat-roofed building of stone, is in front of the principal shrine, and the whole building is approached by a flight of stone steps from the river. The various pagodas are surrounded by a high wall. Thousands of pilgrims from all parts of the country, but chiefly from the coast, flock thither at the annual feast. It generally takes place in April, when the heat is intense and the water is scarce; but that is perhaps the best season for them to escape fever, which at other times is very prevalent in the surrounding country. Cholera, however, frequently breaks out among the pilgrims, and occasions terrible destruction of life.*

DUMAGÚDEM, fifteen miles farther up the river, was for some time the headquarters of the engineering operations on the Upper Godavery. There was then a large but changing population, principally consisting of labourers and other people connected with the works; but since the prosecution of these works has been stayed, the actual number of the population has decreased. A magistrate is stationed there; and it can boast of a post-office, a telegraph-office, and a police station-house. The Koi village, which used to be very near where the works were prosecuted, has been removed to a distance of two or three miles.†

As the scene of the works on the Upper Godavery has been annexed to the District, it is necessary to give here a brief account of the project of opening up the navigation of the river. It was first urged on the notice of the Government by Sir Arthur Cotton in 1851; and, as the expense of the works was found to be very great, they were, in October 1871, finally abandoned before the completion of the scheme. Up to 1861 the sum of £20,000 had been spent on preliminary surveys and other expenses. There are three great obstructions to the navigation caused by rocky barriers. The first is ninety miles above the Annicut, at Dumagúdem, and is twenty miles long. The second is fourteen miles long, and is sixty-eight miles above the first barrier. The third is seventy-five miles above the second, and is thirty-five miles long.

When Colonel Cotton was inspecting the irrigation works in the Rajahmundry District in March 1853, he received intelligence that the Governor-General had determined to sanction the examination of the river with a view to opening up its navigation, and he ascended the river as far as its junction with the Sabari. "It must be observed," he wrote in his Report, "that there is now a deep channel with an imperceptible current in the dry season, showing a dead level for nearly forty miles. This alone is sufficient to show how well worthy of further investigation this point is, when we con-

* Grant's Gazetteer of the Central Provinces, p. 54. Church Missionary Intelligencer for 1861, p. 123.

† Grant's Gazetteer of the Central Provinces, p. 188.

sider that a still-water steam navigation from the sea to Berar would form the cheapest line of communication in the world."

In 1859 Captain Haig, of the Madras Engineers, prepared a very interesting and elaborate report on the navigation of the river for the information of the Secretary of State for India. The following are extracts from it :—

"The Godavery valley, comprehending the greater part of the Nagpore territories, and a large portion of the territory of the Nizam, forms part of the great plain which slopes with a gentle incline from the Western Ghauts to the shores of the Bay of Bengal. It has an area of 130,000 square miles. The line of least descent in it, in a direction from west to east, is that which follows the course of the Wardha to its junction with the Godavery, and thence the latter river to the sea. This is the line of navigation which it is proposed to open. It has its upper terminus at Náchangaon, an important cotton-mart, sixty miles south-west of Nagpore, the head-quarters of the province, and thirty miles east of Umrouti, the principal commercial town of Berar. It passes within fifteen miles of Hinginghat, the chief emporium for the cotton, which now goes northwards *viâ* Mirzapore to Calcutta, and close to the important towns of Woony and Chandah. It runs, in fact, for 100 miles through the finest cotton-fields of India, and may be said to shape its course in a very direct line from the chief cotton centre of the Peninsula to Cocanada, the best and safest port on the eastern coast."

"The length of river is 500 miles. Its slope is fifteen inches per mile from the sea up to Hinginghat, 440 miles; the remaining sixty miles having a greater declivity. The inclination of its bed is not uniform, being interrupted at three points by remarkable barriers of rock, which form rapids which are navigable only in floods. The first of these occurs at a point 150 miles from the sea, the second at 220 miles, and the third at 310 miles. These points excepted, there is sufficient water in the river for navigation during nine months of the year for steamers drawing from two to four feet of water, according to the state of the river. The flood season comprehends the five months from July to October, during which boats may at times draw as much as six or even ten feet. During half the year the current is about a mile and a half per hour. During the other three months it varies between this and three miles, excepting in extreme floods, when, at a few points, and in the middle of the stream, it is as much as six miles; but the river never continues in this state for more than a few days in the year."

"After a careful and repeated examination of the whole line, a project was drawn up for removing all the natural impediments to the navigation. Its estimated cost is £292,000, or for 473 miles of river above the Annicut £618 per mile. An additional 300 miles of the other tributaries will also be rendered available for navigation by the same works during four to five months of the year. The means proposed for the removal of the obstructions caused by the barriers are lateral canals with locks, similar to those in rivers of like character in other countries. The project, after careful scrutiny, received the unqualified assent of the Madras Government, and, on their strong recommendation, was adopted by the late Court of Directors, and ordered to be carried into execution."

About the time Captain Haig's Report was written, Sir Charles Trevelyan, then Governor of Madras, during an official tour in the Delta of the Godavery, ascended the river for a short distance, and in a Minute describing this tour, he warmly and heartily recommended the immediate prosecution of the scheme for opening it for navigation.

The glowing anticipations of increased commercial prosperity in which Sir Charles Trevelyan indulged, have unhappily not been fulfilled. The works were not fully completed; but so far as they were prosecuted, they afforded an additional proof of the engineering skill and indomitable energy of one of the ablest members of the corps of Madras Engineers. The works were ostensibly abandoned on account of the expense of their construction. There was never any hope of the river being made navigable all the year round; but it was expected to be practicable for boats the greater part of the year. "It was thought that a boat might make a trip down in ten days, and return the same season, by being towed up, in two and a half months. Hinginghat is half-way between Bombay and the mouths of the Godavery; and it was calculated that the river would convey cotton at one-third the rate of the railway. Linseed and gingelly oil seed, it was thought, would also be sent by the river, while the importations up-stream would be salt, cocoa-nuts, some European goods, and military stores; but these hopes have been abandoned, so far as a remunerative return on the outlay is concerned."

When Sir Richard Temple inspected the works in 1863, £700,000 had already been expended. He recommended that the works at the first and second barrier, and in the river up to the foot of the third barrier, should be proceeded with, at an estimated cost of £255,000, so that the navigation might be open to the foot of the third barrier.

In a despatch dated August 1871, the Secretary of State proposed that the navigation works should be completed on the smallest possible scale as far as the foot of the third barrier, whence a road should be made to Chanda; but in October of the same year, at the request of the Government of India, the whole scheme was abandoned, as involving expenditure which did not give promise of any adequate return.*

The principal Zemindári in the District is that of PITTÁPURAM, which is situated between the eastern branch of the Godavery and the District of Vizagapatam. The present Zemindár is Venkata Mahapati Gangadhara Ráma Row Gáru. He was very young when his father died, and he succeeded to the estate, which was, consequently, for twelve years under the management of the Collector. It has now been several years under the management of the Zemindar himself.

The family belongs to the Velama caste, and to the subdivision of that caste entitled *Ugrulu*, which is a term applied to those who gain their livelihood by the profession of arms. The Rajah's ancestors are said to have emigrated from Oude. The Zemindári of Pittápuram was bestowed on Rámachendra Ráyanam Gáru, grandson of the original founder of the family, by the Mohammedan Government, in recognition of his services to the State. This grant was made two hundred and twenty-eight years ago, or about 1647; and rewards and favours seem to have been showered on the family by the Mussulman governors during the time it was under their rule. A *parwana* was issued in Hijri 1087 to Jagga Ráyanam Gáru, brother of the original grantee, appointing him to be a sirdar in command of 350 men. Two years afterwards Krishna Ráyanam Gáru, the second owner of the estate, received from the Emperor of Delhi a grant, bestowing on him the village of Samulcotta as a *mokhása*, or rent-free, inheritance to descend to his family, and appointing him a sirdar in command of 150 men.

* Statement exhibiting the Material and Moral Progress of India during 1872-73, Blue Book, p. 79.

The next honour bestowed on the Pittápuram family shows that the Government of the Nizam had some consideration for the feelings of their dependents. It is generally imagined that the gift of an elephant to an indigent Rajah was one of the most cruel kindnesses that could be devised, because of the ruinous expense of its keep. The Nizam appears to have been more considerate to the Rajah Venkatakrishna Ráyanam Gáru. In Hijri 1163 an annual grant of five hundred pagodas was made to him in lieu of the more stately but more costly gift of an elephant. Four years later, two further grants were made to the same Rajah—the first making over to him the fort of Pittápuram, with all its munitions of war, and the second granting him Kápavaram and other villages, as a *jaghir*. The permanent grant of the estate, or, as it was usually called in those days, a Sunnud-i-Mulkeyat Istimrar, was conferred by the English Government in 1802, when the Permanent Settlement was effected, on Venkata Níládri Ráyanam Gáru, who was then in possession of the estate.*

The present Rajah has generously supported the Dispensary and the Anglo-Vernacular School at Cocanada, and other institutions throughout the District. He received the thanks of the Government of Madras for having given the sum of 2000 rupees for the construction of a new house for the Dispensary at Cocanada, and for having contributed forty rupees a month towards its support, and he also received a well-merited tribute of praise from the same Government for having invested the sum of 27,360 rupees in order that the interest might be applied to the permanent support of the Anglo-Vernacular School at Cocanada.† During his minority he was educated at this school, which was originally founded by the exertions of Mr. Purvis, when Collector of the District, and which, after a temporary term of abeyánce, was resuscitated in 1863. In gratitude for the kindly interest taken in him by Mr. Purvis, the Rajah of Pittápuram had a bust of that gentleman prepared in England, and placed in the large school-room. It is a most excellent piece of sculpture, being the work of the late Mr. Noble, the celebrated sculptor, and is an admirable likeness. The Zemindar also made a grant of 2647 rupees for the construction of the present school-house, and supplied the funds for procuring the necessary furniture for it.

* The above details regarding the family were kindly given me by the Rajah himself.

† See Government Orders of February 2, 1866, and November 30, 1867.

The Rajah also gave the money for the building and furnishing a suitable school-house to be used as a girls' school, and bears the chief, if not the whole, of the monthly expenses. He likewise maintains, at a cost of 100 rupees a month, schools in his capital, Pittápuram; and subscribes to Sanscrit and Vernacular schools in Súrayyarowpéta, Triplicane, and other places. Súrayyarowpéta is a suburb of Cocanada, and a large proportion of the sites for building purposes was freely granted by the Rajah, who is the owner of the land. He has further built houses for the accommodation of the Police at Ramanakkapéta,* and he has shown his desire to benefit his people in a practical manner by sinking wells, constructing tanks, and supplying drinking water for travellers in various parts of his estate.

* See Government Order of November 3, 1866.

CHAPTER III.

THE PORTS OF COCANADA AND CORINGA.

DESCRIPTION OF THE PORTS—SURVEY BY MR. TOPPING—LIEUT. WARREN'S SURVEY OF CORINGA—CAPTAIN BIDEN'S REPORT—PROJECTED IMPROVEMENTS—MR. ROBERTSON'S SURVEY AND REPORT—WRECKS OF THE "RAJPOOT" AND "SACRAMENTO."

CORINGA and Cocanada are the two principal ports on the eastern coast of India. Both are situated on rivers, the mouths of which are obstructed by bars, while the outer anchorage is in the Bay of Coringa, which is formed by alluvium brought down by the Godavery and deposited on the coast. The southern side of the bay has thus been thrown up in the course of ages; but, unfortunately, the main branch of the great river, instead of pouring its waters into the sea at right angles with the line of the coast, has, by the united action of currents and of the heavy surf, been forced to change its course to a northerly direction, and now empties itself by one large mouth and several small ones into the Bay of Coringa. An immense quantity of silt is thus annually deposited in the bay, which is slowly but surely filling it up, and destroying its usefulness as an anchorage.

No country in the world is so badly supplied with harbours as India, and if there was any reasonable hope of improving Coringa Bay, or, indeed, any anchorage along the coast, it would be impossible to spend the public money to greater advantage. In the case of Coringa and Cocanada, such a result would be of immense importance. For a long time the trade of the District has been rapidly increasing. The immensely increased area under cultivation since the completion of the Annicut, and the system of water communication in the Delta, and with the neighbouring District of the Kistna, have tended to this end. Cocanada is the port through which this great and increasing trade must flow; and, if the harbour can be made a good one by artificial means, the value of the export trade of the Godavery for one year would be a small price to pay for such a result. But the question is, Whether this is possible?

This question has been discussed during a great number of years. It divides itself into two parts. As to the improvement of the outer Bay of Coringa, and as to the improvement of the bar-rivers on which Cocanada and Coringa are situated. The first is, of course, the main point; and, although it has been discussed for many years, and much valuable time has been spent in drawing up elaborate reports and estimates, yet up to the present day nothing has been done, and it is very doubtful if anything will be done. With regard to the second point, some attempts have been made from time to time to improve the inner anchorages, with partial success.

The earliest survey of the Bay of Coringa was made in 1789. The Court of Directors appointed Mr. M. Topping, astronomer in the service of Government at Madras, to survey the coast adjacent to the mouths of the Godavery. The precise object of his investigations was to determine whether there was a passage for large ships into the river Godavery, and to ascertain what shelter the roadstead of Coringa afforded. To enable him to execute this service, a small cutter of about thirty-five tons burden was placed at his disposal, and the Government requested the Master-Attendant of the port to render him every assistance. Mr. Topping kept a full and accurate journal, in which he entered all the details of his investigations, and several extracts from this interesting journal are appended, as they give an admirable account of the state of the question relating to the capabilities of the harbour at Coringa at the earliest point of its discussion.

"I had not been many days in the Bay of Coringa," Mr. Topping writes, "before I perceived that the charts which had formerly been made of it were extremely erroneous; indeed, so very defective, that they scarcely bore any resemblance to the place they were supposed to describe. It is true considerable changes may have been occasioned by the inundation in 1787; but by no means such as might have happened, had the charts made prior to it been exact delineations. The sea-reef that projects to the eastward of Hope Island, and happily affords shelter to the road of Coringa, is placed by them within (to the north-west) instead of without (to the north-east) of Point Gardewar; a circumstance of perilous tendency, should ships steer by such pretended information. The position, figure, and magnitude of Hope Island is also shamefully erroneous on those charts, being placed at the distance of nearly four miles from Point Gardewar, instead of somewhat less than one mile and a half, its true distance. And this representation, no doubt, led the Honourable Court to expect that a passage for their shipping into the Godavery might be found between it and Point Gardewar, a matter, as will now appear, of utter impossibility. The configuration of the coast, likewise, as well as the depths of water laid down, bear no marks of authenticity, or of their being the result of a genuine survey.

"It appearing to have been a peculiar object with the Honourable Court to get, if possible, their ships into the Godavery, as into a place of undoubted security, I spared no pains to determine the possibility or impossibility of accomplishing that end, and accordingly continued my operations, at the several embouchures of that river, a considerable time after I was even convinced myself of the impracticability of attaining such desideratum; and this I did, because I considered it as my duty to satisfy the Honourable Court in a matter of such importance, past all future doubt.

"It is, however, with great pleasure I inform the Honourable Court that, notwithstanding such hoped-for admission is denied, the exclusion itself is a matter of little moment, being amply compensated for by the safety, commodiousness, and free access of the road of Coringa—a place of great convenience and security at every season of the year. It is true the road is open to the sea from the north to the east points of the horizon, but, besides that, it is defended by its adjacent shores from the effects of winds blowing from the remaining three-fourths of the compass. It is rendered peculiarly favourable to shipping in distress by the mud-banks that are so situated within it as to receive, without injury, such vessels as may, through any misfortune, be driven on shore. It is a common and well-known practice with the natives of these parts to run their shipping purposely on shore in this bay, in order to secure them against the expected violence of the north-east monsoon, to which, it is true, they lie apparently exposed, but from which, it is equally true, they find themselves effectually secured. And this happens not only because they are bedded in the soft mud, but because, during such gales as blow directly on shore, there is actually very little sea running, the fluidity of the water being diminished, and its activity deadened by the accession of mud that rises at such times from the loose bottom. In the month of December last, the wind blew very fresh from the east-north-east for ten days together, when many vessels were lost on various parts of the coast. During the height of this gale, I passed over the sea-beach between Coringa and Jagganaikpuram, and observed, with much surprise, that I could have landed in perfect safety from a small boat as low down as Solinga, although the beach thereabouts is sandy, and the wind blew directly from the open sea upon it. Between Solinga and the mouth of the Coringa river, there is no more surf than on the borders of the Thames.

"Having said thus much of the security and other advantages of the port of Coringa (for I will not scruple to call even the road of Coringa a port), it remains for me to state the only fair objection that can be made to it as a place of rendezvous for shipping. This is the possibility of a future inundation, like that which happened in May 1787; since nothing less than so extraordinary a convulsion of nature can make it insecure. A traditional account of a similar disaster having befallen this part of the country coming to my hearing, I held it my indispensable duty to make what inquiry I could about it, and the only information I could obtain was from a very old man, who called himself Gollapoondi Nagy Chitty (probably Gollapúdi Nágishetti) of the Banian caste. He said he was ninety-four years of age, and that he remembered the former inundation perfectly well.

"The questions I put to this venerable informant, and the answers I received, were to the following effect:—That the former inundation happened in the month of December, eighty-three years ago (1706). That the easterly wind had blown very hard all that and the preceding day. That the water came in the night. That the present town of Coringa had then no existence, being built by Mr. Westcot, a resident of Injeram, about thirty years ago; but that old Coringa stood where it now does, though the ground on which it stands was then much higher than at present, being a sand-bank so much elevated above the level of the sea as to secure every person inhabiting it from the effects of the deluge. That this sand-bank has since gradually worn away to its present form. That people, but in no great number, were lost at Cottapollam (Kottapálem) and the other neighbouring villages; that innumerable trees were thrown down (as by the late storm) and destroyed; the paddy-fields ruined; the springs of fresh water spoiled, and great quantities of salt left upon the ground. That the flood covered the face of the country full three hours. That the villages of Yanam, Nellapilly, Comprapollam, and others, had then no existence, the country about them being at that time a continued forest. That this kind of inundation is called in the Gentoo language *Uppena.* That Gollapoondi Nagy Chitty then lived where he still does, at a village called Dungaroo (Dangéru), about four coss to the westward of Coringa. What degree of credit is due to the above report I cannot pretend to determine, much less can I venture to suggest what influence it ought to have upon the judgment and determinations of the Honourable Court. I could not, however, reconcile to myself the idea of concealing from them what information I could gain upon the subject, of how little importance soever the communication of it may be to their future deliberations and decisions." *

Writing subsequently on the causes of the inundation of May 20, 1787, which, though not so terribly fatal in its effects, was very similar to the inundations at Masulipatam in 1683 and 1864, Mr. Topping says:—

"I have considered with some attention the affair of this inundation, which, though a very extraordinary phenomenon, I do not think could be caused by an earthquake (as is generally supposed at Madras), but am of opinion might have arisen from a combination of other causes, which I take to be as follows: Firstly, From a violent and long-continued gale from the north-east, at a time when the south-west monsoon should prevail, and had actually set in many weeks previous to it, checking the northerly current, and forcing the waters back upon the coast. Secondly, From the configuration of the coast itself, peculiarly favourable to such an accident at such a crisis, as may be seen by inspecting a chart of it from Ganjam to Point Gardewar, particularly noticing the sudden projection of Point Gardewar, and the situation of Coringa in the recess or *cul de sac* of a bay. Thirdly, From the peculiar circumstances of the tides, in which it is to be observed that the inundation not only happened at the spring-tides, but at those of the new moon. That the moon had just passed her perigee. That her declination was about 22° north, and that, consequently, she had passed the meridian for several days together very near the zenith of Coringa. In short, there happened at that fatal juncture a union of almost

* Selections from the Records of the Madras Government, No. xix. On the Harbours and Ports of the Northern Circars, p. 22.

every cause that could have a tendency to elevate the waters of the sea; besides (the most powerful one of all) the furious gale before mentioned, which, I understand, blew during six days without intermission. It appears from observations that the moon not only transited the meridian very near the zenith of Coringa for several days together, but that she had been at her nearest distance from the earth at a previous time very nearly calculated to cause the highest tides that can possibly happen." *

After careful observations and diligent sounding, Mr. Topping came to the conclusion that Coringa possessed very great advantages as a port. "It had a safe anchorage, smooth water, a central situation between Madras and Bengal, on the sea-coast of the Company's own territories, a free and safe communication at all times with the shore; besides the inferior (though not unimportant) considerations of provisions being much cheaper and better than at Madras, equally good water, and, in particular, great plenty of firewood. It is true docks for large ships cannot be made there, because the flat, projecting mud-banks render the river and shores inaccessible to vessels drawing more than ten feet; but ships may be hove down keel out, if necessary, nine months in the year in the bay. . . . It is not possible (in my opinion) for a vessel, either light or loaded, to receive injury by getting on shore in any part of the Bay of Coringa. Vessels, after losing all their anchors and cables, may, and do, run in here, where they find a secure retreat from the heaviest gales that blow, even from the sea-quarter. It is, however, to be supposed that I except such extraordinary and tremendous convulsions of nature as that which happened in May 1787. . . . Captain Anderson has informed me that, in December 1784, when he commanded the 'Greyhound' Packet, that vessel lay in the Bay of Coringa (the 'Pigot,' Indiaman, being in company) during one of the heaviest gales from the eastward he ever knew; that, to his astonishment, he found no sea running, and that his vessel grounded in the soft mud on the lee shore, where she lay perfectly quiet and secure. I, therefore, beg to refer you to the journals of those ships for collateral evidence of what I have positively asserted in my Report of the Bay of Coringa, viz., that it is a place of great security for shipping at every season of the year." †

After taking careful and accurate soundings in that part of the

* Selections from the Records of the Madras Government, No. xix. p. 29.

† Ibid., p. 30.

coast, Mr. Topping came to the conclusion that there was no practicable passage from the sea into the Godavery between the Coringa river and Hope Island. "These soundings," he wrote, "were taken by way of ascertaining, past all possibility of future doubt, the existence or non-existence of a passage for ships into the Godavery this way; and I can now take upon me to affirm that there is not at low water time five feet water in any part of this track." *

Mr. Topping also constructed a tide-table, after careful and elaborated observations. It appears from this that the rise of water was 12 to 45 feet, and that, during the springs, the night tides frequently exceeded by several inches those which happened in the daytime.†

In the year 1802, Mr. Ebenezer Roebuck, a private individual resident at Coringa, constructed a dock there capacious enough to receive any ship of the Royal Navy not drawing more than 14 feet of water. He spent a large sum of money on this work, which he hoped would prove of national importance and utility. This dock was 155 feet long, and capable of receiving a ship of any length. The breadth at the bottom was 51 feet, and 76 at the top. The masonry at the bottom was 5 feet thick, and consisted of large stones and brick, with beams laid transverse and lengthways for the blocks to rest upon. These were nearly 2 feet high, consisting of two pieces for the convenience of shifting when any work was required for the keel. In common spring-tides there were from 13 feet 6 inches to 14 feet of water at the dock gate, and during a great part of the year from 14 feet 2 inches to 15 feet. The gate, which was a floating one, was 48 feet wide. The dock was drained by two steam-engines, so that the rise and fall of the tide was of no consequence so far as related to the dock, and the engines were of sufficient power to drain the dock in a few hours. ‡

H. M. S. "Albatross" and other vessels were repaired in this dock; and as it was considered important that they should be inspected by a scientific officer, the Governor in Council directed that Lieutenant Warren, the Acting-Astronomer and Marine Surveyor, should proceed to Coringa, and make an accurate survey of the river and port at that place. This survey was to be made in communication with the commander of the frigate "Wilhelmina," the Honourable Archibald Cochrane, who was directed by the Commander-in-Chief of the

* Selections from the Records of the Madras Government, No. xix. p. 28.

† Ibid., p. 2.

‡ Ibid., pp. 74, 98.

East India Squadron to make every exertion to get his ship over the flat at the bar of the river and into Mr. Roebuck's dock. After being lightened of her guns and upper masts, she drew 13 feet 6 inches of water, which was rather more than Mr. Roebuck had stated to be conveniently practicable. The attempt was, however, perfectly successful, and the ship entered the river without sustaining any damage whatever. Lieutenant Warren reported most favourably of Mr. Roebuck's dock, and submitted to the Government a most interesting Report on the practicability of large vessels entering the river; but as Coringa has ceased to be used now as a port by the ships of the Royal Navy, and other large craft, it will be sufficient if I reproduce only the conclusions at which he arrived. "I am of opinion," he wrote to the Chief Secretary in December 1805, "that, in the present state of the flat at the entrance of the river, any ship not drawing more than 12 feet 6 inches water may easily enter it in two springs, at any time of the year; and certainly in one, if assisted by anchors previously placed on the passage. I further think that the time of any vessel entering the river will be considerably shortened if undertaken during the north-east monsoon, as there is (particularly in the month of November) a very perceptible increase of water in the bay, when the wind blows south from that quarter. And, lastly, I am of opinion, that if two canals were cut across the windings of the Coringa river, the navigation of the river, which is now in great danger of being destroyed, may be preserved and improved." *

In 1855, the late Captain Christopher Biden, then the zealous and indefatigable Master-Attendant of Madras, paid a visit to the Northern Districts, and prepared a most excellent report on the ports of Coringa, Cocanada, and Nursapore. He had visited the same coast in 1846, and the observations which he then made enabled him to draw up a Memorandum for the guidance of commanders of vessels bound for Cocanada or Coringa, which was published for general information in the "Fort Saint George Gazette" in October of that year. The chief practical result of this report was a clearer marking of the shoal off the harbour of Coringa for buoys. The lighthouse on Hope Island was raised 20 feet, and the illuminating power of the light was increased.

* Selections from the Records of the Madras Government, No. xix. pp. 104, 65.

A survey of the coast in the neighbourhood of Cocanada and Coringa had previously been determined on, and in 1857–58 it was carried out by Lieutenant Taylor of the Indian navy. An admirable chart was prepared by him and Lieutenant May of the same service.

When Sir Charles Trevelyan visited Cocanada in 1859, he put on record that the harbour had been much improved by the simple expedient of straightening the mouth of the river, and extending it into the sea between groynes of rough stone. He thought, too, that the old bed of the river, which is rendered useless by this straight cut, would furnish ample space for enlarging the harbour and making docks.

However, in October 1859, the Madras Government ordered that the suggestion for improving Coringa harbour should stand over for the present. In the same year, Sir Arthur Cotton wrote a memorandum on the importance of the harbour, and Colonel Rundall sent in an elaborate proposal for its improvement.

In 1862 attention was again drawn to the main point, and it was recorded that the only means of preventing the filling up of the harbour by silt was by opening a fresh outlet for the Godavery, and making embankments across the narrow channels by which the river now makes its way into the harbour. In a despatch dated September 16, 1862, the Secretary of State approved of the proposal to cut this new outlet for the river. In consequence of this, Major Stoddard, the District Engineer, prepared a report on the measures necessary for preventing the further deterioration of the harbour, and for its improvement, accompanied by estimates, amounting to £340,000.

The latest report, however, on these ports, was prepared by Mr. Robertson, who was specially deputed to examine and report on all the ports of India. It will be useful to give rather copious extracts from this report, as it contains the most recent information on this important subject. Mr. Robertson arrived at Cocanada on the 31st of March 1871, and left on the 11th of April.

"A report on Cocanada," he writes, "may conveniently be arranged under three heads:—1. Coringa Harbour. 2. Cocanada Harbour. 3. Cocanada Bay.

"1. *Coringa River and Harbour.*—The depth of water on what is called the bar, in the channel leading to Coringa, was carefully taken by Captain Castor during the first springs of my visit. One or two places had only 3 feet 6 inches of water, but the greater part had 4 feet at low water of springs. In the very elaborate chart of Cocanada Bay, made by Lieutenants Taylor and May of the Indian navy in 1857, the depth on Coringa Bay is given as 3 feet. It would appear, therefore, that no deterioration has taken place on this bar during the last thirteen years, whatever might have taken place in previous years. The tide rises from 3 to 5½ feet, so that there is still about 9 feet at high water of springs. Notwithstanding many loose statements about the size of vessels which used to frequent Coringa, I could not obtain reliable evidence that a vessel had ever, at any time, got up to Coringa, drawing more than from 9 to 10 feet; and, even then, only when the north-east monsoon had brought more water than usual into the bay. Vessels now go to Coringa principally for repairs, and not for cargo, because the silting up of the bay has lengthened the channel up to Coringa. When statements are made that vessels of 600, or even more, tons frequent Coringa, it must be borne in mind that they are taken up there with a clean-swept hold, without ballast, and as light as it is possible to make them. It takes many tides to warp a laden vessel, larger than a cargo-boat, up to Coringa. Cocanada, naturally, is now preferred to Coringa for trade purposes.

"The channel ought to be marked out the whole way from Cocanada to the entrance to Coringa river. In such shallow water this can be done for a trifling sum. At present, every vessel has to find the channel for itself, at the expense of great delay and constant grounding. If the channel were properly buoyed off, a watch could then easily be kept on the bar, and the dredger set to work when necessary. I was informed that no dredging had been done at Coringa for six or seven years. There is so little surf in Coringa Bay that there would be no difficulty in keeping a constant depth of 6 or 7 feet, at low water of springs, on the bar, and in the channel up to Coringa river.

"It has been suggested that the head of Coringa river should be closed at Yanam, to prevent the river bringing down silt into the bay. I am decidedly opposed to this. Were it done, the approach to Coringa and Yanam would be converted into a tidal creek, which would quickly silt up. The river, probably, does not bring down very much silt with it from the Godavery, of which it is but a small offshoot, at right angles also to the main stream. I have no doubt whatever, that if the water during floods, which at present scours out a channel through the mud of Cocanada Bay, were to be cut off by a dam at Yanam, Coringa would be destroyed as a port. The other mouths of the Godavery bring down so much silt that it would speedily obliterate Coringa channel, were it not kept open by some scour. We found so little water at the head of the river at Yanam, that our steamer, drawing only 3 feet, stuck just at the entrance from the Godavery, and we had to wait for some hours till the tide rose, before we could get down the river. It would be very easy, therefore, to close Coringa river, at this point, were this desirable; but, instead of closing, I should prefer to deepen it.

"There can be no doubt that the day is not far distant when the channel to Coringa must be regarded as a canal. Were it not for the expense, the best course would be to anticipate the action of nature, and embank the channel, on both sides, all the way to Cocanada, thus shutting out the mud which comes down the neighbouring small mouths of the Godavery.

"2. *Cocanada Harbour.*—The channel at Cocanada has been much neglected of late years. It only requires some attention to keep it in as favourable a state as circumstances admit. It appears to be wider than can be kept open by tidal scour, or freshes, alone; and a good deal of silting has in consequence taken place. The river should be narrowed, by running a wall or bank on the south side, from the bridge downward, so as to make the width of the harbour approach more nearly to the width between the groynes. The north side should either be dredged at regular intervals of time, or have a timber wharf along the line of deep water, at which cargo-boats could lie.

"If the stone groynes on each side of the channel are ever lengthened, I would suggest that they should be curved a little seawards, so as to take the stream more gently into the channel from Coringa, and not so directly at right angles to it.

"During my visit, one dredger of twenty-horse power, and drawing 3 feet, was at work, and Mr. Walford, the superintendent of the dredging-machines, informed me that there had been no dredging for three years previously. Another dredger of the same size was laid up for want of a new boiler. These two dredges, if regularly worked, are perfectly able to keep up the depth of Coringa and Cocanada channels to the full amount which they have ever been. I believe the fuel for these dredges is obtained from the jungle at Hope Island.

"Immediately outside the groyne heads, I found 8 feet of water, diminishing rather rapidly to 5 feet, and then very slowly to 4 feet 6 inches, the least depth at the time of my visit. The dredger, however, had been at work for a short time. This is fully as much water as the chart of 1859 gives, which proves how easily the depth may be obtained with a little attention. A beacon should be erected at the head of the north groyne, for the harbour mouth is not easily seen from a little distance. The lighthouse at Cocanada is now little more than a harbour-light, and is not of much use to ships beating in for the anchorage.

"3. *Cocanada or Coringa Bay.*—The anchorage for ships is now five or six miles to the north of where it was at the time of Warren's survey of 1806, in consequence of the silting up of the bay. Cocanada Bay is situated at the mouth of the Godavery, and receives a great part of the discharge from that river. In time, the bay must become part of a delta.

"I have read all the reports and the many schemes for preventing, or rather delaying, this inevitable result, by diverting the main channel of the river, or closing up some of the minor ones, so as to throw more water to the south. I have also examined the river itself, in a steamer, entering by the Guvalair Nulle, and ascending the main channel as far as Yanam. An excellent view of the delta is to be obtained from the top of Hope Island lighthouse, 81 feet above the sea-level.

"It would be desirable to have another survey made of the neighbourhood of Hope Island, and of the promontory which is in course of formation to the north and east of it. Considerable changes must have taken place during the last fourteen years. It appeared to me as if the tendency of the growth of the delta was to give rather more shelter to Cocanada Bay than is shown in the chart of 1857.

"It would not be difficult, by a considerable outlay, to drain more water into the channel to the south of Hope Island, which the floods would soon enlarge. It has been suggested to put a dam across the river, and to make a new cut for it at the sudden bend, where the river, after running east, turns and discharges to the north, in obedience to the law which regulates most Indian river mouths. The cut could easily be made, and the river induced to discharge part of its water through the cut. But it would be a very expensive and difficult operation to put a dam across the main stream. The width of this is upwards of 1200 yards, and the depth more than 20 feet. The dam would be exposed to the daily ebb and flow of the tide; and, if not completed before the rains set in, and the new cut ready at the same time, the whole country would be flooded, or the dam swept away.

"It is no light matter to interfere with the formation of a delta, or to alter the mouths of such a river as the Godavery. There are not, in my opinion, sufficient data to warrant such an attempt to delay the destruction of Cocanada Bay. How are we to be sure that more actual harm may not be done to the anchorage by such diversion than by the gradual process at present going on? The bay, no doubt, receives all the silt which flows down the mouths of the river discharging into it; but the anchorage, though pushed gradually farther out, is preserved in its full depth, and receives a proportionate degree of shelter from the corresponding growth of Hope Island Point. It is very probable that if the river were to discharge its silt into the sea to the south of Hope Island, the ocean current, which for the most part of the year runs to the north, would convey the silt into the deep water at the entrance to Cocanada Bay, and gradually shoal it up. Part of the silt might be swept by the flood tide into the bay, and part deposited in the eddy which, I think, must occur at the entrance to the bay. This supposition is to a great extent conjectural, I grant; and it would require to be confirmed by a series of experiments with floats, before it is possible to give a decided opinion on the subject.

"There is one point, however, in favour of an increased discharge of water to the south of Hope Island, namely, that whatever silt comes down the river during the months in which the ocean current sets to the south, would be carried altogether away from Cocanada Bay. At present, the bay receives the silt which comes down during the whole year. The rate at which the silting up of the bay takes place, and its effect on the position of the anchorage, will diminish each year as the bay widens out. A certain amount of silt likewise must pass down the irrigation canals, and be deposited over the surface of the deltas. I think that a set of experiments with floats, such as barrels with a flag on them, should be made to determine the exact set of the currents sweeping past the mouth of the eastern channel, which runs to the south of Hope Island. If the floats do not show a decided tendency to enter Cocanada Bay, or to remain in an eddy at its entrance, then, I think, something might be safely done towards the preservation of the anchorage. It would not be difficult, by throwing out a long groyne near the entrance to the Wunka Nulle, to train the set of the stream more directly into the eastern channel, and so discharge more water to the south of Hope Island. To obtain a knowledge of the size and character of the river above the tidal portion of it, I visited the Annicut at Dowlaishweram.

"The formation of the deltas round Hope Island has placed the lighthouse many miles inland. The swampy nature of the jungle there, likewise, makes the light so obscure that it is seldom seen at a greater distance than ten miles. I would strongly advise that another light be placed some seven or eight miles to the north-east by north of Hope Island lighthouse. This light should be a floating one, for two reasons—first, that it may be shifted when required by the increase of the delta; second, that a light on screw piles, at the mouth of a river in flood, is liable to be undermined by the current if the ground is soft, especially if subject, in addition, to the action of breakers. A lighthouse in Morecambe Bay has been abandoned in consequence of this action of the current, and has been replaced by a floating light. The new floating light should have a dioptric apparatus, similar to those supplied by Messrs. Stevenson for the Hooghly, and for Yokohama in Japan. The usual height for the light is 38 feet above the sea, which would show upwards of eleven nautical miles, allowing 15 feet for the height of the eye. From aloft, the light is seen at a distance of nineteen miles. The cost of the dioptric apparatus is about £500 in this country, including certain articles in duplicate and six months' stores. The cost of the lightships on the Hooghly, as well as the expense of maintaining them, will be known to the Government. It will be necessary to keep up the light on Hope Island for some years at least, because it has been there since the beginning of the century, and is marked on all the charts, and referred to in the published sailing directions.

"The Master-Attendant at Cocanada should have a proper sea-going steam-tug at his disposal, for he has to go long distances out to vessels, and to look after the buoys. Part of the expense would be repaid by tugging cargo-boats out to vessels in the anchorage, and larger vessels up to Coringa for repairs."*

The Harbour Conservancy Act was passed on the 13th of August 1855. This Act (No. xxii. of 1855) did not come at once into operation, because a good deal of information was required before it could be applied to the various ports. The Supreme Government, consequently, suspended its introduction for two years, to allow time for collecting the necessary data regarding the limits of the ports, their trade, the amount of collections, and the particular rules to be enforced at each. Fifteen ports were named by the Board of Revenue, in the first instance, as those to which this Act was to apply. Coringa and Cocanada were among these selected ports. They were presided over by the Master Attendant of Cocanada.

An Act for controlling emigrant vessels was also passed. It was found necessary to legislate on this matter, because several irregularities had been found to exist in the matter of emigration. Serious complaints had been made by the authorities in Ceylon and the Tenasserim Provinces of the excessive numbers who had been embarked on board native vessels. Regulations had from time to time been issued on the subject, and these irregularities had been partially checked, and the emigration brought under control; but no penalties could be legally enforced, and evasions were commonly practised. A legislative Act was therefore needed. Cocanada was one of the few ports selected, at which only it became legal to embark native passengers for voyages across the seas. The number of such passengers was limited to one person to every four tons of the vessel's burden.† During the course of the following year, Nursapore was added to the ports from which it was legal to embark native passengers for long voyages.

In consideration of the growing commercial importance of Cocanada, and the increased work connected with the port, it was thought advisable to enlarge the Master-Attendant's establishment, and to raise his salary from 200 to 350 rupees a month. A shipping office was established under Act I. of 1859; and a new building was erected in a more convenient position for the offices of the

* Reports to the Government of India on Indian Harbours, by Mr. George Robertson, p. 71.

† Administration Reports for 1856–57, p. 33.

Master-Attendant and of the Sea Customs-house, the old building being appropriated to the Electric Telegraph Department.* The new building is situated in a fine commanding position on the left bank of the narrow river, up which all boats are obliged to pass in going to and from the shipping.

The lighthouse at Cocanada was completed in 1865. It also is situated on the left bank at the entrance of the river. The total outlay on this work, together with the flagstaff, groynes, &c., was 73,011 rupees.

The increase of the trade in the port in Cocanada grew yearly. In the year 1867 the native navigation had increased so rapidly, and had assumed so much greater proportions than formerly, that the Madras Government took notice of it, and mentioned the fact in their report. A superior class of native craft, of from 300 to 500 tons burden, left the port. These were sheathed with zinc and yellow metal or copper. They were commanded by intelligent natives, who used sextants and chronometers. These commanders came principally from the Maldive Islands, and many of them held certificates. Shipbuilding also was vigorously prosecuted at Cocanada, as the trade and importance at that port increased.

The revolving light which had for many years been exhibited from the lighthouse on Hope Island got very much out of repair in 1870. Though it was actually seen eighteen miles out at sea, the light was eclipsed every half minute, and complaints were made by several commanders of vessels, who stated that these rapid eclipses prevented proper bearings being taken of the light. It was ultimately resolved that a new lighthouse should be erected on screw piles off the east end of Hope Island, and five miles to the north-east of the old light, and a second-class dioptric light exhibited on it.†

This chapter will be appropriately concluded by an account of one or two of the most celebrated wrecks which have taken place on the portion of the coast included in this District.

The fine iron ship "Rajpoot," 1333 tons burden, was wrecked off Nursapore in 1866. This was, perhaps, the most remarkable wreck that

* Administration Reports for 1859-60, p. 109.

† Ibid. for 1871-72, p. 114; for 1872-73, p. 130; for 1873-74, p. 94.

ever occurred on this part of the coast, both on account of the mode of her loss and the magnitude of the interests involved. The loss was entirely attributable to great inaccuracy in the compasses, which seem to have been deranged by the influence of the iron of which the ship was constructed, and to gross carelessness in the reckoning. She was bound from London to Calcutta with passengers, and with a cargo valued at £130,000. The passengers and crew met with no mishap, but were safely landed, by means of jack-stays, run from the mast to the shore. This result was owing, in a great measure, to the exertions of a missionary residing at Nursapore, who had formerly been an officer in a merchant vessel. The cargo was rescued, with the exception of a few tons which were thrown overboard. The vessel was subsequently floated. A formal inquiry was made into the causes of the wreck, and the commander was reprimanded, and it was recommended that the certificate of the chief officer should be suspended for six months; neither of which sentences were confirmed, owing to some irregularity in the finding. The greater part of the cargo was conveyed to Calcutta by the barque "Calliope," Captain Simmons, which was at the time lying in the roads at Masulipatam, and came to the rescue. Two suits were subsequently instituted in the Civil Court for salvage, and for the value of the charter-party for conveying the cargo to Calcutta, both of which were given in favour of the master of the "Calliope."

The most important wreck, however, in regard to the greatness of the loss, was that of the "Sacramento." The "Sacramento" was a fine steam frigate belonging to the navy of the United States, and she was on a voyage round the world, with the object, as one of the officers stated, "of showing the American flag" in the most considerable ports on the globe, at the conclusion of the civil war. She had already been to many places in South America and Africa, and was proceeding from Madras to Calcutta *via* Cocanada when the disaster occurred. She was commanded by Captain Collins, a most distinguished officer, who was supported by a chosen company of officers, naturalists, and savants. At 7.30 on the evening of the 19th of June 1867, she ran on a bank about sixteen miles south of Hope Island light, and two and a half miles off shore. Every assistance was rendered by the marine and other authorities at Cocanada, for which the Government of the United States expressed their hearty thanks. No lives were lost, for the weather was fine, and the sea smooth. A raft containing twenty-nine officers and men drifted out to sea, and they were eventually picked up by Captain Ballantine of the British India Steam Navigation Company's vessel "Arabia," who put back to Cocanada with them—a service which was acknowledged by the Government of the United States by the presentation of a gold chronometer.

CHAPTER IV.

PRODUCTS, MANUFACTURES, AND ETHNOLOGY OF THE DISTRICT.

FERTILITY OF THE DISTRICT—THE DELTA—PRINCIPAL CROPS—GLANCE AT THE ZOOLOGY—FISHES OF THE GODAVERY—MANUFACTURES—GEOLOGICAL SURVEY—HEALTH OF THE DISTRICT—DISEASES OF CATTLE—LANGUAGE—CASTES—CONDITION OF THE PEOPLE—THE KOIS OR HILL TRIBES.

THE Godavery District is exceedingly fertile. With reference to its productive powers it may be broadly divided into two parts—the upland and the plains. In the former there is comparatively little cultivation. What there is consists principally of dry grains, as there is very little irrigation, except from tanks and from the mountain streams. The upland part of the District is, however, very wealthy in forest productions. Abundance of teak is grown on the banks of the river, and a great quantity of timber is floated down the stream from the interior.

The most fertile part of the District is in the plains, and especially in the Deltas, which are under the influence of the irrigation from the Annicut. In fact, this tract is as fertile as any part of Southern India, not excluding Tanjore, which has justly been called "the garden of the south." The principal crops are rice, millet, Indian corn, sugar-cane, cotton, hemp, and gingelly-oil seed.

The staple crop grown in the District is paddy, the chief varieties being white and black paddy. The cultivation of the wet crop is now commenced much earlier than could be the case formerly, when the ryots were obliged to wait for the first fall of rain or the first rising of the river. This rarely occurred before the middle of June. Now the seed-beds, being watered from the channels, are often prepared in May, and the young shoots are ready for transplanting by the time the freshes fill the channels, a month or so later. The harvest is, consequently, hastened, and the first crop of white paddy is reaped by the middle of January, the black being sometimes earlier. The other cereals are raggy, which is generally sown in July, and reaped in November; jonna or millet, sown in October, and reaped in January; korra (*Pannicum Italicum*), and gante or sazza (*Holcus spicatus*), which are usually sown in July, and reaped in September or later; and varagu, which is sown in December, and gathered in February. These crops are grown in dry land, in which also black paddy is sometimes cultivated. The latter is seldom sown alone, but is generally mixed with dhall or with cotton.

The chief green crops are dhall, gram of various varieties, such as Bengal gram, horse gram, green gram, &c.; fenugreek, gingelly-oil seeds, and mustard. They are sown from July to October, and reaped in January and February.

The extent of ground taken up by the cultivation of paddy has most considerably increased of late years. It may roughly be stated as five times larger than it formerly was. The quality of this cereal cannot be said to have improved in itself, but very much more of it is grown. A great proportion of dry land has been converted into wet, and paddy is now produced on it instead of the former dry crops. Rice, which is the staff of life of the great majority of the people, is called by different names in the various stages of its growth. The seed is called *vittulu*; the growing paddy is *vari*; the paddy, *dhányam*; rice, *biyyam*; and boiled rice, *annam*.

The following is a brief statement, showing the extent of the exceptional crops, such as cotton, sugar-cane, and indigo, grown in the District, and the assessment levied on them for nine years, namely, from Fasli 1273 (1863-64) to Fasli 1281 (1871-72).

Fasli.	Cotton.		Sugar-cane.		Indigo.	
	Extent.	Assessment.	Extent.	Assessment.	Extent.	Assessment.
	Acres.	Rupees.	Acres.	Rupees.	Acres.	Rupees.
1273	21,372	58,296	5,387	69,993	423	1,004
1274	39,375	101,884	5,535	74,998	179	449
1275	21,115	49,149	5,810	72,266	460	1,199
1276	33,123	58,187	5,453	59,425	850	1,231
1277	17,445	34,134	6,983	78,559	357	544
1278	24,563	46,695	6,694	70,972	1,080	1,849
1279	29,270	51,009	4,259	46,463	2,210	7,085
1280	23,572	39,773	5,294	55,388	1,747	6,037
1281	22,053	42,386	6,386	59,205	921	2,123

From this statement it will be observed that very little indigo is grown in the District. The much higher rate of assessment on sugar-cane than on cotton is due to the former being grown principally on wet land, and the latter on dry.

Various species of fibrous plants are grown in the District. In the year 1854, during the Crimean War, when the trade with Russia fell off, the attention of the Madràs Government was attracted to the subject of the fibres of India, and they made an effort to point out to the population of this Presidency the advantages likely to result from the more extensive cultivation of fibrous plants. A deficiency was at that time felt in the supply of flax and hemp for the English market. Expectations were raised that India would be able, in a great measure, to meet this demand. Abundance of hemp and other fibrous plants are grown there; but, as their value was not sufficiently appreciated by the ryot and the merchant, too little care had been bestowed on their cultivation and preparation. The Government, therefore, made an effort to stimulate the cultivation of these plants, and to improve the preparation of the manufactures from them, by calling for returns from every District, showing the mode of cultivation and preparation of the fibres, the expense of preparation, the quantity grown, and the capabilities of each district and locality in this respect.

We give the following description of the mode of cultivation and preparation of the principal fibrous plants grown in the District. *Zanumu*, the *cannabis sativa*, or hemp, is planted in November, and cut by the end of March; whether grown in dry or wet lands, it is cultivated as a dry grain, and never watered. Clayey soils, and those situated beyond the reach of inundation, are best suited for its cultivation. About 2200 bundles can be produced in one putti of land, each bundle yielding 1½ viss of fibre, or a total of 3300 viss, or 412½ maunds, and is valued at one rupee a maund. The expenses of cultivation are estimated at Rs. 8-8-0, and those of preparation of the fibre at Rs. 100 a putti of land. The bundles are buried in mud, and left to rot for about a week, when they are taken out and beaten in the water; and, after all impurities are removed, the fibre is collected. The quantity exported during the four years preceding this inquiry was—

	cwt.	lbs.
1851-52	700	62
1852-53	3471	9
1853-54	1149	99
1854-55	4269	63

Gógu is a fibrous plant, the leaves of which are used as a vegetable in curry, and from the fibre of which a coarse gunny is made. It is not extensively cultivated, because it diminishes the productive power of the land on which it is grown. The fibre is prepared in the same way as that of hemp. Each putti is calculated to yield 2200 bundles, each giving about 2½ viss, or 687½ maunds, valued at 687½ rupees, at one rupee a maund. It is planted in July, and comes to maturity in September.

A great number of cocoa-nut trees are grown near the coast, where the sandy soil is most favourable for them. Large plantations are to be seen in every direction, especially in the Taluk of Amalápuram, and the returns from them are exceedingly lucrative.

The following is a brief account of the mode of cultivation. Young plants of a year's growth are planted out, and watered for six years, after which they do not require much water. The trees generally bear fruit about the ninth year after transplantation. The expenses of cultivation are stated to be 668 rupees for a putti of land, namely, 140 rupees, being the price of 600 young plants; 48 rupees being the value of the labour required for planting them; and 480 rupees being the wages of labourers employed to water and tend the trees until they come into bearing. When the trees begin to bear fruit, the value of the produce of a tree, exclusive of the fibre, is estimated at about 12 annas a year, making the total value of the produce in a putti of land 300 rupees. The cocoa-nut tree yields an excellent fibre. The quantity of fibre in the above extent of land is estimated at 150 maunds, yielding Rs. 93-12-0, at 10 annas a maund. The fibre is prepared by the outer covering of the cocoa-nut being moistened, and beaten with wooden mallets, when the fibre has thus been loosened. The coir thus obtained is twisted into ropes. The fruit is exported, but very little of the fibre.*

Palmyras and date-palms are also very abundant, particularly near the coast. Toddy is, consequently, very common. Fruit is abundant. There are large plantations of plantains, pumple-noses,

* Selections from the Records of the Madras Government, No. xxiii. pp. 13, 131.

and oranges, in the Taluks of Amalápuram and Nursapore. Some of the plantains are of a most excellent flavour, particularly the *Tsakara kéli*, which receives this name on account of its peculiar sweetness. The Dutch brought a capital kind of orange from Batavia, and planted it at Palcole. The oranges there still retain the name of *Batái nárinja pandu*, or the Batavian orange. Palcole is also famous for its excellent pumple-noses and pine-apples. A very luscious orange with a loose skin is grown among the hills; but it is so different from the thick-skinned species that it has received an entirely different name in Telugu—*Kamalá pandu.*

NATURAL HISTORY.

Bison are found in the hills, and the range of mountains which runs at right angles to the Gorge, where the Godavery enters the District, is generally called in English the Bison Range, because of the numerous bison to be found there. There are also tigers, cheetas, bears, hyænas, and wild pig in these hills. Wolves are sometimes seen. In the plains there is an abundance of antelope, spotted deer, and other large game, while the various tanks swarm with wild duck, teal, and other aquatic birds. There are a great many alligators in the Godavery.

The Godavery abounds with good fish, some of which come up from the sea, and others are purely fresh water fish. Since the construction of the Annicut, however, the number of fish in the river above it has very much decreased. In 1868, Dr. Day, who had been commissioned to make inquiry into the whole subject of fisheries throughout India, visited the District, and his interesting account is here quoted.

"The fisheries at Rajahmundry are neither farmed out nor let; and from the year 1855 to 1862 only 24 rupees a year were received by Government for them. It appears to be a common scramble who can take the fish, irrespective of their age or condition. At present there is a tax of one rupee on every house inhabited by fishermen. This they appear to consider gives them a right to the fisheries. I applied to the Tahsildar for further information respecting this, and he explained that, since 1862, 'the tax on them was inflicted, and is being collected by the Municipal Department.' About thirty persons fish with cast-nets, and it appears to be a tacit agreement that the fishermen from Rajahmundry do not go to Dowlaishweram, and *vice versa.*

"Before the construction of the Annicut, sea fish were by no means uncommon opposite the town; but now they have become comparatively rare, and it is quite futile to expect to obtain large fish above the Annicut. The anglers appear to have but little sport, they sit hours and hours on the stone wall or elsewhere, baiting their hooks from time to time with coagulated blood, but they as frequently return home without as with anything worth catching. This great diminution in the number and size of fish taken by angling is said to be only of very recent years. I obtained a few sable fish (*Clupea palasa*), C. and V., which had evidently deposited their roe, and about 100 fry of the same species, apparently about a month old, and also the *Sciæna coitor*, H. B., thus distinctly proving that sea fish may either ascend the river over the Annicut, or come up the irrigation channels. There appears to be a large demand for fish, and the sable and other species ascend during the south-west monsoon when the freshes come down.

"Rising 15 feet from the bed of the river, the wall of the Annicut is 14 feet 6 inches broad at its summit. From its rear, or sea face, it forms a smooth curve technically called an "ogee curve." This is 29 feet in length, having a descent of 8·6 feet; whilst beyond this portion are large racked stones, terminating in a retaining wall, the whole of this latter being 35 feet in length, having a descent of 3 feet; whilst still further from the Annicut is a rough stone apron 114 feet in length, with a perpendicular descent of 6·9 feet. It will, consequently, be seen that for the last 29 feet, prior to reaching the Annicut wall, the ascent is a curved and perfectly smooth wall. It is asserted that up this the sable ascend, when the freshes are so high that there is no perceptible ripple over the top of the Annicut, and this, although theoretical, is probable. As to their ascending up the under-sluices it is simply impossible. Since the construction of the Annicut, the fishing for the sable at Dowlaishweram has greatly increased, for they are now detained and captured in large quantities below that structure, whilst waiting for a fresh to enable them to ascend.

"The Dowlaishweram fishermen work in gangs of from nine to twenty in each under one head man. The fish are disposed of by sale, and the proceeds divided into shares. The usual plan appears to be for each gang to possess two boats, with one long net, which is fastened at either end of the stern of each boat. These boats are then paddled round a large circuit of water, and thus taken down stream; and, gradually bringing the outer end of the net round, they tow it on shore. About four hauls are made daily by each gang. I saw forty-five sable fish captured at the first haul by three gangs of eight men each; this was considered only a moderate take. Ten of the fish were out of season from having deposited their ova. They looked dull about the eyes and head, and had a flabby, unwholesome feel. These had, no doubt, dropped their ova below the Annicut, for it is very improbable that, having once passed over it to spawn, they could return the same season, unless down the irrigation channels. Not a single one of the fry was taken below the Annicut on this or on any subsequent occasion. Each adult fish is worth about six pie. The sable is said to be taken in the greatest number in the freshes of July, August, and September, whilst about the middle of October it commences to disappear from the river, which is getting clear. Owing to the comparative sluggishness of the Godavery it can be netted through much of the freshes. Some of the fry leave as late as March, and go down the irrigation canals to the sea. Besides being captured by long seine-nets, the sable are taken by means of cast-nets, and, when the sluices are open, even by baskets which are hung over the river close to the Annicut wall, so that, as they jump, they fall into them.

"The fishermen state that there is no waste of fish taken from this locality; that all captured are sold without any trouble, and they maintain that they could sell three times the amount now taken without the least difficulty. They universally agree that the number captured is much less than it used to be, and that the fisheries have been decreasing since the erection of the Annicut, whilst above that structure large fish have almost entirely disappeared for the last few years.

"I will now detail the various species of fish which I obtained in the Godavery:—

List of Sea Fishes personally obtained in the Godavery.

Scientific and Telugu Names.	Above Annicut.	Below Annicut.	In Irrigation Canals.	Size attained.	Remarks.
Sciæna coitor, *C. V.* Goraku, *Tel.* . . .	Yes.	Yes.	?	7 in.	Breeding.
Clupea palasa, *C. V.* Pulasa, *Tel.* . . .	Yes.	Yes.	Yes.	18 "	Do.
Pristis semisagittatus, *Shaw*	No.	Yes.	No.	Large.	...

"There are other species of sea fish which also ascend; but these

I have omitted, as they come up more for the purpose of preying upon the smaller kinds than anything else; and the Annicut does not interfere with their breeding, but only assists them in procuring food. The fresh-water fishes I obtained were as follows:—

ACANTHOPTERYGÆ.

1. Ambassis, *Akkurati* and *Balimkaku*, Tel.
2. Goby, Gobius giurus (H. B.), *Tsikidundu*, Tel.
3. Nandus marmoratus (C. and V.), *Septi* and *Isoppitai*, Tel.
4. Common walking fish, Ophiocephalus striatus (Bloch), *Sowarah* and *Muttageddasa*, Tel.
5. Fresh-water sand eel, Rhynchobdella aculeata (Bloch), *Bommiddi*, Tel.
6. Spined eel, Mastacemblus armatus (Lacep), *Mudi bommiddi*, Tel.
7. Small spined eel, Mastacemblus pancalus (H. B.), *Páparélu*, Tel.

SILURIDÆ.

8. Scorpion fish, Saccobranchus singio (H. B.), *Márpu*, Tel.
9. Wallago attu (Bloch), *Váluga*, Tel.
10. Eutropius taakree (Sykes), *Salava jella*, Tel.
11. Pseudeutropius atherinoides (Bloch), *Áku jella*, Tel.
12. Pangasius buchanani (C. and V.), *Banka jella*, Tel.
13. Silondia gangetica (C. and V.), *Vanzu*, Tel.
14. Macrones cavasius (H. B.), *Nára jella*, Tel.
15. Macrones aor (H. B.), *Mudi jella*, Tel.
16. Macrones tengara (H. B.), *Saku jella*, Tel.
17. Rita crucigera (Owen), *Gudla jella*, Tel.
18. Bagarius Yarrellii (Sykes), *Ráti jella*, Tel.

CYRINDIÆ.

19. Catla buchanani (C. and V.), *Bochche*, Tel.
20. Cirrhina Leschenaultii (C. and V.), *Aruzu*, Tel.
21. Labeo fimbriatus (Bloch), *Ruchu* and *gandumenu*, Tel.
22. Labeo gonius (H. B.), *Mosul*, Tel.
23. Labeo calbasu (H. B.), *Nalla gandumenu*, Tel.
24. Barbus? *Vagamma*, Tel.
25. Barbus guentheri (Day), *Nilusu*, Tel.
26. Barbus sophore (H. B.), *Chédu perigi*, Tel. or "Bitter carp."
27. Barbus ambassis (Day), *Kalai*, Tel.
28. Crossochilus reba (H. B.), *Pullarazu*, Tel.

29. Thynnichthys? *Kala tala* and *Áku chépa*, Tel.
30. Nuria danrica (H. B.), *Konissi*, Tel.
31. Amblypharyngodon mola (H. B.), *Tallamaya*, Tel.
32. Aspidoparia morar (H. B.), *Ulatsa*, Tel.
33. Rohtee vigorsii (Sykes), *Kunninga*, Tel.
34. Rohtee microlepsis (Blyth), *Kilai*, Tel.
35. Rohtee ogilbii (Sykes), *Kunninga*, Tel.
36. Chela bacaila (H. B.), *Badishaya*, Tel.
37. Perilampus atpar (H. B.), *Áku konissi*, Tel.*

"From Dowlaishweram I proceeded to Cocanada down the canal, and took the opportunity of examining whether the sable fish make use of that communication with the sea as a means of ascent and descent. At its mouth I was able to obtain several specimens of the mature fish, which is exceedingly common at that spot, but above the locks they were absent. Still it is my belief that these may have been the mature of young fry which had come down this means of exit from the Godavery to the sea. Above the first lock from the sea there were a considerable number of the young of the same size as those taken in the Godavery at Rajahmundry, thus conclusively showing that the fry are able to make use of this communication with the sea to descend from the river; for, as already observed, the young fish cannot pass over the Annicut after the freshes are over, the water being too low. The only exit they find at Dowlaishweram is by the canal. The locks are opened several times a day for the purpose of admitting boats passing to and fro; young fry have a natural tendency to go down stream, and thus wait close to the obstruction until it is opened, when they will have little difficulty in descending, provided their capture at these spots is prohibited. I do not think, therefore, that at present it is necessary to incur any expense in building a fish pass at Dowlaishweram, as I found sea fish above that structure, and also traced the young down the canal towards the sea. The destruction of the fry in these canals is, however, on all hands admitted to be most disastrous. They are captured close to the locks, and wherever any impediment exists; whilst when the water is cut off in the canals, and they are closed for repairs, the lower end becomes dry, and the fish must either die there, or pass into the paddy-fields and be destroyed. As these fish pass down from October to January or February, this destruction

* Not having the Telugu words before me, I can be responsible for the transliteration of those words only which I can find in Brown's Dictionary.—H. M.

should be entirely prevented, and this alone would probably be one means of restoring the sable to the river.

"At Cocanada there are about forty fishermen who formerly resided within the limits of the municipality; but as their absence was considered desirable, they were presented with a suitable piece of land on which to erect their village. They consider the best season for sea fishing commences about December, and although they salt fish, it is not of a good quality. They collect the saline effervescence from the marshes, and into this they put small fish, which are allowed to remain in it for twenty-four hours, and subsequently one day's drying in the sun is deemed quite sufficient. The smell of this preserved fish is abominable. It is their impression that good salt is too expensive for it to be profitable to them to use it in curing fish. They have a yearly ceremony about December, when they boil milk and rice together on the banks of the Godavery, which they then worship, and subsequently have a feast off some goats which are killed for the occasion. In the fresh-waters, and tanks fed by the irrigation canals, it is asserted there has of late years been a considerable falling off in the quantity of fish taken, and consequently the price has risen. This falling off of fish, however, can hardly be due to anything but the destruction of the fry, as I was fortunate enough to be able to ascertain. The Collector, Mr. Fraser, kindly allowed me to have one haul of a seine-net in a tank at Cocanada fed by the irrigation channel. For the last two years the water has been used for drinking purposes, and all netting consequently prohibited. In this haul twenty-seven large *Bochchelu* were taken, weighing from 5 lbs. to 9 lbs. each, besides an enormous number of small fish, consisting of the young of this species, and other inhabitants of fresh water. This was most interesting, showing the effects of preservation; such fine fish of this kind it would be simply impossible to obtain from any irrigation channels or tanks which are constantly netted." *

MANUFACTURES.

The chief manufactures of the District are cloths, carpets, and cheroots. Most excellent cloths are made at Uppáda about ten miles north of Cocanada, and in several villages near Nílapalli and Nursapore. The weavers are, however, in a very impoverished condition, and this branch of industry has languished since the abolition

* Proceedings of the Madras Government, Revenue Department, 4th February 1869.

of the close trade in the days of the East India Company's monopoly. The fine turbans made at Uppáda are still in great requisition in the District. Tent cloth of superior quality is manufactured in the villages near Rajahmundry and in the Central Jail. Very good carpets are made in the town of Ellore by the Mohammedan inhabitants of the town, who are descendants of Persian settlers, and they are always kept in full employment, for the carpets are in great demand even in the English market. Excellent cheroots are made from the rich tobacco grown in the District, and are named "lunkas," from the islands on which the tobacco is principally grown. Curious toys, figures, and artificial fruits are made by a family of the Muchi caste at Nursapore. They are rather larger, but quite as lifelike, as the similar figures manufactured at Condapilly in the Kistna District. Excellent saltpetre is manufactured at Ellore, and cocoa-nut oil at Amalápuram.

GEOLOGY.

In the year 1835 Dr. De Benza accompanied Sir Frederick Adam, the Governor of Madras, on a tour through the Northern Circars, and gave an account of the geological observations which he had made during the journey in the number of the "Madras Journal of Literature and Science" for January 1837. His researches did not extend far beyond the high road, as his party traversed the District from Ellore to Tuni. The hills to the north are described as of granite formation, intermixed with gneiss and amygdaloidal trap and calcareous tufa, with a scanty admixture of fine porcelain clay. To the east the hills are of sandstone, containing deposits of iron ore. In the Delta the soil is alluvial.*

The geological survey of the District has recently been made, and it is expected that the results will soon be published. As the complete account, however, has not yet been given, the general character of the geological formation can be gathered only from the fragmentary notices which have already appeared.

Sandstone extends from the Godavery near Bhadráchalam until it is lost, about sixty miles farther south, beneath the coast alluvium in the neighbourhood of Ellore. To the south-east it stretches nearly as far as Rajahmundry, extending to the banks of the Godavery at Pólavaram, below the great gorge, in the metamorphic rocks through which the river runs. At Pangadi, about ten miles due west of Rajahmundry, on the opposite side of the river, the sand-

* Thornton's Gazetteer.

stones are covered by the bedded dolerites of the Deccan trap, just as 300 miles in a direct line to the north-west, the same sandstones in the districts of Chanda and south-east Berar disappear beneath the same traps on the eastern verge of the great basaltic area of the Deccan.

The beds of sandstone extending south of the Godavery towards Ellore and Rajahmundry appear to differ in no important respect from the rocks in Chanda. In the neighbourhood of these towns the sandstones are variegated in a peculiar manner. They are associated with numerous hard bands of ferruginous grit, and compact red and yellow shale. In one instance, they were found to have a semi-vitreous texture, which is very characteristic of some beds in Chanda and Berar. All these indications led to the conclusion that these rocks were representations of the *kámthi* beds of Nagpore and Chanda. "Let it not be supposed," says Mr. W. T. Blanford, who discovered the existence of these rocks, "that this conclusion is a mere abstract scientific matter, interesting to geologists, but of no importance to the world in general. In reality it involves the most serious question, whether coal can be discovered in the Madras Presidency." Hitherto no rocks with which coal has been associated in India had been found south of the Godavery. It was, therefore, very probable that, if sandstones belonging to the great series of the coal-bearing beds of Berar were found, coal would also be discovered, which eventually proved to be the case.

The following are the limits of the *kámthi* sandstone area near Rajahmundry and Ellore. The northern boundary runs nearly east and west from Ráigúdem on the Godavery to Paluncha. Thence turning sharply to the south, it passes first south, and then south-east to Chintalapúdi, twenty miles from Ellore, in the north-western angle of our District. From Chintalapúdi the boundary must be continued to the south, passing just east of Nuzvíd, whence it turns to the south-west, and finally reaches the alluvial plains of Ellore near Krishnavaram, a village sixteen miles west by south of Ellore. *Kámthi* beds stretch along the edge of the alluvium from this point to the Godavery, trap intervening. The beds are, in general, flat or dip at low angles. Rocks of the *Demúda* group have not been discovered among them. The north-eastern limit of the sandstone area extends from the Godavery to Pondigul, twelve miles below Bhadráchalam, through the western portion of the mass of hills which culminate at the trigonometrical station of Rajgota.

Passing a few miles east of Ashwarowpéta, it trends nearly due east, in the direction of a point only a little south of Pólavaram. The part of the Godavery District occupied by it may, consequently, be described as a figure of irregular shape contained between Chintalapúdi, Ashwarowpéta, Pólavaram, Pangadi, and Ellore.

The hills west of Pangadi consist principally of trap, overlaid in part by sandstone or conglomerate; underlying sandstone appears only on their northern edge, close to Dúdukúr. The fossiliferous limestone band is distinctly intertrappean, but at a small height above the base of the volcanic rocks. The trap is fine-grained and compact, decomposing into the usual soft earthy greenish rock. All around, the country is covered with black cotton soil, and agate fragments are scattered about. To the eastward the hills are thickly capped with ferruginous grit and conglomerate, precisely resembling that in the *Kámthis*, and probably derived from their waste. This rock is well seen near Daicharla and south of the bungalow at Pangadi. In the latter place it consists of coarse white speckled felspathic sandstone, yellowish-brown in colour, with ferruginous bands. The trap can be of but little thickness, probably not more than 200 to 250 feet. It is seen on the road from Pangadi to Rajahmundry, and reappears north of the latter town, whilst the overlying sandstone appears to form the hills at Dowlaishweram.

After Mr. Blandford had discovered and cursorily examined the area of brown and red *Kámthi* sandstones, which is to be found to the west of the Godavery opposite Rajahmundry, Mr. King had an opportunity of going more closely over the same ground, but without being able to discover any other locality in which rocks of a distinctly *Barákar* character, that is, of the coal-bearing nature, occurred than the small portion seen by Mr. Blandford. As this was the only part of the Madras Presidency in which sandstones belonging to the Indian coal-bearing rocks had yet been found, Mr. King undertook a more minute investigation of them. The extent of the field was, however, very small, and it at first appeared to be destitute of any absolute indications of coal.

The field of these beds is about five and a half square miles in extent, being situated on the head waters of a large feeder of the river Yerra kálava, with the village of Beddadanole in its midst. It is thirty-eight miles west-north-west of Rajahmundry, and about four miles from the boundary of the Nizam's dominions near Ashwarowpéta. The nearest large village, Ganapavaram, lies a mile and a half to the south. The area of the sandstones itself is covered by thick tree jungle, and is very thinly populated.

The strata extend for some width on either side of the river; on the left there is a width of little more than a mile with a length of something more than four miles, while the patch is narrower on the right, being about a mile wide in the middle and thinning off to the north and south. The rocks are thick and thin-bedded, coarse felspathic sandstones, rather friable, of white or pale grey and buff colours. They occasionally exhibit ferruginous concretions on the weathered surface. The dip is, as a rule, south-west or westwards at low angles of 2°, 5°, and 10°, and there are occasional undulations. In the small stream south of Beddadanole there is a tolerably continuous outcrop of sandstones, having a general dip of 2° to 5° to the south-west, with frequent easy rolls all down the bed, until it debouches on the main stream. Very much the same kind of section is seen of the nullah north of the village, and again in a side stream further north. In the main river there are frequent outcrops of these sandstones below the junction of the first feeder mentioned above, and away in the jungle on either bank; but the best outcrops are seen higher up at the watering-place north-west of Beddadanole, and thence upwards along the river course. Here there is a good deal of sandstone displayed on either side of the stream in thick beds, having an easy dip to the west. These are overlaid by a more compact and hard brown bed, which seems to mark the change upwards into *Kámthi* beds, as it is succeeded by thinner yellow strata, and then by the red purple and brown beds characteristic of that series in this part of the country.

It is very difficult to estimate the thickness of the *Barákars* as developed in the area under notice, owing to the frequent rolling of the strata; but as far as could be made out in the three stream traverses of the Beddadanole side of the field, there must be at least 300 feet without reckoning the strata on either side of the river which are not at all so clearly seen. To the west of the field the land rising to the flat-topped hills of Pirampúdi is all made up of *Kámthis*, under which the Beddadanole *Barákars* may extend for any distance, though they will, if such be the case, be at too great a depth to justify mere trial boring, unless some better evidence of coal can be obtained from the sandstones now exposed. On the whole, it is very much to be feared that there is here only a small patch of *Barákars*, which does not extend far under the *Kámthis*, so that, if coal were eventually struck, the quantity would be so small as to be merely sufficient for local use. The *Kámthis*, considered to be, in part at least, representative of a higher series (Panchet), had thickened out greatly in this direction, and constituted the great area of sandstones to the north of Ellore and the west of the Godavery, which had in no case been found to contain coal. Mr. King advised, however, that borings should be made, though he did not anticipate the finding of coal in any great quantity, in order that the question might be finally settled. The most important point, and indeed the only tangible point, was that the rocks of the Beddadanole area were *Barákars*—that is, they belonged to the lower member of the *Damúda* series, or the coal-bearing rocks of India.*

Coal-boring operations have recently been undertaken. No great amount of money was expended on them during the last year of which accounts have been received; but the exploration is to be renewed with superior tools for the purpose to be obtained from England. A seam of coal of inferior quality, more than four feet thick, was discovered.

HEALTH.

The Godavery District is considered one of the most healthy in the Presidency of Madras. The climate is comparatively equable, and, although it is very hot indeed during two months of the year, it is never very oppressive during the remainder. It may safely be asserted that there is no cooler or more healthy place in the plains than Nursapore. The mortuary returns, all imperfect as they are, are the only means of ascertaining the general health of the District, and they show that it can be compared favourably with that of other parts of India. The following is the death ratio per thousand for the six years commencing with 1866:—

1866 . . .	31·7
1867 . . .	17·8
1868 . . .	14·4
1869 . . .	22·3
1870 . . .	27·1
1871 . . .	14·9

The exceptionally high rate in this District in 1866 and 1870 can

* Records of the Geological Survey of India, vol. iv. p. 49; vol. v. pp. 28, 113.

be accounted for by the destructive visitations of cholera which occurred in those years. Fever also was very prevalent during the cold season of 1869–70.

The health of the District is, to a certain extent, affected by the seasons. On the setting in of the rainy weather and during the rains, rheumatism and chest affections are more common than during the hot weather; and in the cold weather the inhabitants of the District suffer from fever and diseases of the kidneys.

Fever is the most prevalent disease in the District, and occasions the greatest mortality. It is endemic, but is always worse during the cold weather, and more especially during the months of December and January, when chilly winds blow from the north-east over the jungly hills. It is induced by the habit of the natives sleeping outside their houses and exposing themselves to the influence of the wind, and it is aggravated by their practice of treating it by starvation. When attacked, they starve for several days at a time, each period of starvation being called in Telugu *lankhanam*, and the disease has all the more power over them when they are thus weakened and reduced. The fever is generally of the intermittent type. It is accompanied by ague. The hills in the north are peculiarly feverish. The disease is chronic among the inhabitants of these hills, and few persons from the low country can visit them without being attacked by this insidious enemy. It does not show itself generally while the visitor is moving about from place to place among the hills, but it comes out in all its force when he returns to the plains and approaches the sea. The most healthy season is during the hot weather, which is the very reverse of the case in the Wynaad and on the western coast; and the setting in of the rains brings out the malaria from the decayed vegetation, and renders the whole tract of jungle unhealthy. The prevalence of fever in the plains is not so regular and constant. Some seasons are worse than others. At the end of 1869 and the beginning of 1870 it was very bad, and in the following year the late Assistant-Surgeon Wright, in whose early death the Government have lost the services of a most energetic and promising officer, was ordered to proceed to the District, and to make a thorough investigation into the reasons of the outbreak.

It was clearly ascertained by this inquiry that this outbreak of fever was not attributable, as some had erroneously imagined, to the increase of irrigation in the District. It was entirely caused by the malarious winds which prevail during the north-east monsoon. The following are the conclusions to which the Sanitary Commissioner arrived after the perusal of Mr. Wright's Report on the subject:—

"It has seemed to me to be a point of the very greatest importance to determine whether the periodical outbreaks of fever in this District have increased in severity since the Godavery Irrigation Works have been completed. Practically there are no data to show what the health condition of the present irrigated districts was before the Annicut was built. Mr. Wright implies that the tracts now unhealthy formerly bore the repute of being salubrious; but mere native opinion on such a subject as the progressive insalubrity of a locality, without facts or figures in support of it, is of little value, and I am not inclined to attach any importance to it in the face of the actual facts of the last five years, viz., that the fever death-rate has been considerably higher in the non-irrigated than in the irrigated Taluks of the District.

"In order to compare the fever statistics of the irrigated and non-irrigated Taluks of the Godavery District, I have examined the data for the five years ending December 1870, and, as the results for a lengthened period are more likely to be accurate than when taken for a single year, I think the following figures represent the nearest approximation to the truth:—

"In the irrigated Taluks of the District the mean annual death-rate from fever for the five years (1866–70) was	8·12 per mille.
In Zamindari estates, mostly on the seaboard and irrigated	8·5 "
In Taluks above the Delta and not irrigated from the river Godavery . . .	11·05 "

From these figures it will be apparent at a glance that the intensity of fever in the District is most marked in the Taluks which cannot possibly have been influenced by the system of irrigation works, inasmuch as these Taluks are altogether above, or outside of, the irrigated area.

"My conviction is that the periodical accessions of fever in the Godavery District are due to the geographical position of that District in respect to malarious lands to the north and west, and that the fever is due to the northerly winds of the north-east monsoon sweeping over the malarious jungles of the hill tracts of the Northern Circars before they reach the Godavery District. In respect to individual Taluks and estates, Mr. Wright has shown the correctness of this observation, and that the Taluks which are the most open to influences from the sea have the least fever, while those parts of the District which are exposed most to the winds which have blown across unhealthy jungles have had the highest ratios of fever prevalence and mortality. The results of five years' registration demonstrate in a very clear manner that the intensity of fever in any Taluk has no relation to the extent of irrigation of the land, but is solely due to its geographical position and its exposure to malarious winds during the north-east monsoon.

"The irrigated districts do not all suffer in the same degree from fever. Thus, for five years the death-rate in the Rámachandrapuram Taluk was 11·9 per thousand, while in Amalápuram and Nursapore the rates were 6·5 and 4·6 per mille only. The difference I attribute entirely to the position of the Taluks, the former being exposed to the malarious winds from the north, while the latter are exposed mainly to sea-breezes." *

One of the principal diseases of the District is beriberi. The Telugu name for this disease is *ubbu váyuvu*, or rheumatism, with dropsical swelling. Though endemic in many situations, it is frequently epidemic after the setting in of the rains. It has the same origin as fever, namely, the malarious exhalation from rank vegetation. Natives suffer from it much more than Europeans, indeed it is very rare to hear of the latter being attacked with it; and it is more prevalent on the coast than inland. It is a disease of middle life, and is peculiar to males, never having been observed in females. It is both chronic and acute. The acute form is usually attended by intermittent fever; and the chronic form is more frequently the sequel of rheumatism and fever.†

Cholera and smallpox are sometimes very prevalent. The former is merely an epidemic, visiting the District from time to time with fearful virulence, and chiefly invading it from the north, through Ganjam and Vizagapatam. The latter is, more or less, endemic. Cholera very frequently succeeds a severe outbreak of smallpox. The sanitary condition of the houses and of the villages render these

* Proceedings of the Madras Government, Public Department, June 14, 1871. See also Government Order of December 30, 1872, No. 1413.

† Medical Topography of the Northern Division, p. 89.

diseases more widespread and obstinate than they would be if they had not these predisposing circumstances to lay hold of.

The District cannot be said to be very healthy for cattle. So much of the land in all the Delta Taluks is taken up for cultivation that very little has been reserved for pasturage. The ryots in these Taluks make it a practice to send their cattle during the cultivating season to graze in the inner and upland Taluks, where there is a much greater abundance of fodder for them. The grass which grows on the banks of the canals in the Delta is very prejudicial to the health of cattle. This grass, being grown on land watered from the Annicut, becomes very rank, and causes the cattle that feed on it to contract a disease called in Telugu *Jelaga rōgam*, which generally proves fatal. Leeches are bred in the stomach of the animal, and eat into its intestines, death being occasioned by hæmorrhage. The mortality among the cattle in the District is consequently very great. Inflammation of the throat is also another dangerous disease to which the cattle are peculiarly liable. The following table shows the reported mortality among the cattle during a period of eighteen years:—

Fasli.	Number of Deaths.	Fasli.	Number of Deaths.	Fasli.	Number of Deaths.
1264	19,113	1270	17,855	1276	22,357
1265	16,060	1271	27,201	1277	17,364
1266	20,020	1272	12,766	1278	23,580
1267	15,708	1273	17,351	1279	28,294
1268	8,182	1274	14,364	1280	25,403
1269	15,764	1275	23,041	1281	36,090*

LANGUAGE.

The language of the Godavery District is Telugu. About three per cent. of the inhabitants, or perhaps less, are of Mohammedan descent, and speak Hindustani, and Koi is spoken by some of the Hill people in the interior; but Telugu is the vernacular language of the great majority of the people of the District. The Godavery District occupies the centre of the maritime part of the country inhabited by the Telugu-speaking people, and it is spoken there with greater purity than anywhere else. The Telugu people number about thirteen millions, of whom about eleven millions and a half are in the Presidency of Madras, and they extend as far inland as Bellary and

* MS. Records and Settlement Reports.

Mysore. The whole Telugu country may with tolerable accuracy be described as lying within the area contained by lines drawn from the four following points :—Tekkali, in the Ganjam District; Pulicat, a few miles north of Madras; Nandidroog, in Mysore; and Gulbarga, in the territories of the Nizam.

Telugu belongs to the Dravidian family of languages. When the Sanscrit-speaking people, who belonged to the Aryan family, gradually penetrated from the north of India, where they had settled after their immigration from the north-west, and entered on new conquests towards the south, they drove into the hills or subjugated the aboriginal race. The languages of this people are called Dravidian.

Of all the Dravidian languages Telugu is the sweetest and most musical. It is exceedingly mellifluous, and sounds harmonious even in the mouth of the most vulgar and illiterate. It has justly been called the Italian of the East; and though Tamil may, perhaps, be a richer language, and more wealthy in classical literature, we would prefer Telugu on account of its exquisite beauty and melody. Every word properly ends with a vowel. Words of purely Telugu origin are short, and are usually dissyllabic; and the best Telugu consists of such words skilfully mingled with a few Sanscrit derivatives, just as the best and most nervous English is that in which plain Saxon words are used with the least admixture of Latin. The language has, however, been strengthened and enriched by Sanscrit, especially in religious and scientific subjects, which have been imparted by the learning of the Aryan invaders.

POPULATION.

The population of the District, according to the last census, is 1,592,939. The great majority of the inhabitants are, of course, Hindus, 1,555,981 being of that religion, 35,173 Mohammedans, 39 Buddhists or Jains, and 1483 Christians.

The relative number of the principal religious sects is as follows: —1,219,676 Vishnavaites, 323,288 Shivaites, 10,210 Lingayets, and 2807 who were returned as "other Hindus." The proportion of the two chief sects is 78·3 of Vishnavaites, and 20·8 Shivaites in every hundred of the Hindu inhabitants, so that by far the greater number are the special worshippers of Vishnu. Only 5·8 of the Hindus are Brahmins. These are most numerous in the Taluks of Amalápuram, Rámachandrapuram, Nursapore, and Tanuku. The most numerous of the principal castes are the agriculturists and the

Málas or Pariahs, there being 498,373 of the former, and 372,688 of the latter. There are 165,833 toddy-drawers, 65,905 weavers, and 58,809 shepherds. Fuller and more comprehensive statistics will be found in the tables in the Appendix.

The inhabitants of the District in general, and especially the agricultural classes, are most prosperous. The condition of the ryots has decidedly improved since the great extension of irrigation consequent on the construction of the Annicut and the canals dependent upon it. The prosperity of the ryots is evident to the most casual observer. The gradual substitution of tiled houses for thatched, the better dress which is being used by the ryots, the more universal adoption of rice as an article of diet rather than Indian corn and other dry grains formerly in almost universal use, are all silent but certain indications of the improvement of the agricultural and even of the labouring classes.

The ordinary dress of a ryot is very simple. Its cost varies according to the quality of the material; but the average value of a man's costume is from two to five rupees. It generally consists of a lower garment (*dhôvati*), of an upper garment (*uttariyam*), and of a turban or head-cloth (*pága*).

The house usually occupied by an ordinary ryot is as simple as his costume. It consists of one or two rooms, built with mud and thatched with palmyra leaves. The ploughing oxen or the cows frequently occupy part of the same building as the family. A few earthenware pots and brass utensils comprise the whole of the furniture, with the exception, perhaps, of a low cot or "charpoy" with the bottom made of tape. The increase of the family prosperity is chiefly seen in the better quality of the cloths worn, in the superior kind of food eaten, and especially in the greater number of the jewels worn both by the men and by the women, particularly on the occasion of the usual Hindu feasts. A prosperous townsman generally inhabits a rather larger house than the peasant does. His house consists, perhaps, of three or four rooms, with a courtyard in the centre. A raised chunam seat, called in the south a "pial," and in the Telugu country *arugu*, is to be seen on each side of the entrance door, where the owner sits in the cool of the evening to hear the gossip of the day, and to chat with his friends. The utensils are very similar to those in an ordinary ryot's house, only of a better quality and more numerous. There are more brass pots and dishes, and other vessels, all being kept scrupulously bright and clean. Some of the cups may be of silver. Of what we call furniture there is none, except a few chairs in the houses of the most wealthy, who may desire to imitate European manners. Generally there are a few lacquered wooden boxes to contain the family jewels, cooking utensils, and palmyra leaf books, or perhaps a mat or two or a rug to sit on. The general articles of food are rice, dhall, curds, and butter-milk, tamarinds, ghee—that is, clarified butter—and vegetables. Some of the lower castes eat meat and fish. The lowest orders live on raggi or on Indian corn. The average monthly expense of the household of the middle class is about fifteen rupees, and that of an ordinary ryot is four rupees.

The mountains in the north of the District are in a great measure inhabited by an aboriginal race called Kois. This people are of the same family as the Gonds, the Khonds, and the other primitive races of Southern and Central India, and they all are probably the descendants of the former inhabitants of the country, who were driven into the mountains and forests at the time of the great Brahminical invasion.* The Kois themselves say that they are descendants of Bhímadúr; and the local tradition is that, when Bhímadúr accompanied his brother Dharma Rázu to his forest exile, he one day went hunting in the jungle, and there met a wild woman of the woods, with whom he fell in love and whom married. The fruit of their union was the Koi people. The tradition further states that this wild woman was not a human being. Their language has an affinity to that of the Khonds. It is quite distinct from Telugu, which language, however, the Kois living near the Telugu country understand and speak in an uncouth and barbarous manner. It contains a few words apparently of the same origin as the Dravidian languages, but there are more Tamil words in it than Telugu, which is the case in most of the aboriginal languages of the South. The Kois extend some distance inland, and are found on the banks of the Upper Godavery and its affluents on the north, but they are most numerous towards Bustar.

The term Koi is spread over a wide area. The Gonds, with whom the Kois of this District are allied, divide themselves into twelve classes. There are the Raj Gond, Raghuwál, Dadave, Katalyá,

* The Ethnological Commission of the Central Provinces appointed in 1868 divided the aboriginal races to be found in that part of India into two great classes—the Kolarian and the Dravidian. The Kois were classified among the ten races named under the latter head with the Gonds and Khonds.

and others. These four are comprehended under the name Koitor—the Gond, *par excellence.* This term, in its radical form of Koi, is given to the Meria-sacrificing aborigines of Orissa, as well as to the jungle tribes in this District who skirt the east bank of the Godavery as far up nearly as the mouth of the Indravati. Its meaning is evidently associated with the idea of a hill, the Persian name of which, *Koh*, approaches it more closely than the Telugu, *Konda.**

The Kois are a simple-minded people. They look poor and untidy. Their hair, especially that of the women, is usually dishevelled and unkempt. They look emaciated and haggard, which is generally the result of disease. The jungles in which they reside are very unhealthy, and the Kois who live in the Godavery District seem almost to a man to suffer from chronic fever. Their requirements are few, and their wants easily supplied. They lead an unsophisticated, savage life, and have few ideas, and no knowledge beyond the daily events of their own little villages; but this withdrawal from civilized existence is favourable to the growth of those virtues which are peculiar to a savage people. Like the Khonds, they are noted for truthfulness, and are quite an example in this respect to the civilized and more cultivated inhabitants of the plains. They call themselves *Koitors*, the latter part of which appellation has been very easily and naturally changed by the Telugu people, and by the Kois who come most closely into contact with them, into *Doralu*, which means "lords;" and they are always honoured by this title in the Godavery District.

Their villages are small, but very picturesque. They are built in groups of five or six houses, in some places even a smaller number, and there are very rarely so many as ten or fifteen. A clearing is made in the jungle, and a few acres for cultivation are left vacant round the houses. In clearing away the wood, every tree is removed except the *ippa*-trees (*Bassia lattifolia*) and tamarind-trees, which are of the greatest service to the people on account of their fruit and shade. The Kois do not remain long in the same place. They are a restless race. Four years suffice to exhaust the soil in one locality, and they do not take the trouble to plough deeper, but migrate to another spot, where they make a fresh clearing, and erect a new

* Rev. S. Hislop's Aboriginal Tribes of the Central Provinces, edited by Sir Richard Temple, p. 4.

village. Their huts are generally covered with melons and gourds the flowing tendrils of which give them a very graceful appearance, but the surrounding jungle makes them very damp and unhealthy.

When the cultivation season is over and the time of harvest draws on, the whole of the village turn out by families, and live on the small wooden scaffoldings erected in the fields, for the purpose of scaring away the wild animals and birds which come to feed on the ripening grain. Deer and wild pigs come by night to steal it, and flocks of kids by day. Tigers and cheetas often resort to the fields of Indian corn, and conceal themselves among the lofty plants. Poorer kinds of grain are also grown, such as millet and maize, out of which the people make a kind of porridge called *java*. They likewise grow a little cotton, from which they make some coarse cloth, and tobacco. The *ippa*-tree is much prized. The Kois eat the flowers of this tree, which are round and fleshy. They eat them either dried in the sun or fried with a little oil. Oil both for lights and for cooking is obtained from the nut, from which also an intoxicating spirit is extracted.

The Kois have no caste, and profess a very simple and primitive religion. They have no written language, and, consequently, they have no literature, no sacred books, and no systematic worship. They believe in one Supreme Being, but their devotion to Him is of a very vague and indefinite nature. They say they worship the spirits of the mountains, and pay homage to Korra Rázu, their tutelary guardian, who protects them from the ravages of tigers. This is the commonest form of worship among them; but it does not appear to go very deep into their hearts, and is inspired more by the dread of the enemy which is nearest to them, and enters most into their everyday thoughts and feelings. Some say they also worship Bhímadúr, from whom they are said to have sprung. They have no pagodas or sacred places. They call on the manes of their ancestors, and offer them libations of milk. In some places the usual village goddesses are invoked; but these villages are near the country inhabited by Hindus, and are occupied by people who have come in contact with Hinduism. The only image which they appear to possess is called *Neshani*, probably derived from the Hindustani *Nishan*, a flag, which is something like an umbrella, with a flag attached to the handle. It is said to be kept in the mountains, and the people point, when mentioning it, to the part of the country where Bustar is situated. It is reported to be in a village called Gangalúru, and to be kept by a people named *Marmivándlu.* The Kois sometimes go thither on pilgrimage. This image is also called *Velpu.*

The Kois look forward to a future state of existence. They regard heaven in the material form of a large and strong fort, where there is an abundance of rice stored up for those who are permitted to enter. Hell is a place in which an iron crow continually gnaws the flesh of the unfortunate persons detained there. Those who are kind, hospitable, and charitable, are the characters whom they expect to enjoy eternal bliss, and to enter the fortress of heaven.

They permit the re-marriage of widows. Their weddings are exceedingly primitive, and the wedding ceremony very simple. Matches are sometimes made by force. If peaceable negotiation fails, the bride is forcibly seized and carried off, but they prefer the quieter and easier mode of wooing. At the time of the wedding ceremony, the couple have each a triangular mark made on their foreheads. They kneel together, the woman with her head a little lower than the man's, and water is poured over them both. The ceremony is then supposed to be complete.

This simple and interesting people are open to religious instruction, and the missionaries speak very highly of their friendliness and docility, and of the receptive nature of their minds. They feel their own ignorance, and are ready to receive instruction. Sir Arthur Cotton was the first pointedly to call attention to the promising field for missionary labour, which the Kois present in common with the Santals, the Gonds, the Shanars, the Karens, and other aboriginal tribes. A mission to them was commenced in 1860 at Dumagúdem, when the works on the Upper Godavery were being carried on. It was energetically supported by Colonel Haig of the Royal Engineers (Madras), who was at the head of the works, and several European missionaries have resided there. The climate, however, was so prejudicial to the health of European residents that it was for a time considered advisable for the mission to be placed under the charge of the godly and devoted convert, Rázu, who is now an ordained minister of the Church of England. The Rev. J. Cain has, however, recently gone to reside there and to prosecute the mission work.*

* Sixty-first Report of the Church Missionary Society, p. 158; Church Missionary Intelligencer for 1860, p. 152; ibid. for 1861, pp. 124, 310; ibid. for 1863, p. 156; ibid. for 1864, p. 56; Church Missionary Gleaner for 1868, p. 109.

CHAPTER V.

EDUCATION.

FORMER CONDITION AS TO EDUCATION—MR. TAYLOR'S SCHEME FOR ELEMENTARY EDUCATION—APPROVAL OF THE GOVERNMENT—DOUBTS AS TO THE VOLUNTARY NATURE OF THE RATES—DEPARTMENT OF PUBLIC EDUCATION—MADRAS EDUCATION ACT.

RAJAHMUNDRY was one of the first Districts to take advantage of the era of educational improvement which was inaugurated by the despatch of the Court of Directors in 1854. Praiseworthy efforts in this direction had, however, been made in previous years. In the year 1826 the Collector, Mr. Bayard, established, under instructions from Government, three schools, one at Rajahmundry, another at Cocanada, and a third at Nursapore. They lasted ten years, and were then abolished. The school at Nursapore had an attendance of fifty pupils at the date of its abolition, which showed that a good number of the inhabitants were anxious to avail themselves of educational advantages when offered to them. The first advance in the new direction was made at Nursapore. When Mr. George Noble Taylor was Sub-Collector, a society was formed there with the object of advancing the interests of education. An Anglo-vernacular school was established at Nursapore itself, the headquarters of the Sub-Division, and branch schools at the towns of Pálkólu, Penugonda, and 'Atsanta, all of which were supported by local subscriptions.

It having come to Mr. Taylor's knowledge that some of the principal inhabitants of the villages and of the wealthy farmers who frequented the markets at these places had been attracted by the novelty of the schools established in them, he conceived the idea of extending the scheme to the whole of the Sub-Division. In August 1854 he brought the subject to the notice of Sir Walter Elliot, then Commissioner of the Northern Circars, stating that he had received applications for the establishment of primary vernacular village schools from the inhabitants of twenty-four villages. They had come forward, he said, of their own accord to solicit his assistance. They proposed to defray the cost of maintaining the proposed schools by a fixed annual addition to the demand of each village at the time of the annual settlement, which would form a permanent allowance like the allowances given to the village officers, and would be applied solely for educational purposes. "The plan thus proposed," Mr. Taylor wrote, "appears to me to be open to less objection than any that could be devised under present circumstances, and until a general and comprehensive system of public instruction is set on foot by Government. The population of these villages is almost purely agricultural, and it is but fair that the whole body of ryots should contribute towards the support of an institution that would be available for all alike, and the expense is so trifling that it would fall very lightly on each individual member of the community. The influential head-men would have the direction and apportionment of this as well as of every other item of the joint-rent, and its distribution would be regulated under the same checks which are found to prevent abuse with regard to other fixed allowances.

"It might be thought more desirable to leave the people to settle a matter of this kind among themselves without any interference on the part of Government. If, it may perhaps be said, they are desirous to subscribe for a school, let them collect the money and appoint a master; but, from my experience of the native character, and from frequent conferences I have held with those of the ryots who most desire this particular improvement, I am satisfied that voluntary contributions, properly so called, without the direction and sanction of authority, can never be looked for, and that the project would instantly fall to the ground if left to the uncontrolled management even of the most experienced among them. The fact is that, in matters of education, we have left the people too long alone, and it seems to me that when we find them eager and willing to assess themselves for their own improvement, we ought to take advantage of this first effort towards social progress in the most legitimate way that presents itself.

"It is essential that the proposal should emanate from the village itself, and the amount to be so applied fixed by the inhabitants, who in a body should be required to signify their assent to the arrangement. In many instances the amount subscribed will be insufficient to provide a separate school for each village, but, when this is the case, the most central of a knot of villages can be chosen, and their combined funds assigned for the purpose of one school for the use of all. Where the common village schools already exist, one master or inspector might be appointed to visit each in turn. In this way I feel confident that a very great deal may be done for the gradual improvement of the whole population. It will be necessary to satisfy ourselves of the competence of those masters to teach, to point out to them the method we desire to be adopted, and to provide such books and papers as may appear to be best suited to convey sound and useful instruction. The most thriving communities will naturally be foremost in the march of improvement; and, as might be expected, the ryots of those villages which have already benefited by the Annicut are the first to come forward to beg permission to contribute towards the expense of their children's education. The spread of sound vernacular instruction may eventually be not the least among the indirect effects of our works of irrigation." *

Mr. Taylor's philanthropic scheme, of which the above was the first sketch, met with the hearty approval and support of the Commissioner of the Northern Circars, who recommended that schools might be established in those villages where the largest contributions had been offered. "The principle of self-assessment for public objects," he remarked, "has always prevailed in the Circars, and was prohibited in consequence of the improper purposes to which the funds so raised were applied. The present is the first instance in which it has been proposed to use it for a praiseworthy end. Where, therefore, an earnest desire has been manifested for instruction, it is incumbent on the Government to see that the movement is turned to good account, and to supply such assistance as will ensure a favourable result." † The Government, while expressing their approval and desire to afford every encouragement to Mr. Taylor's project, requested him to submit to them a fuller and more detailed scheme.

The chief difficulty which was anticipated was the procuring of duly qualified agents; but Mr. Taylor did not regard it as insuperable. "Qualified agents in the shape of competent masters," he wrote, "are gradually springing up, and there are to be found young men who have acquired sufficient knowledge of a systematic way of

* Selections from the Records of the Madras Government, No. xxvi., Papers relating to the Establishment of Village Vernacular Schools in the Sub-Division of Rajahmundry, p. 1.

† Ibid., p. 4.

teaching to be able to impart the amount of instruction which is necessary as a beginning. Several men of this class are already employed by me, as President of the Nursapore School, and I have no doubt that more will be found as occasion arises. It was this class of men that I contemplated entertaining in the position of schoolmaster in every large and important village of a Taluk, whose duty it would be to supervise, direct, and instruct the village schoolmasters within his range.

"For this purpose a course of instruction, or training, if I may use the word, is already carried on by the Telugu master in the English and Vernacular School at this place, and in a very short time the quickest among the pupils will have acquired sufficient knowledge to become good village teachers. Some of these men are at present instructors in the various vernacular schools in this town, and prepare their scholars for entry into the higher English School. Others, again, when they are far enough advanced, might be employed as the visitors of village schools, or become village schoolmasters where these do not already exist. It will be understood that in every case the master hitherto employed and preferred by the villagers will always be continued, subject to the authority and direction of his superior. In this manner the indigenous village schools will be encouraged, and a system of inspection set on foot which has been found so successful for the promotion of education in the North-West Provinces.

"Over these divisional, or, as they were then called, Samut teachers I would propose the higher grade of Tahsil schoolmaster for every Taluk. He would be stationed at the capital of the Taluk and residence of the Tahsildar, where a school on a superior footing might be established, to which also might be attached a divisional or a village teacher as assistant-master.

"The qualifications of a Tahsil schoolmaster will, of course, be of a higher order than those required in the divisional teacher; and, in the first instance, it will, perhaps, be difficult to find men in every respect fit for the post. Besides a grammatical and critical knowledge of his own vernacular tongue, and ability to teach all such subjects as may be treated in the books supplied to him, such as the ordinary rules of arithmetic, geography, outlines of history, mensuration of land, and calculation of areas, a slight knowledge of English would be of the greatest use, as enabling him to impart elementary instruction in that language, to the most advanced pupils, whose circumstances prevented their attending an English school at a distance. Too much, however, ought not to be attempted at first, the grand object being to give the people improved instruction in their own language, and, through its medium, to lead them to sound and useful knowledge.

"A system of promotion by merit being once organized, the difficulty of obtaining competent teachers would in time vanish, and it would not be very long before we should have a number of well-trained individuals, qualified in a very high degree, to conduct the Tahsil schools. To this end I would propose grades in the divisional teachers, with a regular scale of salary, those men being first promoted who showed themselves most active and attentive to their duties. The village schoolmaster on his pay of a few rupees, the contribution of the inhabitants, should look forward to become a visiting teacher, to rise from the lowest to the highest grade of that class, and eventually to become a Tahsil schoolmaster. With this incentive to exertion a reasonable expectation may be formed of a favourable result.

"So far the plan has provided for the supervision and inspection of the village schools by the divisional visiting teachers, and for the gradual advancement of the latter to the post of Tahsil schoolmaster; but these masters themselves will require constant inspection and control, and, for this purpose, I would appoint an efficient officer as District visitor and inspector, who would be directly responsible for the qualifications of the masters, and for the proper state and efficiency of the schools. He would be constantly on the move, proceeding from one Taluk to another, and from school to school, seeing that one uniform system was adopted, and that instruction was properly imparted. He would be required to furnish a periodical report of the result of his tour, and his leisure hours should be devoted to the preparation of suitable vernacular books, under the direction of the Educational Board.

"It is, no doubt, very desirable that this officer should, if possible, be a European, well versed in educational management, with a good knowledge of the vernacular of the country. I cannot doubt, however, that many a passed proficient of the High School, or other well-qualified native who has received a sound moral education at Madras, would be willing to undertake the office, and would be found equal to the duties expected from him. It is quite true that we cannot fix our standard too high; but it is no less certain that little will be accomplished, unless we make use of the materials which are now at hand. Well trained and educated young men of the class I refer to, have been employed with advantage in every department of the Government; and there is no reason to suppose that they would fail to give equal satisfaction in the educational line. They would require at first a good deal of guidance and direction; but energy, assiduity, and an interest in their work would make up for their want of experience, and much good might be expected to result to their countrymen from their influence and example.

"The Government, adverting to the Commissioner's proposition of a salary of 10 to 15 rupees, remark that no real improvement can be expected in the village schools till qualified and improved masters can be placed in them, and that a much higher salary is necessary to induce persons of that description to take up the profession of a schoolmaster. This is a subject of the very greatest importance, and seems to demand our most serious consideration. It will be observed that the scheme I am now proposing contemplates the improvement of the existing village schools, and the retention of those masters who are approved by the villagers, and who will be paid from the fund subscribed by themselves, one teacher or visitor being appointed in the largest village of a group of perhaps ten or fifteen villages, who will be paid by Government. The instruction conveyed by the former under the guidance of the latter, will necessarily be of the most elementary kind. Very few, if any, but the cultivating and labouring class will attend his school, and the period of their attendance would not average probably more than three hours a day. To carry the natives with us in a measure of this kind, we must endeavour to show them that, while their children are gaining knowledge, the fathers are not losers thereby. The child of six or eight years old, and even younger, accompanies his parents to their field or to their labour, tends the cattle, and assists in various ways in the occupations of the family. He must be allowed to do this still, if the parents desire it, and during the intervals of labour, part of the time which is now spent in sleep or idleness will be more profitably employed in the village school. The schoolmaster himself, being a resident in the village, and, as it were, one of themselves, needs but a small salary; but this salary, which is now dependent upon chance or charity, will be secured to him by the plan of fixing an annual addition to the demand of the village.

It should be paid to him monthly, like the salaries of all Government officials, and not be subject, as is sometimes the case with other village allowances, to be curtailed, or altogether withheld, in the event of an adverse season, when part of the Government demand is not realized.

"The sum of 5 rupees monthly, or 60 rupees a year, is, perhaps, the minimum upon which persons of this class could make a respectable appearance, and, if schools on the present plan were once started, the greater number of villages would soon offer to contribute that amount. The assistance of Government, in the shape of books and a visitor, might be promised to every village, the contributions in which amounted to 60 rupees annually. With this salary of 5 rupees, or even less, the village schoolmaster will be in a better position than he ever occupied before; but I would give him an additional stimulus to exertion by allowing him to receive a fixed fee from every class of persons in the village who do not contribute to the fund assessed upon the land. Two annas a month would probably be a high enough fee. A register of scholars can be kept and periodically inspected by the visiting Government teacher, and the efficiency of the village domine would be judged by the number of pupils attending his instruction.

"I would divide the Government visiting teachers into three or four grades, according to the size and importance of their charge. The salary of the lowest grade of teachers of this class ought not to be less than 15 rupees per mensem, the intermediate grade may receive 20 rupees, and the highest 25. The salary of the Tahsil schoolmaster I would fix at 30 rupees, and that of the District visitor or native inspector, at 75 or 100 rupees. It would be found necessary, in the first instance, at any rate, to place the latter under the direction of one of the European Revenue officers in the District, through whom his reports and diaries would be submitted to Government.

"The Commissioner has recommended that I be allowed to establish schools, in the first instance, in twelve villages, where the largest contributions have been offered. Most of these villages contain more than one thousand inhabitants, and six of them are divisional stations. If, upon this further explanation of my views, the Government are disposed to authorize my accepting the voluntary offers of all villagers to contribute to the Educational Fund, and to appoint a visiting teacher at the principal village of a group, it will not be necessary to place a Government schoolmaster in each of these villages. Those who were the first to come forward ought to be the first to receive encouragement, and I would make an arrangement so that all should benefit by the assistance afforded by Government.

"If I may be permitted to suggest what that assistance should be, I would say—First of all, let a native inspector be appointed. He might, in the first instance, receive 50 rupees a month, and his chief duty for the present would be the preparation and translation of suitable elementary works, and he would assist in the examination and training of the masters intended for the divisional and village schools. Secondly, I would propose the appointment of two Tahsil schoolmasters on the pay of 30 rupees. A schoolhouse should be built at each Tahsildar's station for the accommodation of the pupils. The third point is the entertainment of visiting teachers. I think I can undertake to nominate six who are competent to carry out the object in view, and to direct the masters of the village schools. Their number might be increased as the vernacular schools multiplied, and as men were found competent for the task. Of those six, four might receive a salary of 15 rupees and two of 20, or, if it be thought more expedient, they might all be paid alike. They would be distributed through the three Delta Taluks of the Subdivision, so as to make their services as effective as possible. A small sum would be required for books, and for the purpose of aiding the inhabitants to erect places of shelter near the divisional school. The annual cost of an educational staff, as above detailed, would be 3500 rupees. I have only to state, in conclusion, that I am fully sensible of my inability to meet all the objections that may be raised against the plan submitted; and am not unmindful of the many discouragements we must inevitably meet with in attempting to carry out any general measure of this kind. With a determination, however, to overcome every impediment, and with the united efforts of all classes of the servants of Government, I feel persuaded that any well-considered attempt will be crowned with a large measure of success." *

Mr. Taylor's scheme received the hearty approval of Mr. Goldingham, who had succeeded Sir Walter Elliot as Commissioner of the Northern Circars, and it obtained the sanction of Government. The

* Selections from the Records of the Madras Government, No. xxvi. Papers relating to the Establishment of Village Vernacular Schools in the Subdivision of Rajahmundry, p. 7.

Governor in Council cheerfully recorded his approval of the project, which, being experimental, was at first to be applied only to the three Delta Taluks of the Subdivision of the District as then constituted, namely, Mogalturru, Tanuku, and Undi. The sum of 980 rupees for two Tahsil schoolhouses, schoolrooms in other places, books, and other purposes, was placed at Mr. Taylor's disposal, and an educational staff at the monthly expense of 210 rupees was sanctioned; and, as the readiness of the people to submit to an extra assessment on their land to further the design was considered an evidence of their appreciation of the advantages which the scheme promised to confer on their children, the levy of such a rate was authorized as would ensure the regular monthly payment of the salary of the village schoolmasters; who were to receive, in addition, a fee of two annas a month from all those who did not contribute to the fund assessed upon the land. It was hoped that the Government would be in a position to consider the expediency of adopting the plan on an extended scale, should the execution of the proposed educational scheme entrusted to Mr. Taylor prove a success. The Government stated, however, that they could not agree with Mr. Taylor with regard to the non-admission of the Málas, whom he was unwilling to see admitted into schools, the cost of which was defrayed by their superiors. "Perfect equality in educational matters, and the admission of all sects and castes to its benefits on equal terms, are principles," they said, "of paramount importance. Experience has shown that these principles can always be successfully maintained if asserted with judgment and firmness." * Subsequently, a salary of 100 rupees a month was sanctioned for an Inspector of Vernacular Schools in the Subdivision instead of 50 rupees.† S. Nadamoony Moodeliar was appointed the first Inspector, and he held the office and performed the duties with zeal and efficiency for many years, until he was transferred to the Revenue Department.

In his first Report, which was for the half year commencing April 1855, the Inspector was able to give an encouraging account of the progress made. In April the number of pupils was only 112 out of 38,546, which was the estimated number of all the male juvenile population in the three taluks. By the end of October there were

* Selections from the Records of the Madras Government, p. 25. Extract from Min. of Cons., March 3, 1855. No. 288. Public Department.

† Ibid., p. 29.

1422.* The principal schools increased from three to eight, and fifty-four village schools were taken under Government supervision and control. The two chief obstacles at the commencement were the idea that all the schools were to be free to all classes, and the difficulty in getting the agricultural population to allow their children to attend. The people in general imagined that Government had established the schools, and intended that they were to be free to all classes of the community, without making any distinction between the non-agriculturists and the rural population who contributed for their maintenance. A little tact, and the clear explanation of the nature of the assistance really afforded by Government, seem to have removed this difficulty. The other impediment was more important, and more difficult to overcome. The agricultural portion of the community, for whose benefit in the first instance this scheme was projected, preferred to take their children to their fields, or to set them to watch the cattle, rather than to permit their attending school. Though this objection had been anticipated, and the hours for attendance at school had been named so as best to suit the convenience of these people, yet so strong was the hold their occupation had on them, that most of the ryots of the lower grade were disinclined to dispense with the services which their children could render in the fields. It was, therefore, found necessary to assemble as large a number as possible of this class, and to explain to them the benefits they would derive, so as to conduce to the advancement and improvement of their own pursuits. Their attention was drawn to one important advantage—that of knowing their rights and ceasing to be the dupes of the village scribes, who not unfrequently had recourse to fraudulent means to impose on these illiterate people. This attempt was attended with satisfactory results. The number of pupils increased, and free entrance into the schools was sought by the under-tenants also as the dependants of the ryots, who, being subscribers to the schools, were alone charged no fees for the education of their children. The main object of the scheme being to educate this section of the population, the desired privilege was allowed, and the attendance became very satisfactory.† A dim superstitious fear of coming results also proved an obstacle at first. The ryots in some localities felt a reluctance to send their children to the schools where a new and as yet unintelligible system was introduced. The village priests foreboded evil,

* Selections from the Records of the Madras Government, p. 73.

† Ibid., No. xxvi., p. 66.

and their representations produced an undefined feeling of dread in the minds of the more indifferent and ignorant. This panic seems to have speedily passed away.*

Mr. Taylor left the District at the beginning of 1856. At that time the scheme which he had projected was in full force. The Central School at Nursapore was in good working order, and a European master was on his way from England to take charge of it. The number of the boys then attending the Central School was sixty. There was also a Telugu Normal Class for the instruction and training of village teachers, who were to be sent out, from time to time, to the villages where schools under the new system might be instituted. This class was held in the building belonging to the Central School. In the same building there was a class studying practical geometry and land-surveying, which included many village scribes, from whom a small fee for this extra instruction was demanded.† There were two Tahsil schools, the head masters of which were paid by Government, and were to devote a portion of their time to the duty of inspection. There were six divisional schools in central villages, the masters of which were also to be paid by Government, and, besides carrying on the instruction of their own schools, were to act as visitors of the neighbouring village schools. And, finally, there were fifty-five village schools, situated in those places where the inhabitants were willing voluntarily to contribute 60 rupees a year, which were to be added to the annual revenue demand. There were thus concentric circles of schools established and in full play, wheel working within wheel, and forming one united whole of educational machinery, which reflected the purest lustre on Mr. Taylor's administration of the Subdivision of Rajahmundry. He had also a small printing press attached to his office at Nursapore, from which were issued, from time to time, small pamphlets in Telugu for the use of the various village and other vernacular schools, such as "The People's Magazine," and "The Daily Lesson Books."

With regard to the question of the willingness with which the contributions for these schools were paid by the ryots, it is interesting to quote the remarks made by Mr. Taylor in his final Report. "The scheme," he wrote, "is evidently one which could only be introduced with success in a District moderately assessed, and among

* Selections from the Records of the Madras Government, p. 35.

† Ibid., p. 42.

a thriving and improving population. It were useless to attempt to force education upon communities struggling for a bare subsistence. Once supplied with a sufficiency of food and clothing, with the comforts, and, to them, the luxuries of life, the people of this country will, like others, seek education as the means of social improvement. To the altered circumstances of the agricultural population of the Rajahmundry Delta, consequent upon the abundant and certain irrigation from the Annicut, I attribute their consent to tax themselves for the education of their children.

"I desire also to state that, in every instance in which a school has been established, the inhabitants have cheerfully offered to support it, and have also willingly purchased the books that have been introduced. Every precaution was taken to ascertain their real wishes in the matter, and I declined to open a school wherever there was the least hesitation or difference of opinion on the part of the community. Discontented spirits will always be found, and, as might have been expected, there have been a few complaints from the disaffected, and appeals both to myself and to higher authority, which have received immediate attention, but have usually ended in the objectors consenting with the majority that the schools should remain."

It can easily be imagined that the Tahsildars, the village accountants, and others in authority, perceiving what was likely to please the Sub-Collector, would induce the villagers, in some instances, to contribute against their will; but I believe that, in the great majority of instances, the villagers contributed cheerfully, or were willingly guided in the matter by the leaders of public opinion in their small rural communities.

In 1855 an officer was appointed to be Director of Public Instruction in accordance with the orders of the Government of India in pursuance of the Court of Directors' Educational Despatch of July 19, 1854. Mr., now Sir Alexander, Arbuthnot, was the first Director of Public Instruction at Madras. From that moment a strong and healthy impetus was given to the cause of education. Systematic exertions were made to advance it in every possible way.

Vernacular education was one of the first projects which the Court of Directors desired to foster. This branch of the education of the people was quite in its infancy. But little had been done throughout the Madras Presidency. In this District, however, there was a marked and brilliant exception. The experiment of establishing elementary vernacular schools by means of a voluntary cess raised by the inhabitants had been tried, as stated above, and it had proved a decided success. At the close of the first year of the Director of Public Instruction's official career, there were two Tahsil schools, seven divisional schools, and seventy-seven village schools, in full working order, with an attendance of 1870 pupils.* In the following year they were reported on most favourably by the Inspector of Schools for the First Educational Division. The number had increased to 86, and the pupils numbered nearly 2000. The number in the following year increased to 99. On the 30th of April 1861, the number had reached 101, with 1928 pupils.

A question arose at this time regarding the true character of the rate by which these schools were maintained. It was commenced on the understanding that it was a voluntary rate, and that the schools were established at the request of the people themselves. Mr. Davidson, who was then acting as Sub-Collector of the District, represented that it was not voluntary, and that much difficulty was experienced in collecting it. After inquiry into the matter, the Director of Public Instruction came to the conclusion that the voluntary character of the rate was rapidly disappearing, if it had ever existed, a fact which he considered very doubtful. Referring to the suggestion made in Lord Stanley's Despatch of April 7, 1859, as to the expediency of providing for elementary education throughout the country by means of an educational rate, he strongly recommended that the rate in question should be converted into a compulsory tax. The Government were decidedly opposed to such a measure. They objected on principle to a tax for educational purposes as being calculated to excite suspicion and distrust. Captain Macdonald, the Inspector of Schools, reported that, "in many of the villages, the ryots stated that their payments were made cheerfully, and the accounts showed that there were no arrears worth mentioning. In others, the villagers mentioned, either that they had never voluntarily agreed to the subscriptions at all, or that they had agreed to them, on the understanding that they would last for only one year. In these cases, the ryots appeared to have been all along resisting the payments of the rate, and often successfully." He considered that these schools had done an incalculable amount of good, and that, at the lowest estimate, they did not cost the people more than their own indigenous schools. He was of

* Madras Administration Report for 1855-56, pp. 27, 37.

opinion that, in consequence of the assessment having been raised on account of the water rate, and in consequence of the new Survey and Settlement, the collection of the rate would be attended by more opposition than had previously been experienced; and the Board of Revenue corroborated this opinion, stating that the new assessment was not of that light character which would admit of cesses being superadded for every special object.*

In the correspondence which ensued on this subject, the question was raised as to the authority of the Sub-Collector to enforce payment of the rate. Mr. Taylor considered that the rate, when once agreed to, became a fixed permanent addition to the village demand; but none of his successors in the Sub-Collectorate acted on this theory, and it appeared clearly that no such power could legally be enforced. It was, therefore, considered necessary, in order that the schools should be maintained, that some change should be made in the plan originally sanctioned for providing the requisite funds.

On full consideration, the Director of Public Instruction came to the conclusion that some plan should be adopted to modify the present system, and to render it free from all legal objections. He, therefore, framed a Bill which was intended to have the effect of legalizing the rate, whenever a certain proportion of the inhabitants might be willing to continue it, and also to facilitate the application of the system to other districts. This Bill was based on the principle of the Municipal Act of 1850. It dealt, in the first instance, with the existing schools in this District, and provided for a course of procedure being adopted with regard to them somewhat different from that which was to be adopted in the case of places where it might be proposed to establish new schools. It prescribed, in the former case, for the immediate enforcement of the Act, unless the majority of the inhabitants should petition against it within a certain time. It prescribed, in the latter case, that the Act should not come into force until the majority of the inhabitants made an application to that effect. "The measure now proposed," Mr. Arbuthnot observed, "furnishes the most satisfactory means of solving the difficulty which has so long been felt in regard to maintaining the schools in the Godavery District. Wherever the inhabitants are sincere in their professed desire to maintain the schools, the Act will give them the means of doing so, and wherever the present rate is really in opposition to their wishes, it will be taken off. In other districts

* Administration Reports for 1860-61, p. 128, and for 1861-62, p. 87.

it will furnish a machinery for the establishment of schools of any grade, whenever there may be a desire for them; and while it provides for the permanency of the schools by means of local taxation, it will not be in any way incompatible with the extension of the grant-in-aid system; but, on the contrary, will aid the development of that system by giving a permanency to the local funds, in aid of which grants will be made, and which, in the case of schools supported by natives, does not at present exist. It may prove, like the Municipal Act, which has been taken as its model, to be altogether, or, in a great measure, a dead letter; but, if it fails, it can do no harm, and, if it should succeed, it will prove a very useful and simple means of promoting the diffusion of popular instruction." *

The proposed Bill became law in 1862. The new Act provided in regard to this District that, in any town or village in which one of the rate schools was in operation, if a majority of the inhabitants should not, within two months from the passing of the Act, petition for the discontinuance of the school, the Government were to declare the Act in force for a period of five years, and to appoint Commissioners for the assessing and collecting the rate, and managing the affairs of the schools supported by it. The Commissioners were to be the Inspector of Schools for the Division, the Deputy-Inspector of Schools for the District, and such number of resident householders as the Collector might appoint. They were to make rules for the levy of the rate, its amount, the parties who were to pay it, the mode of collection, the appointment, remuneration, and dismissal of teachers, and the branches of learning to be taught. Such of the rules as related to the collection of rates were to be subject to the approval of the Governor in Council; and those which referred to the appointment of teachers, or to the subjects of instruction, were to be approved by the Director of Public Instruction. Power was given to the Commissioners to recover the rate by distress and sale of the goods and chattels of defaulters. The Act was to be in force, in each case, for a term of five years; and, on the expiration of that time, the application of its provisions was to be renewed by the local Government, if, within two months from the date of such expiration, a majority of the inhabitants should not apply for its discontinuance. In the case of new schools, the Government was to be satisfied, before the Act could be applied, that its application was in

* Administration Report for 1861–62, p. lxxxvii.

accordance with the wishes of the inhabitants.* In the first year the Act was applied to seventy-two schools. In thirty-three villages the majority of the inhabitants objected to the introduction of the Act, and the schools were closed.†

The working of the Act was not satisfactory. Its machinery was found to be ill adapted to the purpose for which it was intended to be applied. It was intended for the maintenance of elementary schools in villages where the people were chiefly agricultural. The Commissioners appointed under the provisions of the Act were not persons likely to stimulate and encourage education. "They are ignorant ryots," observed Mr. Bowers, the Inspector of Schools, "who care nothing for the schools, and neglect their duties." The proper remedy could not easily be discovered. "The only way," he added, "in which they can be prevented from causing the abolition of the schools by simple inaction, is to place them, in their capacity of School Commissioners, as they are in their capacity of village scribes, under the authority of the Sub-Collector; but, in that case, the Act becomes a dead letter and a superfluity. This would be virtually a return to the ante-Act state of things, and would be an admission that these schools could never have been voluntarily maintained. Up to a very recent date, many of the masters had received no salaries for months." The Director of Public Instruction himself was requested by the Government, after this state of affairs had been brought to their notice, to make an inquiry as to the actual working of the Act, and as to the wishes of the inhabitants of those villages to which it had been applied. They particularly requested it to be understood that they did not wish it to be applied to any town or village, where its application was not clearly in accordance with the express desire of a considerable majority of the inhabitants, or where competent School Commissioners were not available.‡ As the result of this inquiry, eleven more village schools were closed in the year 1866, it having been found that the assent of the inhabitants to the application of the Act had not been voluntary. It was, moreover, made evident that the Madras Education Act was not adapted for being successfully applied to small villages, whatever might have been the case in large villages and in towns where intelligent men could be obtained to act as Commissioners.§

* Administration Report for 1862–63, p. 143.

† Ibid. for 1864–65, p. 95.

‡ Ibid. for 1865–66, p. 101.

§ Ibid. for 1866–67, p. 98.

The schools throughout the District are now under the Municipal Commissioners and the Local Fund Boards. The Towns' Improvement Act and the Local Funds' Act, which were both passed in 1871, were intended, among other objects, to promote the cause of popular education, and the funds collected under them were to be mainly appropriated to its extension and improvement. The Godavery is the only District in the Presidency in which the lower-class schools, managed by the Local Fund Boards, are numerous; and in all other respects it stands very fairly in comparison with other districts. There were, at the close of the year 1874-75, 391 schools of all grades in the District, containing an aggregate of 10,460 pupils, the particulars of which will be given in the Appendix. Among other institutions, there are two elementary schools which have recently been established for the benefit of the Mussulman community—one at Rajahmundry, where there is an attendance of 52 pupils, and another at Ellore, where the number is 51, but where also the advantages of education for the Mohammedans are greater than in any other town in the District.*

* Report on Public Instruction in the Madras Presidency for 1874-75.

CHAPTER VI.

HISTORY OF THE GODAVERY ANNICUT.

ORIGIN OF THE SCHEME—SIR ARTHUR COTTON'S PLAN—APPROVAL OF GOVERNMENT—COMMENCEMENT AND PROGRESS OF THE WORKS—OPINION OF THE PUBLIC WORKS' COMMITTEE—A CIVILIAN'S TESTIMONY TO THE VALUE OF THE WORKS—COMPLETION OF THE ANNICUT—DESCRIPTION OF THE STRUCTURE.

THE Godavery Annicut is, perhaps, the noblest feat of engineering skill which has yet been accomplished in British India. It is a gigantic barrier thrown across the river from island to island, in order to arrest the unprofitable progress of its waters to the sea, and to spread them over the surface of the country on either side, thus irrigating copiously land which had previously been dependent on tanks or on the fitful supply of water from the river. Large tracts of land, which had hitherto been left arid and desolate and waste, were thus reached and fertilised by innumerable streams and channels.

The District owes this invaluable boon to the genius of Sir Arthur Cotton. The first idea of the scheme, however, originated with Mr. Michael Topping, who, before the close of the last century, brought to the notice of Government how desirable it would be to throw a dam across the Godavery, so as to raise the water, and thus make it available for irrigating the country near its banks.* This project was permitted to slumber for half a century; but, in the year 1844, it was revived under the following circumstances. About that time the District had fallen into a state so far below even the then generally sad state of the northern districts, that, as will hereafter be related, Sir Henry Montgomery was deputed, as special Commissioner, to take charge of the District, and to report what could be done to raise it from its lamentable state of depression. That experienced officer having come from Tanjore, where he had seen the great results

* First Report of the Public Works Commission at Madras, 1852, p. 100.

of attention to irrigation, after he had put the revenue arrangements into better order, strongly urged the examination of the Delta by an experienced Irrigation Engineer, with a view to the execution of such a complete system of works for the regulation of the water as would effectually lead to the realization of the wonderful amount of produce which the large tract of fertile soil might be expected to yield, if it were supplied with water, relieved from floods, and provided with navigation. On this report Captain, now Sir Arthur, Cotton, of the Madras Engineers, who knew the works in Tanjore, was ordered, in 1845, to take charge of the District as engineer, and to report professionally upon the matter; and, upon his representation, the Governor of Madras, the late Marquis of Tweeddale, so strongly urged the project on the Court of Directors, that the work received their sanction. The models which Captain Cotton purposed to follow were the Annicuts across the Coleroon in the district of Tanjore, and his first suggestion was, that a barrier of the same kind should be thrown across the river Godavery above the town of Rajahmundry; but, in a subsequent and fuller Report, he stated that he had selected the present site, which was manifestly better and more suitable for his purpose.

In his first Report Captain Cotton had drawn attention to the neglected state of the District of Rajahmundry, its destitution of artificial works of irrigation, and the lamentable result of leaving the land dependent merely on the natural supply of water to be drawn from the great river which ran through it. In his second Report he entered more fully into detail, and it seems advisable to allow him, as far as possible, to describe in the following narrative his own project in his own words.*

The magnificent river which was thus about to be utilized, after a course of several hundred miles across the Peninsula, enters at about sixty miles from the sea the alluvial country which it has itself formed. "This alluvial land does not immediately expand to a great width from the point at which the river leaves the main range of the hills, there being still rising grounds and detached patches of hills at a distance of from half a mile to five miles from the river, for the distance of twenty-three miles further; at the end of which distance, two or three detached hills come close to it, the river

* Professional Papers of the Madras Engineers, vol. iii. Copies of Documents relating to the Works of Irrigation on the Godavery River, &c., Printed by order of the House of Commons, April 1853.

divides into two streams, the alluvial country spreads out on both sides, and the Delta may properly be said to commence, extending on the west side till it meets that of the Kistna at the Colair Lake, about forty miles, and on the east side about thirty-two miles to the shore of Coringa Bay." This was the Delta which was to benefit by the projected increase of irrigation.

The slope of the Delta towards the sea is gradual and regular. It commences near the hills with a foot-and-a-half per mile, and diminishes to one foot as it approaches the sea. There is also another slope, which is rather more rapid, namely, a fall from the river perpendicular to its course. It was, moreover, ascertained by examination of the levels, that the highest part of the Delta in the immediate neighbourhood of the river was only eight or ten feet above its bed.

The breadth of the river, Major Cotton reported, varied from about two thousand yards, or one mile and one furlong, to seven thousand yards, or nearly four-and-a-half miles, which latter breadth, however, included islands to the extent of about one thousand or fifteen hundred yards. Notwithstanding this great breadth, there were everywhere great facilities for constructing an Annicut, from the vicinity of hills containing good stone and lime, especially at the head of the Delta, where there was a hill of a most suitable kind of stone, and hydraulic limestone of excellent quality in the immediate neighbourhood. From these advantages, and the low price of labour in the District, a vast mass of masonry might be executed for a comparatively moderate sum.

The country which was to be irrigated by means of the proposed Annicut consisted, with the exception of a strip of sandy land bordering on the sea, of a noble expanse of rich alluvial land fit for almost any cultivation, if well supplied with water. It was estimated to contain about 1,300,000 acres, out of which, deducting one-fourth for sandy tracts near the sea, sites of villages, and channels of rivers, there would remain 1,000,000 acres fit for cultivation with paddy or sugar-cane.

On a consideration of the capabilities of the land and of the resources of the river, Major Cotton was of opinion that three fundamental points had been established:—That there was an ample supply of water for a rice-crop in all the land forming the Delta of the Godavery, and there was certainly water enough in the river for a very large extent of cultivation, probably not less than 100,000 acres, all through the dry season. That there was a vast extent of fertile soil, not less than 820,000 acres within the District of Rajahmundry, and nearly as much in Masulipatam, to which the water might be applied. That by means of an Annicut of a very moderate height, and main channels only two or four miles in length, the last drop of water in the river might be brought to the surface of the country at a level which would command the whole tract.

The important question, whether the cost of the proposed works would be repaid in their effect on the District, was next considered. The original estimate, which was subsequently exceeded by a large amount, was 475,572 rupees. The works then proposed were an Annicut across the river; the head sluices for two main irrigating channels, one on the west of the Annicut, and the other at the head of the Central Delta; locks at each end for passing boats round the Annicut; and those for carrying them past the head sluices into the irrigating channels. The following details of the original estimate cannot fail to be interesting, even at the present time, when the magnitude of the work has been indefinitely increased, and its utility proved beyond a doubt:—

	Rs.
Annicut	388,005
Five locks . . .	18,419
Two head sluices . . .	13,148
Excavations . . .	14,000
Superintendence . . .	12,000
Contingencies . . .	30,000
	475,572

Estimating the area of culturable land in the District of Rajahmundry at 81,600 acres, and the gross value of the produce at 3,020,000 rupees a year, and the revenue at 1,510,000, Major Cotton calculated that there would be a fair opening, after the construction of the Annicut, for an increase of the revenue to the extent of 20 lacs, and of produce to the extent of 124 lacs, in the Government lands alone. "If it be asked," he said, "how is this great sum to be obtained, the answer is, by simply converting the water of the Godavery into money, instead of letting it run into the sea. At this moment water is paid for by the sugar-growers at about one rupee for 800 cubic yards, the cost of raising it by artificial means. There are now about 420,000 cubic yards of water per hour flowing into the sea, worth, at the rate at which it is now actually and profitably purchased, 500 rupees per hour, or 12,000 per day, which, for 240 days (the portion of the year in which the District is not supplied at all), gives 2,880,000 rupees. The water, if applied to the land, would be worth to the cultivators full fifty lacs. The whole of this is at present lost. Through the remainder of the year, that is, during the cultivation of the great crop, about four times this quantity, or one and three-quarter million cubic yards per hour are allowed to flow into the sea that might profitably be applied to the land, and in this way it may be understood by anybody how easily one hundred lacs a year may be lost.

"The only question is, What expenditure is required to give us the full benefit of our natural advantages? My rough estimate for the whole of the works required to put the Delta in good order, is—

	Lacs
Present estimate for the Annicut, &c.	5
Embankments to the river	1
Irrigation channels	2
Drainage works	1
Sluices, locks, and other small works of masonry	1
Roads and bridges	2
Total lacs	12

"Upon the due consideration of these calculations and statements," he continued, "surely there cannot be a doubt as to the results of the construction of an Annicut, considered separately from the other works which the Delta requires. Estimating it to cost 480,000 rupees, it seems certain that within a very few years it will yield at least two and a half lacs, or 50 per cent.; and that, when the sugar cultivation has extended considerably, 100 per cent. would be by no means an improbable return; and, when to this we add the immense change it would make in the circumstances of the people, there seems to be no possible room for doubt as to the advantages derived from such a work being such as to counterbalance the outlay several times over. Take the case of one single year of famine, and consider the dreadful amount of suffering which it involves, to say nothing of the lasting injury to the revenue, which is the certain consequence of it, and the incalculable blessing that an Annicut would be to the District may well be imagined.

That such a thing as a famine in any of the districts near the Godavery should ever take place, is, indeed, the deepest reproach to us. The consideration that such a time has been, and that it will inevitably occur again within a few years if an Annicut is not built, ought alone to be sufficient to induce us to build one, even if there were no returns in ordinary years. This work would not only secure this District from famine, but would necessarily much mitigate it in the neighbouring districts. Indeed, it would effectually secure the whole of these districts from the fearful extremities of starvation to which some of them have been exposed so lately. Had this work been in existence during the last twenty years, undoubtedly much more than 100,000 lives would have been saved by it.

"In the present case, we may confidently expect that the Annicut now estimated, with some trifling sums for small channels, will, within a year after its completion, produce an increase of one lac, and that, by the tenth year, there will be an increase of five lacs, or cent. per cent. on the outlay."

This full and deeply interesting report of Major Cotton's project is concluded with his own summary of the benefits which he anticipated from it.

"We may consider the Annicut as laying the foundation for the complete irrigation, for a rice crop, of the whole Delta of the Godavery, and part of that of the Kistna, in all 3000 square miles, or nearly 2,000,000 acres; and providing for leading out on the land of every drop of water of the Godavery, in the low freshes, and thus making use of what is now totally lost. Thus the produce of this tract, which at present probably does not exceed 30 lacs, would, when full advantage is taken of the water thus distributed over it, be increased to at least 200 lacs. This tract, which now pays with great difficulty about 22 lacs, would then, with great ease, pay 50 or 60. A complete system of internal navigation, intersecting the whole Delta, would be established throughout the year. Every village would be furnished with a stream of pure water for the people and cattle at all seasons. The present estimate provides for the full irrigation of all the tracts at present partially irrigated by the principal channels of the Godavery. It will give us at once the use of a large portion (about one-third) of the water of the low freshes during the whole of the hot weather, thus providing for sugar cultivation to the extent of about 30,000 acres. It will give a constant supply of water to those tracts which are situated near the present channels, but which receive no benefit from them at all. It will put a famine in this or the neighbouring districts out of the range of probability. It will provide immediately two or three most important lines of water communication from Rajahmundry through the heart of the Delta to the sea, available at all seasons. It will have the important effect of showing the people what can be done for them. At present they have no idea of the water being thrown into the channels during the hot season; and, from the first moment that water is seen passing through any villages in the low freshes, the whole people of the Delta will be awakened to its great capabilities, and will be prepared to welcome the opening of channels throughout the whole tract, and to extend the cultivation, which is at present limited by the want of water. It may be estimated to yield one lac of rupees, or 20 per cent. on the outlay in the first year, and at least five lacs, or cent. per cent., within ten years.

"Upon the whole, we have almost everything that the most timid could desire to encourage us to prosecute this undertaking. On the one hand, the most perfect success, and almost unprecedented results from precisely similar works in Tanjore; and, on the other, immediate returns for what has already been done in this District, more than ten times as great as would have been an ample return for the expenditure. What this District may become, if this matter be taken in hand with only a small part of the energy it deserves, it is not easy to conceive. The unfailing river, an immense expanse of the richest soil, a safe and accessible port, a complete internal water communication with teak forests, and abundance of labour at 1½d. a day, form such a combination of advantages as, I suppose, cannot be found in the world, and certainly not under such a Government as ours."

The project which was thus enthusiastically advocated by Major Cotton was warmly supported by the Collector of the District, by the Board of Revenue, by the Chief Engineer, and especially by the Marquis of Tweeddale, the Governor. The Collector, while he heartily approved of the scheme, differed from the estimate made by Major Cotton of the area of the lands of the Delta, of the culturable land, and of the anticipated profits to be derived from the Annicut. The Board of Revenue thus state these differences of opinion, and compare them :—

"The Collector's accounts of the area of the Delta differ considerably from the estimate of Major Cotton; but their several statements of culturable lands more approximate, the difference between them being only from 40,000 to 50,000 acres. It is sufficient for the purposes of this Report to assume as true the lowest estimate of the culturable lands, namely, 616,000 acres, which, if brought under the influence of the Annicut, would immeasurably repay the cost of all the works.

	Puttis.
District accounts of Delta lands . .	91,284
Deduct unfit for cultivation . . .	14,381
	76,903

which, reckoning the putti at the lowest rate of 8 acres, amounts to 615,216 acres.

"In estimating the gross produce of the District, the Civil Engineer assumes the average collections at 18½ rupees the putti, but the Collector states the true rate to be 24 rupees. The value of the produce of the whole area is, according to the Collector's measurement, 2,768, 508 rupees, or, according to Major Cotton's measurement, 3,019,200 rupees. In both these calculations, however, it is assumed that the whole culturable area is cultivated, which is by no means the case.

"The total annual increase to be expected from the construction of the Annicut only, being on a low estimate, 30,000 rupees, and the cost of the work 475,000 rupees, the return in the first year would be one-sixteenth of the outlay, in the second one-eighth, in the third three-sixteenths, and so on, or 6, 12, and 18 per cent. One per cent. may be deducted for repairs in the second and each succeeding year. In ten years, according to these calculations, the Annicut would produce 830,000 rupees. The cost of the work being taken at 480,000, the compound interest on that sum at 5 per cent. for ten years would be about 300,000, and the cost of repairs about 50,000—total, 350,000; and the work would thus, under the most limited and unfavourable view of the subject that can well be taken, pay for itself in ten years, and afterwards yield a clear profit of fully 90,000 rupees per annum: and in this estimate the prevention of further declension in the existing revenue is not taken into consideration."*

* Letter from the Board of Revenue to Government, dated April 9, 1846.

These early calculations both of the projector of this noble undertaking himself and of the Board of Revenue, have been given not only on account of the interest which they possess in themselves; but also on account of the light they throw on the subsequent controversy regarding the utility of the Annicut after its construction, and of the results derived from it.

The sanction and approval of the Government of Madras were cordially given. "This great undertaking," they said, "appears to have been projected with the utmost care and circumspection. In 1844 the Government had under examination the general state of the Rajahmundry District, and entered upon a review of the causes which led to the deterioration of the revenues and the depressed state of the ryots; and it appeared that the total neglect of the works of irrigation under the Zemindari system, the apathy displayed by the Zemindars towards the improvement of their estates, and the evils attending the temporary and partial management of the local revenue officers, were amongst the chief causes of the impoverishment of a province on which nature has bestowed so many advantages in soil and situation. The time has arrived for the introduction of such measures of improvement as will tend to promote the prosperity of this rich but hitherto neglected province, and his Lordship in Council feels satisfied that no measure is more calculated to produce an extensive beneficial effect than the project now under consideration.

"There seems no reason to doubt that an Annicut across the Godavery will be as advantageous to the Rajahmundry District, as the Coleroon Annicuts have been to the Tanjore and Trichinopoly Districts; and it may confidently be expected, not only that a large annual amount of revenue, now difficult to collect, will be secured to Government without pressure on the ryots, but that a vast extent of the richest land will be made available for the cultivation of sugar and other valuable products.

"The difference between the calculations of the Collector and the Civil Engineer as to the probable increase of revenue that may be anticipated from the Annicut, is considerable; but if it had no other effect than that of securing to Government the sum of 90,000 rupees now annually lost, the object of its construction would be sufficiently gained. But when it is considered that, exclusive of the extent to which Major Cotton is of opinion the District of Rajahmundry will be benefited, the Annicut will enable nearly 820,000 acres of land to be brought under perfect irrigation in the District of Masulipatam, it seems impossible to estimate, or to limit, the prospective advantages to the people and to the Government that the completion of such a work is calculated to produce.

"One other point affords the strongest argument in favour of Major Cotton's project, that is, the frequent visitations of famine with which the Rajahmundry District has been afflicted, and from which the inhabitants have so dreadfully suffered; and if, as there is reason to believe, the proposed Annicut will preserve the population of that province from this frightful scourge, there cannot be a question but that its construction should be advocated. His Lordship in Council resolves, therefore, to bring the correspondence on the subject of the projected undertaking to the notice of the Honourable Court of Directors, with the strong recommendation of this Government that sanction be granted for the disbursement of the estimated amount, namely, 475,572 rupees, and that their orders be communicated in time for the commencement of the work at the beginning of the ensuing year." *

Directly sanction had been obtained for proceeding with the work, Major Cotton threw his heart into it with all the energy and zeal of his character. Some modifications of the original plan of the structure were made. It was at first intended that a large quantity of cut-stone should be used; but it was ascertained that the number of stone-cutters procurable was not sufficient to carry forward a work of such magnitude with any prospect of its being completed within a reasonable time, and it became necessary to substitute a mode of construction which would avoid this evil result. The form of the section in the original plan was that of an elevated mass of masonry, broader at the base than at the summit, over which the accumulated waters of the river would rush, and fall vertical on a platform on the lower side. The surface of this platform was to be formed of large rectangular slabs of granite or other hard stone, smoothed at the top, and carefully dressed in the joints, the whole being built upon masonry wells sunk in the bed of the river. Subsequent experiment showed that the work could be more expeditiously and reasonably constructed of ruder materials. Rough stone and rubble plastered over with chunam were proposed as substitutes for cut-stone. Another material alteration was also

* Minutes of Consultation of the Madras Government, Revenue Department, under date September 1, 1846.

proposed. This was to give the whole work a breadth of 18 feet in the clear at the top, so as to provide both an ample road-way during the time that the river was low, and also to allow of a bridge being carried along it. The broad surface of the Annicut was to be two feet lower than the crown of the work, a wall being built two feet high on the upper side, to keep the road-way dry, and to prevent accidents. The under-sluices being of great capacity, they would discharge a large body of water, so that none would go over the work, except while the freshes were high.

The Chief Engineer proposed a modification of this second section submitted by Major Cotton. "In the new weirs proposed for the improvement of the river Shannon," he wrote, "the section is so constructed that there is no fall whatever of any body of water, the down stream being built concave, and having a slope from its summit to its lower extremity, down which the water rushes, till it reaches the level of the river's bed. Under the foundation of the extremity of the slope, a row of piling is driven, and the surface of this section is composed of large rough stones, built in regular stages, their ends being placed outwards, and their lengths or joints perpendicular to the curve. In this form of Annicut the wear and tear is reduced to the lowest amount possible, and the structure seems incapable of any further improvement, it being as strong as possible. I am, therefore, of opinion that, if such a section be substituted in the Rajahmundry Annicut, not only will all the evils of an unnecessary delay be avoided, but also the stability of the work will be increased." *

A few months afterwards the work was in vigorous progress. A staff of engineer and other officers were employed on it. A detachment of the corps of Sappers and Miners was posted at Dowlaishweram, in the immediate vicinity of the works. A civilian had been appointed to the District as Sub-Collector, whose principal duty was to superintend the employment and payment of labourers, and to procure the necessary supplies. A quarry had been opened. Tramroads from the quarry to the river were nearly completed. A small steamer had been obtained from Calcutta. Thousands of labourers had been assembled. The hitherto quiet little village of Dowlaishweram had been converted into a bustling town.

"Upon the whole," Major Cotton writes, on August 18, 1847, "I

* Major Cotton's letter, dated February 17, 1847. Report by the Chief Engineer, dated June 8, 1847.

think we must consider the works to have gone on well, considering our circumstances. Our principal difficulty has been, and is, the keeping the people to their work. There has been very considerable waste in some part of the operations, especially in the embankment, from their idling; but as this has arisen mainly from the great numbers of people employed before we had sufficient superintendence, and from things being at first in disorder, compared with the state we may hope to get them into after a time, we may hope that, in this respect also, there will be nothing to complain of, particularly with the additional European superintendence that we shall now have.

"That we have made the progress which we have, is entirely owing to Mr. Henry Forbes, the Sub-Collector, whose vigorous and active measures have already roused the District to a degree that could not have been expected; and it may be said, indeed, that as respects the getting public and private improvements effected, the District is ten years in advance of what it was a few months ago. The people have come freely from all parts of the District, and both they and the native public servants now fully understand that great improvements can be effected. The actual use of the Godavery water from the new channel, as far as Samulcotta, over an entirely new tract, has also, no doubt, helped to enable the people to realize the practicability of improving the state of the District.

"With respect to the estimate, as we have not yet trenched on the largest items, I cannot speak confidently, but, so far as we have gone, I think there has been a fair result for the money expended. About one and a half lacs of rupees will be laid out in railways, boats, buildings, and machinery, all which will be of use in the execution of the remaining works included in the estimate of twelve lacs." *

The estimate was, however, insufficient. About a year later Major Cotton reported that from various causes, such as want of stone to complete the rough-stone dams, and inability to use steam on the railways, because the locomotives had not been supplied, the expenditure had greatly exceeded the estimate, although the works were not half finished. He requested sanction, therefore, to expend 139,100 rupees more. The Government of Madras, while soliciting the orders of the Court of Directors for this sum, observed that the Civil Engineer had not sufficient data in the present state of the works for estimating the ultimate expenditure, and that they

* Report, dated August 18, 1847.

believed a larger sum than that now estimated would be required to bring them to completion. The Court, in a despatch dated September 20, in the same year, confirmed this supplementary estimate, bringing the total amount sanctioned for this work up to that time to 614,852 rupees.

Meanwhile Major Cotton, prostrated by the exhausting, wearing labour of the past few months, had been compelled to leave the District, and Captain Orr was appointed to act in his stead. One of the first objects to which he turned his attention after assuming charge of the works, was the excavation of a portion of the main channel to lead from the Annicut down the central tract of the Delta. Major Cotton had, previous to his departure, submitted an estimate amounting to 19,550 rupees for this purpose, this being a necessary part of the scheme for irrigating the Delta which was dependent on the Annicut. "In this part of the Delta," he wrote, "there is no artificial or natural channel for many miles from the site of the Annicut; so that the excavation will be a very heavy one, and it can only be accomplished by degrees. The estimate now forwarded provides for a channel only five yards broad at the bottom (since considerably increased), and extending eleven miles, till it meets with what is probably a natural channel." At the same time he requested information from the Board of Revenue regarding the mode of procuring sanction for future estimates, because he wanted to submit estimates for completing two main lines of irrigation and navigation from the Annicut, namely, to Coringa on one side, and to Nursapore on the other; for commencing the high level channel to Ellore; and for making various small connecting cuts to lead the water from the Annicut into the old channels in the lower parts of the Delta. These formed part of the rough estimate of 12 lacs for the minor works connected with the Annicut. Captain Orr submitted a revised estimate for 34,013 rupees for this portion of the work.

The great work of constructing the Annicut itself was progressing slowly, but the amount sanctioned was insufficient. In his Report of September 16, 1848, Captain Orr submitted an estimate for the probable expense of completing it, amounting to 356,376 rupees. After entering into details regarding his future mode of operations, he adds: "In this manner, two years would be fully employed; and I have thus entered into detail that the insuperable obstacles which must oppose any attempt at a too speedy progress may be readily understood. These obstacles consist principally of the great difficulty, till the working season is far advanced, of disposing of the large body of water coming down the river, and of so managing it that there shall always be enough for the purpose of navigation, while at the same time the stream must be diverted from the neighbourhood of the building operations, and the water drained from the foundations. From the nature of the river, and the great extent of the Annicut, the only means of overcoming these obstacles and attaining the desired objects, are by the formation, at much expense and loss of time, of large temporary dams above, and by the excavation of drainage canals below, the site of the work, which operations are so dependent upon the state of the river, that no amount of expenditure alone will hasten them many days. There is, also, if too much be undertaken, the uncertainty of being able to transport daily a sufficient quantity of stone to complete the work in due time, although this year we shall have greatly augmented means of transport by boats, and have more use of steam power. . . . Full use of the Annicut will be obtained next year during the monsoon months, which is the only season, when any cultivation will be carried on for some time, till the people become accustomed to having a regular supply of water during the hot weather. . . . Having endeavoured to explain the nature and difficulties of the undertaking, I may be permitted to add that there can be no doubt as to the practicability of constructing the Annicut, and that time and money alone are required to complete this great work."

This Report was followed by one from a Committee which had been appointed, in obedience to orders from the Court of Directors, to examine and report on the actual condition of the works on the Godavery, and the plans proposed to be pursued for completing them. The Committee's Report, which is dated January 3, 1849, enters into much detail on the "State of the Works," "Apparatus for carrying on the Works," "Past Expenditure," "Machinery," &c. 503,703 rupees is the amount said to have been actually expended up to November 1848, 6690 rupees extra being chargeable to a supplemental estimate, and making the total 510,393 rupees. The Committee, which consisted of Captains Buckle, Bell, and Orr of the Madras Engineers, and Mr. Henry Forbes of the Civil Service, strongly recommended that the additional sum of 407,506 rupees might be sanctioned. They stated that they had instituted a minute inquiry into the new data for the different descriptions of work, and found that they had been prepared with a careful specification of the items of expense of the last season. The data were considered correct, barring contingencies which it was impossible to foresee. The Committee appended a table exhibiting the total anticipated expenditure, compared with the sanctioned estimate, which is reproduced below for future reference and comparison.

Work.	Anticipated Expenditure.		Sanctioned Expenditure.	
	Quantity.	Rupees.	Quantity.	Rupees.
	Cubic yds.			
Masonry..............................	151,283	311,346	130,534	284,170
Loose stone..........................	177,542	103,941	220,143	82,561
	No.			
Wells..................................	4,963	24,074	8,032	37,088
Lock-gates and sluice-shutters	...	16,197	...	6,074
Plastering and other items......	...	2,632	...	2,450
Earth work, including dams....	...	56,386	679,362	21,229
Superintendence...................	...	45,067	...	12,000
Sundries..............................	...	50,549	...	30,000
Contingencies.......................	...	50,000	...	...
Plant..................................	...	178,046	...	...
Unproductive........................	...	18,252	...	...
	Tons.			
Stone for railway embankments	21,000	4,993	...	...
Advances.............................	...	34,953	...	...
Materials on hand................	...	21,463	...	...
		917,899		
Deduct Captain Orr's expenditure mentioned above as "supplemental"................	...	6,690	...	...
Total.................................	...	911,209	...	475,572
Past expenditure..................	503,703			
Supplemental estimate..........	407,506			
		911,209		

In making this recommendation, the Committee remarked, "It is scarcely necessary to add that time itself in the construction of the Annicut is money. If the work is to increase the revenue, the sooner the increase begins the better: if the increase has been in any measure rightly estimated, it will speedily pay a much larger interest upon the extra expenditure than the rate at which the Company borrow money; and a single year of drought, which may happen at any time, would compel all to acknowledge the Annicut to be of incalculable value."

With reference to the "Plans of the Works," it was remarked :—
"With reference to the most important point, the section of the

Annicut, the Committee, after a minute consideration of the subject, are satisfied that the work may be carried forward with safety and success upon the section hitherto followed, with some improvements recommended by Captain Orr. The section is novel, and, considering the adaptation to the description of available material, and to the necessity of rapid construction, appears to the Committee highly creditable alike to the theoretic and practical knowledge of Major Cotton. Its stability has been remarkably demonstrated by the events of the late season; all the works that were not actually raw, having, though much of it was hastily constructed, suffered but little damage under even extraordinary trials. The excellence of the mortar made from the hydraulic lime of the neighbourhood, is an important element of the stability of the works; and the experience already obtained in the management of this lime will render it more valuable for the future. The only change in this section which the Committee recommend, is a narrow wall, as originally intended by Major Cotton, in lieu of the stones and boards afterwards suggested. The latter are open to several objections; and the Committee are of opinion that the increased breadth of the loose stone apron will neutralize any extra force of overfall caused by the proposed wall."

In submitting their Report, the Committee recommended that the works might be prosecuted with all possible diligence, and that the opening of the Ráli and other irrigating channels, required to extend to all parts of the District the benefit of the Annicut, might also receive early sanction.

This Report having been submitted to the Court of Directors by the Government of Madras, the Court, in a despatch dated July 18, 1849, gave their sanction to the further outlay required, "making an aggregate expenditure of 911,209 rupees, or 435,639 rupees in excess of the sum originally sanctioned for that purpose."

The Government of Madras had given the Acting Civil Engineer authority to increase the expenditure on the works in anticipation of the sanction expected from Leadenhall Street, and that officer, in reporting on the works in April, states :—

"At the beginning of February, everything being in a state of preparation, no time was lost after the receipt of authority for increasing the rate of expenditure, in resuming operations on an extensive scale; and by the middle of that month the works were all in full progress. Very satisfactory advance has since been made, considering that, as a preliminary to building in the bed of the river, we have had to execute what is certainly the most difficult and most discouraging branch of our labour, and that which caused so much anxiety to Major Cotton, and so much expense and delay to the work last year; namely, the construction of large temporary dams and canals, to keep the river from the portions of its bed to be built across, and to give command of water-carriage for the transport of materials. These dams have been completed with comparative facility; and the river now, at the same time that it is held back from the line of masonry, is kept at such a level, as to afford a perfect means of water communication direct from the end of the railway on the left bank of the river to the wing-walls of the Vijéshwaram or right side.

"Any one acquainted with the power of a large body of water like that contained in the bed of this river, will appreciate the difficulty, labour, and expense involved in the construction of these dams; but, by those not conversant with the subject, little idea can be formed, but by personal inspection, of the obstacle to our progress which the necessity of the formation of these dams presents. To give, however, an impression of the magnitude of these operations, I may mention, that the dam across the Vijéshwaram branch contains from 40,000 to 50,000 cubic yards of sand, all carried a considerable distance; is three-quarters of a mile in length; is rivetted throughout on both sides with rollers of grass; and that it could be formed only after a strong dam of sand, grass, and stone had been thrown with much labour across one main branch of the river two miles above.

"The uses of these dams and channels are, however, obvious, and the necessity for their formation was foreseen. I merely recur to them, that it may be seen what is the extent of the work we have performed, which, though indispensable, does not appear in a Statement of Progress; and that some perception may be entertained of the causes of an expenditure which, though not explicitly calculated nor valued in my estimate, has been incurred at the very beginning of our proceedings, thereby raising the cost of work already done beyond what may seem a fair proportion."

On September 16, 1849, an unprecedented rise in the Godavery occurred, accompanied by a very severe gale of wind, but the nearly completed Annicut firmly stood the unwonted strain. The highest mark on the standard register at Rajahmundry was 31 feet, but this year the fresh rose to 33 feet 5 inches there, and to the height of

29 feet 4 inches at Dowlaishweram. The works came out of this very severe trial comparatively uninjured, although a good deal of damage was inflicted on the buildings of the establishment connected with them.

The project and construction of the Annicut have hitherto been described in the words of those who were most closely connected with it, and, consequently, from an Engineer's point of view. It will now be viewed from the stand-point of a civilian observer. Mr. Forbes, as already stated, had been appointed Sub-Collector of the District with the object of assuming civil charge of the works. On the 8th of June 1850, he left Dowlaishweram, being appointed elsewhere on special duty, and he thus wrote regarding the progress and present condition of the Annicut:—

"It may be of some interest briefly to review each year's operations, and more immediately within my province, to notice the numbers and classes of people who have been employed at various times, and the quantities of the different supplies which have been furnished from the resources of this District. Operations were first vigorously commenced in April 1847; and, although all that was then done was but in preparation for the actual building of the Annicut and its works, yet these preparations were of necessity so vast that at no subsequent period were so many labourers and artificers employed as between April and July of that year. The quarry had to be opened, and two lines of double railway were formed from it to different points on the river bank; the embankments on the islands were thrown up, the head of the Dowlaishweram main channel formed by an extensive embankment to the head of the Vémagiri island; many boats were built, and railway waggons completed. During the progress of these preparatory works, there were at one time present as many as 10,200 labourers, 500 carpenters, and the same number of smiths. The preceding season had not been a good one, and the pressure of want sent a large number of labourers to the work: many of them, however, were women and children, who, although able to perform the common earth-work then required, could not be employed when building operations commenced. Since the first season, therefore, men alone have generally been employed, and the average number at work during the seasons of 1848, 1849, and 1850, has been 6500.

"In the season of 1848, the Dowlaishweram and Maddúru Annicuts were built, the former 1400 yards in length, and the latter

520 yards, both being raised to the height of 9 feet. A good deal of work was also done to the Dowlaishweram and Vijéshwaram sluices; and from July to November a party of labourers was constantly employed in the quarry in repairing and relaying the railroads, and preparing stone for the operations of the ensuing year.

"In 1849 the Vijéshwaram Annicut was built to a height of 9 feet, being 900 yards in length. Circumstances prevented the commencement of this work until the 10th of February, and a breach occurred during the progress from a sudden rise in the river. Extensive temporary dams had to be erected to turn the river from that branch, and canals excavated for the purpose of navigation. It is the furthest from the quarry, the source of the supply of stone, and from Rajahmundry, where all the limestone is found: the work was, however, completed before the end of May; and the season's operations included the repair of 80 yards in the Maddúru Annicut, an addition of 1½ foot of masonry to that work, the entire completion of the head and under-sluices and locks both at Dowlaishweram and Vijéshwaram, and of the under-sluice and wing-walls at Ráli, and also of about 50 yards on each end of the Ráli Annicut. At a later period of the season, a breach of not a formidable character was made in the Dowlaishweram Annicut, in consequence of the current along the front of the work, caused by the long wing-walls and longer embankment on the side of Pichika island, which materially narrowed the water-way; and, as this would have been a lasting source of anxiety, it was determined to remove the impediments to the free passage of the water, and to lengthen the Annicut by 250 yards.

"At the commencement of the present season, therefore, the position of the works was as follows:—An Annicut 9 feet high had been built across the Dowlaishweram branch of the river, 1400 yards in length, with a wing-wall and high embankment 250 yards in length uniting it to Pichika island; an Annicut of similar height, and 900 yards long, closed the Vijéshwaram branch; and that at Maddúru was closed also by an Annicut 520 yards long and 10½ feet high. The subordinate works were all completed, excepting the head-sluice and lock at Ráli. Thus the only escape for the whole stream of the Godavery was down the Ráli branch of the river; and it was in that very branch that an Annicut was to be built. A temporary dam formed of loose stone had been made in 1848, and strengthened in 1849, both to keep up the water for the purposes of navigation, and to prevent the stream cutting too deep a course in the bed of the river. The water escaping both through and over this rough stone dam, the objects to be attained were to make it water-tight, and of such a height as would turn the stream down the Dowlaishweram and Vijéshwaram branches, where the water could escape through the head and under-sluices. The building was carried on at both ends simultaneously, a small part of the temporary dam being closed with clay and sand as the masonry advanced. The river breached the dam for about 50 yards in February; and no sooner was the damage repaired, than a more extensive breach of about 80 yards was made: this was closed to within 25 or 30 yards, when again the water proved too powerful, and the breach was a third time widened to 80 yards. Measures were then adopted which proved perfectly successful. The Godavery, with a million and a half cubic yards of water passing every hour, was turned aside; and on the 25th of May the Ráli Annicut was completed to a height of 10½ feet.

"The estimate provides for the entire work being covered with cut-stone, for which a quantity not less than 560,000 square feet will be required. There is every reason to believe that the whole of the Dowlaishweram work will be covered this season, and at all events the slope of the Vijéshwaram Annicut and some portion of the top. The season's work is not, however, yet all enumerated. The wing-wall and long embankment on Pichika island have been removed, and the Dowlaishweram Annicut has been extended 250 yards; its total length now being 1650 yards, independent of the head and under-sluices.

"I cannot leave without regret a work which has been my daily occupation, and a source of constant interest to me, for four successive years; but I have seen it advanced to such a point that my regret is unmingled with anxiety. Difficulties are now at an end; the Godavery is dammed from bank to bank; and to complete whatever may be left of the cut-stone work at Vijéshwaram and to cover with cut-stone the Ráli and Maddúru Annicuts, alone remains to be done.

"From March 1, 1847, to April 30, 1850, there has been expended among the labourers working for daily hire, 239,130 rupees; the total number of daily labourers employed having been 3,054,413, or the total population of the province five times told. In addition to this, there has at all times been a large number, particularly in the quarry, on regular monthly wages; and in the present year, when the building operations have been most extensive, there have been in constant employ 641 bricklayers and 365 stone-masons, of whom 308 bricklayers and 231 masons have been supplied from this District. Of the coolies working on daily hire, and taking the average at 6500, about 1200 have been furnished from Masulipatam and 5300 from Rajahmundry. In this District each Taluk has been called upon to supply a fixed number with reference to its size and population. The village officers have among themselves arranged the details of the quota from each village, and also for the regular relief of the parties at intervals of one month.

"I am unwilling to close this Report and all connection with the Godavery Annicut, without stating my great obligations to Captain Orr and all the officers of his department for such a cordial co-operation and so good an understanding that, during the whole time of our association, no single point of difference has ever been allowed to occur."*

Lieutenant-Colonel Cotton resumed charge of the Civil Engineer's Office, 1st Division, in the middle of 1850. In one of his earliest letters, after submitting an estimate for the extension of the Vijéshwaram branch of the Annicut to the length of 400 yards, he writes :—

"I am happy to say that the Annicut is in effective operation, so far as the channels are opened, and that they have now had water in them without intermission for six months instead of for twenty or thirty days only, as formerly; and I hope the work of this year will not require us to lower the water in the river much, so that the channels will be supplied throughout the dry season for the first time. I am happy to state that the District is prospering beyond all my expectations."

The time of Colonel Cotton's connection with the District as Civil Engineer was drawing to a close, and before leaving to assume charge of the more important and influential office of Chief Engineer, he had the satisfaction of reporting that the Annicut was completed. This Report is given below with but few omissions :—

"I have the honour to report for the information of the Board of Revenue the following results of an examination of the Annicut lately made by Captains Orr and Hutchinson and myself. Commencing from the Dowlaishweram side. The lock is in perfect order: no expense has been incurred on this work from the first,

* Professional Papers of the Madras Engineers, vol. iii. p. 146.

namely, a period of five years. I cannot help here mentioning the excellent workmanship of the lock gates, as I think they reflect much credit on Captain Hutchinson. Considering that no one here had any experience in such work, and that the locks are 15 feet wide and 22 feet high, it is remarkable that they should have been made and hung so as to act perfectly without the slightest difficulty or alteration from the first.

"Head sluice in good order, and without repairs from the first. Under-sluices, the same, with the exception that we have had to throw in a prodigious quantity of rough stone for the apron. It has repeatedly sunk one or two yards, and must now contain an enormous quantity of stone. It seems, however, now to be nearly settled, as it has sunk very little of late. Both these sluices have two defects. One is that, being on the lee-side of the river, in the freshes vast quantities of drift wood accumulate against them, and often prevent their being shut close. No evil has arisen from this as yet; but it seems very desirable to free them from anything which might tend to endanger them. Various plans have been thought of, but none that seemed to me in all respects satisfactory. However, one seems so promising that I propose to try it this year. It is a boom of logs of timber, to float on the water, and extend from the end of the Annicut up the river, a little inclined to the bank, and about 1000 feet long, so as to cut off the lock and sluices from the rest of the river. It will be fixed at both ends to upright posts, by iron rings, to admit of its rising and falling with the water: the drift striking against this will be conducted over the Annicut. The other evil of these sluices is, that the shutters are not sufficiently manageable. They are very large, and, with a heavy head of water, they require so much force to drive them down as to endanger the shutters.

"The Dowlaishweram branch of the Annicut with its wing-walls. This work was first built to the height of 9 feet in 1848; and the water went over it while the people were still at work on it. Owing to the excellence of the chunam, however, it received no injury till the great flood at the end of the monsoon of that year, when the water got under the front wall of the work so freely as to press against the under surface of the masonry of the top and slope of the Annicut; and this blew it up. This was only for a short distance near the western wing-wall, and it was owing to the embankment having been carried too far into the river. This was certainly a mistake; but it was necessary to make every effort to complete this great length of dam, 1600 yards, before the monsoon; and this point was gained by shortening the masonry, and lengthening the earthen embankment. But in the great flood, the water scoured along the front of the work so violently as to cut away the sand from the wall, and get under it too freely. The front wall, however, was not undermined or breached. In the following year this end of the Annicut was extended 200 yards, which completely remedied the evil. This branch has since been covered with cut-stone, making it 12 feet high. The section given to it has answered very well; and, excepting at the end near the wing-wall, there has been no injury to the work. The rough-stone apron has sunk, but not very much, and has been raised and extended. During the last monsoon I cannot perceive that it has undergone the least change; but still I propose throwing in a small quantity of additional rough-stone for greater security. This branch has, however, one defect: from the vast quantity of stone required for covering it, and the gradual deterioration of the quarry preventing its due selection, a great deal of the cut-stone is evidently too soft, and wears under the friction of the sand and gravel passing over it. Last year a great number of the soft stones were replaced with harder ones; and it has not worn so much this year, so that it is not necessary to replace any. The soft stones should, however, be gradually all removed. This does not in the least affect the stability of the work. The wing-walls are in good order.

"The embankment across Pichika island is in good order; but I propose to widen it 4 yards. It is now 6 yards broad at the top. It seems advisable to do this, both to render it more convenient as a road, and also to make it more secure from the heavy sea to which it is exposed, when a high fresh is accompanied by a storm.

"Ráli branch with its wing-walls. This is where the great breaches occurred repeatedly in the first rough-stone dams thrown across to retain the water for navigation in the bed of the river. Where these breaches occurred, holes were cut by the water from 20 to 30 feet deep, which were again filled with loose stone. It is very remarkable that this is the only part of the foundations that has caused any trouble. Where the work rested on sand, it stood well; but these deep rough-stone foundations allow the water to pass through in large quantities; and repeatedly we have found, from moisture appearing in the joints of the masonry, and from heavy jets of water, a foot or more high, appearing through the rough-stone apron, that the water was pressing against the under side of the masonry of the Annicut, though, from its great thickness in its finished state, it can resist the pressure effectually. When first this branch was built, the rough-stone which had been thrown into the breaches was not carried up to the point where the solid masonry commenced; but it was covered with some feet of sand washed in with water, and the masonry laid on that. It is to be observed that the masonry of all the rest of the Annicut is laid on sand between the front and rear retaining walls; but in other parts it cannot be washed away. Here the water passed through the stones under the front wall, and carried the sand under the masonry away. The consequence of this was, that the masonry in these places cracked, and in one spot sank till it rested on the rough stone. When the work was examined, it was found to be hollow underneath for a considerable distance. This is very instructive. There is no better foundation for masonry than sand, if it is secured from currents of water. It is indestructible and incompressible, and so far is just as good as rock; but in situations where currents of water can get at it, as it is not, like rock, immovable, it is the worst of all foundations. All the part of the work thus undermined was broken up, and the masonry laid solid on the rough-stone: still this did not prevent the water passing under the work as before. A heavy bank of clay was thrown in front of the Annicut last year, so as to cover the whole of the loose stone, and this stopped the leaks at the time; but they appeared again this year, and the water spouted through the rough-stone apron strongly. We have now covered the front of the rough-stone with a heavy bank of the tough clay mixed with chippings of stone from the spoil heaps in the quarry; and the leaks seem effectually stopped. I am of opinion, however, that it would have been better to have mixed the quarry clay with the "lunka earth," as it would have made it more perfectly water-tight. The work does not appear at all endangered by these leaks. This work has been completed with a cut-stone covering, which is not much worn, partly because there was time to select the stone more carefully, and partly, I believe, because as yet less sand and gravel have passed over it than over the Dowlaishweram branch.

"Under sluices. This work was undermined and ruined in 1850. I was not here when this occurred, and do not clearly understand how it happened; but it was perhaps owing to the front apron being too narrow, and the eddying of the water in front of the vents scooping out the clay to the bottom of the wells on which the work rests. Yet the width of the apron was the same as at the Dowlaishweram under-sluices. However, in rebuilding them we took the precautions of making both front and rear aprons wider, and of putting a double row of wells under the front retaining wall. This work is in perfect order. The rough-stone apron has sunk repeatedly, and taken an immense quantity of rough-stone as at Dowlaishweram; but it is probably now nearly settled.

"Ráli lock. In perfect order; has had no repairs. Head-sluice the same. Ráli embankment requires to be widened as the Pichika island embankment does.

"Maddúru branch and wing-walls. This work was in a half-finished state when the fresh came down in 1848, and was then breached. It was completed to 10½ feet high in 1849, and since then has received no injury. This year it has been covered with cyclopean work, instead of cut-stone, like the others, chiefly on account of its being harder. The parts covered with cut-stone had required repairs, owing to the stone wearing, while those in which the rough rubble masonry had been unprotected received no injury. The cyclopean work is also not more than half the cost of cut-stone. This work is just now being finished, excepting the front yard, which I have left, to receive the iron posts which it is proposed to place along the whole Annicut. The channel of the river below this branch was formerly very shallow; but it has gradually deepened, and is now nearly at its proper level. The rough-stone apron will require to be somewhat strengthened consequent upon raising the work. Maddúru island embankment, the same as the others.

"Vijéshwaram branch. This branch of the river was 2 feet deeper than the Dowlaishweram one; so that the work was, in fact, 2 feet higher, causing a much more powerful overfall. The Annicut was built in 1849; and on the freshes passing over it in 1850, the rough apron sunk so much as to cause some alarm for the work. A large additional quantity of stone was, however, promptly thrown in during a very short interval which providentially occurred after the first fresh; and the work continued in that state through the monsoon. The great overfall had caused a deepening of the channel below, and this, of course, tended again to increase the overfall. To diminish the fall, it was proposed to lengthen the work 400 yards; but, in consequence of the sanction being received too late, the Government ordered the work not to be executed. With the help of the money sanctioned as an advance, I had done everything I could think of to secure the work without extending it. A very strong rough-stone apron was laid by Captain Orr of a great breadth, packed and secured in every way; and the result was entirely satisfactory: not a stone was moved, and not the least alarm occurred through the monsoon. The difference of the level of the upper water and the lower bed, when no water passes over the Annicut, is nearly 16 feet, making the force of the overfall here more than double what it is in the Dowlaishweram branch. This work has been covered with cut-stone, except the slope at the western end, which was left in the expectation of that part being broken up, if the works were extended. The covering of this is provided for in this year's estimate. The work will be exposed to a still more severe trial this year in consequence of raising the Maddúru branch 1½ feet, which will be equivalent to raising this branch half a foot. I am not, however, afraid of it, but shall take the precaution to add some rough-stone to the apron.

"Vijéshwaram island embankment, the same as the others. Under-sluice: this work, in consequence of its being out of the bed of the main river, and having a long narrow channel leading to and from it, has never been exposed to any trial like the others. The channel below, also, passes over such tough clay, that the water can scarcely touch it, whatever velocity it has. The rough-stone apron has never sunk at all. The floor of this sluice has never been covered with cut-stone: this should be done, when time can be found for it. Head-sluice: this work is in good order; but by some oversight, the main piers, which are built of brick, were not provided with stone grooves for the shutters, in consequence of which they got chipped. The first time the channel is closed for any purpose, grooved stones ought to be let into the brick-work. Vijéshwaram lock: in perfect order, and has received no repairs. The sluices in the gates of all these locks are disproportionately small; and they take a long time to fill and empty, which will be a great disadvantage, when the high level channels are completed, and there is much passenger traffic. They can be easily enlarged, and they should be, as soon as an opportunity offers. The channel leading to this sluice and lock is not sufficiently capacious; if a small cut is made, it can easily be enlarged by opening the under-sluices, and causing a strong scour through it.

"The total ordinary estimate for this year, allowing for 20,000 tons of rough-stone for the apron, &c., amounts to 33,835 rupees. It should be particularly observed that out of this nothing, excepting the repair of the trifling injury to the Vijéshwaram under-sluice, is properly repairs. Throughout the whole work not a rupee is required to repair damage sustained by the work last year. Only a quantity of stone had to be thrown into the apron of the Vijéshwaram under-sluice during the monsoon. This state of things is to me highly satisfactory. It seems to give a fair prospect of the actual cost of keeping the work itself in order being very insignificant. The alterations and additions proposed this year are all such as would not occur again; and they only amount to 3½ per cent. upon the total cost of the work. There is certainly every prospect that, including every alteration and improvement that can be thought of hereafter, the permanent annual expenditure on it will not be 2 per cent. upon the cost. One part of the work has now stood four monsoons, and in one of them an unprecedented flood; and I think we may thus consider the Annicut as fairly established. It is also to be considered, that a work like this is not like a bridge or a building, which is liable to be utterly destroyed. Almost the worst that could happen to it would be a breach of 50 or 100 yards, which could be repaired for 10 or 20,000 rupees; a trifle in comparison with the first cost. It is also observable that no alteration has been made in the original section of the work, excepting that the rough-stone apron has been enlarged. The Dowlaishweram branch is just as originally planned, and no alteration of any consequence has been made in the others.

"Can we see this large and important work, calculated so substantially to promote the real comfort of a million of people, thus brought to completion through so many difficulties and contingencies, without heartily acknowledging the goodness of God in thus prospering us, and bringing the project so far to a successful issue, notwithstanding the opposition it has experienced from quarters from which I had every right and every reason to hope for, and from which I did confidently expect, most cordial and energetic support, in carrying out a work of such unequalled magnitude in India, a work approved and ordered by the home authorities, and calculated to be in every way so vast a public benefit? May we not hope that its accomplishment, with the abundant effects which have already resulted from it to the District, will lead to the adoption of such extensive works for the improvement of the country and the promotion of the welfare of the people entrusted to our care, as will lead to an increasing appreciation of a Christian Government? There is nothing that the natives more thoroughly appreciate, after peace, than public works, and especially those that furnish them with water; and I cannot but trust that this is only the beginning of a series of works worthy of our nation, our knowledge, our religion, and the extraordinary power God has been pleased to put into our hands. I say our religion, because I am sure it ought to lead us to do our utmost in every way to care for those who are thus committed to us.

"It remains for me to speak of the state of the bed of the river above the Annicut, which will require to be carefully watched. When the work was commenced, the passage of the water to the Maddúru and Ráli branches was very much obstructed by the large island of Waddevani, and its adjacent sand-banks; so that in low freshes the water reached those branches by very circuitous routes on both sides. There was then a complete channel between the head of the Delta proper and the same island. Great changes have now taken place hereabout. A clear and broad channel has formed close to the western side of that island, leading direct to the Maddúru branch; and another is rapidly forming on the east side, leading direct to the Ráli branch, while the sand has accumulated between the head of the Delta and the island; so that, in another season or two, it seems evident that the head of the island will, in fact, be the head of the Delta, nearly three miles above its former head and above the line of the Annicut, while the water will flow in a clear and direct channel to every branch of the Annicut. This is a desirable state of things; and had not the river shown such decided symptoms of accomplishing it without help, it would have been well to have assisted it. There are, however, banks forming which require to be removed. The principal one is opposite to the eastern end of the Vijéshwaram branch, which, if left to itself, would extend and throw the stream upon the western wing-wall of the Annicut. It has been customary for the inhabitants of the villages near the river, whenever a bank began to form and threaten mischief to the opposite bank of the river, to hasten the evil prodigiously by planting the sand with prairie grass, which rapidly increases it, and it speedily becomes a high and solid island. The object of this is to form new tobacco land; but, of course, it is done at the expense of the land on the adjoining bank of the river, which is cut away proportionately; and not only so, but every deviation from a direct course thus produced tends to cause a series of sets on the alternate banks of the river below. This ought never to be tolerated in a civilized community. Wherever such banks form, and tend to throw the current upon the bank of the river, not only ought grass not to be planted; but, if it grows naturally, it must be rooted up, and, if necessary, channels cut through the bank to facilitate its dissolution by the current. This is especially necessary in the neighbourhood of the Annicut; and if not done, the river would inevitably set on one or other wing-wall, and cut away the adjoining island, till it got round the masonry. I have provided for rooting up the grass, and cutting channels through two newly-formed banks this year. In the first years, in consequence of the indirect course of the stream, the heads of Pichika island and Maddúru island were rapidly cut away, and it became necessary to protect them by loose stone-work; but, in consequence of the changes above mentioned, this danger has now ceased. There is rather a set upon the bank near the village of Dowlaishweram, and it may be necessary to protect it by loose-stone groins; but at present the action of the water there is not serious. Below the Annicut, there is, in a certain state of the river, a strong set on the Dowlaishweram bank; but several groins have been thrown out there, and it seems now pretty well protected. It must be observed that these changes from the action of the river on its banks, are much slower in the Godavery than in the Coleroon and Cauvery, and as it seems also in the Indus and Ganges, so that there is plenty of time to take the necessary precautions; and the stone we have here at hand is a material for barriers far beyond the power of the stream to remove, even though in pieces of the size of the fist. In comparing the present state of the river with the map constructed thirty years ago, it will be seen how very slowly the encroachments of this river proceed.

"The Maddúru branch being now covered, and the extension of the Vijéshwaram branch given up, the only work remaining to complete the Annicut is the line of iron posts and planks along the front. I am now taking the opportunity of covering the Maddúru branch to place the posts along it. The rough-stone apron of the Annicut throughout seems to be well established; there is no appearance of any sinking or disturbance of any consequence this year in any part. It is generally from 15 to 20 yards broad. I am now, however, throwing in additional stone, strengthening each branch according to the proportionate force of the water over it. To the Maddúru branch, as it is now higher than it has been hitherto, I purpose adding considerably, and also to the Vijéshwaram branch, which ought to have an abundantly large apron.

"I have now the honour to request that the establishment which I have recommended for the conservation of this important work may, if approved, be appointed without loss of time. A body of thoroughly trained men, under efficient superintendence, permanently resident on each portion of the work is essential, and should be immediately appointed and housed, that they may be fully prepared for their duties before the freshes. No water-works of any kind can ever be trusted to take care of themselves, and both the cost of this work and the vast amount of property dependent upon it demand that no risk should be run about it." (April 14, 1852.)

Soon after the receipt of this Report through the Board of Revenue, the Government of Madras passed the following congratulatory order:—

"1. The Right Honourable the Governor in Council has received with much satisfaction the Report of Colonel Cotton on the state of the Godavery Annicut, which may now be said to have arrived at completion through the unceasing exertion and energy of Colonel Cotton and the officers associated with him in this great undertaking.

"2. It must be a highly gratifying termination of Colonel Cotton's immediate connection with the 1st Division that he should have been enabled to notify to Government the complete stability of the Annicut, and the success which has up to this period attended his plans; and in congratulating that officer on these happy results, the Governor in Council has much pleasure in recording his obligations to Colonel Cotton, Captain Orr, and the officers of the Department under their orders, for their services on this occasion; and it will be his agreeable duty to bring the same to the notice of the Honourable the Court of Directors.

"3. The Right Honourable the Governor in Council has not failed to remember the very valuable aid rendered by Mr. Forbes, late Sub-Collector of Rajahmundry, during the progress of the work. By the vigorous execution of the responsible duty assigned to him, the constant requirements of the Engineer Department were supplied; and, by his judicious arrangements, order and regularity were preserved among the vast assemblage of artisans and labourers congregated at Dowlaishweram."*

In connection with the Annicut, and in furtherance of the great scheme of artificial irrigation of which it is the basis, sanction was given to two projects for the extended irrigation of the Delta at an estimated expenditure of 138,646 rupees and 176,357 rupees respectively. Besides the expenditure on these subsidiary works, large sums have been sanctioned from time to time, during the progress of the Annicut, as "ordinary repairs." By a statement of the Madras Government, dated February 22, 1853, it appears that the sums sanctioned for the works from their commencement to December 4, 1852, were as follows:—

	Rupees.
For the Annicut	883,258
For the Subsidiary works . . .	581,900
	1,465,158
Ordinary estimate for repairs of works connected with the Annicut since their completion .	51,918
Total	1,517,076

An additional sum of 17,876 rupees was sanctioned in the following month for erecting a new lock at Vijéshwaram, making a total for these works of 1,534,952 rupees up to January 1853.

We conclude this chapter with a brief description of the noble work, the progress of which we have hitherto been tracing. It consisted of four divisions, each being complete in itself. The first, or the Dowlaishweram division, extended from the left bank of the river to Pichika Island, and consisted of the entrance lock into the Canal on the extreme left, the head-sluice, the under-sluices, and the Annicut itself, with its wing-walls, which was 1650 yards long and 12 feet high. The second, or the Ráli branch, extended from Pichika Island to Bobba Island. The Annicut itself, with its wing-walls, was 940 yards long and 10½ feet high, and in the latter island were the lock and head-sluice for supplying the Central Delta Canals. The third, or the Maddúru division, extended from Bobba Island to Maddúru Island, and was 520 yards long and 10½ feet high. The last, or the Vijéshwaram division, extended from Maddúru Island to

* Extract from the Minutes of Consultation, Revenue Department, under date the 27th of May 1852.

Chiguru Island, adjoining the right bank of the river. The Annicut itself was 900 yards long and 9 feet high, and there were under and head-sluices, and a lock on the extreme right of it. Each of these divisional weirs consisted of solid masonry work laid on wells 6 feet deep dug in the sand. In front was a strong retaining-wall, from which the building sloped towards the back retaining-wall, the whole being crowned with a covering made of cut-stone in three of the branches, and of cyclopean work in the fourth. At the back was a rough stone apron from 15 to 20 yards broad.

The whole breadth of the river at this spot is 7000 yards, or 4 miles, and the quantity of stone used in the work was about 800,000 tons, besides some millions of bricks. Some idea can be formed of the extraordinary cheapness of work in India at that time from the expenditure of £90,000 on such a mass, amounting to only a little more than two shillings a ton of stone, including all the temporary work and other charges.

An endeavour has thus been made to give a brief, and, it is hoped, clear description of this invaluable work as an appropriate close to the history of its construction. It would be difficult to enumerate all the benefits it has been the means of conferring on the people of the District, who still cherish the recollection of its founder in their household converse, and in their popular songs. "Peace hath her victories no less renowned than War," * and few of her victories have such an enduring monument as the Godavery Annicut.

* Milton.

CHAPTER VII.

ACCOUNT OF THE IRRIGATION DEPENDENT ON THE ANNICUT.

DESCRIPTION OF THE FORMER SOURCES OF IRRIGATION—PROJECTS FOR WATERING THE EASTERN DELTA—THE CENTRAL DELTA—THE WESTERN DELTA—ACCOUNT OF THE PRESENT CANAL SYSTEM THROUGHOUT THE DISTRICT.

WHILE the main work of the Annicut itself was being diligently pressed forward with all the ardour of men thoroughly in earnest, plans for the complete irrigation of the country dependent on it were not neglected. On the 3d of August 1849, the Acting Civil Engineer forwarded to the Board of Revenue a Report on the various channels previously existing in the Delta, or formed during the last few years, and on those which it would probably be necessary to construct, in order to give full effect to the Annicut. We refer to this Report, because the old channels are described in it as well as projects for new, and the former condition of the District as to irrigation can be understood from it as well as the proposed improvements.

The irrigated portions of the Delta had hitherto derived their supply of water from the local rains, aided by the river. The latter source, however, was very limited, owing to the defective nature of the channels, which, having been excavated to within not more than 12 or 15 feet of the deep bed of the river, received water only so long as it remained at that height, or for about fifty days in the year. The channels on the eastern side were the Túlayya Bhága, the Tsoppella, the Téki, and the Muskapalli channels. The central tract was wholly destitute of the means of river irrigation, water being admitted on the land only during a very few days in the year, through small sluices constructed in the river bank. On the western side there were the old and new Apparow Channel, falling into the Vaiyyéru, which itself led off from the river some miles above Rajahmundry; the Usulumarru, feeding the Gósta Nadi; the Bhúppaya, leading off at Kákaraparru, ten miles below the head of the Delta; and the Pémulu, with several heads, the principal at Kandavilli, Siddhántam, and Átsanta. Of the above, those channels which alone derived immediate advantage from the Annicut were the Túlayya Bhága, and its branches on the east, and the Vaiyyéru, by means of the old Apparow Channel on the west.

The Túlayya Bhága seems to have been originally a natural hollow, of which advantage was taken to form the bed of an irrigating channel by cutting a head to it from the river, and throwing earthen banks across it at various places to raise the water to the necessary height for commanding the adjacent country. It led off from the intended main feeder about a mile below the head-sluice, and conveyed water to the Kápavaram, Bikkavólu, and Rámachandrapuram Taluks, terminating in the salt water creek which flows in from the sea near Cocanada, two miles from which place a bank was erected to exclude the tide, and to retain the fresh water brought down from the floods of the Godavery. The head of the channel had recently been deepened and widened for a distance of ten miles. In 1846 the project was carried out of leading off, from near the village of Kadayam, a branch which should flow with only a nominal fall as far as the town of Samulcotta, thirty miles distant, and water the strip of land contained between it and the Túlayya Bhága—an area of about a hundred square miles. As this project brought an increased quantity of land under irrigation, it became necessary to enlarge the capacity of the head of the Túlayya Bhága, which was done, and the channel was rendered capable of watering 50,000 acres. In 1848, Major Cotton received sanction for the project of rendering the Túlayya Bhága navigable by the construction of locks at Chintapalli and Kovvúru; but the execution of the work was not completed till later. This channel, when the water in the river was 12 feet deep, had a section of 52 square yards, and its velocity then being about 2000 yards per hour, it carried down upwards of 100,000 cubic yards per hour, one-third being taken off by the Samulcotta channel.

The Vaiyyéru, the principal channel on the western side, was nearly similar in its conditions to the Túlayya Bhága, except being of much more considerable dimensions. It first branched from the river at about four miles below the hills, and followed a course nearly parallel to it, as far as the site of the Annicut, where it received two feeders, called the old and new Apparow channels, and then, running in a westerly direction, terminated in the Colair Lake. From the low level and deep hollow in which the Vaiyyéru flowed, very small advantage was derived from it, until it had proceeded a considerable distance. Thus, although skirting the Tanuku Taluk along its whole length, it contributed nothing towards its cultivation.

The following works were considered necessary to complete the project by conducting the water over the whole surface of the Delta, taking advantage of all the existing channels, when available for the purpose, by connecting them with the main feeders, which had their heads already excavated, and furnished with large regulating sluices. On the eastern side of the river, it was proposed to carry the main feeder, with a considerable and uniform section, as far as the village of Kauléshwaram, taking advantage of a former natural arm of the Godavery, which, fortunately running for eight miles in the right direction, as far as the village of Tsoppella, saved the great mass of cuttings always attendant on the excavation of the first few miles of such channels. From Kauléshwaram this main channel was to diminish in size, until it reached its probable termination near Muskapalli, where it would end, and supply the channel at that village. From the main channel about a mile below the Annicut, the Túlayya Bhága branched off. Eight miles further down, near Tsoppella, the second branch was to lead off, by means of which it was intended to irrigate the land as far as Rámachandrapuram, an extent of about fifty square miles.

The third was the Têki Channel, by which it was proposed to convey water to the greater number of villages in the Rámachandrapuram Taluk, an extent of about a hundred square miles, terminating it with a lock in one of the tide water creeks leading from Coringa to near the village of Dugadúru. This channel was to consist of two branches, one of which would lead off towards the town of Rámachandrapuram, and be carried on until it met, close to the village of Vélangi, a salt-water creek, near the mouth of which it would be necessary to construct a calingulah (and, perhaps, eventually, a lock), in order to prevent the entrance of the tide, and to allow the bed to be filled with fresh water, that would then supply the villages in the neighbourhood, and bring under cultivation a good deal of neglected land. The other branch was to keep its direction towards the village of Dangéru, and from thence to Paikéru, where it was to fall into a very considerable salt-water creek that ran from Coringa, and would serve as an excellent navigable termination to the main channel, where a lock was constructed there.

As the Godavery was navigable at all seasons from the sea as far as the village of Kauléshwaram, but the navigation was very intricate, and in the hot weather almost impassable between that village and Dowlaishweram, it was considered advisable to construct a calingulah, and to transfer to the neighbourhood of Kauléshwaram the site of the lock into the river for turning the flank of the Annicut. By the above-mentioned arrangement of channels, the Samulcotta received the drainage of the high lands immediately above it, and the Túlayya Bhága that of the lands lying between it and the Samulcotta channel, discharging its surplus water into the Cocanada river, whence it would probably be made useful as a means of scouring out the bar. The Téki channel received the drainage of the lands irrigated by the Tsoppella and Túlayya Bhága, and discharged its surplus into the Coringa river, while the drainage of the lands irrigated by its own water was carried off partly in the direction of the creek at Vélangi.

In the central portion the main feeder led off from the head of the tract, and did not come to the surface of the land until six miles down, near the village of Vasantaváda, continuing to run along the centre of the tract as far as Ráli. Two branches then issued from it, one leading down the western side in the bed of a channel which originally received water in the freshes, but having had its head closed by the formation of the river embankment, was cut off from the supply. This channel was apparently a natural formation, and required but little additional cutting, as it was already of a fair capacity. It was intended to supply the country along its whole length, and its termination at Batalapálem was considered an eligible site for a large aqueduct, by which it was proposed to convey water to the Nagaram Taluk. At this village it was also proposed to construct a lock to allow of boats passing into the western branch of the river from above the Annicut, as the navigation of the river upward from that place is in the summer very intricate and, indeed, almost impossible.

The other branch of the main feeder fell, near the village of Kottapéta, into an already excavated channel which led down the centre of the Amalápuram Taluk, and terminated in the Godavery near the village of Pérúr, where it was thought necessary to construct a calingulah to prevent the entrance of the tide, and to discharge the surplus water of the channel. From Kottapéta it was considered requisite to lead off a branch parallel to the river for the supply of several small channels which already existed, though they received water in the high freshes only. This branch was to terminate near Komanapalli, discharging over a calingulah its surplus into the branch of the river flowing past that village. From these main feeders all the existing small irrigation channels of this division of the Delta could be supplied.

On the western side of the river it was proposed to supply the existing channels by carrying the main feeder from the Annicut in a direction nearly parallel to the course of the river, closing up the heads of such channels as then received water direct in the freshes, and making arrangements similar to those previously described for the irrigation and drainage of the lands on the eastern side. As there was a considerable portion of land west of the Vaiyyéru commanded by the Annicut, and as that channel itself ran in too deep a hollow for its water to irrigate the lands immediately on its banks without the aid of calingulahs, it was thought necessary to supply those lands either by conducting water from the main channel by aqueducts over the Vaiyyéru, or by taking off a branch from the latter nearly opposite the junction with it of the old Apparow channel, carrying this branch on a high level with little slope to its bed. Such a high level channel would irrigate all the lands between itself and the Vaiyyéru. The main leader was to lead off from immediately above the Annicut, and to run nearly parallel to the course of the river until it met, near the village of Doddipatla, with a head of the Pémulu channel, with which, being united, it was finally to terminate at the village of Yelamanchili, where a lock and calingulah would be necessary to render the main channel navigable as a route for all the traffic hitherto carried on by means of the river between the port of Nursapore and the interior.

The first channel which the main feeder was to supply was the Vaiyyéru and its branches. The second was the Usulamarru, which then led off from the river at the village of that name, and carrying the water of the Godavery direct to the Gósta Nadi, which ran through the head of the Tanuku Taluk, watering, however, a very small portion of it, but conferring much benefit on the Undi Taluk. The country through which it ran being, however, all below the level of the crown of the Annicut, could easily be supplied by means of calingulahs thrown across this channel, or else by leading off fresh cuts from a higher level.

The third which the main feeder intersected was the Bhúppayya, already of a large capacity, which, from the improvements made to it in 1840–43, was productive of considerable advantage to the Undi Taluk, although affording but a very irregular supply of water, being fed in the freshes only; whereas, if supplied by the main feeder, it would receive water all the year round. The fourth and last channel, the Pémulu, then filled by two or three cuts from the Godavery at the villages of Kondavilli, Siddhántam, and Átsanta, appeared to have been originally a natural hollow, of which advantage had been taken. It ended in a large reservoir at Yelamanchili, where a lock and calingulah were required.

In the above description the details of the proposed eventual distribution of the water from the Annicut have been given; but a plan for partially supplying the Gósta Nadi and Bhúppayya channels immediately with water from the Annicut was also proposed, thereby conferring considerable benefit on the Tanuku and Undi Taluks before the main feeder could be excavated and brought into full operation. The Gósta Nadi had hitherto received a partial supply from the Vaiyyéru when, in the height of the freshes, the latter overflowed its banks, and ran down a hollow from a pond called the Rálla Madugu, near the village of Nidadavólu, until it reached the former channel. By rendering this communication more perfect, and by forming an excavation for a few miles only, the Vaiyyéru would be, it was considered, able to contribute immediately to the Gósta Nadi; and again, by making a small cut from the Gósta Nadi, near the town of Tanuku, to the Bhúppayya, near the village of Gontéru, the latter channel would also immediately participate in the benefit of the Annicut.*

The above is a brief description of the means of irrigation then existing in the Delta and the proposed improvements. The District Engineer, in submitting this scheme, requested sanction for eleven lacs of rupees in addition to the nine lacs required as the cost of the Annicut, in order to complete the perfect irrigation of the District,

* Professional Papers of the Madras Engineers, vol. iii. p. 116.

and to render each of the larger irrigating channels navigable as highways for the transport of produce and merchandise. A less sum was subsequently sanctioned.

Following the plan adopted in describing the construction of the Annicut, I propose to give an account of the scheme for the irrigation of the District as far as possible in the very words of the professional officers who devised and executed it. Soon after his return to the District, Lieut.-Colonel Cotton submitted an occasional estimate, amounting to 76,396 rupees, for works of irrigation on the western side of the Godavery. "At present," he said, "the water from that end of the Annicut is conveyed by the new and old Apparow channels into the Vaiyyéru, by which river it is conveyed only to those lands that are not many feet above the level of the sea. The upper part of the river has too deep a channel to admit of the water being led to the lands adjoining it. I should observe that a fundamental point in the distribution of the water is that the old channels, which are chiefly natural ones, are on too low a level to water the adjoining lands without dams; but they are quite convenient for conveying the water required for certain lands down to such a point as will admit of that water being led to them. That is, if the lands are 20 feet below the Annicut, the water may, of course, be led by the natural channels till they reach nearly that level. These channels may thus be made great use of; and it will be much cheaper to convey the water by them, and construct dams across them at the points where portions of it must be diverted to particular tracts, than to carry entirely new channels the whole way from the Annicut. The Vaiyyéru is very capacious, and will conduct a large body of water to the lower lands. The Gósta Nadi also, which commences near the Vaiyyéru, and joins the Bhúppayya, will, with its branches, carry a good quantity of water. But for the lands near the Annicut new channels must be cut.

"The works I now propose are as follows:—The head of the western main channel must be somewhat enlarged. I provide in this estimate to make it capable of leading off 150,000 cubic yards of water per hour when there is 2½ yards depth of water in it—the greatest depth I propose at present to admit into it. This I consider sufficient to secure the crop on 150,000 acres. This will flow by both the old Apparow and the new cut leading to the new Apparow into the Vaiyyéru, down which it will pass as far as the head of the Gósta Nadi. The bed of the Vaiyyéru at this point is 9 feet below the floor of the head-sluice. Here I propose to make a capacious

Annicut with dam stones, which will provide for the water being retained 13½ feet above the bed, that when the water stands 7½ feet in the channel, there will be a fall of 3 feet to the Niddadavólu Annicut, a distance of 6½ miles. This will not be too much for the navigation of the channel. The first branch to be led off will be the Kákaraparru channel, to lead the water to the high lands adjoining the river. The level of the country will suit for this channel at a point between the head-sluice and Niddadavólu. It will be carried with a slight fall of 4 inches per mile till it reaches the bank of the Tipparru, where it will fall into the channel already cut in making the embankment of the river, along which it will flow, having the natural fall of the country. It will water all the high part of the Tanuku Taluk and the narrow strip of land lying between the bank of the river and the Nakkala channel. At the head of the latter I propose a lock and calingulah to turn a portion of the water down the latter channel, both for irrigation and to provide for the navigation by that line to tide-water at Nursapore. From the head of the Nakkala channel the remainder of the water will flow on by the river bank to Yelamanchili. The new part of the Kákaraparru channel is calculated to convey 30,000 cubic yards of water per hour, or to provide for 30,000 acres. The continuation along the river is at present incomplete, and not of sufficient capacity; it will be enlarged in the upper part, and the section gradually diminished to the lower end. The land to which this line of channel will convey water is at present unirrigated, excepting near the lower end of the Nakkala channel. It will supply a large portion of the rich land of the Tanuku Taluk peculiarly fitted for the richer productions, and also the lands already watered by bullocks for the sugar cultivation near Yelamanchili.

"The next branch will be the Gósta Nadi. This is also a natural channel; but in high freshes of the Vaiyyéru that river overflows into it, and my predecessor cleared it out for some miles near its head, without, however, cutting through into the Vaiyyéru. With the height I propose for the Niddadavólu Annicut, if the head of the Gósta Nadi is cut through, the water will flow down it freely. This channel will lead the water into the Bhúppayya and other channels, and their branches; so that a considerable extent of land will receive it at once, and trifling cuts will distribute it to all the other villages in the neighbourhood of Pálakollu. About 30,000 cubic yards per hour may be thrown into this channel.

"The next branch from the Vaiyyéru will be the Venkayya channel. This was cut some years ago by a native proprietor, but it has been neglected. It requires to be cleared and straightened. It conveys water to many villages, and some of their shallow tanks towards the Colair. In the freshes this channel breaches near the village of Ipparru into the Upputéru, the main drain of that part of the country, which enters the sea near Gollapálem. As soon as the monsoon is over, the people close this breach, and retain the water at a level of seven or eight feet above that of the Upputéru. At this point, therefore, a calingulah should be built with a lock. This channel will form the best line for the navigation from the Godavery towards Masulipatam, completing the communication with that port by the ordinary vessels of the bay, which could go out by the Sambaldivi mouth of the Upputéru into the bay, and enter the Masulipatam branch of the Kistna. There would thus be at once a water communication between the two ports of Coringa and Masulipatam, and all the intermediate country. The remainder of the water, after supplying the Venkayya channel, will pass down the Vaiyyéru into numerous branches; this part of the country being the only part that is tolerably well supplied with small channels. The surplus water from this river will find its way by various small creeks across the swamp to the Upputéru.

"The whole of these works are, therefore, calculated to attain the following objects. First, to throw about 150,000 cubic yards of water per hour into a tract of country containing about 300,000 acres of arable Delta land, filling all the channels, large and small, at present existing, and also a new channel, of thirty miles in length. Secondly, to open two main lines of navigation from above the Annicut, one to tide-water at Nursapore, and the other to that at Gollapálem, and the bay of Masulipatam.

"The cost of this part of the works will, therefore, amount to about a quarter of a rupee per acre (81,000 rupees for 300,000 acres). The share of the cost of the great works, the Annicut and embankments, chargeable to this tract, will be about three-tenths of ten lacs, or 300,000 rupees, or 1 rupee per acre, making a total of 1¼ rupee per acre. The works required to complete the operations here will be:—A large work for the drainage of the very flat lands near the salt swamps and the Colair. Enlarging the main channel from the Annicut, to admit of its conveying 300,000 cubic yards per hour. Numerous small works of detail, village channels, sluices, &c., and I estimate the cost of these at about 150,000 rupees.

"It is to be observed that another tract remains to be watered on this side of the river, namely, that lying between the Annicut, Ellore, and the Colair. The most important work in this tract is the high-level channel to Ellore, on the line of the great northern road, which will meet the line from the Kistna Annicut, and form part of a navigation of 220 miles, parallel with the coast, and connecting the Kistna and Godavery direct.

"I think that two rupees per acre will be ample to complete the whole project, generally, consisting of :—

1. Annicut.
2. River embankments and protection.
3. Works of distribution.
4. Do. of drainage.
5. Navigation.
6. Roads, which will, of course, be comparatively insignificant, as all the main traffic will be by water." *

In the following August, Colonel Cotton submitted an estimate for the irrigation of the Central Delta, amounting to 138,647 rupees. "The works already executed in this portion of the country commanded by the Annicut," he wrote, "consist only of the main channel, cut to a depth of 10 yards at bottom, with a fall of 4 inches per mile, with its head-sluice and lock. At eight miles from the Annicut this channel divides into two, one leading into the old channel called the Kausika, flowing within a few miles of the bank of the eastern Godavery, passing near Amalápuram, and terminating in the small branch of the Godavery, which separates from the western main branch near Gannáram, thirteen miles from the coast. This branch falls into the sea at Bendamúrlanka. The Kausika has been cleared out for several miles near Ráli. The other branch of the Ráli main channel terminates in the Gorinkala channel, which flows within a mile or two of the bank of the Western Godavery, and falls into the same branch of the river at Gannáram, a mile below its head. This channel also had been allowed to silt up, and that so completely, that for two miles there was no distinct mark of a channel at all; and, consequently, throughout the monsoon, the water spread over

* Professional Papers of the Madras Engineers, vol. iii. p. 159.

the land for a mile or two. The sum of about 1200 rupees has been expended in clearing this channel.

"The clearing of these two old channels is by no means completed. Merely as drains they require to be greatly enlarged and straightened; but they will be used also for a considerable portion of their length for conveying the irrigation water. At present, indeed, they are used for both purposes; and, by opening and closing the head-sluice, the water can be kept at a convenient level. They also form lines of navigation from the Annicut to tide-water on the Nursapore side, thus completing the water communication between Cocanada and Nursapore.

"The works now proposed are:—The further cutting of the main channel to the extent of 5 yards broad, to provide for the additional branch channels now to be cut, estimated at 12,500 rupees. The enlarging and straightening the Gorinkala channel, to carry on a portion of the water, amounting to 2083 rupees. The construction of a lock and calingulah two and a half miles below Ráli, both to diminish the current for the sake of the navigation, and to raise the water to the proper level for two branch channels. By constructing a lock at this point, we avoid the necessity of leading off the water from a point several miles higher up, and the consequent cutting of the channel for that distance. It is, of course, important, as far as possible, to use the lines of the old channels, both to avoid the division of the lands, and also to save land. Amount of estimate, 5940 rupees. A branch channel leading from above the lock on the east side, to be conducted along the middle of the tract between the Kausika and Gorinkala channels for its irrigation. The extent of this tract is 22,000 acres, exclusive of 24 per cent. allowed for sites of villages, &c. Amount of estimate, 8569 rupees. A lock with waste small surplus channel, led off on the eastern side of it, at the mouth of the Gorinkala channel, to lower the navigation down to tide-water. At present there is much too great a fall at this point; so that, when the river is low, it is scarcely practicable for boats. With this lock, the navigation will be rendered very good between all the different parts of the Delta; tide-water of all the branches being connected with each other, with the river above the Annicut, and (by the works now in progress on the Vaiyyéru) with tide-water within twenty miles of Masulipatam. The lock must be furnished with an upper bay closed with reversed gates, to exclude the floods in high freshes. Amount of estimate, 8765 rupees. A second branch channel leading from the western side of the lock, and flowing on the highest ground close to the river bank of the Western Godavery. This will convey all the water for the irrigation of the strip of land between the bank and the Gorinkala channel, 7500 acres, and also for the whole Taluk of Nagaram (the minor Delta lying between the Bendamúrlanka and Nursapore branches of the Godavery) 66,000 acres, in all 73,500 acres. Amount of estimate, 8340 rupees. A small aqueduct to convey this channel over the Gorinkala channel, immediately below the Udumúdi lock. This channel cannot be carried on so high a level as to allow of the passage of boats under it in the high freshes. Estimate included in No. 5. A large aqueduct across the small branch of the Godavery near Gannavaram (popularly called Gannáram), to convey the water into the Nagaram Taluk. This is the only large work that will be required in the Delta. The estimate for it is 73,200 rupees. The plan prepared contains 39 arches of 40 feet each. The breadth of the channel to be 15 feet, so as to be just navigable for boats, with a towing path 9 feet wide on each side. It is calculated to convey 70,000 cubic yards of water per hour, which is considered to be sufficient for the Taluk of Nagaram. By increasing the fall through it, of course, any quantity of water might be passed through it; but the breadth has been regulated by the navigation, that is, the width given to it and velocity allowed are such as will admit of its being navigated without inconvenience. This work is not a simple aqueduct, but rather an aqueduct sluice, that is, the water in floods will rise above the crowns of the arches. It is evident that it would be both very expensive and dangerous to carry the bed of the irrigating channel (above and below the aqueduct) much above the level of the country; and, as the floods rise to the surface of the ground on each side, at least, the thickness of the arches must be below the surface of the water in the river at such times. The work is accordingly planned as a sluice, that is, with a flooring and apron. The obstruction offered by it to the water is about the same as that of the Annicut in the highest freshes, that is, the proportion of water way to the whole section of the river at that point is about the same as the proportion of the water way over the Annicut bears to the section there. Of course, in ordinary freshes, before the water reaches the crowns of the arches, the obstruction will be only that of a common bridge. Thus the head of water caused by the work and the force of the current through it, will be, when it is most, that is, in the highest freshes, about the same as it is at the Annicut when it is least. This gives us, therefore, a good measure of the power the water will have on the bed of the river below. Now, long before the force of the Annicut is reduced to this, the power of the water upon the apron is quite insignificant. I have allowed for a front apron of 10 yards broad, and a rear apron of 20 yards, supported by a line of wells along its whole length, with some loose-stone also below them. There will be a floor of large packed stone also under the arches, with a line of wells along the lower side from pier to pier. This work will be constructed within the limits of tide-water; and it will be necessary, therefore, to bank out the river on both sides; and the expenses connected with laying the foundation will, perhaps, be considerable, for which I have allowed in the estimate. The foundations must, of course, be wells: the piers to be of bricks, both as safer than rubble masonry, where the weight of arches is to be borne, and, also, probably, cheaper, as the stone must be conveyed thirty miles from Dowlaishweram. From the aqueduct a single channel will be cut for four miles along the narrow part of the Taluk, after which it will divide into two branches, following the banks of the rivers, and terminating in tide-water. Amount of estimate, 17,183 rupees.

"The total cost of these works is thus estimated at 138,647 rupees, and they provide for the irrigation of 95,000 acres, being at the rate of nearly 1½ rupee per acre, which, with its share of the cost of the Annicut, about 1 rupee per acre, makes 2½ rupees per acre. The works that will remain to complete this portion of the Delta works will be very trifling, consisting chiefly of small branch channels and drains, and will probably not amount to more than ¼ rupee per acre, making a total of 2¾ rupees per acre. The average for the whole Delta I estimate at 2 rupees; so that this will exceed the average by ¾ of a rupee. This is, of course, owing to the large aqueduct, the Nagaram Taluk being the only tract in the Delta that requires a masonry work of any magnitude. On the other hand, I consider this by far the most important part of the Delta to lead the water to, as it contains a large extent of the richest land, and is extensively cultivated." *

During the next month Colonel Cotton prepared a scheme for the irrigation of the eastern side of the river, the estimate of

* Professional Papers of the Madras Engineers, vol. iii. p. 166.

which amounted to 156,630 rupees. "The works contained in this estimate are the cutting of a small high-level channel from the eastern main channel, about 5 miles from its head to the Túlayya Bhága, at the head of the Samulcotta channel, 4 miles from the head of the Annicut. This channel will be 4 miles in length, and will water the highest lands that can be reached from the Annicut in that part of the Delta, about 3000 acres. Another branch from the eastern main channel, commencing at 5 miles from the Annicut, and extending to near Vudurupáka, a distance of 14 miles. This branch will water about 16,000 acres. Another branch from the eastern main channel, commencing at 11 miles from the Annicut, and extending to a distance of 14 miles. This channel is to water about 22,000 acres. Another large branch commencing near Álamúr, 15 miles from the Annicut, and terminating near Coringa, a distance of 24 miles. A branch from the last, commencing at Chellúru, 9 miles from its head, and extending a distance of 6 miles. A second branch from the same channel, commencing at Rámachandrapuram, 11 miles from its head, and terminating near Gollapálem, a distance of 11 miles. A lock and calingulah, at the head of the large branch channel near Álamúr, to keep the water at the proper level for that branch, and to admit of the navigation of the main channel on towards Yanam and the tide-water of the eastern Godavery. A lock and calingulah at the lower end of the same branch channel near Coringa, to connect it with tide-water there. A small branch from the old channel into which the eastern main channel falls, about 4 miles below Álamúr, and extending to tide-water near Injaram, 16 miles. A continuation of the eastern main channel at Kauléshwarapuram, carried along the line of the bank of the river from Kauléshwarapuram to the French territory at Yanam; 21 miles, to water 32,000 acres. A draining channel of 12 miles, along a slight natural hollow, from the Túlayya Bhága, near Marumonda to Téki. Widening the head of the Túlayya Bhága. A lock and calingulah in the cut just mentioned, and another calingulah across the old course of the Túlayya Bhága. From the calingulah last mentioned, a branch led from the old Túlayya Bhága nearly to Cocanada, 21 miles. Excavating the new cut below the lock last mentioned, to the depth required for the fall at that work, for a distance of 4 miles. A branch channel leading from the north bank of the Túlayya Bhága, at a point 16 miles from its head, extending 12 miles to the Yéléru, near Samulcotta. This will leave about a mile breadth of land to be watered by the Samulcotta channel throughout its length. That channel being carried on a level to reach the highest lands has scarcely any fall, and consequently very little current. It is, therefore, advisable to water only such an extent of land from it as cannot be reached by another channel having a greater current.

"Numerous irrigating sluices and small calingulahs, and several small bridges, are allowed for all these channels. The total extent of land included within these limits is 240,000 acres, exclusive of the Pittapore estate and of the island on which Coringa stands. The total sum expended on this tract will thus be 283,630 rupees. This will give an expenditure of rather more than one rupee an acre, besides its share of the cost of the general works, which is less than one rupee an acre, making a total of two rupees an acre.

"After these works are executed there will remain some very small branches to be cut to particular villages, and probably some small drainage works, but the cost of these will be very trifling, and probably will not add a quarter rupee per acre to the average. It must, however, be expected that many small improvements may continue to be made by degrees, as the country becomes fully occupied and cultivated. The main channel will also, no doubt, require to be eventually widened."

It will be observed that in the above scheme the navigation of the canals was provided for as well as the irrigation of the land. On further information on this subject being required by Government, Colonel Cotton thus enters into further details :—

"With respect to the cost of making these channels capable of being navigated, I should state :—The channel running parallel to the great northern road, and the canal leading from Dowlaishweram to the ports of Coringa, Cocanada, Nursapore, and Masulipatam, are being made first-class lines, with locks 100 feet by 15. The first-class lines extending to tide-water require three locks to reduce the current to a mile an hour. All the upper parts of these lines require to convey so much water for irrigation, and all their lower parts so much drainage water, that they would ultimately be amply capacious for navigation also. When the locks are constructed, calingulahs must, at all events, be built to raise the water sufficiently to lead off the branch irrigating channels. Hence the works that can properly be charged to navigation are the locks, three in each channel to tide-water, costing each about 8000 rupees on an average, with some small portion of the excavation, perhaps, in all 30,000 rupees for an average of 35 miles of first-class channel, or under 1000 rupees a mile. Supposing the traffic on all these lines to be, on an average, only 20 tons a day, or 7000 a year, the charge would be a quarter pie per ton per mile, the cost of land carriage being two annas a ton per mile for carts. We have now nearly completed, so far as to be practicable, about 600 miles of water communication. If 20 tons a day were conveyed along it on an average, such a traffic would by land cost 1500 rupees a day, or 5 lacs a year; by the channels it would cost about 40,000 rupees a year. I should not be surprised if, after a few years, the traffic were to average 50 tons a day.

"On the lines of channel not leading directly to some important place, I propose to use smaller locks, namely, 65 feet by 11½, and to allow a greater current, namely, two miles an hour, for which about two locks, at 4000 rupees, would be sufficient for lines to tide-water of 35 miles, or, including some excavation, 300 rupees a mile. The navigation of the channels formed part of the original project, and is, indeed, an essential part of any project for raising this country to a state worthy of a civilized Government." *

Besides these schemes for irrigation and navigation, the subject of the drainage of flooded lands, which was of scarcely less importance, engaged Colonel Cotton's attention. The principal project of this kind was for draining a large tract of land to the east of the Colair Lake, which was then in the District of Masulipatam, but a part of which is now included in the Godavery District. This tract was described as "flooded by the waters of the Vaiyyéru, and those of the Tamaléru and Budeméru below the Colair. Nothing of any consequence," continued Colonel Cotton "has ever been done for relieving it from the vast body of water brought down to it from the extensive basins which drain to it. It is more than usually exposed to both the evils of drought and flooding. On the one hand, the rivers that supply it, rising within 70 miles of the coast, fail when the local rains do; on the other hand, when the rains are general, the floods in them have hitherto concurred with the floods of the Kistna and Godavery, and a vast accumulation of water has thus been brought over this tract, where the two basins meet.

"So far as the irrigation is concerned, an ample supply of water

* Professional Papers of the Madras Engineers, vol. iii. p. 192.

can now be led from the Godavery Annicut to this tract at all times. It remains, therefore, to provide for the floods to which it is exposed. The tract in question, though very flat, is yet not without slope. The Colair, though considerable, is totally inadequate to carry off the floods of three rivers.

"The works that I now propose for the removal of this evil are:— Clearing and enlarging the partial line of channel leading from Pipparru on the Vaiyyéru, straight to tide-water in the salt swamp near Yenamaduru. A cut through the land that bounds the Colair, near the point where the Upputéru approaches nearest to it. There has not hitherto been any means of emptying the lake. It is sometimes very nearly, if not quite, dry in the dry season; and at those times, as is usual with lagoons, what little water remains is brackish. It is, of course, desirable to let off this water and not allow it to mix again with the water of the ensuing monsoon, as the productiveness of the land is decidedly impaired by it. The Upputéru should be embanked on both sides from near the Colair to a point near Kaldindi. Near Kaldindi the Upputéru makes a turn at right angles to its former course, and thus increases the length of its course to the sea. By making a cut, therefore, direct to the flats, which are level with high water at a distance of five miles from that point, a great additional discharge will be obtained." *

Sanction was accordingly granted for the prosecution of these works at 66,060 rupees, being at the rate of about one-third rupee per acre, making with its share of the cost of the Annicut, one rupee and a half per acre.

The various channels, with the locks and other appliances for rendering them efficient both for irrigation and navigation, were pushed on with rapidity. The work of the most considerable magnitude was the aqueduct across the branch of the Godavery at Gannáram in the Taluk of Nagaram, which was built by Lieutenant, now Colonel, Haig, whom Colonel Cotton considered his most able and energetic officer. This work of 800 yards long, forty-nine arches of 40 feet, crossing a navigable channel of 28 feet and 5 feet deep, was completed in six months from the time of beginning to make bricks, and watered many thousand acres, and conveyed the produce to the port that year.

Meanwhile Colonel Cotton had been appointed to the office of

* Professional Papers of the Madras Engineers, vol. iii. p. 168.

Chief Engineer, the headquarters of which were at Madras, and his brother, Major F. C. Cotton, succeeded him as Civil Engineer. At the request of the Government, Colonel Cotton inspected all the works on the Godavery, and, in May 1853, presented a Report upon them. We quote from this Report, as it shows the progress made on the works in the District of Rajahmundry up to the above-mentioned date. "I remained in the District from the 7th to the 28th of March, having in company with the Civil Engineer navigated the Samulcotta channel, the eastern main channel as far as the new lock near Álamúr, the Ráli main channel, and Nagaram channel to within four miles of the sea, 44 miles, the western main channel, Vaiyyéru, Venkayya, and Bhímamavar channels, 34 miles, and a branch of the Vaiyyéru to the Colair, crossing which I landed within five miles of Ellore. In the course of these voyages, almost all the principal questions respecting the progress and prosecution of the works were brought under discussion in communication with the various officers and overseers in executive charge. It is with great satisfaction I am able to state that, according to my views, the undertaking is proceeding most favourably. I found everything in far better order than I left it, and a much greater progress made than I could have hoped for.

"With respect to the progress of the works, commencing from the eastward, the Samulcotta channel, which had been stopped short at the outside of the town, has been carried round it, so as to discharge its surplus water into the Yéléru. In the Túlayya Bhága, the new lock and cutting away of the great bend, about ten miles from its head, has been completed; by which the water has been retained at a higher level, to throw a better supply into the Samulcotta channel, and also into the branch now about to be cut in the opposite side of the Tulayya Bhága. The only work of any consequence now required to this most important line of channel is the opening out of the last two miles, from the Kovvúru lock to Cocanada, to avoid the winding and shallow tide-water channel by which the boats at present proceed, and also to convey fresh water to Cocanada. This cut will now be completed. The traffic is very considerable, averaging for the last few months 54 tons of boats a day, through the western lock, with a very great number of rafts; so much so, that it has become a serious question what to do about them, they so greatly encumber the channel, and occupy the locks. The opening of the Coringa line will, however, divide this traffic, and, indeed, take the principal part of it, leaving the Túlayya Bhága chiefly to convey other merchandise.

"In the Central Delta, the aqueduct has been completed, with the exception of the towing-path. The channel above it, which had been almost destroyed by the river breaking in upon it in the flood, has been put into complete order, the main channel leading from it has been continued to tide-water, within four miles of the sea, and several miles of branch channels have been cut. It was highly interesting to pass over this aqueduct in a boat, and see an ample stream of water thus thrown into the richest part of the District, in the height of the dry season, when a year before not a brick had been burnt towards the erection of this large work.

"The Annicut is in perfectly good order. The apron had nowhere sunk seriously, though it was slightly disturbed in some places, and had sunk a little also. The wearing of the stones in the surface of the work by the sand and water passing over it had not continued to any great extent, showing that, in general, the stones are sufficiently hard to resist this action. A few of the softest should be replaced, from time to time, with harder ones. The whole of the iron posts have been cast, and two branches have been completed with them: they have been carried nearly all along a third branch, and will soon be all placed. There is no serious change in the bed of the river above the Annicut, excepting that the current has set powerfully on the island above the eastern wing-wall of the Vijéshwaram branch. This will require to be carefully protected with groins; and the grass must continually be rooted out of the sand-banks that form on the opposite side of that branch. I was in hopes that the river would have made itself a direct channel to the head of the Báli channel, to which it had evidently had a tendency of late; but during the late flood there was an accumulation formed above the head-sluice, which it took some time to cut through; and I am afraid now there will be some trouble in future in keeping the head of this channel clear. By care, however, there is no doubt that the stream of the river may be led more direct to the under-sluices; and when once a direct flow is established to them, there will be no difficulty in keeping it there; and the head of the main channel will continue open. The bed of the river will, however, always require care, though, excepting in those years in which heavy floods occur, the changes will not be rapid.

"The other new works on this side are, the extension of the river bank channel to tide-water near Nursapore; the completion of the lock near Kákaraparru, and the clearing of the Nakkala channel, leading from it to Nursapore; the Palkole channel, leading from the Bhúppayya to Nursapore; the completion of the double lock and calingulah at the end of the Venkayya channel, and of the embankment of that channel; the cutting of the large drainage channel from the Vaiyyéru at Pipparru direct to tide-water near Bhímavaram, and that of the other drainage channels near the Colair. The communication with Nursapore is not yet completely open. The lock at the lower end of the Nakkala must be built to make this quite effectual; but when a little more work has been executed in clearing the Nakkala, the water will be turned into it, and will, I am in hopes, make a practicable navigation. The connection of the port of Nursapore with the rest of the District is very much required. The completion of the Parimella lock at the end of the Venkayya is very important: it makes the communication good into the Colair, and the lower part of the Vaiyyéru.

"The principal works that now remain to be executed are:—The completion of the Colair drainage works now under execution. The main drainage line, and navigation by the Nakkala to Nursapore. The Coringa irrigation channel, and other branches in the Eastern Delta. The embankment on the western side of the eastern Godavery, and the channels in that neighbourhood, for the irrigation of the Amalápuram Taluk. The extension of the eastern high level channel towards Vizagapatam, and the cutting of that to Ellore. The channel connecting the high level channel at Samulcotta with Cocanada, completing, at the same time, the drainage of that part, and forming a road. The channel connecting the Colair with Masulipatam, I can only once more express a hope, that the whole project, as ordered by the Court, will now be carried out without any further questioning, and with some of the vigour and energy which the extraordinary success, so far, ought to produce in all who have anything to do with it. All the works connected with it in any way ought also to be prosecuted."

In the above Report, Colonel Cotton referred to the great increase of revenue in the District of Rajahmundry, as a proof of the success of his scheme. A doubt was raised as to the accuracy of his statements on this point, and one member of the Civil Service proceeded so far as to denounce the Godavery Works as a "gigantic swindle." The Madras Government, in consequence of these disputes, instituted an inquiry into the whole matter. This led to a long and acrimonious discussion, which it is unnecessary to reproduce, and the results of which were perfectly unsatisfactory.* The best evidence to show the value of these works is to give a clear and brief statement, comparing the revenue of the District, and the value of the exports and of the imports, in the year before the construction of the works with those in the year when the re-arrangement of the Districts of Rajahmundry and Masulipatam was effected. Comparison with later years would not be sufficiently fair and accurate, because a large portion of the old Masulipatam District has since been transferred to the Godavery, and an exact account of the increase of revenue thereby afforded cannot be ascertained. A reference to the Comparative Statement in the Appendix will, however, show the improvement in the revenue since the change. Other causes contributed, in a measure, to the increased prosperity which this statement exhibits; but it seems unquestionable that the increase of land revenue, and of the export and import trade, has resulted chiefly from the enormous development of cultivation under the stimulus given by these hydraulic works, and from the advantages which have, indirectly as well as directly, followed their construction.

	Before the Annicut, A.D. 1846–47.	After the Annicut, A.D. 1859–60.	Increase.
	Rupees.	Rupees.	Rupees.
Collections of land revenue in the Delta Taluks	998,011	1,634,569	636,558
Collections for the whole Rajahmundry District	1,230,665	1,937,519	706,854
Sundry sources of revenue in the District	407,748	731,493	323,745
Value of exports	1,356,336	4,214,745	2,858,409
Value of imports	411,365	641,509	230,144

Colonel Cotton's Report, previously quoted, narrates the progress of the canals and the various channels in the District up to the commencement of 1853. In 1857, in consequence of the great Sepoy War, a restrictive order was passed arresting the works for financial

* Reports on the Direct and Indirect Effects of the Godavery and Kistna Annicuts. Madras, 1858.

reasons. In 1859 Sir Charles Trevelyan, then Governor of Madras, visited the District, and left on record the impression made on his mind by these works in a Minute, in which he cordially recommended the immediate and active prosecution of them. "The irrigable area of this Delta," he wrote, "has been variously estimated; but, after making every deduction, it probably amounts to about 1,100,000 acres. A considerable portion of this has been irrigated; and that the remainder has not yet been so, is partly owing to the deficiency of population; partly to the insufficiency of the main channels, and the want of subsidiary channels for the detailed distribution of the water; and, still more, to the uncertainty in which the agricultural population is kept by the delay in the settlement of the land revenue. Nevertheless, the people have already greatly profited by the new facilities which have been afforded for their industry, and I have never seen, in any part of India, such evident marks of personal comfort and advancing prosperity. In the Godavery Delta the first difficulties have been overcome, and the primary and more expensive works have been executed. Secondary works of distribution alone remain to be provided; and these are so eminently profitable, that, if we have not means in hand to do them, it would be greatly for our advantage to borrow money for the purpose." *

Sir Charles Trevelyan's counsel was followed. In 1864 an extension of the line completing the water communication between the Godavery and the Kistna rivers was sanctioned, and since that, improvements have been executed from loan funds. The aggregate length of all the canals in the District is 528 miles to irrigate 780,000 acres.†

This chapter will be concluded by a brief statement of the various canals which, according to the latest returns, at present intersect the District.

There are three main canals, called respectively the Eastern, Central, and Western Delta Main Canals.

The Eastern Delta Main Canal divides into two branches, about 800 yards below the head sluice on the left flank of the Annicut;

* Minute by Sir C. Trevelyan, dated October 15, 1859.

† In the Blue Book, showing the Moral and Material Progress of India during the year 1872-3, p. 69, the length of the canals is given as 840 miles; but the assertion in the text is made on the authority of a Statement recently received from the District Engineer's Office, which will be found in the Appendix.

of these, one branch forms the Cocanada and Samulcotta Canals; the second, the Bank and Coringa Canals. The Samulcotta Canal takes off from the Cocanada Canal 4 miles from the head, and is a high level channel, being carried up to Samulcotta without locks. From Samulcotta it is continued on to tide-water at Cocanada, there being three locks in this section of the Canal. The Cocanada Canal has three locks in its length of 29½ miles; the last 2½ miles are a natural salt creek embanked and improved. At 6½ miles from the head, the Mandapéta Canal, which joins the Coringa Canal at its twentieth mile, is taken off. The Bank and Coringa Canals separate 13 miles from the head; the former, which is carried on to Yanam, is at present navigable for 22 only, out of its total length of 38 miles. The Coringa Canal has three locks, and is carried into tidal water at Manjéru. From its twenty-second mile a branch canal 10 miles long is led off to Injaram.

The Central Delta Main Canal is 8 miles long, and then divides into the Bank, the Amalápuram, and the Gannáram Canals. The former is not navigable at present except between June and December, when there is navigation for 35 out of its total length of 41 miles. The Amalápuram Main Canal is navigable to Amalápuram, one mile above which the Bendamúrlanka Canal is taken off, which is navigable only for 2 miles at present. It is proposed to extend the navigation on these canals to Sallapalli and Bendamúrlanka respectively. The Gannáram Canal is navigable for 36 miles. It crosses the Vainatéyam branch of the river by a large aqueduct at Gannáram. It is proposed to extend the navigation of this canal to Sakinédapalli opposite Nursapore, or 46 miles from the head.

The Western Delta Main Canal is 6 miles long from the head sluice on the right flank of the Annicut to Chittapéta Weir. At this point the canal separates into the Kákaraparru and Ellore Canals, which afterwards subdivide, the former into the Gósta Nadi, Mukkámala, Bank, and Nursapore Canals; the latter into the Attili and Vaiyyéru Canals. The Kákaraparru Canal is 10 miles long from Chittapéta to Peraveli; at 1¼ miles from its head, the Gósta Nadi takes off; 9 miles from the head, the Bank and the Mukkámala Canals take off; and from Peraveli downwards the canal is called the Nursapore Canal. The Gósta Nadi is an improved natural channel, and is navigable for 28 miles. The Mukkámala Canal, one mile long, is dropped into an old natural channel called the Nakkala, and is not navigable beyond Mukkámala. The Bank Canal is navigable from its head (9 miles of the Kákaraparru Canal) to the Godavery at Lakshméshwaram, where it is connected with tide-water. The Nursapore Canal is navigable to Mogalturru, and has two connections with tide-water, being connected with the Godavery at Nursapore, and with the Upputéru at Mogalturru. The total length of the canal is 30 miles from its head at Peraveli. The Ellore Canal is 40 miles long from Chittapéta to Ellore, where it joins the canal from the Kistna Annicut at Bézwáda. At half-a-mile below the Chittapéta Weir the Attili Canal takes off, and at 2¼ miles the Vaiyyéru Canal. The Ellore Canal is a high level channel; there is only one lock in it, which is situated at Ellore, and by which the Kistna Canal is dropped into it. The Attili Canal is 15¾ miles long, and is navigable up to the village of Attili. The Vaiyyéru Canal is navigable to Yélúrupád, where a tidal lock connects it with the tide-water of the Upputéru. It is also connected with the Colair Lake by a lock at Chinnakkaparam. At 10½ miles the Undi High Level channel takes off. The Undi Canal, 18 miles long, is navigable to Undi, the 5 miles of the channel below Undi not being navigable.*

I have thus endeavoured to describe both the Annicut itself and the system of irrigation dependent on it, and to give an historical account of their construction. Little need be added in conclusion. It is impossible to overrate the value of these beneficent works. No one who has witnessed the very great advantage which they have proved to the people will consider that they have been the result of wasted or misspent money. The noble river, which formerly ran in comparative uselessness to the sea, has been restrained, and bridled, and sent abroad in a thousand channels to fertilize the land. The fluid, which is so precious in the arid climate of the East that it has been felicitously likened to "liquid gold," has been converted into capital that has been repaid in what has proved better than the most enormous rate of interest, and has carried the blessings of fertility and contentment and peace to a region which, as in the great famine of 1833, was formerly desolated by the most terrible scarcity and drought.

* The above statement has been kindly supplied by Mr. J. W. Rundall, who has had great experience in the Public Works Department in this District.

CHAPTER VIII.

ANCIENT HISTORY.

THE DRAVIDIAN RACE—THE ARYAN INVADERS—BHUDDISM—TRAVELS OF HIOUEN-THSANG—THE CHÁLUKYA DYNASTY—KINGDOM OF VENGI DÉSHAM—CONQUEST OF THE CHÓLA DYNASTY—KINGDOM OF TELINGANA—APPEARANCE OF THE MOHAMMEDANS.

THE present Godavery District is almost equally divided into two portions by the beautiful river from which it receives its name. These portions have been connected by historical events with the countries which they severally adjoin. Thus we find that the eastern division, which is slightly the larger, was frequently invaded by the kings of Orissa, and was, from time to time, annexed to the extensive dominions of the "Lords of the Elephant," who ruled at Cuttack; the other division generally belonged to the kingdom of 'Andhra or Telingana, which extended inland; and thus we shall have our attention directed alternately to the fortunes of the adjoining dominions, as each division is affected by them.

This part of the Indian Peninsula was inhabited in pre-historic times by the great Dravidian race, which spread itself over the whole of Southern India. The Telugu-speaking people were the most numerous branch of this section of the human family. Indeed, there are traces of their having extended in very early times almost as far north as the mouths of the Ganges, and they reached as far to the south and west as they do now. They spoke a distinct language, and not a mere dialect of the same language as the Tamilians and the other inhabitants of the south spoke.* Telugu can be detected even in the brief notices of the people mentioned in Ptolemy and Pliny. The latter makes mention of "an island in the Ganges named Modogalingam." His informants most likely referred to the Delta

* Dr. Caldwell's Comparative Grammar of the Dravidian Languages, 2d edition, p. 29.

of the Godavery and the adjacent country, for that river is considered by the natives to have the same source as the sacred stream of the Ganges, and is frequently called by that name. The correct reading of the word Modogalingam is probably "modo Galingam," the latter being equivalent to Kalingam; and on the supposition of "modo" being a corruption of "múdu," three, the name would mean "the three Kalingas." Tri-Kalinga, or "the three Kalingas," is a term applied to the Telugu country on inscriptions.* The country thus mentioned by Pliny was called by Ptolemy "Triglyphum" or "Trilingum," which is synonymous with Trilingam, or the more modern Telingana. The river Godavery was also known to Ptolemy, although he was ignorant of the direction in which it flowed. He had received information regarding the Goaris, as he called it, but imagined that it flowed into the Gulf of Cambay.†

Kalinga was mentioned by Pliny the Younger in his work on Natural History. He mentions the Calingæ as occupying the sea-coast of India below the Mandei and Malli, and the famous mountain Mallus, which was probably Mahéndragiri in the District of Ganjam. The passage runs thus:—"Multarumque gentium cognomen Brachmanæ, quorum Maccocalingæ. Flumina Prinas et Cainas, quod in Gangem influit, ambo navigabilia. Gentes Callingæ mari proximi, et supra Mandei, Malli, quorum mons Mallus, finisque tractus ejus Ganges;" ‡ or, in the quaint translation of Philemon Holland made in 1635, "Also the Brachmanæ, a name common to many nations, among whom are the Maccocalingæ. Of rivers there are Pinnas and Cainas, the latter of which twain runneth into Ganges, and both are navigable. The people called Calingæ coast hard upon the sea. But the Mandei and Malli, among whom is the Mountain Malus, are above them higher in the country." § Perhaps the rivers intended are the Kistna and the Godavery. Towards the south, the country of the Calingæ is said to have extended to the promontory of Calingon and to the town of Dandaguda, or Dandagula, which was 625 Roman miles from the Ganges. The following is the quotation from Pliny:—"Ab ostio Gangis ad pro-

* Mr. C. P. Brown's Carnatic Chronology, p. 85. Dr. Caldwell's Comparative Grammar of the Dravidian Languages, 2d edition, p. 32.

† See Smith's Atlas of Ancient Geography. Col. H. Yule's "Description of India."

‡ C. Plinii Secundi Naturalis Historia, lib. vi. 21, Bibliotheca Teubneriana.

§ Translation of Pliny's Natural Historie, p. 126.

montorium Calingon et oppidum Dandaguda DCXXV mil. passuum." "From the mouth of Ganges, where he entereth into the sea, unto the Cape Calingon and the town Dandagula, are counted 625 miles."* The distance and the similarity of the name of the promontory indicate Coringa. General Cunningham is of opinion that the town of Dandaguda may fairly be identified as Dántapura of the Buddhist chronicles, which may, as the capital of Kalinga, be, with much probability, regarded as Rajahmundry. Mr. Fergusson is inclined to adopt the suggestion that the Calingon of Pliny is Coringa; but he considers that Rajahmundry cannot be identified as Dántapura, as placing the scene of the enshrining of the relic of Buddha so far south would violate every probability of the narrative.†

The Dravidian people entered India long before the Aryan immigration. It has not been determined by what route they entered; but they probably came from the north-west, because there are traces of a Dravidian element in the language of some of the people who dwelt beyond the Indus. They sprang originally from some distant part of Upper Asia. As they settled down in the Peninsula of India they fell into separate nationalities, each having its own language and institutions. In very ancient times they established empires, celebrated for their high civilization; but these kingdoms are too remote to come within the cognizance of historical research. That the people dwelling in the Telugu country, of which Rajahmundry is now the centre, were a civilized, though a simple and pastoral, race, is proved by almost every requirement of men gathered together into a well organized society, being capable of expression in pure Telugu, without the assistance of the more refined language of the Aryan invader. Before Sanscrit was spoken in the Peninsula, village communities, with the usual functionaries of these miniature republics, existed in the maritime plains on the coast of the Bay of Bengal. Women drew water for the daily use of their households; men ploughed their fields, or drove their flocks to pasture; and every avocation of daily life has its appropriate representation in the speech which has been handed down to us. Remnants of the ancient, simple, yet idolatrous, religion still linger among the people. Village and household deities are to this day worshipped in every hamlet; every one has his own patron god;

* Nat. Hist. vi. 23.

† Journal of the Royal Asiatic Society, New Series, vol. vi. p. 251.

and the serpent is feared and worshipped.* This pre-historic race, however long and quietly it may have inhabited the land, so completely gave way before the Aryan invaders, that it has lost all remembrance of its former ethnical existence.†

The date of the Aryan invasion is as little known as that of the Dravidian immigration. The Aryans evidently entered India from the north-west, and established themselves firmly as far as the valley of the Ganges before they attempted to penetrate towards the south. They represented the former inhabitants of the country as monkeys, genii, and wild men of the woods, evidently referring to a people less advanced in civilization than themselves. The collision between the nature-worship of this Aryan people and the worship of the simpler Dravidian race, resulted in Brahminism, or the service of a supreme spirit named Brahma, by the sacred caste of Brahmins. The inhabitants of this District gradually conformed to the faith and to the manners of the conquerors.

The first that we hear in native chronicles of the eastern portion of the Godavery District is in the account of the kingdom of Orissa. It is stated that Gautama Déva, the Rajah of Orissa, at an early period, added to his dominions all the country from the Mahéndra Hills to the Godavery. His son, Mahéndra Déva, is said to have founded the town of Rajahmundry, which was called after him, Rája-mahéndra-varam, or "the gift of the Rajah Mahéndra."‡ Rajahmundry was the great king's southern capital. This is, however, merely native tradition. Local tradition ascribes the foundation of Rajahmundry to Vijayáditya Mahéndrudu, one of the sovereigns of the Chálukya dynasty.

Local traditions in South India are, however, peculiarly uncertain. The only reliable evidence regarding the ancient history of the country is derived from inscriptions. The earliest extant documents of this nature in the Telugu country refer to a dynasty of sovereigns, to whom no title can be assigned, but who ruled in the kingdom of Vengi, which extended from the Kistna to the Godavery, and probably included the deltas of both rivers. The names and dates of these monarchs cannot be ascertained; but they appear to have reigned from about the second century of the Christian era, until this country was conquered by the eastern Chálukya kings,

* Wheeler's History of India, vol. iii. p. 12, 13.

† Dr. W. W. Hunter's Dictionary of the Non-Aryan Languages, Preface.

‡ Stirling's Account of Orissa, "Asiatic Researches," vol. xv. p. 258. Dr. W. W. Hunter's Orissa, vol. ii. p. 183.

probably at the commencement of the seventh century. Two grants of these sovereigns have been given by Dr. Burnell.*

The next great change that came over the people of this province was the rise and rapid spread of Buddhism. Deriving its origin from Gótama Buddha or Sákya Muni, a sage of Northern India, the profession of this religion was disseminated rapidly over the country. It took such firm hold of the Telugu people, that it seems quite to have superseded the old Vedic and early Brahminical beliefs. The depth to which Buddhism had descended into the mind of the people is proved by the very extensive Buddhist remains which have been discovered in the Telugu country, especially on the banks of the Kistna. The most magnificent ruins of the kind were found at Amrávati on that river. Beautiful sculptured marbles and caskets of crystal were discovered. Similar remains on a smaller scale were found in the Zemindari of Pittapore, when excavations were being made among the foundations of an ancient temple in 1842 and 1843.† Buddhism was so firmly established in Kalinga, as this part of the country was then called, that King Asóka thought it unnecessary to issue in that province the stringent edicts which he had published in other parts of his dominions in his zeal for the propagation of this religion.‡ It flourished till the seventh century of the present era, when it began to fade, and continued gradually to decline till the middle of the following century, when, under the pressure of persecution, it disappeared even with more marvellous rapidity than it had arisen.

A most interesting account of Southern India as it was in the seventh century is given by a Chinese traveller named Hiouen-Thsang. He was a Buddhist priest, and visited India for the purpose of studying Buddhist literature, and of making a pilgrimage to the holy places of Buddhism. He was fifteen years in the country, namely, from A.D. 629 to 644, and travelled from Cabul to Conjeveram, or even as far as Negapatam, visiting most of the places in which he was interested on the way. On leaving Northern India he passed through Ganjam and, perhaps, Vizagapatam, then forming part of the kingdom of Kalinga; and, after visiting Central India, he

* Elements of South Indian Palæography, pp. 12, 14, 86.

† See Sir Walter Elliot's paper in the "Madras Journal of Literature and Science," vol. xi. p. 304. A plate representing the figures found in these vases appears in vol. xv. of the above journal, but there is no description of them.

‡ Journal of the Asiatic Society of Bengal, vol. vii. p. 269.

traversed the kingdoms of 'Andra and Dhanakachéka, proceeding by the sea-coast to the south.*

From Hiouen-Thsang's account, we learn that Southern India was divided in the year 640 into nine large kingdoms. The only kingdoms which there is any necessity to mention here are the three northern—Kalinga, 'Andra, and Dhanakachéka, as the Godavery District was situated within the limits of the first and last, and it adjoined the kingdom of 'Andra.

The kingdom of Kalinga, as described by the Chinese traveller, probably extended from beyond Ganjam to the Godavery.† 'Andra was to the west, and Dhanakachéka to the south and west. This kingdom was 833 miles in circuit. The capital was stated to be from 233 to 250 miles south-west of Ganjam. Merely reckoning by distance, this would indicate Rajahmundry or Coringa. General Cunningham is of opinion that the former is meant, because it was once the capital of that part of the country.‡ Mr. Fergusson, however, considers that the correct site of the capital of Kalinga is in the neighbourhood of Kalingapatam, as the traveller would scarcely have gone so far south as Coringa or Rajahmundry, and then retraced his steps to visit Kósala. As the next place he visited was in the Central Provinces, I think it much more likely that he turned inland before he reached this District rather than that he attempted to traverse the impenetrable forests on the north of Rajahmundry.

Passing through part of the kingdom of Kósala, Hiouen-Thsang entered the kingdom of 'Andra. This territory partly corresponded with the modern Telingana, and the capital of it was probably Warangole.§ It was 500 miles in circuit, but no boundaries are given. The inhabitants are mentioned by Pliny under the name of Andaræ,|| and he states that they possessed thirty fortified cities, 100,000 infantry, 2000 cavalry, and 1000 elephants. The Chinese pilgrim mentions that, although the language was different from

* M. Julien's Life and Pilgrimage of Hiouen-Thsang. Cunningham's Ancient Geography of India, vol. i. pp. ix., 515. Wheeler's History of India, vol. iii. p. 259.

† From the map which accompanies Mr. Fergusson's article in the "Journal of the Royal Asiatic Society," New Series, vol. vi., he appears to consider that this District was situated altogether without the kingdom of Kalinga.

‡ Ancient Geography of India, vol. i. p. 515.

§ Dr. Burnell is of opinion that P'ing-k'i-la or Vinkhila stated by the pilgrim to be the capital, represents Vengi ló, ló being the Telugu locative suffix, which was mistaken for part of the name.

|| "Validior deinde gens Andaræ," etc., Plin. Nat. Hist. vi. 19.

that of Central India, the written characters were the same, so that probably the Devanagari alphabet was then generally in use, instead of the more easy and rounded characters of Telugu.*

The next kingdom which Hiouen-Thsang traversed was Dhanakachéka. He describes it as 1000 miles in circuit; and it seems to have extended from Gulbarga and Pennakonda on the west to the sea on the east. The southern boundary was in the district of Nellore, and the northern boundary was the Godavery, the kingdoms of 'Andra and Kalinga being on the north. It is very probable that, at that time, there were two capitals in this kingdom—the political capital, which was probably at Vengipuram, or Végi, near Ellore, and also the religious capital, near the conventual establishment at Amrávati, on the Kistna. Mr. Fergusson has come to the conclusion that the political capital of Dhanachéka was situated on the site now occupied by Bezwáda. It must, however, be borne in mind that the eastern branch of the Chálukya family was, probably, ruling at Végi at the time of Hiouen-Thsang's visit.

Not many years before the visit of the Chinese pilgrim, the country between the Godavery and the Kistna was invaded and conquered by the Rajput family of the Chálukyas. This tribe founded the oldest and the strongest line of kings that ever reigned in Southern India. The elder branch settled in the country of Kuntala, having their capital at Kalyán, 100 miles west of Hyderabad; and the younger branch, in the person of Kubja Vishnu Vardhana, the hunchback, or the dwarf, made new conquests towards the east, in the country of Vengi. The united families were thus rendered masters of the whole table-land between the Nerbudda and the Kistna, and of the line of coast from the Godavery to Nellore. Their power lasted about five centuries.† The conquest of Vengi may be dated at the commencement of the seventh century of the present era.

The branch of the Chálukya family, which had settled in Vengi, extended their conquests eastwards and northwards to the frontiers of Orissa, and ultimately established their seat of government at Rajahmundry, which, in the preface to the Telugu translation of the Mahábharatam, is called the "central gem of Vengi désham." In a Telugu paper among the Mackenzie Manuscripts, it is stated

* Cunningham's Ancient Geography of India, vol. i. p. 527.

† Sir Walter Elliot in the "Madras Journal of Literature and Science" for April 1840, p. 313. Journal of the Royal Asiatic Society, New Series, vol. i. p. 250.

that the earlier Chálukya kings resided at Birudánkaráyapuram, on the site of the present village of Bikkavólu, where there are extensive ruins, and that subsequently Vijayáditya Mahéndrudu, the thirteenth in the list of these kings, constructed a strong fort, called Yómagiri Droog, in the neighbourhood of Dowlaishweram, and built the town of Rajahmundry. There would be little use in giving here the bare list of these sovereigns. It will be sufficient to say that more than one revolution appears to have occurred; but the ancient family regained power, and retained it until it passed by conquest and by matrimonial alliance into the hands of Rájéndra Chóla, the dominant sovereign of Southern India, under whom the Chóla dynasty attained the zenith of its power. The Chálukyas were of the Lunar race, and were apparently Vaishnavites. They assumed much outward show of dignity and state. The symbol of the boar appears on all their coins, and distinguishes them from those of all other dynasties.*

The ancient capital of Vengi was situated about 8 miles north of Ellore, and I give the following account of a visit to it and of the local traditions regarding it which are current at Ellore:—"About 8 or 10 miles north of Ellore is situated the village of Pedda Végi, half-an-hour's walk to the north of which is Chinna Végi, and 5 miles south of these is another village, named Dendalúru, with several hamlets attached to it, named Ganganagúdem, Senagúdem, &c. According to the local tradition, all these formerly constituted one large city, in which were numerous temples dedicated to Siva. The ruins of about fifty fanes sacred to this deity still exist in Dendalúru, and likewise four statues or idols of Vignéshwara, one of which, very large, is on the southern side of the village, near a tank surrounded by date trees. A high mound of earth, called 'Bhímalingam Dibba,' is found on the east side of the village, and a tank, named 'Makalamma Cheruvu,' to the north, has a mound in the centre, on which are two stone bulls. There is another tank to the west of the village, called 'Narikalavári Cheruvu,' on the banks of which are two *sila sásanams* standing upright, and two more which are prostrate. Between Pedda Végi and Chinna Végi is another remarkable mound."† It is evident from the ruins here described that Vengi in its palmiest days must have been a very extensive

* Taylor's Catalogue Raisonné of Oriental MSS., vol. iii. p. 510. Madras Journal of Literature and Science, vol. iv. p. 82.

† Madras Journal of Literature and Science for April 1840, vol. xi. p. 304.

and magnificent city. The fort at Ellore was constructed with the stones from the ruined pagodas at Dendulúru and Végi, which the Mussulmans destroyed and utilized in this manner.

Rájéndra Chóla was succeeded by his son, Vikráma Déva. On the death of his uncle, who had acted as his viceroy in the north, Vikráma Déva sent his son, Rája Rája, to assume the office of viceroy; but, after one year of power, the latter resigned in favour of his younger brother, Víra Déva Chóla, who assumed the title of Kulóttunga Chóla.* His grants have been found in great numbers, extending from the year A.D. 1079 to 1135. There was a partial restoration of the Chálukya dynasty about the end of Kulóttunga Chóla's authority; and they maintained their power up to the latter part of the twelfth century, when their territories fell under the dominion of the Kákatíya or Ganapati dynasty of Warangole. †

This dynasty, which produced several most powerful and illustrious princes, ruled in the extensive country best known as Telingana, or, from its principal capital, Warangole. The family is said to have traced its genealogy from the ancient line of Hastinapuram. Two brothers, then in power in the north, quarrelled, and one of them, quitting his paternal dominions, migrated into the Deckan, and settled south of the Godavery. At first merely pastoral chieftains, he and his successors gradually acquired wider territory and power, and at length established a kingdom, the capital of which was Anumakonda. The seventh in descent from the one who assumed the regal dignity was named Kákati Pralaya, and from him the line received its original name.

The kings of this dynasty were frequently engaged in warfare with the Rajahs of Cuttack. At first this warfare consisted of forays on the flocks and herds of the southern people; but it appears to have soon attained wider and more destructive proportions. In the MSS. Records there are constant entries of attacks from the Rajahs of Cuttack resisted, or retaliative forays made into Orissa. At length, in the year 1132, Chor-ganga, apparently one of the Kákatíya dynasty, whose name is still preserved in one of the quarters of the sacred city of Puri, made a successful expedition into Orissa, and founded the Gangetic dynasty in that province. He carried his

* Professor Wilson's Descriptive Catalogue of the Mackenzie MSS., vol. i. p. 118.

† Sir Walter Elliot in "Madras Journal of Literature and Science," 1858. Taylor's Oriental MSS., vol. iii. p. 79.

victorious arms into the western districts of Bengal; and under his sway, and during that of his successors, the kingdom of Orissa extended from the Delta of the Ganges to the Delta of the Godavery. During this period, which lasted till the extinction of the Gangavamsa line, the eastern and northern portion of the Godavery District formed a part of the kingdom of Orissa, Rajahmundry being the southern capital. The southern strip of territory extending from the Chilka Lake appears to have cost the Rajahs of Cuttack an infinity of trouble. As early as 1164 a rebellion is reported under Alla Reddi, and frequent expeditions were despatched to reduce this turbulent province to subjection. The Reddiwars, in the neighbourhood of Rajahmundry, were continually in arms, and the *Reddivári Samasthánam*, as their line is locally designated, attained to considerable power.* The kings of Orissa, nevertheless, continued to exercise supremacy over this maritime territory until the beginning of the sixteenth century. They built temples, gave grants of land to Brahmins, and their names occur in the local list of kings as far south as the Godavery.†

The territory west of the Godavery still remained in the possession of the Ganapatis of Warangole. Kákatíya Pralaya was accidentally slain by his eldest son, who succeeded him, but was dethroned and put to death by his uncle, Mahá Déva. Mahá Déva for some time ruled in conjunction with his nephew, Ganapati Déva, another son of Kákatíya Pralaya; but, on his being slain in battle, Kákatíya Pratápa Ganapati Rudra Déva became the sole occupant of the throne and of the regal power. He has left even a more illustrious name than his father, and, like him, bestowed a name, or rather a title, on the royal house to which he belonged. His memory is preserved not only in the appellation of the dynasty, but lso in the traditions of the people. He is stated to have enclosed his capital with stone walls, and to have made it almost impregnable. He lavishly patronized literature, and built numerous cities and pagodas. He appointed secular Brahmins to the office of village scribe. He extended his kingdom towards the south, and conquered the country as far as Nellore, where he built several forts, and constructed a large tank. He waged war against the Rajah of Dévagiri, by whom his uncle had been slain, and, after he had conquered him, espoused his daughter, Rudramma Déva. He seems to

* Mr. C. P. Brown's Carnatic Chronology.

† Dr. W. W. Hunter's Orissa, vol. i. pp. 277-316.

have spent a happy life with his illustrious consort, but they had no son; and, on his death, he was succeeded by the queen, who ruled the country well and vigorously for about thirty years, until her daughter's son, Pratápa Víra Rudra Déva, was of age to ascend the throne.*

In the reign of this queen we obtain a glimpse of the estimation in which she was held in the south from the accounts of her given to the Venetian traveller, Marco Polo. The short passage in which mention is made of her is here quoted, because it throws a little stream of light from Europe on the sovereign and the kingdom to which the western portion of this District then belonged. "When you leave Maabar," wrote the traveller, "and go about a thousand (or, as some copies have it, five hundred) miles in a northerly direction, you come to the kingdom of Mutfili. This was formerly under the rule of a king, and since his death, some forty years past, it has been under his queen, a lady of much distinction, who, for the love she bore him, never would marry another husband. And I can assure you that, during all the space of forty years, she administered her realm as well as ever her husband did, or better; and as she was a lover of justice, of equity, and of peace, she was more beloved by those of her kingdom than ever was lord or lady of theirs before. . . . In this kingdom also are made the best and most delicate buckrams and those of the highest price; in sooth, they look like the tissue of a spider's web. There is no king or queen in the world but might be glad to wear them."†

This beloved queen transferred the royal authority to her grandson on his attaining his majority, in the year 1292 or 1295. This prince is known to the Mohammedan historian, Ferishta, by the name of Luddur Deo, and he was the last of his family who exercised any political influence. His dominions are said to have extended from the Godavery to the Palar, and as far westward as the Western Ghauts. This great power excited the jealousy of the

* One MS. account says twenty-eight, and another thirty-eight years.

† Col. Yule's Travels of Marco Polo, vol. ii. p. 295. Dr. Burnell, in a note appended to this passage, states that the kingdom to which Marco Polo refers was evidently the kingdom of Telingana, then ruled by the Kákatíya or Ganapati family, whose capital was at Warangole; and suggests that, as the Venetian traveller's custom was to give the name to the countries he visited from some place in them which he or his informants had seen, the name "Mutfili" might have been taken from the village of Motupalli, in the district of Guntoor, which was then included in the kingdom of Telingana.

Mussulmans, with whom he waged continual warfare, in which he was frequently victorious. He was at last taken prisoner, and sent captive to Delhi in A.D. 1323, but he was ultimately released, and died at Warangole.* With him the glory of the celebrated family of Ganapati princes departed, and within a few years the whole of their vast territory passed into the hands of the Gajapati Rajahs of Orissa.

The native chronicles term the successive dynasties of this province the Narapati, the Gajapati, and the Aswapati dynasties, or the "masters of men," the "masters of elephants," and the "masters of horses," by which term the Mohammedans are intended. The glory of the Narapatis, or the sovereigns of Warangole, was at this time passing away. The Gajapatis of Orissa scarcely extended their power beyond the banks of the Godavery. The rule of the owners of legions of horses was about to commence in Telingana, which was ere long merged in the Mohammedan principality of Golconda; and the power of this new and formidable people in time extended over the whole of the eastern portion of the Godavery District and of the neighbouring kingdom of Orissa.†

* Taylor's Catalogue Raisonné of Oriental MSS., vol. iii. p. 480.

† Wilson's Descriptive Catalogue of the Mackenzie MSS., p. 125.

CHAPTER IX.

EARLY ENGLISH SETTLEMENTS.

ESTABLISHMENT OF A MANUFACTORY AT MASULIPATAM—EARLY VOYAGES—SETTLEMENT AT VIRAVÁSARAM—FACTORY AT MADAPOLLAM—MR. STREYNSHAM MASTER'S TOUR AND VOYAGE—FACTORIES AT INJARAM AND BENDAMŪRLANKA—ABOLITION OF THE COMPANY'S MERCANTILE ESTABLISHMENTS.

THE first factory established by the English on the eastern coast of India was at Masulipatam. This town, once the seat of a flourishing trade and a place of political importance, is situated so close to the Godavery District, and is so intimately connected with Ellore and the contiguous country, that some notice of its early history and subsequent progress is essential to the thorough knowledge of the District with which this work is more immediately concerned.

The factory at Masulipatam was established in 1611. It soon became not only the centre of the trade in that neighbourhood, but also the principal emporium belonging to the English on the eastern coast. The very earliest notice of this factory is to be found in two letters addressed by Lucas Antheuniss, at Pettapollee (probably Peddapalli) or Nizampatam, to Peter Williams, a factor at Masulipatam, in which the particulars of certain petty mercantile transactions are mentioned. These letters are dated respectively December 29, 1611, and January 8, 1612.*

In January 1611 Captain Hippon was despatched by the Directors of the East India Company in the ship "Globe" to open a trade with the people on the Coromandel coast. A Dutchman, named Peter Williamson Floris, who was in the English Company's employ, accompanied him in the capacity of factor, with authority to conduct all commercial transactions. After touching at Pulicat, where Floris and Hippon were unsuccessful in opening trade, the "Globe" sailed for Masulipatam. Thence she departed, laden with cotton cloths and

* Calendar of State Papers, East India, 1513 to 1616, Rolls Series, p. 233.

other delicate fabrics, for Bantam and Siam. In the following year (1613) she returned to Masulipatam. Floris has left an interesting account of these voyages, and a quaint extract from the narrative of his second visit to the principal mart of the Northern Circars is appended.

"On the 19th of *December* they arrived at *Masulipatan*, where they found an *English* ship and two *Hollanders*. They understood that *Mir Sadardi* was out of place, and that *Atmakhan* and *Busebulleran* did govern. The ship was the *James*, sent expressly to second them in their voyage. The 21st, the Author and others went on shore, where they were met by *Wentakadra*, son to Busebulleran, with the *Shah Bandar* and other *Moors*, by whom they were well received, being presented with several Tesseriffes. The Director Warner and the Author had each a fine Horse given them. *Floris* refused his, suspecting their treachery, but was compelled to accept it. He took a Kaul at four *per Centum*, and landed goods. The 25th of *January*, the *James* departed for *Petapoli*, and on the 7th of *February* from thence for *Bantam*. On the 18th Mr. *Floris* went to *Narsapur Peta*, and the 19th, the ship was brought into the River, drawing 9¾ feet, and having 10½, contrary to the Reports of some who wished no good to the English. The 23d, the Author returned to *Masulipatan*.

"The 29th of *July*, there arrived four persons, as Ambassadors, along with *Wengali*, from the great King of *Narsinga*, or *Velûr*, who brought Mr. *Floris*, the king's *Kaul* with his *Abestiam* (which is a white Cloth, bearing the impression of his own hand, in sandal or saffron); likewise one from the Queen of *Paleakate*, besides several Letters from *Jaga Raja*, *Tima Raja*, *Apokandaia*, and others. The King's Letter was written on a Leaf of Gold, wherein he excused the Offence given the English at Paleakate; and invited them to come to his Country, giving them leave to choose a Place for building a House or Castle to their liking, besides other Privileges. As an earnest of his good Will, he bestowed on Mr. *Floris* a Town, yielding an income of about four hundred pounds a Year, promising to do more for him at his next Arrival. The Hollanders did all they could to obstruct these Favours; but their Influence was not great enough. The inhabitants, grieving to see every year English ships pass by without reaping any Benefit from them, filled the King's Ears with Complaints, and procured these friendly Offers. Mr. *Floris* kept the Envoys with him, and bore their Expenses, till the Ship came into the Road. His Man *Wengali* had spoken in Person with the King, who laid his Hand on his Head and presented him with a Tesseriffe.

"In *August*, there happened in *Narsapur Peta*, and thereabouts, a greater Overflowing than had been seen in twenty-nine Years. The whole Salt Hills, Towns, and Rice were drove away, and many thousand Men and Cattle were drowned; the Water rising three Yards above the Highway. The 4th of October, the Ships being sheathed, came into the Road of Masulipatan; and *Floris* gave order for loading the Goods. On the 25th, came News of the Death of Wenkatadrapa, King of Velûr, after fifty years' Reign, and that his three Wives (of whom *Obiama*, Queen of *Paleakate*, was one) had burned themselves with the Corps. Great Troubles were apprehended. The *Hollanders* were afraid of their castle newly built in *Paleakate*." *

From the above extract it will be observed that Nursapore, where, if the obstruction of the bar across the entrance of the river could be overcome, there is an excellent harbour for ships of the largest size, was well known more than two centuries ago for its docks for the building and repair of large vessels. Being situated on the bank of the Godavery it has always been exposed to inundations during the high freshes of the river.

So early as 1617 the value of the commerce between India and the Spice Islands was perceived. It was seen that large quantities of goods from Cambay and Masulipatam might be disposed of at the factories in the island of Sumatra, and that in return gold, camphor, pepper, and benzoin could be obtained. This traffic proved so profitable that, in 1627, the President and Council at Batavia recommended that 300,000 rials in money should be sent annually to the Coromandel coast and Masulipatam, as stock to be invested in cloths, which could be exchanged in the Eastern Archipelago for gold and camphor and spices.†

The Company's servants at the newly-opened factory were not permitted to traffic in peace. The native authorities threw every hindrance in their way, stimulated, no doubt, by the jealousy and intrigues of their Dutch rivals. In consequence of these troubles, they removed in 1628 to Armegam in the present District of Nellore,

* Journal of Mr. Peter Williamson Floris, Cape Merchant in the Voyage of Captain Hippon. Translated from the Dutch. "Collection of Voyages and Travels," vol. i. p. 443.

† Bruce's Annals of the East India Company, vol. i. pp. 188, 279.

where a factory had been founded three years before; but Masulipatam was not deserted long. Armegam was found to be a position of far inferior commercial advantages. The Governor of the province in which Masulipatam was situated having continued in a course of determined opposition to their interests, the English merchants applied to the King of Golconda for a firman to protect them from the extortion of his officers. A firman was granted according to their request in November 1632. It authorized the English to re-establish their trade at Masulipatam, and, in general, allowed them the liberty to trade at the other ports in his dominions. Among other provisions, the curious one occurs that the English were to enter into an obligation binding them to import into the king's dominions Persian horses and "other rarities," of which he was to have the preference of purchase. This firman was accompanied by an order to the Rajah of the District, enjoining implicit obedience to the king's commands. This document was called the Golden Firman.*

Not satisfied with this favourable decree, the English made further demands on the generosity of the king. An application was made for an enlargement of the privileges and facilities for trade which they already possessed, and a fresh firman was obtained in 1634 or 1635. On the strength of this still more favourable grant, the merchants at Masulipatam entertained the project of establishing an agency at Verasheroon, situated about forty miles to the north of their now flourishing factory, at which they anticipated the purchase of coarse cloths at reasonable rates. Accordingly we find in the records of 1650 that a factory had been established at that place.† Verasheroon was probably Viravásaram, a large and flourishing village situated near a broad lagoon, a few miles west of Nursapore. It was formerly the capital of the Taluk of Undi.

Notwithstanding the favour extended to them by the King of Golconda, and the issue of firmans on their behalf, the English were still annoyed by the oppression of the local authorities. Their Dutch commercial rivals were the instigators of every annoyance. The merchants of Masulipatam were consequently obliged to search for a quieter and more convenient position on the coast, and this led to the acquisition of land further south and to the foundation of Fort St. George at Madras, which subsequently became the capital

* Bruce, vol. i. p. 315.

† Ibid., vol. i. pp. 326, 454.

of the English possessions on the eastern coast. This position had hitherto been held by Masulipatam.

Other reasons besides the rivalry of the Dutch caused the trade at Masulipatam and Madras to fluctuate. In 1648 and 1649 a desultory war occurred between the kings of Viziapore and Golconda, which almost caused the ruin of the cloth trade at the principal towns in the neighbourhood of the northern port. The East India Company determined, however, to use every effort to resuscitate it, and not only recommended that Fort St. George should be strengthened, but also increased the establishment and strengthened the factories at the subordinate establishments of Masulipatam, Verasheroon, and Pettapollee.* This activity was not very long-lived. In 1653 we find the Company sending out stringent orders regarding economy and the reduction of expenditure. These orders were obeyed by the abolition of the factory at Pettapollee, to the south of Masulipatam, and by the reduction of the number of the Company's servants at Verasheroon to the north.

The report of a consultation of the English authorities at Masulipatam on December 4, 1655, has been preserved. It is remarkable as containing the first mention of a Protestant chaplain at Madras; and, as it is curious in many respects, I think it is worthy of being reproduced here. Mr. Edward Winter must have been the President of the Council at Masulipatam, and the abolition of the factory at "Pettapollee" could not have been carried out immediately after it had been decided on. "Next was had into consideration what proportion of means was thought needful to be allowed to such of the Company's servants as are to reside at Madraspatam and Metchlapatam, and the subordinate factories, for their necessary expenses, charges, garrison, &c., excepted, it was agreed that thirty old pagodas should be allowed to Mr. Edward Winter to uphold the Company's houses at Metchlapatam, Verasheeroon, Pottapollee, Daleepadee, and sixty new pagodas for the president and two factors, the minister and his wife, and chirurgeon, at Fort St. George." †

About 1670, a Dominican Friar, named Fernandez Navarette, visited Masulipatam on his return journey from China to Europe. He had been sent by his order to exercise his ecclesiastical functions in the Philippine Islands and China, and he returned by a rather

* Bruce, vol. i. pp. 454, 484.

† Kaye's History of the Administration of the East India Company, p. 628, *note*.

circuitous route. From Malacca he went by sea to "Madrasta Patan," and thence by land to Golconda and Masulipatam, at which port he embarked for Surat. He gives the following description of Masulipatam and the people there, which, I think, will be interesting, as a glimpse of life at this settlement at that early period, by an independent observer :—"The city *Musulapatam* is famous all along the Coast of *Coromandel*. It is situated sixty Leagues North of *Madrasta*, a very populous Place, and of great Trade. The *English* and *Dutch*, and at present the *French*, have erected Factories there. Some years ago, besides these, the *Danes* had one too. Some *Portuguese*, *Mungrels*, and Blacks, who are Catholicks, live there, and have a little Church, where there was a Father of the Order of St. Augustin. Some *English* and *Dutch*, who have discharged themselves from their Companies, have settled there, and live with their Families. The Climate is very bad and unhealthy. They said the Heat from April to August was intolerable. All the Country abounds in Wheat, Rice, Sheep, Hens, Geese, Fish, and Fruit, all at reasonable rates. I stayed with my *Chinese* in the *French* factory, where I said Mass to them every Day, and din'd and supp'd at their Table; they treated me in Health and a small Sickness I had with extraordinary Kindness, Love, and Affection. The Ship that was to sail for Suratte lay six Leagues lower at *Rosipor* (probably Nursapore). It was to be sheathed, and they had not yet begun to work on it, which troubled me extremely. The city is singular, and there being such a diversity of Natives, there falls out something new every Day among *Persians*, *Armenians*, *Moors*, &c. That city resembles *Babel*, in the variety of Tongues, and differences of Garbs and Customs, but I liked the natural Inclinations of them all. I sometimes went to the Church, which was a considerable distance from the Factory, met several People by the way, and they were all courteous and civil. I talked with some *English* and *Dutch*, visited them, because it was necessary, and found them very obliging in their Words, and some no less in their Actions." *

The earliest volume of records in the Government Office at Madras commences with a letter from the Court of Directors addressed to "our Agent and Councell in Fort Saint George," and dated November 7, 1670. Among other subjects, the following mention is made

* An Account of China, written in Spanish, by the R. F. F. Dominic Fernandez Navarette. Translated in "Collection of Voyages and Travels." London, 1704, vol. i.

of the investments and of the trade to be carried on at Masulipatam and the adjacent country. "We have continued to supply you," the Directors wrote, "with the great stock, in reguard you write you have opertunity to make great investments, and our desires to have a full trade carried on at your port, Mesulapatam, and the Bay, in the commodities hereafter mencioned, and in reguard ye Dutch do so fully fall in with the Calicoe trade that they had the last year 50,000 pieces of Long cloth, the French also putting hard for the trade, and the Danes and Portugals viewing theirs, so that for us to bring a small quantity, and sell it dear, would be but to hold the candle to them." *

Later in the same month, the following letter was sent, "To our chiefe and factors at Mesulapatam:"—"Hoping that Mr. Mohune has arrived, and that Mr. Jearsy has been called to account, and made satisfaction for what of our property came to his hands, and what damages we have sustained by him. That you attend to our instructions to promote the sale of our goods, and to procure a vent for English manufactures, that you are not making any new disturbance concerning place and precedency, but observe our orders, and that you speedily dispatch our ships from your port." †

In this letter we find an allusion made to jealousy between Masulipatam and Madras with regard to precedence. Five years later, the Directors remark on the "aversion" of their Agent and Council at the Fort for Masulipatam. They direct the immediate dismissal of Mr. Mohune, and inquiry into his counter-charges against Mr. Mainwaring, who had been appointed Chief at Masulipatam, and, generally, into the conduct of their factors at Masulipatam, who were said to have driven a great trade in calicoes to the South Seas, and other places, "contrary to our express orders and their covenants." They trust that Major Puckle, whom they had sent out by last year's ships to that end, may have already made this inquiry. Major W. Puckle was to be Chief at Masulipatam, and his salary to be £100 per annum. ‡

Before Major Puckle proceeded to assume his appointment at Masulipatam, he drew up various rules for the guidance of the

* Notes on and Extracts from the Government Records in Fort St. George, Madras, Public Department. Madras: printed at the Government Press, 1871, No. i. p. 2.

† Ibid., p. 4.

‡ Ibid., p. 7.

establishments at that factory, and at the places subordinate to it. There had been frequent and most unseemly dissensions between the Company's servants at Masulipatam. Mr. Mainwaring, the Chief whom Major Puckle succeeded, had been accused of evil living, and of abuse of his official position and influence for his own advantage in trade; and he had brought similar counter-charges against Mr. Mohune, who had preceded him. There had been "endless debates and mutual aspersions," and the dispute had gone so far that the Court of Directors remark in a despatch from England, "We find a complaint against Mr. Wales and Cullen about throwing a brickbat into Mr. Mainwaring's window. We shall not," they add, "permit any of our servants, of what quality soever, to contemn our authority, which those do that contemn any that act by it." *

In the proposals which Major Puckle laid before the Agent and Council at Madras, it was suggested that the establishment at Masulipatam should consist of a Chief, a second for accounts, a third for Godowns—these being the members of Council,—a secretary, two factors, a steward, three writers—each of the Council to take charge of one,—a physician, and a minister; and that there should be eleven servants at Madapollam (Mádhavayapálem), one at Verasheroon, and one at Pettapollee, "to keepe possession."

With reference to the out-stations under the authority of the Chief and Council at Masulipatam, the Directors, in a letter dated December 12, 1677, authorize the Agent at Fort St. George to rent Madapollam and Verasheroon. But before the receipt of this letter, the Agent and Council, in their anxiety to obtain the land on which the factories at these places were built on advantageous terms, passed the following characteristic minute :—

"The King of Golcondah, being about to visit Mechlipatam, resolve to instruct the Chief and Councel at Madapollam, if they find it necessary, to present him with a considerable sum of money to endeavour to obtain in return—1st. Leave to coin rupees and pice at Madras, to be current throughout the King of Golcondah's dominions. 2d. That all English goods and trade in the Cornatt (Carnatic) country, shall be free of tunkah, or custom, as they are in Masulipatam and those parts of the *ancient* kingdom of Golcondah. 3d. To get Verasheroone or Madapollam, one or both, settled on the Company rent free, or else at a moderate rent, by a Phirmaund

* Extracts from Government Records, No. i. p. 14.

to pay the rent to the Divan and to no other, and that the set rent shall never be raised."* (May 23, 1678.)

As this is the first occasion on which the Chief and Council of Madapollam are mentioned, I conclude that they had been appointed since Major Puckle's visit of inquiry had taken place. There was certainly a chief there three years later, but I was not aware that he was assisted in his deliberations by a Council. The Chief and his Council must, however, have still been subordinate to the authorities at Masulipatam.

These instructions, unfortunately, were of no avail. On the 3d of June another minute was written. "Besides former instructions to Chief and Council at Madapollam, how to comport themselves on occasion of the King's visit, resolve further to propose their obtaining for us rent free, or on a moderate rent, oñ a Phirmaund from the king, Trivitor, Egoomooroo, and St. Thomâ, and the villages under them. . . . News that the King of Golcondah, in consequence of the great heat and water *scarcy* for his following, has deferred his journey 'to the joy of all his subjects.' "†

Hitherto Madapollam, though possessing a Chief and Council of its own, had been subordinate to Masulipatam; but it was soon to become independent.‡ As there had been a good deal of dissension and confusion in the north, and the interests of the Company had consequently suffered in a great measure, it was considered advisable that the Agent of Fort St. George should make an official tour of inspection, and visit all the factories in that quarter. On the 3d March 1679, the Council met in their chamber at Fort St. George, and passed the following resolution:—

"Upon consideration of the Honourable Company's affairs at Metchlepatam and the adjacent factories, it was resolved to be necessary, and for the Honourable Company's interests, for the Agent to visit those factories subordinate to this jurisdiction, a vacancy in business now happening for this conveniency. Three other Members of Council to take charge of the Company's affairs at this place, and Mr. Richard Mohune, the Minister, Secretary, and some of the young men to accompany the Agent on his journey, which is to be commenced as soon as befitting preparations can be

* Extracts from Government Records, No. i. p. 74. † Ibid., p. 75.

‡ It may be mentioned here that the cloths for which this place was celebrated are still called in the English market "Madapollams."

gott ready, it being necessary for the reputation of the Nation to go in a handsome Port and Equipage."

I am tempted to give several extracts from the Journal, or "Memoriall," as it is called, of this interesting tour. The company consisted of Streynsham Master, Esq., Agent of the Coast and Bay, Mr. Timothy Wilkes and Mr. Richard Mohune of Councill, the minister, the chirurgeon, the schoolmaster, the secretary, and two writers, an ensign, six mounted soldiers, and a trumpeter—in all, seventeen persons in the Company's service; and four freemen, who went with the Agent's company for their own pleasure and at their own charges. This little retinue started from Madras on March 11, 1679, and passing through Pulicat, Nellore, and Nizampatam, arrived at Masulipatam on the 26th. "At the town-gate they were met by the Company's Merchants, and entered the town in a handsome equipage with a great train. The Chief of the Dutch, Signor Outhorne, sent excuses for not meeting them, but would make his visit next day. The Governor of the Town, Aga Telloll, was not in town, but five or six days' journey off.

"The Chief of the Dutch came to visit the Agent, and he and his company were entertained at a banquet, and went home again about eight at night. 'Signor Outhorne discoursing with the Agent, among other Bravadoes, delivered this as remarkable, that their Company has so many Islands and Castles in the South Seas—many of which he named—that they were as Emperors: they had hitherto made Kings, and now lately they had made an Emperor, viz., the Mataran, who has several kings under him, and he has given their Company all the sea-ports upon the coast of Java: when they wanted men, upon their call, the kings brought their armys to fight for them, as a great Prince of Macassar, whom he named, has brought a great army to Battavia to fight the king of Bantam by land, and they intended to block it up by sea, and when 'twas objected that their Company at home would not approve of a warr with Bantam, he replyed he knew better, for he came from Battavia this yeare about January last.'

"On April 2d, Aga Telloll, the Governour, returned from Narsapore and those places under his Government," and on the 4th, a "visit was received from, and return visit paid to Aga Telloll, who came with a train of Persians, and was very civil, entertaining the Agent at a 'plentifull supper,' giving a horse, and offering Tashrifs, which could not be accepted as only to be received by an inferior from a superior." It was considered advisable, however, to present a bribe to this distinguished Mussulman official, and the following ingenuous entry appears in the diary :—"Being a person rising in favour at Court, 250 pagodas, ready money, is given to Aga Telloll privately, which will be much more acceptable than a greater summe publickly."

"The Agent started at four P.M., on the 7th of April, for Madapollam," after he had placed the affairs at Masulipatam on what, he considered, a satisfactory footing, "and crossing the Enteer river on the morning of the 8th, forded another small river, and thence by sea (the back-water) to Peddy Gullypollam (Pedda Gollapálem), 22½ English miles, and passing through Collypatam (Kálipatnam) and Mootullpellee (Mótapalli), arrived at Madapollam on the 9th. In the evening viewed the warehouses, gardens, and yards, which are all well situated upon the side of the great river which goes into the sea about five miles from the factory. The towns, Madapollam and Narsapore, are joined together.

"Narsapore visited; many large substantial houses built by Englishmen, but some deserted, and all in danger from the encroachments of the river. The Dutch Chief at Pollicull (Pálakollu) stayed the day in the Dutch House at Narsapore, and visited the Agent, informing him that 'he who was aforetime King of Orixa was risen with a great army of 35,000 horse, upon the coast and country of Gingerlee, who has besieged the Seir Lascar or Gratt of the King of Golcondah in a castle, and has taken away 500 laest of Paddy, of the Dutch Company's.'"

"April 15. One John Heathfield, Chyrurgeon of Madapollam and Metchlepatam, having married the widow of Mr. Fleetwood, who had taken the town of Narsapore to farm three years since, which is against the Honourable Company's order, is ordered to quit the farm.

"The Braminy of the Factory and his two sons committed under guard in the Factory for disrespectful behaviour, the former 'having cast out slighting speeches on the Agent.'"

"April 16. The former contract with the merchants made void, and a new one entered into. Conappa, the Braminy, and his two sons released on paying 500 pagodas, and dismissed the Company's Service.

"There being conveniency in this place for ye breeding up of spotted deer which the Hon'ble Company doe every yeare order to be sent home for His Majesty, it is ordered that care be taken to breede them up in this Factory to be sent home accordingly." The king whom the Company were thus anxious to please, was Charles the Second.

"The Dutch House and compound at Narsapore visited. Iron works, where three hundred smiths may work. Many vessels lying in the river employed in the great rice trade of Gingerlee."

Having finished his inspection of the Company's factories, the Agent started on his return journey to Madras. He did not propose to return by the route he had come, but "intended to go the upward inland way, and to make an elbow to take a sight of the Dimond Mines."

His first stage was to Verasheroon, which is stated to be nine miles from Madapollam. This place has already been identified as Víravásaram, and the distance given in this Diary, and the direction in which the Agent is said to have travelled, proves that this identification is correct. "The Company had two houses here," both having at this time partly fallen into disrepair. "It was thought the Company might, with advantage, rent the place of the King, there being accommodation for weavers, but the place is now ruined and empty of people through the tyranny of the Government.

"Passing through Pentepoll (most probably Pentapádu) on the 18th, the Agent reached Elloor, one of the greatest towns of this country, 'where are made ye best carpetts after ye manner of those in Persia, by a race of Persians which they told us came over above a hundred years agoe.'" After visiting the diamond mines, the Agent and his party returned to Madras through Nellore, thus bringing to a close a very pleasant, as well as a very interesting, trip. They reached Madras on the 4th of May, where they were met by the people, and received with much ceremony, "returning in good health (God be praised) from a journey which, though troublesome hath been of great advantage to the Honourable Company."

One of the principal fruits of the Agent's visit was, that the factory at Madapollam was rendered independent of that at Masulipatam, a position which it had not hitherto enjoyed, and was placed directly under the orders of the Agent at Fort St. George. On the 7th of July the following order, carrying this decision into effect, was passed :—

"The Hon'ble Company's orders in their letter, January 3, 1679, 'concerning the settlement of their investments at Pettepollee and

Madapollam, independent one of another, and subordinate to the Fort, and that the charge at Metchlepatam be retrenched, and only three persons left there, the grandeur of the Factory to be laid aside, and the charges to be curtailed to 5 or 600 pagodas per annum,' being read and debated, it was resolved that, before the investment could be transferred to Pettepollee, new houses and warehouses must be built; as for the rest, the orders to be carried out." *

It was soon considered advisable that the Agent should pay a second visit to Masulipatam, and should also inspect the other settlements in the Bay of Bengal. On this occasion he went by sea. The following extracts are taken from

"The Memoriall of Streynsham Master, Esq., Agent of the Coast of Chormandell and Bay of Bengall. His voyage to Metchlepatam and the Bay to visit those Factorys, &c., belonging to the Hon'ble English E. I. Company.†

"August 1st. Embarked on the 'Golden Fleece,' with Mr. Richard Mohun of the Council, Mr. Richard Elliot, Chaplain, the Secretary, two writers, an ensign, and 13 soldiers, besides peons and pellanqueen boys. On board the other Ships went other Factors and Writers. Sighting Pulicat at daybreak next day, they arrived in the Masulipatam Roads on the forenoon of the 4th. Mr. Christopher Hatton, Chief of the Council, and others of the Factory and Freemen came on board, but the wind blowing fresh off land, they could not go ashore that day.

"The wind continuing to blow off the land so strong, and likely to continue so, the Agent being unable to land, resolves to conduct his business and give instructions on board for the Factories of Metchlepatam and Madapollam separately. The Council and Establishment for each Factory, and rules for their guidance, prescribed in accordance with the Hon'ble Company's orders. Orders for the year's investment at Madapollam. As to the retrenchment of the charges of the Factories, the Agent finds that the charges are much less than they have been of late years, while the business is larger than heretofore; but the Councils are warned to be frugal both in Table Expenses, and to dispense with as many Peons and servants as may be, 'the Dutch having last yeare put away their Drums, Pipes, &c., and many peons.' 300 bags of Gram, each 5 maunds, and 100 Collars of Bandaloors covered with leather."

* Extracts from Government Records, Second Series, p. 8. † Ibid., p. 36.

To show that the severance between Masulipatam and Madapollam was complete, "the Chiefs of those places are directed to obey the orders of the Deputy-Agent at Fort St. George during the Agent's absence." The above directions and instructions were sent "unto Mr. John Field, Chief, &c., Councell for ye affairs of ye said Hon'ble Company at Madapollam. Directions for the investment, orders for good Government to the Chief at Masulipatam. Orders to take care of the houses and gardens at Verasheroone, so that right and title in them be not lost, but no further charges be incurred for them, and to get in the bad debts thereabouts. A present is to be given to Kishnapa, the Brahminy Governor of Dasheroon (Dowlaishweram), and those parts, as was done last year, he having been very respectful to the Hon'ble Company's investments. One or two ships to anchor off the Narsapore River, and good, strong, and tight boats, and some cattemarans to be procured in connection with that service."

With regard to the prospects of the trade in those parts, notwithstanding the keen rivalry of the Dutch, the Agent writes :—

"At Metchlepatam the Dutch have landed this yeare a very great stock of Silver, Copper, and Spices, wherewith it is reported they intend to carry out vast investments to the prejudice of the English business, having advanced 10 per cent. on the usual prices of all sorts of calicoes, and with the gold coined some months past at Pullicat paid off all their debts upon the Coast, and do now in all their Factories make their investments with ready money advances, which they never did heretofore. Notwithstanding which our merchants goe on cheerfully in their business, not questioning, but to comply with the contracts made with them by the Agents at Metchlepatam and Madapollam."

After visiting the other factories in the Bay, the Agent anchored off Nursapore on January 7, 1680. On the following day the Agent landed, and went to the factory, where he examined the accounts and the cash-chest. The regulations for the ordering of the Company's affairs at Madapollam were given to the Chief. They were similar to those issued to the other factories in the Bay, and the following abstract will give our readers a good idea of the spirit in which they were written. A public table is to be kept, at which all single persons of the factory are to diet themselves, and no diet-money is to be allowed to single persons, but only to those that are married and wish to diet apart. No candle or bottle to be allowed, such as has hitherto been allowed under the name of "Settlement Charges." Candles are to be allowed only to the Chiefs and those of Council, to the Chaplain, and to the Surgeon. Lamps are to be allowed to every chamber. No Chief is to be permitted to remove from his factory to any other without leave from Fort St. George. No house-servants (such as Vakils, Banians, and Writers) are to be removed or entertained without an order of Council, "it being observed to be of bad consequence to turn off old servants."

While Mr. Master was on shore, he held a consultation with Mr. Field, the Chief, regarding the affairs of the factory, and the various matters discussed were recorded. "After much debate the merchants agree to a standing contract for the investments, on certain terms which are stated. Two boats of about twenty tons a piece ordered to be built at Nursapore, to be sent next year to Balasore for the trade there and for service in the Bay. A flag-staff to be set up, as a mark for ships to anchor by, at the river mouth. Tashrifs (presents) of broad and fine cloth given to the principal merchants. Gruaraz, the former chief Bramini of the Factory, having died, a successor is appointed, and a pension of 20 pagodas per annum is granted to his widow for her life, to be paid out of the Bramini's part of the Dustoor. A house in Madapollam, belonging to Mr. Robert Fleetwood, deceased, purchased for 40 pagodas. A large house at Nursapore offered for 300 pagodas: resolved to wait and see whether the latter cannot be bought for less. Presents from and to Nursaraz's son. The contract, in full, with the Madapollam merchants for the investments. It is agreed that the contract shall be 'for many years' continuance without alteration, unless it shall be caused through warr, famine, or other such like inevitable necessity;' but shall not be varied on account of fluctuations in prices, or of loss or gain to one party or the other." All these trivial details are of value, because they throw light on the mode of living and of conducting business in the country stations two centuries ago. We can imagine grave Mr. Streynsham Master seated as president of the little Council in the dining-hall of the factory, which was most probably situated on the bank of the river with the view opened to the sea, where the "Golden Fleece" lay at anchor. Tradition states that it was built on the mound on which the bungalow attached to the house occupied by the present Assistant-Superintendent of Police now stands, though this tradition may be erroneous, as a great portion of the old town of Madapollam has been carried away by the encroachment of the stream. The cheerful noise of repairing and building vessels is heard from the adjacent dry docks. The Komitis are ushered into the presence of Mr. Master and Mr. Field, and present their offerings and receive gifts of cloths in return; and then the solemn business of Oriental bargaining is begun. After a long discussion the contracts are finally agreed to, and they are pronounced to be perpetual. All is life-like and real.

The following day the Agent embarked on board the "Golden Fleece," and, after visiting Masulipatam, reached Fort St. George on the 26th of January, "and so ended this troublesome voyage."

During Mr. Master's visits, Mr. John Field appears to have been the Chief of Madapollam. He must have been of some standing, because, on the death of Mr. Christopher Hatton, Chief of Masulipatam, Mr. John Tivill was appointed to succeed him "without prejudice to Mr. Field's seniority, the precedency of place being his right." * Mr. John Davis was the next Chief of Madapollam. His little daughter died there in 1681, and the stone erected to her memory is still to be seen in the grounds attached to the former public bungalow, which is now used as the Deputy-Collector's office. The following is a copy of this inscription:—

Here lyeth the Bo-
dy of Katherine Davis
the daughter of John Davis
Chief of *Mada-*
pollam who depart-
ed this life the 24th
August anno 1681
Aged 17 months.

In 1690 Mr. Elihu Yale, then Governor of Madras, received a cowle or firman from Zulfikar Khan, one of the Emperor Aurangzib's most famous generals, for the English possessions on the coast. Zulfikar Khan had been sent by the Emperor to attempt the capture of the stronghold of Gingee, then held by the Mahrattas, and had been at the same time appointed Soubahdar of the whole country. The following is a translation of part of this cowle:—

"Whereas in the time of the late shameless and faithless rebellion, the President of the English, Elihu Yale, Governor and Captain of Chinnapatanam, protected and assisted Mahmoud Ali and

* Extracts from Government Records, Second Series, p. 30.

other servants of the Mogul, and supplied me with powder with other services; in consideration whereof I have made and given this my Cowle or grant, that the rent of the Fort and Factory of Chinnapatanam with accustomary privileges, the English Factories of Metchlepatam, Madapollam, Vizagapatam, &c., within the territories of the Golconda country, also their other settlements, according to the former custom and the usual practice of the English, let it remain undisturbed." In April 1692, Mr. Yale received firmans from the Vizier Assad Khan, who was with the imperial army before Gingee, confirming the above grant, and bestowing additional privileges, such as the power of coining.

Injaram, on the eastern branch of the Godavery, was made a settlement in 1708. Captain Alexander Hamilton, who visited India at the beginning of the eighteenth century, stated that the best and finest long cloth that India afforded was made there; but that the inland countries lying near the river were in the hands of different Rajahs, each of whom, being sovereign in his own small dominions, made such impositions and exactions on the cloth which came down the river that they ruined the profitable trade of Injaram. "In 1708," he says, "the English from Vizagapatam settled there; but, whether the factory was starved for want of money, or whether the constituent and constituted chiefs of the factories disagreed about dividing the bear's skin, I know not, but the factory was soon withdrawn, and the project lost." * This settlement must, however, have speedily revived, for there was a factory there in 1725, and, during the French War, a little later, there was a factory at Injaram. †

Besides the English factories at Madapollam and Injaram, there was also a settlement at Bendamúrlanka. This was in a most healthy situation, about a mile from the sea, and eighteen miles due east from Nursapore. A factory was there in 1757; ‡ but it had been removed before 1786, when the Committee of Circuit sent in their Report on the Havéli lands dependent on Masulipatam. §

The East India Company's mercantile establishments were abolished in the year 1829. Up to that year there had been Residents at Injaram and at Nursapore to manage the mercantile

* New Account of East India, by Captain Alexander Hamilton. Pinkerton's "Collection of Travels," vol. viii. p. 397.

† Orme, vol. ii. pp. 218, 261.

‡ Ibid., p. 261.

§ Report, § 14.

affairs of the Company independently of the Collectors, who were appointed in 1794. The investments, as they were called, which were annually made at the factories, caused a steady and continuous impetus to the staple industry of the people, and constituted one great means for promoting the prosperity of the District. On an average, seven lacs of rupees were yearly expended on the purchase of muslins and cloths during the twenty-four years previous to their abolition. In some earlier years the annual disbursements amounted to ten, eleven, twelve, and, in one year, exceeded fourteen, lacs of rupees. The abolition of the factories had for some years a most prejudicial effect on the prosperity of the District. For a time the shock thus inflicted on the mercantile community was partially alleviated by the incitement which private enterprise received by the opening the withdrawal of the Government from commerce afforded; but the main trade in cloth was superseded by the manufactures of Europe, and the flourishing trade of the weavers, for which this part of India had attained a celebrity throughout the whole world, was almost annihilated.*

* Report on the Rajahmundry District, by Sir Henry Montgomery, § 37.

CHAPTER X.

THE DUTCH AND FRENCH SETTLEMENTS.

THE DUTCH EAST INDIA COMPANY—TRADE OF THE DUTCH IN THE EAST—FACTORIES AT MADAPOLLAM AND PALKOLE—DUTCH LIFE IN INDIA—DISPUTES WITH THE ENGLISH—THE FRENCH EAST INDIA COMPANY—FACTORIES AT MASULIPATAM AND YANAM—FRENCH OCCUPATION OF THE NORTHERN CIRCARS—DESCRIPTIVE ACCOUNT OF YANAM.

THE Dutch were among the first European nations to engage in Oriental commerce by the newly-discovered route round the Cape of Good Hope. Before the close of the sixteenth century, several voyages had been made to the Eastern Archipelago by enterprising Dutchmen, and various companies had been formed to continue and develop this profitable trade. The beginning of the new century, however, saw the commencement of a new era of commercial enterprise in Holland as well as in England. The Dutch East India Company was established on the 20th of March 1602, and a general charter was granted to the directors of it by the States General, incorporating the different companies which had previously existed into one great association, and conferring on it the exclusive privilege of trading to the East.* The new company soon acquired a considerable degree of power. As was subsequently the case in England, it became a new and formidable power in the State—a magnificent *imperium in imperio.* "It was," as a philosophical French writer remarked, "a new state erected within the State itself, which enriched it and increased its strength abroad, but might, in time, weaken the influence of the democratical principle, which inspires the love of equality and economy of the laws, and of one's own countrymen." †

* Beveridge's Comprehensive History of India, vol. i. p. 223.

† Abbé Raynal's Philosophical and Political History of the Settlements and Trade of Europeans in the East and West Indies. Translated by J. Justamond. Second Edition. 1767. Vol. i. p. 174.

The enterprise of the Dutch attracted them principally to the Eastern Archipelago, where they established a flourishing trade with the Spice Islands; but they had also several settlements in India which were, however, subordinate to their Eastern capital, Batavia, in the Island of Java.* The English also traded to the Spice Islands, but their chief settlements and entrepôts of trade were in India. The rivalry between the two nations was painfully keen; but their interests gradually parted asunder, and the Dutch remained masters in the Spice Islands, while the energy and the power of the English were concentrated on the continent of India.† In 1658 the Dutch took Negapatam from the Portuguese, and it became their chief settlement on the coast of Coromandel. It was the central place to which all the linens and other commodities collected by the Dutch Company from the other places on the coast were brought for exportation. The extravagance of the expenditure, however, prevented the trade being profitable. By the end of the seventeenth century the value of the articles exported from the eastern coast, which are described as "iron, lead, copper, calico, pepper, and spices," amounted to £43,750, but the expenses swallowed up the profits.‡ In corroboration of this assertion, it is stated in another account that in 1776–77, or a century later, the profits were 427,131 francs, while the charges amounted to 452,133. The Dutch East India Company's possessions were at that time divided into seven governments. The seventh was that on the Coromandel coast. Negapatam was the capital, and under it were the other factories on the coast—Sadras, Palkole, Jagganaikpore, and Bimlipatam.§

Palkole (Pálakollu) and Jagganaikpore (Jagannádhapuram) are villages in the Godavery District. Palkole is situated about five miles north of Nursapore. It is now on the canal from Vijéshwaram to Nursapore. The soil around the village is very fertile, and the Dutch took advantage of it to plant oranges, pumple mosses, and plantains in abundance. The Dutch settled here before the middle of the seventeenth century. In the quiet little graveyard, shaded by orange-trees, there are several tombs still in good preservation,

* Bruce's Annals, vol. i. p. 29.

† Lindsay's History of Merchant Shipping, vol. ii. pp. 160, 172.

‡ Ibid., vol. i. p. 222.

§ Account of Java and Batavia from the Voyages of Stavorinus. Pinkerton's "Voyages," vol. xi. p. 202.

and I append copies and translations of the two most ancient inscriptions upon them.

HIER LIŸE BE	HERE LIES IN-
GRAVEN DZOON VAN	TERRED THE SON OF
DEN ADS^{t} LAMBERT	THE ASSISTANT LAMBERT
HEMSİNCK GEN-	HEMSINCK GEN-
GERRALRI, GEBOREN	GERRALRI, BORN
IN Palicol ADIJ 17^{den}	IN Palicol 17th
OCTOBER A° 1660 EN	OCTOBER A° 1660
OVERLEDEN DEN	DECEASED
9^{den} November A° 1662.	9th November A° 1662.

HIER LEŸT BEGRAVEN SŸMON	HERE LIES INTERRED SYMON
VAN GROENEWEGEN VAN DELFT	VAN GROENEWEGEN OF DELFT,
IN SŸN LEVEN COOPMAN EN	DURING HIS LIFE MERCHANT AND
OPPERHOOFT TEN COMPTORE	CHIEF OF THE FACTORY,
PALICOL OBIJT ADIJ 3^{en} IVNIJ	PALICOL, DIED 3^{d} JUNÊ
A° 1665.	A° 1665.

Mr. Streynsham Master, the Agent at Fort St. George, paid a visit to Nursapore in 1679, as already stated. The Dutch had an iron factory there, and they owned a house near the English factory at Madapollam. On the 10th of April the Dutch Chief of Palkole came and stayed the day at the Dutch House at Nursapore, to pay his respects to the English Agent. On the 14th the Agent returned the visit at Palkole. He recorded that "the Dutch have there a Factory of a large compounde, where they do dye much blew cloth, having above three hundred jars set in the ground for that work; also they make many their best paintings there, the town being first rented by them at 2000 old Pagodas, and is now given them free by the king." The Agent also visited the Dutch house and factory at Nursapore.*

Jagannádhapuram, now really a part of Cocanada, also belonged to the Dutch. "Daatijeroon" was the original name of the place where the factory stood. The ground on which Jagannádhapuram was built, together with the factory and two villages near it, which were used for bleaching calicoes and other piece-goods, was the

* Notes on and Extracts from the Government Records of Fort St. George. 1871. Second Series, p. 32.

Company's own property. The factory was defended by rude ramparts of earth.*

The Dutch also had a factory at Masulipatam, where, probably, the cloth made at Palkole was manufactured into chintzes, and whence it was exported. Masulipatam is thus described in an old book of travels, and the account is given for the sake of the picture of Dutch life in India which succeeds it:—"*Masulipatam* is a City seated near a large River, where the *English* and *Dutch* have their Factories. It is very populous, and the residence of a Governour, who pays a certain yearly Tribute to the King of *Golcondar*, which he squeezes out of the Inhabitants, especially the *Gentives*, which are sorely oppressed by the *Persians* and *Moors* here, who farm all the Weaving Trade from the great Persons; wherefore there is scarce any Trafficking here without Profit, unless you have a Patent from the King, which is not easy to be obtained, because the Governours (who pay 140,000 *Pagodes* of annual tribute to the King) constantly oppose it; and it is a difficult matter to approach the King (who keeps his Court at a great distance hence) without purchasing their Favour, or some other Government Men's at Court. For the rest, this City is a Place of great Traffick, where most of our Commodities, as also those transported hither from the *Moloques*, *China*, &c., are sold at a very good rate. Here is also a great Concourse of Merchants from *Cambaja*, *Suratte*, and other Places under the jurisdiction of the *Great Mogul*, as also from *Gou*, *Orixa*, *Bengala*, and *Pegu*. Here is also a considerable Traffick in Diamonds and Rubies." †

Then follows an amusing account of Dutch life in the factories on the coast. "As the manner of Living of the vulgar sort among the *Dutch* in the *East Indies* is none of the best, so we will be satisfied with giving an account of those of the better sort. They commonly rise with the Sun—Sleep after Sun-rising being accounted very unwholesome here in the morning. Some have a Custom of washing their Heads, nay, the whole Body, with cold Water, immediately after their coming out of bed; others do it

* Account of Java and Batavia from the Voyages of Stavorinus. Pinkerton's "Collection of Travels," vol. xi. p. 203.

† A True and Exact Description of the most Celebrated East India Coasts of Malabar and Coromandel. By Philip Baldores, Minister of the Word of God in Ceylon. Translated from the High Dutch, printed at Amsterdam, 1672. "Collection of Voyages and Travels." London, 1704, p. 655.

with lukewarm Water three or four times a week; the last of which I have found the best by Experience. Brandy or any other strong Liquors are not much used by the wiser sort in the Morning, unless it be a Spoonful just before Dinner, and a little at Night before they go to bed.

"The *Tea* (always used fasting by the *Chineses*) has got a mighty Ascendant over the *Hollanders* of late years. Its chief Virtues are to disperse the gross Vapours of the Head and Stomach, and consequently to exhilarate our Spirits. The ordinary drink of the *Hollanders* is a Mixture of Water and Sugar boil'd together. Some fill certain Earthern Vessels over night with Water, and add to it three or four Glasses of *Spanish* Wine, which, exposed together all night in the Dew, turns white, and affords a pleasant Liquor, but is a little too cool, for which reason some put a certain quantity of Mum in the Vessel. The *Brunswick* Mum is both more pleasant and wholesome here than in Europe. Among the wines, those of *Spain* are most in request. It's true they sometimes inflame the Gall, but against that they make use of *Rhubarb* and *Cremor* of *Tartar*. The French and Rhenish Wines are not strong enough in these hot Countries, where the Stomach requires more lively Cordials, as a little Brandy, or a moderate share of Canary. Their ordinary Food is Goats, Sheep, Fowl, Hares, Peacocks, and such like.

"The *Hollanders* most generally take their Afternoon's Sleep here, as the *Italians* and some other *Europeans* do in hot Countries, a thing sufficiently commendable in the Indies, where the heat of the Sun Beams invites the Inhabitants to pass away the middle of the Day (when they are unfit for Business) at their ease. They have also a constant Custom of washing their Mouths after Dinner. About three or four a Clock in the Afternoon they take their Tea, and after that a Walk; the Evenings and Nights being pretty cool and very pleasant here, especially when the Moon shines. They sup commonly about seven or eight a Clock, but very moderately, and go to sleep about ten or eleven upon Quilts, Feather-beds being not used in the *Indies*." *

The above description gives a pleasing impression of the quiet life pursued by the Dutch in their up-country settlements. It is not unlike the mode of life such as may be seen in most Indian stations at the present day, although, perhaps, our Dutch pre-

* Ibid.

decessors were more quiet and phlegmatic than we are. Their early rising, their careful observance of ablutions, their generally abstemious habits, their afternoon tea, and quiet evening walk, would very fairly answer to the description of the life which is adopted by English families at retired out-of-the-way stations like Palkole.

With all their quietness of life in private, however, the Dutch were very tenacious of rank, and particular as to ceremonial in all official affairs. They wisely considered the success of their East India Company as a matter which concerned the whole nation, and they granted to their officials every power and privilege which they thought it necessary to bestow in order to insure the respect and attention of the people among whom they might reside. No people were more jealous of liberty at home, and yet they invested the Company with absolute sovereignty in India. No people ever affected less grandeur at home, and yet they obliged the Governor-General at Batavia and the Governors in India to appear in public in all the pomp of Oriental magnificence, in order to place them on the basis of equality with the princes with whom they might have to treat.* The following account of the mode of reception at the Government House will give the reader some idea of the punctilious ceremony which was observed by the Dutch officials in India, mingled with a ludicrous familiarity of manners:—"The Governor-General receives his guests sitting at the step at the door, dressed in a black waistcoat, with a stiff linen cap on; and, when they have all come, the General says: 'Friends, pull off your coats;' upon which every one takes off his coat, hat, and sword. They then sit down on chairs placed in a row on the step, every one according to his rank; and if it should happen that any does not observe this, he is told by the General, 'That is not your place, you must sit there.' Every one has then a glass of beer, and the toast is, 'A pleasant evening to you;' after that a pipe of tobacco, and then the conversation begins, but in such a manner that each speaks to his neighbour, without daring to speak so loud that the supreme commander may hear, who only converses for that evening with the person who sits next him, and who is, consequently, the highest in rank; and all that the General says aloud is, 'The ladies' health.' As soon as he has said this, every one jumps from his seat with a glass of wine which he had already in his hand, forming all

* Essay on the East India Trade, 1770, p. 9.

together a large half-circle, and, with their heads bent forward, they call out, 'The General's lady's health;' then follow the healths of every person present, each rising and bowing when his health is drunk. This ceremony is prolonged by the General till the clock strikes nine, when every one receives his hat, coat, and sword again, and obliging himself to drink to the General's health, who receives it with, 'Thank ye for my health.' Every one then takes his leave." * The consideration of rank among the English in India is great, but it never runs into the desperate extreme which it appears to have attained among the Dutch.

In 1686 the Dutch, irritated by real or fancied affronts received from the King of Golconda, quietly took from him the town of Masulipatam, and the Dutch Governor at Pulicat announced the capture of it to the English Government at Madras in very imperious terms. The King of Golconda was engaged at the time in a harassing war with the Emperor of Delhi.

"Upon the Coast of Choromandel," wrote one who undertook to vindicate the honour of his country at that time, "the English Company have a Sovereign Regency under His Majesty over a great City and a strong Fort and Garrison with above 200 guns mounted: Notwithstanding which, as soon as the Dutch Company had taken *Metchlepatam* (an open town upon the same coast), they did immediately, with insufferable insolence, forbid the English the Trade of the place, on purpose to lay the English low in the Eyes of the Natives, according to their usual Treatment. The particulars of this appears by the following Transcripts from the Originals, viz.:—

"A letter sent by the Dutch Governour and Council of *Palliacatt*, to the English Governour and Council of Fort St. George, bearing date the 3–13th of August 1686.

"It cannot be unknown to your Honours, how our honourable Netherlands East India Company, for some years on this Coast of Choromandel, by the great Ministers of State and other lesser Governours and Servants of the Gulcondah Crown Bearer, as well in the Low Lands of the North from Orixa to Metchlepatam, as also in the Lands of Carnatica, are Abused and Affronted in many unspeakable manners which we principally regard. . . . Whereupon the Right Honourable Council of *India* cannot swallow such innumerable overgrown injuries, and have been forced to resolve the better to

* View of the Present State of the Dutch Settlements in the East Indies. London, 1780, p. 5.

come by our right, in recompense of our great loss, and for the injuries and affronts done us, to take in possession (by the forces now sent us) the City of *Metchlepatam*. . . . Which resolution of the High Honourable to take in possession the City of *Metchlepatam* is put in execution, and by God's blessing and the Companie's Arms, so effected that we now for our Company this 26th of July are Masters of the aforesaid City of *Metchlepatam*; wherein, according to our Orders and to the maintaining our Friendships, we shall not incommode or hinder your Honours to imbarque in your Ships from your Factory at *Metchlepatam* what goods you have ready by you as you have occasion, and to disimbarque all your Provisions and Merchandize which are brought by your Ships to *Metchlepatam*, and lay them up in your Factory; but not to carry them without the City to dispose of them to Merchants or Subjects of the King of *Gulcondah*, so long as our Company hath not satisfaction from the King and keep possession of the Town.

JOHN PITTS.
JOHANNES HUYSMAN.
REHNIER JACOBSON."

Tall 3–13th August 1686.

Believing that the only object of the Dutch was to "ruinate and destroy the English trade," the Council of Fort St. George sent the following indignant and energetic reply:—

"We have received a large Declaration from your Honours of the State and pretended grounds of the quarrel between His Majesty the King of Gulcondah and the Right Honourable the Netherlands East India Company, you have also acquainted us that you have taken into your possession His Port of *Metchlepatam*: And because we are strangers to the particular causes of this Warr, we can say nothing to it; yet we are not ignorant of your farther design therein, and we wish it may not be your design to overthrow the Right Honourable Company's Trade there, which has been practised already too much, particularly at *Bantam*, for we have ever observed that, in all your Contracts with the Kings and Princes of these Countries, you endeavour to exclude our Trade in their Ports. . . . We must tell you that 'tis too great of you to appoint us what we have to do in reference to our Trade at *Metchlepatam* (though you have possession thereof), for we know of no obligation to observe such directions, the house and ground of our Factory being our Right Honourable Company's inheritance bought with their money.

In the meantime we shall endeavour to follow our Trade, and we shall not want them that are appointed to give us an account of the least obstruction thereto, which we advise you not to do, because of the ill consequences that may be to your own interests.

W. GYFFORDS.
ELIHU YALE."

The Dutch very naturally endeavoured to justify their proceedings, and asserted that the English merchants at Masulipatam had, of their own accord, retired from the town for fear of their property being burnt. "The English had also," they said, "divers other Lodges more, by or not far from *Metchlepatam*, where they could, without any molestation, drive their Trade." * One of these "Lodges" was Madapollam.

In 1787, when the Committee of Circuit wrote their Report on the Zemindaris dependent on Masulipatam, Palkole was still in possession of the Dutch. Previous to the war, which had then recently ended, the Committee ascertained that they had annually provided at their factory at that place 400 bales of white long cloth of from 12 to 24 punjums, for the market in Europe, besides quantities of chintz, and other stained goods for the trade in the Indian Archipelago. † The Dutch East India Company also possessed at that time the villages of Jagannádhapuram, Gollapálem, and Gundavaram, in the Zemindari of Pittapore. At the factory at Jagannádhapuram, the Dutch annually imported about a lakh of Madras pagodas, partly in specie, and partly in goods, one-half being in gold, and the other in copper and spices. Forty thousand pagodas out of this sum were expended on the purchase of *chay* goods, by which is probably meant articles dyed with the chay-root, and six thousand pagodas to the furnishing of white long cloth at this place and at Palkole. Private individuals likewise exported coarse *punjum* cloths to the eastward, and some fine long cloth, manufactured in the Delta, and as high in price as twenty pagodas the piece, were

* Justification of the Directors of the Netherlands East India Company. London, 1687. Appendix.

An impartial Vindication of the English East India Company from the Unjust and Scandalous Imputation cast upon them in a Treatise intituled "A Justification of the Netherlands East India Company; as it was delivered over unto the High and Mighty Lords the States General of the United Provinces," 1688, p. 168.

† Report of the Committee of Circuit on Zemindaris, § 19.

sent to Batavia. Although the Dutch paid quit-rent to the English East India Company for these villages, yet they had long been in the habit of collecting an import duty of 5 per cent., and an export duty of 3 per cent., in the Cocanada river. The Committee of Circuit confessed that they could not ascertain upon what grounds the Dutch claimed this privilege; and stated their opinion that, as the Dutch possessed only one side of the river, it seemed inconsistent for them to collect duties on merchandize exported from and imported at Cocanada, where the Zemindar then levied land customs.*

A few years later, all the Dutch possessions were ceded to Great Britain. The Dutch had joined the "armed neutrality," which was really aimed at the overthrow of the naval supremacy of England, and war was declared against them. Negapatam and the other Dutch settlements were taken during the warfare which ensued, and were ceded to the English at the peace of Versailles in 1783. Their factories in the Godavery District, however, were retained in their possession on the condition of their paying a quit-rent to the East India Company, and were not finally ceded to England till 1804.

Minor disputes sometimes occurred between the Dutch and the English authorities. A ludicrous example of this is to be found among the records of 1788. Mr. Revell, the Collector at Mogalturru, reported to the Chief and Council at Masulipatam that a complaint had been made to him by the Renter of Customs in Attili and 'Atsanta of "impediments having been thrown in his way by the Dutch at Palkole in the collection of the established 'Juncan,' who had before regularly conducted his business without interruption." The Dutch authorities, Messrs. Van Haefton and Vanquel Diton, at Palkole, on learning that the Renter had preferred a complaint against them, took his gumasta, or assistant, into custody, and sent him to Mr. Revell in charge of the peons belonging to their factory with the following letter:—"Some days ago it was here spread abroad that the Jonquender Vamoory Kistnamah was of intention to stop in this place the 'schandy' or market-day. To-day being Saturday, he has made in reality some preparations thereto, and hindered many people to bring their merchandizes in this place. He is gone even so far that he has sent the Bram who we send you by these under the guard of four of our peons, to menace strongly the people

* Report of the Committee of Circuit on Zemindaris, § 7.

who were already in our town, and to engage them to leave the market-place. We cannot believe that this is done by your orders, but are confident that you will do us justice by a good punishment of him who is the author of this disturbance, that he might never undertake more such and other like brutalities under our flag or colours." This letter and the answer to his communication convinced Mr. Revell that the matter was political, and that the Dutch were striving after an increase of power, or an alteration of the system under which they held these villages. It was, however, merely a local matter of minor importance, the Dutch being indignant at the "shandy" or market being closed, and the Renter irritated at one of his assistants being arrested. The Dutch declared solemnly that they were not "of intention to bring any the least hinderance to the foreign jungunder's to raise the duties in this place; nevertheless, under this special restriction that he must comport himself decently, and not do any impertenanties to any people who bring their merchandizes to our market-place, nor do the least thing that may be against the esteem that one nation owes to the other." *

So long as Palkole and Jagannádhapuram remained in possession of the Dutch, they paid a small tribute to the English, more as an acknowledgment of the sovereignty of the East India Company than as a recompense for their possessions. This custom originated in a present annually made by those factories on Christmas Day to the Mohammedan Governors on condition of their being furnished with "dustucks," or passes, to enable them to pass the merchandize of their Company duty free. In 1794, the Chief and Council at Masulipatam requested payment of this tribute, namely, 286 pagodas, being 143 pagodas for Fasli 1271, and the same amount for Fasli 1272 from Palkole, and pagodas 434, being 217 for each Fasli from Jagannádhapuram. The amount from Palkole was readily paid; but the Dutch authorities at Jagannádhapuram requested exemption on the ground that their Company had abandoned all commerce on this coast for the past two years, and would probably give up their establishments altogether. "We are ordered," they added, "by our superiors to try if we, upon that fundament, can be free of paying all contributions." †

The only other European nation with whom the English came into contact in the north were the French. The French East India Company was established by the letters patent of King Henri IV.

* MS. Records. † Ibid.

in 1604, the same period which saw the birth of the East India Companies of England and Holland. At first the new Company did not prosper. The opposition against it was strong, and great difficulty was experienced in raising the funds which were required to carry it on with advantage. The letters-patent were renewed by Louis XIII. in 1611, and the Company recovered itself and began to flourish under the powerful patronage of the king's great minister, Cardinal de Richelieu.* It was afterwards placed on a still firmer footing by Colbert, minister of Louis XIV. in 1664.

In 1669 Marcara, a Persian in the service of the French, obtained permission to establish a factory at Masulipatam, where both the English and the Dutch had for some time possessed commercial emporiums. He had been sent on a mission to the King of Golconda to enter into negotiation for this purpose, and to obtain from him the privilege of trading throughout his dominions. He was successful in his endeavours, notwithstanding the opposition of his English and Dutch rivals. On the 5th of December he obtained a firman from the king, which gave the French East India Company the privilege of carrying on all commercial undertakings in the dominions of the King of Golconda without payment of duty either on imports or exports. He also received a licence permitting him to establish a factory at Masulipatam.† In 1693 a small square was built, which received the name of Francepéta, and which, I believe, still remains in the possession of France, though it is entirely surrounded by the town, and can be of no commercial or political advantage to that country.

Besides their factory at Masulipatam, the French also possessed a factory at Yanam (Yánám), which was apparently subordinate to their chief at the larger and more important town. Yanam still belongs to France. It is a clean, pretty, carefully-kept little town, situated on the left bank of the eastern branch of the Godavery. It is not far from Injaram, where the English had a factory at the beginning of the eighteenth century. This locality must have been most favourable to trade, for a great many weavers resided there, and it was the centre of the trade in cloths which chiefly found its outlet at the port of Masulipatam. Yanam, however, is quite a modern town. It was not in existence in 1706, when a fearful inundation of the sea created great devastation in the neighbourhood.

* Essay on the East India Trade, p. 11.

† Malleson's French in India, pp. 15, 31.

The site of the present town and that of the neighbouring villages of Nílapalli and Komprapálem was then a continuous forest.* It is not known exactly when the French occupied Yanam, but it must have been early in the eighteenth century, not long after the English had opened their factory at Injaram.

The French factory was established there some time before 1750. In that year Nazir Jung, the then Subahdar of the Deckan, sent orders to seize the houses and effects which the French Company possessed in Masulipatam and Yanam. His orders were obeyed with scrupulous exactness, and his officers took possession of the French property at both places without plundering anything, and sealing up all that they took.† Masulipatam was afterwards taken by the French.

When Salabut Jung was raised to the throne, one of his first acts was to confirm all the grants which his predecessor had made to the French, and he also added to their possessions in gratitude for the assistance which he had received. He gave them a grant of the lands attached to Nizampatam and other villages, and also those attached to Nursapore, in this District. He also gave instructions that all the factories at Yanam, which his brother had taken, should be restored to them.‡

Yanam followed, of course, all the vicissitudes of the French in the north. For a time the whole district was under French control; and Yanam changed masters as often as the fortune of war permitted, being restored to France with the other French possessions in India at each successive peace. In 1787, when the Committee of Circuit made their report on the Zemindaris dependent on Masulipatam, the annual export from Yanam amounted to between two and three thousand bales of white long cloth, principally of the coarser kind, the greater part of which was paid for in specie.§

Yanam is the only place in the District which belongs now to the French. I am indebted to the present Chief for the following excellent descriptive account of the settlement:—The factory of Yanam is situated in 16° 43′ N. lat. and 80° 5′ E., 140 leagues N.N.E. from Pondicherry. It is built at the point where the Coringa river issues from the Godavery, and is bounded by those rivers on the east and south. The area of the territory is 2258 acres. It extends along

* Selections from the Records of the Madras Government, No. xix. p. 24.

† Orme, vol. i. p. 146.

‡ Malleson's French in India, p. 274.

§ Report on the Zemindaris, § 5.

the banks of the above two rivers for two leagues and a half, and its breadth varies from 390 metres to 3 kilometres. The soil is very fertile. The temperature varies from 20° to 26° centigrades from November to January, from 27° to 36° from February to April, from 36° to 44° in May and June, and from 28° to 34° from July to October.

Up to 1857 the territory of Yanam was farmed out to a single agent, who was called the farmer-general. He alone was responsible to the Government, from whom he received the rent, and he leased out the land to the ryots. In that year this system was superseded by the Government dealing directly with the ryots instead of through the farmer-general. The object of this novel measure was to bring the proprietor into immediate contact with the producer—the State with the cultivator. It was, however, not put into force until July 13, 1858, corresponding with the first day of Fasli 1268. This interval was intended for the expiration of the contracts which had been entered into between the ryots and the late farmer-general, and for the settlement of the land-tax.

An order was issued in 1871, by which the ryots were permitted to become permanent proprietors, and which also assured to the agricultural population stability in the occupation of the land. They now receive the advantage of all the improvements which they may desire to make without running the chance from time to time of being dispossessed, instead of the precarious tenure which they had under the renting system. After this order had been issued, the land was divided into wet land, dry land, and pasture land, let out on contract by public auction. This contract, which had the effect of conferring on the new holders the full and entire ownership of the land, involved the obligation of paying the land-tax, which is fixed at one-fourth of the raw produce. The amount of the contract for the land is remitted to the treasury in five instalments at the same time as the land-tax. On condition of the full payment of the price of their possessions, and of the revenue due, the proprietors of Yanam are permitted, under the conditions and restrictions published in the above-mentioned order, to undertake any kind of cultivation, and to obtain as much as they can out of their land without the amount which has been imposed upon them being increased at any time or under any circumstances. The government of Yanam give the ryots, without any additional tax, the water from the Dowlaishweram canal, which flows through their territory. In a word, the condition of the ryots at Yanam has been considerably ameliorated since these measures have been put in force.

The Chief, who is appointed by the President of the Republic, governs under the control of the Governor-General of the French possessions in India. He presides over the council instituted for the discussion of the budget. He has under his orders a priest, a head of police and other administrative affairs, a collector of taxes, who also acts as treasurer and receiver of unclaimed property, a medical man, and a registrar. The Chief fulfils the functions of President of the Criminal Court, of commerce, and of the magistracy and police. There is also a European civilian in charge of the registration of births, deaths, and marriages.

The area of the territory is about 1429 hectares. The population is estimated at 5460, divided as follows:—Yanam proper, 4221; Kanakalapéta, 441; Mettakúru, 133; Kursammapéta, 527; Adavipálem, 138. It contains 29 terraced houses, 108 tiled houses, 90 thatched houses, and some hundreds of huts.

In November 1839, a terrible hurricane, accompanied by an inundation of the sea, laid the town waste, and destroyed all the official records.

There are three schools in Yanam—a girls' school, superintended by four nuns of St. Joseph of Lyons, paid by the State; a school for caste girls, under the same superintendence; and a free school for boys for instruction in Telugu and French.

The police consists of a commissioner, a cutwal, a head-peon, and eighteen constables. There is a jail and a dispensary. The latter is supplied every six months from Pondicherry. It is under the care of the medical officer, and supplies the wants of the people of the town and neighbourhood. The medicines are given gratis to all who may require them.

The average number of criminal cases a year is 16, and of civil trials, 60. The average revenue for the last nine years has been 45,500 rupees. The principal item was the import duty, which amounted to about 17,500 rupees a year.

CHAPTER XI.

THE MOHAMMEDAN PERIOD.

FIRST INVASION OF THE DECKAN—THE BAHMANI DYNASTY—INVASION OF ORISSA—MOHAMMEDAN OCCUPATION OF RAJAHMUNDRY AND KONDAPILLI—DIVISION OF TERRITORY—SIEGE AND CAPTURE OF RAJAHMUNDRY—MOHAMMEDAN RULE—WARFARE IN THE SOUTH—THE FRENCH OCCUPATION.

THE first invasion of the Deckan attempted by the Mohammedans was undertaken by Allah-ud-din, nephew and successor of Jelal-ud-din, the first Emperor of the house of Khilji. After his accession to the throne of Delhi, he despatched an army through Bengal to attack Warangole, the capital of Telingana; while he sent another army, under his favourite general Malik Kafur, to Deogiri. The former expedition failed; but Kafur was commissioned to retrieve the disaster. He invaded the north of Telingana, gained a signal victory over his opponents, took the fort of Warangole, and compelled the Rajah to become a tributary of the Emperor of Delhi.*

The hold of the Mussulmans on the country was then neither lasting nor secure. After the murder of the last sovereign of the house of Khilji, Ghazi Khan Toghlak, Governor of the Punjab, succeeded to the imperial throne. The Hindu rajahs of the Deckan had, during this time of confusion, asserted their independence, and Juna Khan, the emperor's eldest son, was sent to restore the emperor's authority. His expedition was successful until he reached Warangole, where the garrison withstood his attacks for several months. Even his own officers deserted him, and he was forced to make an ignominious retreat. In the following year he was more successful; and

* Elphinstone's History of India, 2d edition, vol. ii. pp. 43, 46.

he not only captured Warangole, but took the rajah prisoner and carried him captive to Delhi.

Two years afterwards, Juna Khan ascended the throne, and attained an infamous celebrity as emperor under the title of Sultan Mohammed Toghlak. His insane cruelties and fantastic caprices induced his subjects, both Mohammedan and Hindu, to revolt. Among others, the Rajah of Telingana effected his independence, regained possession of Warangole, and expelled the Mussulman garrisons from his country.

Hussan Gangu, who, in 1347, was the Mohammedan leader of the revolt against the Emperor Mohammed Toghlak, was the founder of the Bahmani dynasty, which flourished in the Deckan for several generations. He was a man of low origin, and in early life farmed a small piece of land from a Brahmin astrologer. Finding some treasure in his field, he informed his landlord of the discovery, who was so much pleased with his honesty that he recommended him to the king, with whom the Brahmin was in favour. Hussan Gangu never forgot this kindness, and, when he himself succeeded to power and founded a kingdom, he added to his other names the word Bahmani or Brahmini, by which his dynasty has been distinguished. He was at first materially assisted in his endeavour to throw off his allegiance to the emperor by the Hindu rajahs of Warangole and Vizianagar. This alliance was not, however, of long duration. The warfare between Mohammedan and Hindu which ensued was unceasing, and lasted throughout the entire rule of the Bahmani dynasty. In 1421, Ahmed Shah, the reigning sovereign, defeated the Rajah of Telingana, captured Warangole, and thus deprived the Hindu Rajah of the ancient capital of his race.*

Mohammed the Second ascended the throne in 1463, and proved one of the most energetic and warlike of the house of Bahmani. In 1471 he availed himself of the internal dissensions of the Hindu rajahs of Orissa to send Mussulman troops into that province, and to acquire the two fertile districts of Rajahmundry and Kondapilli, so that the whole of the Godavery District must have come into his possession, and nominally formed a portion of his dominions. The Rajah of Orissa had died without issue, and the succession to the throne was disputed by Mangal Rai, his adopted son, and Ambar Rai, one of his cousins. The latter applied for

* Elphinstone, vol. ii. pp. 580, 641.

assistance to Mohammed Shah, promising to become his tributary, if he should prove successful by the aid of the Mussulman arms. Mohammed Shah gladly complied with this request, for he already coveted the province of Orissa, and the present offer seemed most opportunely to favour his designs. The person whom he selected as commander-in-chief of his troops was Mallik Hussan Bheiru, upon whom he conferred the title of Nizam-ul-Mulk, which afterwards became one of the most renowned Mohammedan titles. The new commander was a converted Hindu, who had been taken prisoner in infancy, and brought into the royal palace as companion to the king when a prince. Mohammed Shah adopted the policy of enrolling foreigners of various races in his service, and he had a personal body-guard of 2000 Abyssinians and Indians, of whom Mallik Naib Nizam-ul-Mulk Bheiru was considered the leader.*

Nizam-ul-Mulk at once marched towards Orissa with a large army. He was joined by Ambar Rai, with his troops, on the border of that province, and the Hindu pretender became the guide to the invading forces against his relative. Mangal Rai was defeated, and Ambar Rai placed upon the throne. Nizam-ul-Mulk proceeded, after this conquest, to reduce the two districts of Rajahmundry and Kondapilli. He was accompanied in this expedition by Ambar Rai; and having, under the instructions of his sovereign, established efficient military garrisons in the two chief towns, he permitted Ambar Rai to depart to his own country, while he himself returned to court with the rich spoils of the conquered districts. On this occasion, Nizam-ul-Mulk was confirmed in the government of all Telingana, and received the districts of Rajahmundry and Kondapilli as a personal estate.†

In the following year, or, perhaps, a little later, the country was visited by a severe famine. The wells dried up; no rain fell for two years; and the towns in consequence were nearly depopulated. During these two years no grain was sown throughout Telingana and the whole of the Bahmani dominions; and, in the third, when, as the Mohammedan historian says, the Almighty showered His mercy on the earth, scarcely any farmers remained in the country to cultivate the soil.

Not long after this appalling visitation, while the country was slowly recovering from its effects, intelligence was received at the

* Briggs's Ferishta, vol. ii. p. 491.

† Ibid., vol. ii. 492. Elphinstone, vol. ii. p. 654.

court of Mohammed Shah that the garrison of Kondapilli had mutinied. It was stated that they had murdered their governor, seized the property of his dependents, and given up the fort to Bhíma Rázu, a person who had originally been patronized by the king. When he found himself placed in possession of this important fort, Bhíma Rázu sent an embassy to the Rajah of Orissa, representing that, if he desired to recover his hereditary dominions in Telingana, this was the most favourable opportunity, because the resources of the Deckan were exhausted by two years' famine, and the Mohammedan armies were considerably reduced in number. Bhíma Rázu also promised to join him, if permitted to share in the conquests which might be made, and to retain the fort of Kondapilli. The Rajah of Orissa willingly availed himself of these offers. He collected without delay an army consisting of 10,000 horse and 8000 foot; and, having summoned a neighbouring rajah to his assistance, entered Telingana. Nizam-ul-Mulk, who had returned to Rajahmundry as the Governor of the two districts, was unable to oppose so large an army with his own insignificant resources. He shut himself up in the fort of Rajahmundry, and sent intelligence to the king of the desperate situation in which he was placed.

Mohammed Shah resolved to march against the enemy in person. Having, therefore, advanced one year's pay to his troops, he began his march with all practicable expedition. As he drew near Rajahmundry, the enemy withdrew, being apprehensive of meeting him in the open field. Bhíma Rázu retired to the fort of Kondapilli, and the Rajah of Orissa retreated to his own dominions. Indignant at the insult which had been offered to him, Mohammed Shah left his son, Prince Mahmud Khan, and his faithful prime minister and adviser, Khwaja Mahmud Gawan, at Rajahmundry, and invaded the province of Orissa. He penetrated as far as the capital, desolated the country, and collected contributions from the people. He also conceived the project of permanently occupying the province, and summoned his son and his Dewan with the object of establishing them there. The Rajah of Orissa, however, entered into negotiation with him, and succeeded in purchasing his withdrawal. The Rajah sent him a splendid embassy, and most costly presents; but the Mussulman monarch was not content with less than a gift which the Rajah prized more highly than anything else. This royal offering consisted of twenty-five elephants which belonged to his predecessor, and which he valued more than his life. The precious offering, however, was made, and the Mohammedan invader withdrew from the province.

Mohammed Shah, returning to Kondapilli, engaged in the siege of the fort. The siege lasted six months. At last Bhíma Rázu surrendered, and the Mussulman troops occupied the fort. The king, incensed at having been baffled so long, and filled with zeal for his intolerant faith, entered one of the temples, and with his own hands massacred some of the officiating Brahmins. He built a mosque on the ruins of the desolated pagoda, distributed alms, and read prayers in it; and, at the instigation of his Dewan, assumed the title of Ghazi, of which he was very proud.

Mohammed Shah remained at Rajahmundry three years after these events, settling the country and establishing military posts in it. Having expelled or reduced all the refractory Zemindars in the District, he left to prosecute his conquests towards the south. Before leaving he re-appointed Nizam-ul-Mulk governor of Rajahmundry, Kondapilli, and the surrounding country; but that nobleman, disappointed at being made governor of only a portion of Telingana and not of the whole, requested permission to follow the king, or, as expressed by the native historian, attend his stirrup; and his son, Mallik Ahmed, was appointed as his deputy in the north. The king was victorious in the ensuing campaign, and extended his conquests over the whole country of Ahmednuggar, being one of the several kingdoms which were established on the dissolution of the Bahmani dynasty. This was completed during the reign of the profligate king Mahmud, who died in 1518, though for a few years three or four princes nominally occupied the throne.*

In the early part of the sixteenth century, Krishna Ráya, the illustrious Rajah of Vizayanagar, whose memory is still venerated in the south as one of the most beneficent and intellectual of Hindu princes, invaded Orissa and penetrated as far as Cuttack, where he wedded the daughter of the Rajah, as a bond of the peace which he demanded. He had captured Kondapilli and Rajahmundry and other fortresses on his northward march, and, on conclusion of this alliance with the Rajah of Orissa, he restored to him those two strongholds, which had lately been held by the Mohammedans.†

* Briggs's Ferishta.

† Wilson's Descriptive Catalogue of the Mackenzie MSS., vol. i. p. cxlv., 296.

This event is commemorated in an inscription in the Pagoda of Simháchalam, near Vizagapatam, in which it is recorded that "the illustrious Maharajah Krishna Déva, who filled the throne of Vizayanagar, had set out to conquer the eastern country, and had subdued Udayagiri, Kondavídu, Kondapilli, Rájamahéndravaram, and other fortresses; and had come to Simhádri, where, on the 12th of Chaitra Bahula of the year Dháta, being 1438 of the Sálivάhana era, or A.D. 1516, he had presented a benefaction to the temple."*

On the death of Mahmud Shah, the governors of the several provinces threw off the slight semblance of allegiance which they had paid to the late king, and asserted their own independence. Among others, Sultan Kuli Kutb-ul-Mulk, who still outwardly continued his profession of allegiance to the shadow of royalty that remained, retained possession of the province of Telingana, of which he had been the governor, making Golconda his capital. He was originally a Turcoman soldier of fortune, and had entered the household troops of the Bahmani sovereign, in which he had distinguished himself.† During the early years of his rule he was engaged in the reduction of the neighbouring Zemindars of Telingana. It was his usual practice, when advancing into a hostile country, to feign a retreat, after having made his observations, in order to draw his enemies into an ambuscade, from which they seldom escaped. When first invited to seize on the Bahmani territory in the vicinity of his government, he refused, contenting hinself with the estates conferred on him, and aggrandizing his power by the reduction of the Hindu Zemindars alone, because they were the enemies of the Mohammedan faith. The spirit in which he conducted his warfare will be clearly seen from the following speech towards the close of his career:—"It is now," he said, "nearly sixty years since I was first engaged in spreading the banners of the faithful and reducing the infidels of Telingana from the borders of Warangole to Masulipatam and Rajahmundry, having taken between sixty and seventy forts by force of arms, such as Rajkonda, Kondapilli, Ellore, and Chicacole. I also swore by the Prophet and his descendant Ali, that, if ever I succeeded in establishing my independence, I would promote the faith of the followers of the twelve Imams in parts where the banners of the faithful had never before waved."

After he had been chosen king, one of his first exploits was the

* Carmichael's Manual of Vizagapatam, p. 350.

† Elphinstone, vol. ii. p. 662.

conquest of Sítápati, Rajah of Kammamet. Sítápati fled northward with the remnant of his followers, and took refuge with Rajah Rámchandra, son of the Rajah of Orissa, who then ruled over the whole territory extending from the sea coasts of Telingana to the confines of Bengal. The Rajah assisted him with an enormous army, which, being reinforced by the irregular levies of the principal Hindu chiefs of Telingana, is said to have amounted to 300,000 infantry and 30,000 horse. Allowing that these numbers are the result of Mohammedan exaggeration, a very considerable force must have been collected. The Mohammedans were hard pressed, and the issue of the battle was at one time doubtful; but Sultan Kuli Kutb himself, as other Mussulman sovereigns have frequently done, knelt down publicly before the assembled hosts and prayed for victory. He then led his troops forward, and, as the Persian historian says, drove the affrighted Hindus before him like a flock of timid sheep.

After this battle he captured the fort of Kondapilli. He then took Ellore, and proceeded to Rajahmundry. As he drew near this town, he received information that the enemy were lurking in great numbers among the neighbouring hills and jungles, intending to make a night attack. He encamped, therefore, on the banks of the Godavery, with the headquarters of his army, and sent detachments under his generals, Futteh Khan and Rustoom Khan, to watch the enemy, and, if possible, cut him off. A sanguinary engagement ensued, in which the Hindus lost two thousand men. The defeated army fled to the hills.

Vishwanádha Déva, Rajah of Orissa, hearing of the defeat of his son and his allies, sent an embassy to Sultan Kuli Kutb Shah, with a humble message of submission. A treaty was subsequently concluded, by which it was agreed that the river Godavery was in future to be the boundary between the Mohammedan kingdom of Telingana and the Hindu kingdom of Orissa. The seals of the King and of Vishwanádha Déva having been affixed to this treaty, the district of Ellore was placed in possession of the Mohammedans. Peace having thus been concluded, Sultan Kuli returned to Golconda.* His conquests to the west of the Godavery seem never to have been disturbed, and Ellore and the south-western portion of the Godavery District were completely subjugated and incorporated into his dominions. He reduced them

* Briggs's Ferishta, vol. iii. p. 352.

to the form of provinces, and modelled them on the same principles of internal government as prevailed till the time when they were added to the English dominions.* He was murdered in 1543, at the age of ninety, by his son and successor.

The most illustrious monarch of this house was Ibrahim Shah, who ascended the throne in 1550. He had a Hindu minister named Jaggadéva Row, whom he implicitly trusted; and most of his infantry and all his garrisons are said to have been composed of Telugu men of the same race as Jaggadéva Row's. This trusted minister, however, deserted the cause of his master and patron, and fled from his court to Berar. There he joined the army of Ráma Rázu, the mighty sovereign of Vizayanagar, and induced him to enter into a confederacy against Ibrahim Shah, with other Hindu and Mohammedan potentates. The allied armies invaded the country of Golconda, and caused Ibrahim Shah to take refuge in his capital, where they closely hemmed him in.

While the confederates were thus attacking Ibrahim Shah in the heart of his dominions, Sidrázu Timmappa, Rajah of Kondbir, considered that it afforded him a favourable opportunity for recapturing the fort of Kondapilli; while Sítápati and Vidiádri from Rajahmundry advanced to Ellore and laid siege to the fort. Dilawur Khan, Governor of Ellore, made a brave and determined defence. He repeatedly sent messengers to the king to inform him of his desperate situation, and of the straits to which he was reduced. After Ibrahim Shah had concluded peace with the confederates who had attacked him, and was free to act on the offensive again, he immediately sent a reinforcement of two thousand men to relieve Dilawur Khan, and he authorized him, when he had repulsed the besiegers, to build a fort at Nidadavólu for the better protection of the frontier. With this assistance Dilawur Khan was enabled to defeat his enemy, and he at once set to work to build the new fort according to the royal instructions which he had received.

After the construction of this fort, Dilawur Khan represented to the king the advisability of attacking Rajahmundry, which was only eight miles distant from it, and making an effort to recover it and the adjacent province. On the dissolution of the Bahmani dynasty, Vishnadéva, then Rajah of Orissa, had occupied the whole country as far as the Godavery, and had thus united under his sceptre all the

* Mr. Grant, Appendix to the Fifth Report.

ancient territories of his family from the confines of Bengal to those of Telingana. Rajahmundry was included in this reconstructed kingdom, which had hitherto proved itself strong enough to resist all attempts upon it from the Mohammedans, whenever they endeavoured to exact the tribute which had formerly been paid. At this time, however, Rajahmundry was under the government of a Reddi, who was considered to be a vassal of the Gajapati dynasty, and who was probably Vidiádri, mentioned by Ferishta; and, as he considered himself to be, in a measure, independent of his more influential relative on the throne of Orissa, his power of defence was lessened, and the province became an easier prey to Ibrahim Kutb Shah.* There were likewise disturbances in Orissa, and the country had been invaded from Bengal.† Treachery also was at work. Vatsavay Mussalee, ancestor of the Zemindars of Peddapore and then the manager of the Rajahmundry Reddi's possessions, was induced to further the ambitious projects of the Sultan Ibrahim by the promise of the farm of Himúru, which served as the foundation of more extensive acquisitions in the future.‡

The political condition of the province induced Ibrahim Shah to grant the request of the Governor of Ellore with ready alacrity. He was pleased at the opportunity now afforded of winning back the territory which had formerly belonged to the Mohammedans under the Bahmani dynasty, and of extending his conquests on the eastern coast against their former enemies in Orissa. He selected one of his most distinguished commanders named Ruffut Khan Lary, on whom he had bestowed the title of Mullik Naib, to be the commander-in-chief of the projected expedition. He directed Ruffut Khan to proceed at once to Nidadavólu with 10,000 horse, and to hold himself in readiness for an immediate advance to Rajahmundry. Alarmed at these preparations, Vidiádri and Sítápati summoned to their aid the Rajah of Kásimkóta and other Hindu chieftains in the neighbourhood. They responded cheerfully to the summons, and swelled the army at Rajahmundry by reinforcements amounting, according to the Mohammedan historian, to 100,000 infantry, 2000 horse, and 2000 musketeers. The Hindus then crossed the river and offered battle to the Mohammedans. A sanguinary engagement ensued in which the Hindus were signally defeated, and Vidiádri and Sítápati fled to Rajahmundry.

* Mr. Grant, in the Appendix to the Fifth Report.

† Elphinstone, vol. ii. p. 664.

‡ Mr. Grant, Appendix to the Fifth Report.

The Mohammedan general was not long in following up his victory. He must have crossed the river near Dowlaishweram, for the capture of that place was his first exploit after taking the offensive. It appears that he made it his headquarters during the subsequent operations, and all his heavy baggage was left there. After having made arrangements for securing the headquarters of his army at Dowlaishweram, Ruffut Khan made an attack on the fort of Tátipáka, which was in the possession of Narasinga Row, a powerful Zemindar. The fort was protected by a deep moat, and the siege occupied the Mohammedans a whole month. Emboldened by thus keeping the invaders at bay, Narasinga Row made a determined sally with 10,000 infantry and two or three thousand horse. His army was, however, defeated, and was compelled to retire into the fort; and there he was subsequently taken prisoner. When the king received intelligence of the check which his troops had received at Tátipáka, he issued directions that they were to fall back on Dowlaishweram and to remain there during the rainy season. When the monsoon was over, Tátipáka was again attacked, and on this occasion successfully. The country around Rajahmundry was reduced; but, as the Mohammedan troops were looking forward to the assault of that town, directions were received that they were to return at once to the capital in order that they might take part in the more extensive operations which were then being undertaken against Ráma Rázu, Rajah of Vizayanagar, and his confederates, and which culminated in the decisive battle of Tálikóta. This enables us to fix the date of the events above described as about A.D. 1564.

Twelve months afterwards the king again sent Ruffut Khan to Rajahmundry. His army consisted of 10,000 horse. When Ruffut Khan reached Dowlaishweram, he learned that Sítápati was busily engaged in sending reinforcements by night to the garrison at Rajahmundry from Peddapore and Rájanagaram. Ruffut Khan determined, therefore, to advance at once to Peddapore, both to attack Sítápati, and to cut off the reinforcements for Rajahmundry. On the way he encountered the Hindu army in force, and a severe battle ensued. The Hindus were completely defeated, and fled to Peddapore. The Mohammedans pursued them with promptitude, and took the fort of Peddapore by escalade. Sítápati and his family made their escape to Rájanagaram through the woods. The Mohammedans continued the pursuit on the following day; but they could not make a very rapid advance, because of the narrowness of the paths and the thickness of the jungle. They were unable to advance more than two miles a day, and they lost more than 300 men from the enemy's skirmishers. They at last succeeded in cutting their way to the fort of Rájanagaram, and in taking it. Sítápati again fled, and took refuge with Vidiádri, the Rajah of Rajahmundry, in his fort.

The Mohammedan general immediately proceeded to attack Rajahmundry. A desperate battle took place near the town. Ruffut Khan was opposed by the united forces of Vidiádri and the Rajah of Kásimkóta, amounting to 30,000 infantry, and an equal number of horse. At first the issue of the battle was doubtful. At their first onset the Hindu soldiers broke the right wing of the Mohammedan army; but the reserve of the latter coming up, the fugitives rallied, and returned to repulse the foe. The Hindu army took refuge in the fort of Rajahmundry, and Ruffut Khan laid siege to it. The siege lasted four months. At length the fire of the cumbrous artillery of the Mussulmans took effect, and a breach of nearly fifty paces was made in the curtain. The besieged then sent a flag of truce. An offer of surrender was made through Yellu Pandit, one of the Hindu accountants in the Mussulman army, who was permitted for this purpose to enter the fort. The conditions were, that Vidiádri and Sítápati might be permitted to go wherever they pleased with their families. This being granted the fort was surrendered, and Vidiádri proceeded to Kásimkóta and Sítápati to Vizayanagar. This event took place in A.H. 979 or A.D. 1571–72, and the following sentence in Persian commemorates the date: "The temple of the infidels has fallen into our hands."*

On the fall of Rajahmundry, the king sent instructions to Ruffut Khan to continue his victorious progress, and to march forthwith to Kásimkóta, the Rajah of which place had, by his assistance, so materially aided in the defence of Rajahmundry. The general, instead of taking the more practicable route by the sea-coast, kept inland, and probably followed the direction of the present high road. On the way he encountered the Hindu army again, and another battle took place. Twenty thousand Hindus under Ven-

* Briggs's Ferishta, vol. iii. p. 423. I have also in my possession a Telugu distich, in which the date of this siege is given as the 5th of Áshádha Shuddha in the year Ángirasa, being 1495 of the Sálirábana era, or A.D. 1572. See Mr. C. P. Brown's Carnatic Chronology, p. 66.

kata Rázu opposed his progress; but they were defeated. After he had spent some time in reducing various forts in the country round Rajahmundry and Kásimkóta, he proceeded to attack Vizayanádha Déva, the Rajah of Orissa, whom he overcame, and reduced to accept his own terms of peace. Ruffut Khan then returned to his headquarters at Rajahmundry. All the territory on the coast which had been recovered by the Hindus during the confusion that ensued on the disintegration of the Bahmani dynasty had been conquered, and the country from Masulipatam to Orissa had been brought again under the dominion of the Mohammedan king.

In the reign of Mohammed Kuli Kutb Shah, the Rajah of Kásimkóta having died, his son, Mukanda Rázu, a youth twelve years of age, refused to continue paying tribute. He attempted to seize the Mohammedan governor, and to detain him as a prisoner. General Mir Zain-ul-Abidim Rusamdar was deputed to proceed against the youthful rebel, who had received countenance and support in his enterprise by many of the neighbouring Hindu rajahs. An obstinate, and at one time doubtful, battle took place near Rajahmundry. Shankam Rázu, Mukanda Rázu's cousin, was killed; but the Mussulmans were very nearly worsted. The fate of the day hung in suspense for a long while, but the victory was obtained by Amin Jumla Amin-ul-Mulk, who had previously taken the command, turning the flank of the Hindu army by a successful charge with a large body of cavalry which he had kept in reserve for this purpose. This was a dearly bought victory, for the Mohammedan conquerors lost a great many brave officers and men. It secured peace, however, for Mukanda Rázu fled to Kásimkóta, and, on being pursued thither, he finally abandoned the country, and took refuge in Bengal.

When the troops were withdrawn from Rajahmundry and Ellore for the prosecution of this campaign, the Reddis, who resided in the hills, and have frequently since made predatory incursions into the plains, took advantage of the opportunity thus offered them, and plundered Ellore, Nidadavólu, and Baharzalli. The inhabitants fled for security to the neighbouring jungles. A general, named Amil Khan, was sent against the marauders. Directly an organized attack was made upon them, the Reddis, who were most probably aided by the Kois, dispersed according to their usual custom, but reassembled in difficult passes and ravines. At one time 20,000 are stated to have made a stand on the banks of the river. A delay was occasioned by waiting for a supply of muskets and rockets from

Rajahmundry; but on receiving this assistance, the Mohammedans were able easily to disperse the undisciplined hordes which followed the Reddis. They rallied here and there at stockades which they had erected in the hill passes; but they were at length subdued, and tranquillity finally restored.*

The conquest of Ellore and the country west of the Godavery was complete; but the Mussulman hold on Rajahmundry and on the country to the east of the river was very insecure, and the conquest of that province was very far from complete. The island of Nagaram, in the Central Delta, for instance, is stated to have remained unsubdued by the troops of Ibrahim Shah; nor could the interior of the province be sufficiently protected from the ravages of the ejected landed proprietors, who had been driven to take refuge in the unhealthy fastnesses situated in the hills. They frequently gave trouble by predatory expeditions such as I have just described, and the Mohammedans were unable to keep them in check, because they were destitute of a sufficient standing force.†

Nevertheless, the emperors of Delhi included Rajahmundry, as far as the river, in their imperial dominions, reckoning it as part of the province of Orissa. Rajah Man Sing, the Emperor Akbar's delegate in Bengal, having partially subdued the northern portion of Orissa, included in his conquests the southern dependencies of Chicacole and Rajahmundry, valuing the latter at 125,000 rupees, and it was entered in the Ayeen Akbari as yielding that amount annually. The Mogul arms, however, did not really penetrate beyond the Chilka Lake, and the fanciful assessment of this District and Chicacole, merely serves to evince the imperfection of that famous rent-roll.‡ But whatever nominal claim the emperors of Delhi may have asserted over this District as a portion of Orissa, it really belonged to the King of Golconda, who employed a feudatory force in it to collect the revenue. This force subsisted on lands exempt from taxation, on undue exactions from inferior subjects of the State, or on plunder unscrupulously taken from the people. This desultory government, resulting from a nominal military occupation of the District, lasted for rather more than a hundred years, from 1571, when it was taken by Ibrahim Kutb Shah, to 1687, when the kingdom of Golconda was subverted by the victorious arms of the mightiest of the Mogul emperors, Aurangzib.§ Little change could,

* Briggs's Ferishta.

† Mr. James Grant, in Appendix to the Fifth Report. ‡ Ibid. § Ibid.

however, have been experienced by the unfortunate people. It was merely the exchange of the military yoke of one sovereign for that of another. Aurangzib was too busily employed during the last twenty years of his reign to visit his recently-acquired territories, and they must have been governed in a manner very similar to that employed by the kings of Golconda.

On the disintegration of the magnificent empire of Aurangzib, this District formed a portion of the province of Golconda, which was one of the two-and-twenty provinces composing the Subah of the Deckan. It was usurped by Kumr-ud-din Assuf Jah, the first and greatest of the Nizams, who fixed his capital at Hyderabad, and reigned in nominal subjection to the emperor at Delhi, but in real independence, under the title of Nizam-ul-Mulk, or the Regulator of the Kingdom. Golconda comprised the Nabobships of Arcot, Kurnool, Rajahmundry, and Chicacole. The Nizam created Anwar-ud-din, father of the well-known Mohammed Ali, Nabob of the Carnatic, Nabob of the two latter districts.* His administration was vigorous and severe. His energy was actively seconded by his subordinate, Rustum Khan, who seems chiefly to have resided at Rajahmundry. The people, however, must have looked back with longing regret to the laxer, but milder, sway of their own Reddis, or of the undisciplined mercenary forces of the kings of Golconda, if a tithe of what is related of these new rulers is true. I append an extract, referring to this reign of terror, which was written by Mr. James Grant, who was resident at Hyderabad at the commencement of the present century, and who had excellent opportunities of examining the official records there, and of making himself fully acquainted with the facts. I give the passage entire, because the curiously ironical style in which it is written would lose its force by abridgment:—

"At length the memorable battle of Shuckerkerd (A.D. 1724) gave a transient repose to the Deckan, and transferred in fact, though not in form, the sovereignty of this great limb of the Mogul Empire to Assuf Jah. Great were the benefits derived from the vigour and integrity of Rustum Khan, who, from 1732, for seven successive years, ruled, with the most ample delegated sway, Rajahmundry, with the other four more southerly provinces. There the Zemindars generally had availed themselves of the surrounding distractions on the death of Aurangzib to usurp the rights and feeble authority of

* Orme's History of Hindostan, vol. i. pp. 53, 158.

their Mohammedan superintendents. To correct these dangerous abuses, and restore the necessary forms of interior administration, were the arduous tasks assigned to this new Zillahdar; and the conduct of the man so fully justifies the Nizam's choice, that even to this day it is held up and considered by the inhabitants in general as an example worthy of imitation for necessary policy, considerate humanity, and rigid and universal justice. At the same time as the Zemindars defrauded the public treasury, they squeezed with the iron hand of oppression the industrious husbandmen and manufacturers. The first object, therefore, of Rustum Khan's government was the total extirpation of such merciless tyrants. Those who escaped the sword were proclaimed as traitors, and a reward being offered for their own, with their adherents' heads, a sufficient number was soon collected to erect two of those shocking pyramidical monuments, called Kulla-minar, near each of the provincial capitals, for one of which kind, though on a larger scale, the cruelty of Nadir is held in Europe so justly in abhorrence. The inhabitants in general feared and admired him, and the severe administration of Rustum Khan, which he now further distinguished by substituting ameens, or temporary collectors, in the room of the refractory Zemindars, was proverbial for exemplary excellence in the Northern Circars." *

The Nizam Assuf Jah died in 1748, at the advanced age of seventy-seven. He was succeeded by his second son, Nazir Jung, whose claims were disputed by his nephew, Mirzapha Jung. In this memorable contest the French and English took opposite sides. The former supported Mirzapha Jung, and the latter Nazir Jung. At first the French were victorious, and succeeded in seating their candidate on the throne of Hyderabad. Unwar-ud-din, who had been transferred a few years before from the Northern Circars to Arcot, was killed at the battle of Amboor, and his son, Mohammed Ali, was at once acknowledged by the English as the Nabob of the Carnatic, in opposition to his rival, Chunda Sahib, the friend and ally of the French (1749).

While Nazir Jung was at Arcot engaged in this harassing warfare, he sent instructions to his officers in the north to seize the French possessions at Masulipatam and Yanam. As Monsieur Dupleix felt that Masulipatam was a place of considerable importance, and that the interests of his country would suffer if he did not

* Grant, in Appendix to the Fifth Report.

make an effort to recover his position there, he despatched a small force of sepoys and French troops to recapture the factory and to take the town. This expedition was completely successful, and the French flag was again hoisted over the factories at Masulipatam and Yanam.*

Near the close of the same year, Nazir Jung was treacherously killed by one of his dependents during an attack on his camp by the French and their allies; and the French proceeded at once to install his rival, Mirzapha Jung, as Subahdar of the Deckan. A magnificent ceremonial took place at Pondicherry on the occasion of his installation in this high position, in which M. Dupleix was the principal actor. Gorgeously arrayed as a Mussulman potentate, he made obeisance to the monarch of his own creation, and in return received a declaration constituting him Governor of all the Mogul territories south of the Kistna, including Masulipatam and its dependencies.

Mirzapha Jung did not long enjoy his triumph. Taking into his service a detachment of 300 Europeans and 2000 French sepoys, under the command of Monsieur Bussy, the most eminent military genius the French ever had in India, he set out on his return to Golconda. He had not proceeded far when he was slain, while endeavouring to quell a rebellion of his troops; and M. Bussy proclaimed Salabut Jung, third son of the great Assuf Jah, as his successor. Immediately proceeding northward, the new Subahdar made a triumphal entry into his capital, Golconda, on the 2d of April 1751, and on the 18th of the following June he made a still more magnificent entry into Aurungabad, the city in which afterwards he principally resided.

After assisting Salabut Jung for some months with his sagacious counsel on military matters, M. Bussy was compelled to repair to Masulipatam for the purpose of recruiting his impaired health by a sojourn on the coast. He was not permitted, however, to enjoy for any length of time the invigorating sea-breezes which the debilitated state of his health required. The Nizam's Dewan, who had long entertained strong feelings of prejudice and dislike to M. Bussy himself, and to all of the French auxiliaries, took advantage of his absence and instituted various intrigues to drive them out of the service. M. Dupleix, perceiving that the influence of

* Orme, i. p. 146. Malleson, p. 252.

the French was declining in the councils of the Nizam, wrote to urge M. Bussy's immediate return to Aurungabad, even at the expense of his health. "Le Sieur de Bussy," he wrote with artful and plausible flattery, "was too zealous a patriot not to sacrifice even health itself for the benefit of the State." * M. Bussy at once responded to this appeal. Without a moment's hesitation he left his sea-side retreat. Though still ailing in bodily health, he hastened to Hyderabad, where his troops were waiting to receive him. Directly the rains had ceased, he proceeded to Aurungabad, a march of over 300 miles. On the approach of the French, the Dewan tendered his submission. The Nizam received M. Bussy with true Oriental splendour; and the reconciliation between them was complete. After the French officers had presented their offerings to the Nizam, M. Bussy and he came out of the princely pavilion where the interview had taken place, holding each other by the hand. Bussy assisted him to mount his elephant, and they proceeded together in state to the palace. There a royal grant was presented to Bussy bestowing upon him, on behalf of his nation, the maritime provinces which are generally known by the name of the Northern Circars, from the revenues of which the French army was henceforward to be maintained. This grant was ratified in the house of the Dewan. The terms of it were, that "the provinces of Mustaphanagar, Ellore, Rajamundrum, and Chicacole should be given for the support of the French army; that the sums which Jaffir Ali Khan, at that time governor of those provinces, might have collected before M. Bussy should be able to settle the administration of them, should be made good from the Soubah's treasury, in case Jaffir Ali Khan himself should delay or evade payment of them; and that the French troops should, as before the separation, have the guard of the Soubah's person." † The patents for these four provinces were prepared without delay, and M. Bussy sent them to M. Moracin, the French chief at Masulipatam, with instructions to take immediate possession. At the same time a force of 150 Europeans and 2500 sepoys was sent to enable him, if necessary, to enforce his authority. ‡ Thus the Godavery District passed into the possession of the French in November 1753.

The acquisition of this territory, added to that of Masulipatam and Kondavídu, which they already possessed, gave the French the

* Malleson, p. 367. † Orme, vol. i. p. 334. ‡ Malleson, p. 372.

largest dominions that had yet been acquired by any European nation in India. It made them masters of the eastern coast for a distance of 600 miles; furnished them with a magnificent revenue more than sufficient for the maintenance of their troops in the north; and placed in their power a country easy of defence against any enemy from the interior, from which it was separated by an irregular chain of mountains, and, in most parts, by impenetrable forests.

Jaffir Ali Khan, Governor of the four ceded provinces, determined to resist the French, and, if possible, to prevent their taking possession. Finding that Gajapati Vizayaráma Rázu, Rajah of Vizayanagaram, the most influential landholder in the province of Chicacole, with whom he was then at war, was of the same disposition, he made peace with him, and they both united their forces to offer a combined opposition to the French; but M. Moracin bribed Vizayaráma Rázu to desert the cause by proposing to lease the provinces of Rajahmundry and Chicacole to him at a favourable rent. Jaffir Ali Khan, finding himself so speedily and easily deserted by his recent ally, immediately quitted the country. Meeting a party of Mahrattas as he was proceeding towards the west, he induced them to join him, and to make an incursion into the territories which he had just left. Guided across the mountains by a dispossessed and discontented Polygar, he re-entered the country, through unfrequented passes, with his marauding band; attacked the Rajah of Vizayanagaram near his capital; passed through the lower part of the province of Chicacole and the province of Rajahmundry, plundering as he went; and, finally, quitted this District by the town of Ellore.

Directly he heard of this rapid, but calamitous, incursion, M. Bussy came from Hyderabad to Masulipatam with the object of assisting in the settlement of the ceded provinces. In August he proceeded to Rajahmundry, as better adapted for that purpose, owing to its central position. The French were now the acknowledged rulers of these provinces without a rival or competitor, for the Mahrattas, satisfied with the plunder they had gained, showed no further inclination to assist Jaffir Ali Khan in the recovery of his government, and that astute courtier, convinced of the present futility of his designs, had proceeded to Aurungabad to make his submission to the Nizam.*

* Orme, vol. i. p. 374.

Meanwhile, the French Government had recalled M. Dupleix, and had sent out M. Godheu, as commissioner, to treat with the English. M. Godheu arrived at Pondicherry in August, and assumed charge of the French possessions. A provisional treaty was entered into between him and Mr. Saunders, the Governor of Madras, which was referred to Europe for the confirmation of the Governments of their respective nations. It is beside the object of this work to enter into the details of this and similar treaties, and it is proposed to refer to them only so far as they concern the history of this District. Among other provisions in this treaty, it was stipulated that each nation was to possess four or five subordinate factories, or simple houses of trade, in the provinces of Rajahmundry and Chicacole. The following are the clauses which relate to the Godavery District :—

"The navigation of Nursapore river shall be free. The English may carry their settlement upon the banks of the said river or keep Bandermalunka, but they shall possess only one of those two places. The French shall have a settlement on the same river. The districts shall be equal between the two nations.

"The entrance of Ingeram river shall be free; neither the French nor the English shall possess the islands of Coringe and Yellacatipa. The English shall have their factory at Suncrapollam with its districts, and a warehouse at Nellepelly, the fortifications of which shall be razed.

"The French shall have their factory at Yanam with districts equal to those of Suncrapollam, and they shall be at liberty to have a warehouse on *terra firma* in case they judge it necessary for the convenience and ease of their trading business." *

It was agreed on both sides that the provisions of this treaty were not to be definitively binding; but were to be the basis of a truce which was to continue until they were confirmed and ratified in England and in France.

Bussy received the same powers from M. Godheu as had been granted to him by M. Dupleix; and he remained till the end of the year in the newly-acquired provinces, which, according to the tenth article of the above treaty, were to remain for the present in possession of the French. He was engaged in settling the government, and was constantly employed in petty warfare with the hill

* Aitchison's Collection of Treaties, Engagements, and Sunnuds, vol. v. p. 187.

Zemindars, who would never pay the tribute imposed on them except at the point of the sword. He sometimes accompanied the expeditions which he was compelled to send against these refractory chiefs.*

This is, perhaps, the most appropriate place in which the French administration of the Northern Circars under Bussy can be reviewed; and the following extract from Mr. James Grant's Report, which has already been quoted, will give the best idea of the impression which it made on the courtiers of the Nizam :—"This able politician and commander found himself under the necessity, but always with true civilized humanity, of going over the same ground with the best of his Mohammedan predecessors in re-establishing order and the indubitable rights of Eastern sovereignty. Zemindars were as usual dismissed from their employments, but generally permitted to enjoy, under French sunnuds, their *russums* and *saverams*, or conditional hereditary privileges; and there are more instances of new creations than total extirpation of the necessary officers of Government. The union of these several possessions under one head appeared the most eligible system of administration, and Vizayaráma Rázu rendered himself the most useful and acceptable man to act in the capacity of chief." The revenue had hitherto been very much understated, and the Mohammedan rulers appear to have collected what they considered to be due to them without any system or order. The French made some effort after system. "A complete survey and *hustabood*, or detailed account of the gross collections of the whole country, were formed, and put M. Bussy in the knowledge of resources entirely beyond the reach of his Mohammedan predecessors, and greatly exceeding, perhaps, the general belief of modern financiers. But moderation was necessary. The *jummabundy* or annual settlement was, therefore, only doubled in Chicacole and Rajahmundry. Besides which, as a temporary expedient, the Zemindars were bound to maintain the public peace; defray all charges of collections; and keep on foot a *Sibbundy* corps of 12,000 infantry, which, over and above the ordinary services of preserving the three yearly crops, or enforcing their equal division between Government and the tenants, were liable to be called on to repel any invading foe. All this, however, we believe to have been only the first step towards establishing a more adequate *jumma kaumil*, or revenue stan-

* Orme, vol. i. p. 404.

dard." Mr. Grant concludes his estimate of M. Bussy's financial arrangements with the statement that he did not desire to exact a larger amount of revenue than was sufficient to carry on his government. "Nothing," he adds in a style of curious satirical grandiloquence, "nothing beyond a splendid family subsistence, with just such a surplus of income as might serve to support official dignity, consequential appearance, personal pre-eminence, and gentility. This we believe would have been the equitable result of M. Bussy's system of finance, if he had been allowed to complete it."

The brief administration of the Northern Circars by the French reflected much credit on M. Bussy; and it may confidently be asserted that, if these provinces had remained much longer under his command, he would have distinguished himself as greatly as an administrator as he had as a general. He seems to have exerted himself to the utmost to establish a regular form of government without violently subverting the system of the Mohammedan rulers, but skilfully adapting it to his own purposes. He endeavoured to effect something approaching a regular revenue settlement, and to introduce an equitable administration of justice. It is doubtful, however, whether the continued possession of the country by the French would have been advantageous to the people. They become more speedily Orientalized than the English. They would have amalgamated more readily with the natives, and, perhaps, have sympathized more fully with them; but it is not likely that they would have exhibited the impartiality, the unimpeachable integrity, and the earnest desire for the good of the people, which have characterized the English administration in this province as well as in other parts of India.

CHAPTER XII.

EXPULSION OF THE FRENCH.

BRILLIANT SERVICES RENDERED BY BUSSY TO THE NIZAM—HIS RECALL BY LALLY—EXPEDITION FROM BENGAL—BATTLE OF CONDORE—ADVANCE TO MASULIPATAM—DEFEAT OF THE FRENCH—CESSION OF THE NORTHERN CIRCARS TO THE ENGLISH.

AT the beginning of the following year, Monsieur Bussy returned to Hyderabad, where Salabut Jung was collecting his forces for an advance on Mysore. Thither Bussy accompanied him, and marched with him as far as Seringapatam, where a treaty was dictated to the Mysoreans under the very walls of their capital. Next year this indefatigable soldier gave Salabut Jung his invaluable assistance against the Mahrattas and against the Nabob of Savanore. The Nizam, however, entertained no feelings of gratitude towards him. Notwithstanding his brilliant services, Salabut Jung was induced, principally by the intrigues of Jaffir Ali Khan, the late Nabob of Rajahmundry, to dismiss him and his brave French contingent. This took place in July 1756. As they were advancing towards Masulipatam after this ungracious dismissal, they were closely beset by the enemy, and Bussy resolved to make a determined stand at Hyderabad. Posting his brave little army in the summer palace and garden of Charmaul, he made a vigorous resistance. For fully six weeks he kept the enemy at bay. At the end of that time he was relieved by M. Law, who had been sent to his assistance with troops from Pondicherry and Masulipatam. A reconciliation ensued between Bussy and Salabut Jung, and among the first to make submission was his old enemy, Jaffir Ali Khan.

Having re-established his influence at the Court of the Nizam, he thought it time to retrace his steps to the provinces now belonging to his nation. His presence was required there to quell disturbances, and to complete the establishment of the government. He commenced his march on the 16th of November, and took with him an army of 500 French soldiers and 4000 sepoys.* He arrived at Rajahmundry on the 19th of December, having taken the route by Bezwada and Ellore. M. Bussy had recently raised a nobleman, named Ibrahim Khan, to the government of Rajahmundry and Chicacole; but Ibrahim had deserted his cause during the trying period of the siege of Charmaul, and now, dreading his resentment, quitted the country at his approach. Vizayaráma Rázu, however, who had adhered faithfully to him, came to meet and welcome him, accompanied by several other chiefs and landholders. Taking this influential chieftain in his train, Bussy proceeded to the north, and was engaged for some months in petty warfare in the province of Chicacole. During this campaign the tragical siege of Bobbili occurred, which still lives in the traditions and in the ballads of the people. He returned to Rajahmundry at the end of 1757.†

During Bussy's absence in the north, about the time that the battle of Plassey was fought, the French garrison of Rajahmundry, reinforced by troops from Masulipatam, took the three English factories at Madapollam, Bendamúrlanka, and Injaram. No English garrison occupied these places, with the exception of a party of twenty men at Injaram, and they prudently offered no opposition. The provisional treaty, to which reference has been made when describing the relative position of the French and English in this District after the departure of M. Dupleix, was little more than waste paper, and the two nations were now in open hostility against each other, the Seven Years' War having broken out in Europe during the previous year. The capture of these factories must have been for the time a serious blow to the English interests in this District, as they annually furnished 700 bales of excellent cloth for the Company's market in England.‡

Bussy's absence was severely felt at the Court of the Nizam. His enemies now obtained the opportunity they had long desired to weaken his influence over the mind of that irresolute potentate, from whom one of his brothers, named Nizam Ali, had succeeded by the exercise of skilful intrigue in obtaining all real authority and power. When the tidings of these events reached Bussy, he hastened from Rajahmundry to the assistance of Salabut Jung with all his available force. His little army consisted of 700 Frenchmen and 5000 sepoys, with ten field-pieces; and they performed the

* Malleson, p. 486.

† Orme, vol. ii. pp. 253-63.

‡ Ibid., vol. ii. p. 261.

march from Rajahmundry to Aurungabad in the incredibly short space of twenty-one days. They proceeded to Ellore, and thence across country by a route never before attempted by European troops. This was one of the finest marches on record in India. It extended nearly along the entire length of the Godavery, Aurungabad being situated not much farther from the source of that river than Rajahmundry is from its mouths.

Bussy's tact and influence, and the salutary fear inspired by the presence of the French army, restored Salabut Jung to all his former power. At this critical juncture, however, Bussy was summoned to the Carnatic by M. Lally, the new Governor-General of the French possessions; and in obedience to this mandate, he proceeded with his army to the neighbourhood of Masulipatam. At Réyúru, on the Kistna, on August 3, 1758, he delivered over the command of the troops and the government of the Northern Provinces to the Marquis de Conflans, who had been nominated his successor, and went at once to join Lally in the Carnatic. No step could have been more inopportune or more ruinously fatal to the interests of the French in the Deckan and in the Northern Circars. Great as an administrator, and still greater as a soldier, Bussy had been the life and soul of the French cause. His removal was an irreparable blow.

His departure from the Northern Circars was the signal for a revolt against the government of the French. Vizayaráma Rázu, Rajah of Vizayanagaram, the faithful ally of the French, was assassinated at the siege of Bobbili, and was succeeded by a cousin, named Ananda Rázu. Ananda Rázu felt much dissatisfied at the arrangements which M. Bussy had made at the time of his predecessor's decease. As soon, therefore, as the French general had left for Aurungabad, he took Vizagapatam, and made overtures to the English at Calcutta and Madras, offering to render them every assistance in his power if they would send an expedition to invade the Northern Circars. Clive, who was then in Bengal, favourably entertained the Rajah's proposals contrary to the opinion of his whole Council, and they were supported by the representations of Mr. Bristol, who had been Agent at Cuttack, but had lately gone thence to Injaram. An expedition was at once arranged, and the command of it conferred on Colonel Forde. His army consisted of 500 Europeans, including artillerymen, 2000 sepoys, and 100 Lascars.

This armament reached Vizagapatam on October 20, 1758. The town of Vizagapatam had been surrendered to Mr. Johnstone, the

English representative, on the 12th of the previous month. The English force marched from Vizagapatam on November the 1st; joined the Rajah at Kásimkóta; and, in conjunction with him, advanced to meet the French, who had assembled in force at Rajahmundry for the purpose of making an attack on the Rajah. Some delay, however, occurred, owing to the difficulty of entering into satisfactory arrangements with Ananda Rázu. Mr. Andrews, who had formerly been the Chief at Madapollam, had been sent from Madras to re-establish the factory at Vizagapatam; and he hastened to join the army for the purpose of conducting the negotiations, and he succeeded in obtaining a treaty, in which it was agreed that "all the countries which might be conquered should be delivered to the Rajah, who was to collect the revenues; but that the seaports, and the towns at the mouths of the rivers, should belong to the Company, with the revenues of the Districts annexed to them; that no treaty for the disposal or restitution, whether of the Rajah's or the English possessions, should be made without the consent of both parties; that the Rajah should supply 50,000 rupees a month for the expenses of the army, and 6000 for the particular expenses of the officers." *

Satisfactory arrangements having thus been made, the army continued its advance. On the 3d of December it came in sight of the enemy, who was encamped at Gollaprólu, a village near the fort of Pittapore, about forty miles from Rajahmundry. His force consisted of 500 Europeans, 6000 sepoys, and a great number of the local troops, of which 500 were cavalry. The whole were under the command of M. Conflans. On the 6th, the English occupied the village of Chambole (Chébólu), four miles from the enemy; but the commander of each army, considering his forces too securely posted to hazard an advance, remained stationary for three days. Colonel Forde then came to the determination that an effort had better be made to outflank the enemy by a movement to his right, and, skirting the low hills in that direction, to regain the road to Rajahmundry in the rear of the French, where the ground was unsuited for cavalry. This movement was commenced very early in the morning of the 9th. The village of Condore (Chandurti), near the foot of the hills, three miles from Chambole, was reached by eight o'clock. The English army was still four miles from the French camp; but it had now better ground to manœuvre on, and midway there was

* Orme, vol. ii. p. 376. Cambridge's Account of the War in India, 2d edition, 1762, p. 268.

a village, which, it was hoped, would afford a strong advanced post. Imagining that the object of Colonel Forde's movement was to obtain possession of this village, M. Conflans crossed the plain with his army to anticipate him. Colonel Forde, however, remained where he was, with the intention of regulating his own movements by those of the enemy. M. Conflans supposed that this inaction was a sign of conscious weakness, and that the English were about to return to their encampment at Chambole; and he caused his whole army to form line and advance. This onward movement of the French was performed in great haste and in much disorder. The two armies were now brought face to face. The way in which they were drawn up was very similar. The Europeans in the centre with the artillery on their flanks, and the sepoys on either wing, the Rajah's troops on the English side being some distance behind and beyond the flanks of the sepoy battalions.

The English advanced in steady order under a heavy fire from the French. The French, on the other hand, bounded forward with all their national impetuosity, outmarching their artillery. A mile from Condore, Colonel Forde halted to prepare for action. At that moment the whole of the European battalion was behind a field of lofty Indian corn, by which it was entirely concealed; while the sepoys on either flank were fully exposed on the plain. The French, dashing forward with spirit, outflanked the English sepoys on both sides, and their Europeans, instead of advancing straight forward towards the centre, where they might have imagined the English battalion would be, inclined to the right, and encountered the sepoys of the English left flank, whom they mistook for European troops. Finding themselves outflanked and unable to withstand the impetuous advance of the French, the sepoys turned and fled, eagerly pursued by the enemy's horse. The French were preparing to pursue them and to follow up their supposed victory, when they saw a line of men, with shouldered arms, marching in firm and steady array, from behind the field of Indian corn. This was the English battalion quietly advancing to occupy the ground which the sepoys had just abandoned. The French vainly attempted to reform their broken line; but they were unable to withstand the rapid fire of the English infantry, and fled precipitately to regain their guns, which had been left half a mile in the rear.

The eagerness of the victors to pursue was so great that they were unable to keep their ranks, with the exception of one division, which was made to advance in a steady and orderly manner, so as to form a reserve, in case the too hasty pursuit of the others should end in their being discomfited, as their opponents had been at the first. They went straight at the guns, where the French had rallied, and had reformed their broken ranks. At the first discharge of the artillery, Captain Adnet, who commanded the Europeans, fell mortally wounded. His men rushed on, drove the enemy from the guns, and, as each division followed up the assault with equal vigour, every gun was taken. The French retreated to their camp. The sepoys of their right wing, seeing that the Europeans who had been following them had been routed, retreated to the rear of their guns by a circuitous route, and joined their European comrades in flight. The contest was hotter on the English right. There the sepoys, under the command of Captain Knox, who subsequently distinguished himself greatly in Bengal, were at first stubbornly opposed by the enemy's sepoys. The latter, however, fell back, when the French deserted their guns, and Captain Knox and his men, with those whom he was able to rally from the scattered fragments of the left wing, were set free to follow the pursuit.

So soon as the necessary dispositions could be made, Colonel Forde advanced to attack the enemy's camp. At first it appeared most probable that the French would make a determined stand in defence; but, just as the English drew near and their guns came within range, the French abandoned their position, and fled in the wildest confusion. Thirty pieces of cannon were taken, together with the camp equipage and ammunition; but the treasure had previously been sent away and secured. Six French officers and seventy men were killed in this engagement, and about the same number were taken prisoners; while one officer and fifteen men were killed on the English side, and a few were wounded. M. Conflans, the French commander, galloped all the way from the field of battle to Rajahmundry, where he arrived before midnight, though the distance was fully forty miles. This was the most important battle fought in this District. The ultimate result of it was the release of the Northern Circars from French dominion, which, brief though it was, left such an impression that, even so late as 1857, when an incursion of Rohillas from the Nizam's country was apprehended, the current rumour among the people was that a French army was coming over the border.*

* The 1st Madras Fusiliers, now 102d Regiment of the Line, bears the name of

The French army, discomfited and dispirited, fled to Rajahmundry. Colonel Forde at once sent forward 1500 sepoys to occupy that town. They arrived there at daybreak the following morning. The French, imagining that they constituted the whole of the pursuing army, instead of being only its advanced guard, immediately abandoned the fort, which was of no great strength. One boat laden with several Europeans was in the middle of the stream, and some others with a few small field-pieces had just reached the opposite bank, when the English arrived. The sepoys opened an ineffectual fire on them from the walls of the fort, which deterred them from carrying off these pieces or remaining in the vicinity. Fifteen Europeans were taken prisoners within the fort, with a quantity of ammunition and stores.

Colonel Forde arrived soon afterwards with the remainder of the army; but the Rajah and his forces, which had really taken no part in the engagement, lingered in listless apathy near the battle-field. The English army crossed the river on the 23d, with the object of following the French at once, and taking advantage of the recent victory. The Rajah, however, could not understand the wisdom of this energetic action. He had failed to pay the portion of the subsidy which he had promised to give on the fort of Rajahmundry being placed in his possession; and Colonel Forde, much to his disgust and chagrin, was compelled to relinquish the pursuit and to recross the river. The Rajah, supposing that Colonel Forde had returned to take vengeance on him, fled to the neighbouring hills, probably in the direction of Rampa; and the English commander was obliged to retrace his steps as far as Pedda-

this victory on its colours. With reference to this, Captain Broome, in his "History of the Rise and Progress of the Bengal Army, 1851," remarks that, although this distinction was awarded to it, only one officer, and not a single man belonging to it was present in the engagement (p. 220). On the other hand, the author of "The Historical Record of the First Madras European Regiment" (London: Smith, Elder, & Co., 1843, p. 147), who states that he compiled his work from the old official and regimental records, asserts that the regiment was engaged in this battle. No records are to be found in the India Office old enough to verify either assertion; but the very fact of the name of this battle being emblazoned on its colours is in itself the strongest proof that the regiment was engaged, and it is most improbable that the Madras Government would have perpetuated an error by saying in G.O.G., No. 48, dated March 12, 1841, which was republished by the Government of India on the regiment's leaving the country in 1870, that "it greatly distinguished itself at Condore under Colonel Forde in December 1758."

pore, in order to keep open his communications with Vizagapatam. Mr. Andrews, who had returned thither, was sent back for the purpose of negotiating with the Rajah, whom he visited in his retreat among the hills. The Rajah was mollified by Mr. Andrews' representations, and was induced to rejoin the English camp at Peddapore. The treaty was in some points altered to terms more favourable to his interests, and it was agreed that "whatsoever sums he might furnish should be considered as a loan; and that the revenues of all the countries which might be reduced on the other side of the Godavery, excepting such as belonged to the French, either by establishment or grant in propriety, should be equally divided between him and the English." *

At length, after the loss of much valuable time, the army moved from Peddapore on the 28th of January, and reached Ellore on the 6th of the following month. The Rajah, however, lingered on the way, occupying himself by levying contributions from the surrounding country. During the interval which elapsed while waiting for him, Colonel Forde sent Captain Knox with a battalion of sepoys to take the French factory at Nursapore, where there was a garrison of 100 Europeans and 300 or 400 sepoys. The Zemindar of this District, probably the Rajah of Mogulturru, which is close to Nursapore, was invited to join the expedition; and he heartily responded to the invitation, met Captain Knox on the march, and rendered him every assistance in his power. The French had relied on the Zemindar's help, and, on finding it fail them, they quitted the factory, after having sunk in the river all the ammunition which they could not carry away. Leaving a few men to take charge of the factory, Captain Knox returned to Ellore, where the Rajah of Vizayanagaram was still detaining the army by his dilatory conduct.

Meanwhile, at the earnest request of M. Conflans, Salabut Jung had advanced to his assistance, and was approaching by the valley of the Kistna. Undeterred by the advent of this more numerous army, Colonel Forde marched straight to Masulipatam, and, after a siege which lasted just one month, carried the fort by a brilliant assault. On the 14th of May he concluded a treaty with Salabut Jung, who, awed by the English success, and harassed by disputes with his brother, was glad to retrace his steps to Hyderabad. The following were the stipulations of this treaty, by which a consider-

* Orme, vol. ii. p. 473.

able territory around Masulipatam came into the possession of the English :—

"A COPY of REQUESTS made by Colonel Forde to Nawab Salabut Jung, and his compliance thereto, in his own hand :

"The whole of the Circar of Masulipatam, with eight Districts, as well as the Circar of Nizampatam, and the districts of Condavir and Wacalmanuer, shall be given to the English Company as an enam (or free gift), and the Sunnuds granted to them in the same manner as was done to the French.

"The Nawab Salabut Jung will oblige the French troops which are in his country to pass the river Ganges (the Godavery) within fifteen days, or send them to Pondicherry, or to any other place out of the Deccan country, on the other side of the river Kistna; in future he will not suffer them to have a settlement in this country on any account whatsoever, nor keep them in his service, nor assist them, nor call them to his assistance.

"In all cases the Nawab will not assist the enemies of the English, nor give them protection.

"The English Company, on their part, will not assist the Nawab's enemies, nor give them protection.

"*Dated Moon Ramadan the 16th, Hegira* 1172, *which is the 14th of May* 1759." *

Colonel Forde's brilliant successes had not been without fruit. By this important treaty the French lost all their possessions in the Northern Circars, and never regained them.

Little more remained to be done against the French. The sick and wounded of Colonel Forde's army had been left at Rajahmundry, under the command of Mr. Bristol. He was also in charge of some treasure which had been received from Bengal. A small French force, which M. Conflans had named his "army of observation," had been watching, at a safe and convenient distance, the movements of the English commander; and, directly he proceeded to Masulipatam, it made a dash at Rajahmundry, and easily recaptured the fort. Mr. Bristol, hearing of its approach, sent his

* Aitchison's Collection of Treaties; vol. v. p. 11.

treasure to Cocanada, which was then in the possession of the Dutch, and ordered such of his men as were able to march direct to Vizagapatam. The French pursued the latter a short distance, but soon gave up the pursuit, and returned to join the army of Salabut Jung.

Colonel Forde remained with his victorious army at Masulipatam until the month of October, when he sailed for Calcutta. On the 11th of November, M. Moracin, who had been sent from the south with reinforcements for Masulipatam, but, on hearing of the fall of the fort, had gone on to Ganjam, landed at Cocanada with a small French force. Jaggapati Rázu, a relative of Ananda Rázu, who was then in possession of that part of the country, moved by enmity against his cousin, took the side of the French, when Ananda Rázu invited the assistance of the English. After the victory at Condore, where he had fought on the French side, Colonel Forde bestowed his territory on Ananda Rázu, who, however, had not attempted to take possession, and Jaggapati Rázu still continued in arms on the east of the Godavery, and entered into correspondence with Mr. Andrews, now the chief of the English factory which had been re-established at Masulipatam. M. Moracin, on his landing at Cocanada, sent agents to Samulcotta, where he had a fort, and to his camp, with the hope of entering into negotiations with him. They were, however, unsuccessful; and M. Moracin, discouraged by the desertions of some of his men, and by want of provisions for the remainder, was compelled to re-embark and set sail for Pondicherry.

In the following month another small French force came from Ganjam, under the command of the Chevalier Poete, who landed 50 Europeans and 100 sepoys at Cocanada, with the object of entering into negotiation with Jaggapati Rázu. Meanwhile, the army at Masulipatam, which had been considerably reduced by disease and desertion among the Europeans, and by the departure of many of the sepoys to their homes, had started on its return march to Bengal. Captain Fischer had succeeded Colonel Forde in the command. On his arrival at Rajahmundry, he heard that the French detachment had landed at Cocanada, and he proceeded thither at once. He found the French posted in a village two miles from the Dutch fort. They did not wait to be attacked, but precipitately ran to the factory, into which they were admitted by the Dutch. They were eagerly pursued by the English, who invested the factory, and demanded the surrender of the fugitives. On the following day the Dutch surrendered them under protest. Those of the French troops who had not been disembarked sailed with the Chevalier Poete for Pondicherry. The English army marched from Cocanada to Vizagapatam, whence the European portion of it sailed for Calcutta, while the sepoys continued their march thither by land. Thus ended this short but decisive campaign. The whole of the Northern Circars had been freed from French dominion in the space of a few months, and had reverted to the government of the Nizam, with the exception of Masulipatam and its dependencies, which were retained by the English East India Company.

The weak and irresolute Nizam was left completely paralyzed by the withdrawal of his French allies. Two years afterwards, in 1761, he was deposed by his younger and more energetic brother, Nizam Ali, who had for some time previously given him incessant anxiety by his turbulent and rebellious conduct. After his usurpation of the throne at Hyderabad, the English Government at Madras entered into negotiation with Nizam Ali, with the object of obtaining possession of the Northern Circars. At one stage in these negotiations it was proposed that the East India Company should rent from him the whole of the provinces on the terms of a division of profits. Nizam Ali at first consented, then retracted, and finally all negotiation was broken off, and the provinces were leased to Hussain Ali Khan, to whom they had been let on lease after the French occupation had ceased. The authority of Hussain Ali Khan was, however, little more than nominal, and the English Government entered into an engagement to establish it by force of arms. Some troops were despatched to the Northern Circars for this purpose; but most of those destined for the service were detained in the Carnatic by the invasion of Nizam Ali, who retreated, however, when he discovered that he would be opposed by the English as well as by his nominal opponent, the Nabob of the Carnatic.

One instance of daring at this time deserves to be recorded. Lieutenant, afterwards Sir Henry, Cosby was sent to Rajahmundry in command of a detachment consisting of 200 sepoys and 12 artillerymen to assist Hussain Ali Khan in maintaining his authority. There were at the time rival claimants for the position of Nabob, and considerable jealousy was entertained of the influence of the English. A near relative of one of the claimants was commandant of the fort at Rajahmundry, with 500 Arabs under him, ready for any mischief. He had entered into a conspiracy to take the town and hold it for his relative. Lieutenant Cosby acted with promptitude and vigour. Directly he heard of the plot, he went with his sepoys to the commandant's residence, took him prisoner, and effectually defeated his designs. Mr. Pybus, the Chief of Masulipatam, on hearing of this, immediately sent reinforcements; and, when the country was shortly afterwards ceded, Lieutenant Cosby was the first to hoist the English colours on the fort of Rajahmundry.*

Meanwhile, Lord Clive had returned from England to perform the last services he was to render to his country in India. At the representation of the Government of Madras, he entered into negotiation for the cession of the Northern Circars; and, on August 12, 1765, he received a grant for them from the Emperor of Delhi on the same occasion as he received the virtual sovereignty of Bengal, Orissa, and Behar.

The Madras Government hesitated to avail themselves at once of this imperial grant, alleging that there was no immediate necessity for taking possession, as Hussain Ali Khan had realized the revenues by their help, and that but little more could be obtained that year. In the following March, however, they published the Emperor's Firman, and sent General Calliaud to the Northern Circars to take possession. On hearing of this, the Nizam threatened to retaliate by invading the Carnatic, on which the Government, imagining that it was the best policy to temporize, directed General Calliaud to proceed to Hyderabad, and there to enter into negotiation with the Nizam. A treaty was concluded with that potentate, in which, curious to say, no reference was made to the Emperor's Firman. The Nizam agreed in this treaty to place in possession of the East India Company the whole of the Northern Circars, with the exception of the Circar of Moortizanugger or Guntoor, which had been granted for life to his brother, Basalat Jung, on condition of their paying him a large tribute, and affording him military assistance whenever required. The following is the portion of this treaty by which the present Godavery District, then situated in the Circars of Rajahmundry and Ellore, was made over to the Company, dated November 12, 1766:—

Treaty with the Nizam.

"The Honourable English East India Company, in return for the

* East India Military Calendar. London, 1823, p. 2.

gracious favours received from his Highness, consisting of Sunnuds for the five Circars of Ellore, Siccacole, Rajahmundry, Moostafurnugger, and Moortizanugger, expressing the free gift thereof on them and their heirs for ever and ever, do hereby promise and engage to have a body of their troops ready to settle the affairs of his Highness's government in everything that is right and proper, whenever required.

"The Honourable English East India Company do further engage and promise that, in whatever year the assistance of their troops shall not be required, they will pay to His Highness, as a consideration for the free gift of the above-mentioned five Circars, for ever and ever, the following sums, by kists, as specified in the 8th Article of this Treaty, viz., for the three Circars of Rajahmundry, Ellour, and Moostafurnugger, 5 lakhs of rupees; and for those of Siccacole and Moortizanugger, as soon as they are in their hands, and the settling the same is well effected, 2 lakhs each; in all 9 lakhs of rupees per annum.

"In consideration of the fidelity, attachment, and services of the aforesaid Company, and the dependence His Highness has upon them, his said Highness, out of his great favour, does hereby entirely acquit the above-mentioned Circars of all arrears and demands, down to the present date of these writings." *

Nizam Ali proved thoroughly faithless. He had entered into alliance with the English against Hyder Ali, who was by this time firmly seated on the throne of Mysore, and had made himself a too formidable neighbour of the Nizam and of the Nabob of the Carnatic. Nizam Ali, however, treacherously deserted his allies, and joined Hyder Ali against them. Alarmed at the result of the campaign which ensued, and at an expedition from Bengal which had penetrated so far as Warangole on its way to Hyderabad, he sued for peace; and a second treaty, more favourably than he could reasonably have expected, was concluded with him on February 23, 1768. The former treaty was confirmed by it, and the imperial grant of the Northern Circars to England was mentioned and acknowledged.

* Aitchison's Treaties, Engagements, and Sunnuds, p. 14.

CHAPTER XIII.

EARLY ENGLISH ADMINISTRATION.

COMMENCEMENT OF THE ENGLISH ADMINISTRATION—GENERAL CONDITION OF THE COUNTRY AT THE TIME OF THE CESSION—THE ZEMINDARS—THE HAVÉLI OR GOVERNMENT LANDS — PROVINCIAL CHIEFS AND COUNCILS—COMMITTEE OF CIRCUIT—DISTURBANCES IN PÓLAVARAM—ARREARS OF REVENUE—LAX ADMINISTRATION—ABOLITION OF THE PROVINCIAL COUNCILS.

No little difficulty was experienced by the East India Company in consolidating their authority in the Northern Circars. The government of the Nizam had hitherto been little more than nominal; the great Zemindars were turbulent and refractory; and the new officials of the Company were, from the very nature of the case, but imperfectly acquainted with the customs and feelings of the people, and with the art of governing them. It was considered advisable, therefore, to administer the government for the present in exactly the same way as it had been hitherto administered. Rajahmundry, Ellore, and Kondapilli were, under this system, continued on lease to Hussain Ali Khan, who had previously rented them from the Nizam. The authority thus conferred upon him endued him with the same magnificence as a viceroy under the English Government as he had enjoyed under the Nizam.*

Hussain Ali Khan's administration came to an end with the lapse of his lease in 1769, and the newly-acquired territory was then placed under the direct management of the servants of the Company. The agents of the old factories and their subordinates were converted into Provincial Chiefs and Councils, and Rajahmundry and Ellore were put under the Chief and Council of Masulipatam. This system of government continued in force for five-and-twenty years, and during the whole of that period the entire political, civil, and revenue administration of the Northern Circars was under the

* Fifth Report on East Indian Affairs, p. 204.

Provincial Councils established at Masulipatam, Vizagapatam, and Ganjam.

At this juncture a pause may appropriately be made to consider the general condition of the country at the time when it came into the possession of the English. The great Zemindars or land-holders come prominently into view in the foreground of the picture. These influential personages can scarcely be said to have even been in a state of subjection to the ruling power at all. The anarchy which ensued on the death of the powerful and despotic Emperor Aurangzib, the comparative weakness of the successive rulers of the Deckan, and the continual warfare which had prevailed during the period preceding the transfer to the English, had emboldened and encouraged the Zemindars to usurp almost independent power, and their position nearly resembled that of tributary chiefs. The administration of justice had become so thoroughly disorganized that, to use the strong expression employed by the Select Committee of the House of Commons in their Fifth Report, "not only the forms, but even the remembrance, of civil authority seemed to be wholly lost." *

The Zemindars were not, however, as was erroneously supposed by the English authorities on the acquisition of the country, merely tributary chieftains and the hereditary proprietors of the estates which were then in their possession. They were, on the contrary, only the agents of the ruling Mohammedan power; and though they were generally permitted to continue generation after generation in possession of their estates, they were really removable at pleasure, and were frequently punished by dismissal for acts of disobedience. They had originally been created by the Mussulman rulers to stand between themselves and the actual cultivators of the soil, in order that the heavy demands of revenue might more easily be realized. The Zemindars were, it is true, in many instances the descendants of the ancient Hindu princes who formerly ruled over the country; but the greater number were originally mere dependents of the Mussulman Government, whose revenue it was their business to collect. They had, however, become so powerful of late that they had usurped hereditary rights, and regarded themselves as the legal owners of the soil. The pretensions which they put forward very naturally misled the English authorities on assuming charge of the administration; and, although a juster view of their rights was

* Fifth Report, p. 211.

obtained after closer investigation of the matter, the English Government has acted kindly and wisely in continuing to them their privileges, when these have not been forfeited by actual oppression and misrule.

The practice was for the Zemindars to appropriate to themselves the whole of the revenue on condition of paying a certain fixed sum to the Government. Many of the Zemindars resided among the hills, and it was very difficult to approach their mountain fastnesses, when occasion required, on account of the unhealthiness of the climate, as well as on account of the almost impenetrable jungle with which they were surrounded. The chief of these hill Zemindars in the Circar of Rajahmundry were the Rajah of Pólavaram and the Mansabdar of Rampa. Others resided in the plains. The principal of these were the Rajahs of Peddapore, Pittapore, Kóta, Rámachendrapuram, and Mogulturru. Each Zemindar maintained the semblance of state. He usually resided in a mud fort of no great strength, in which his palace was situated. Whenever he went out, he was accompanied by a retinue of peons bearing matchlocks and pikes. He was generally borne in a richly-embroidered palanquin, with a curved pole in front ornamented with a silver figure-head of the sacred swan, or of some grotesque deity; or he rode on the houdah of a gorgeously caparisoned elephant. Men went before him shouting aloud his titles, as he passed through a village or drew near the house where he was about to visit. His relations and his followers accompanied him on horseback or in palanquins. Grand ceremonials took place on the occasion of a wedding, the adoption of a son, or other necessary rites. Great sums were given away in presents to Brahmins and in largesses to the multitude. Lavish expenditure required large revenues, and it was imperative that as much as possible should be squeezed from the cultivators of the soil, from whom, as in all Eastern countries, the bulk of the revenue was derived. No real care was bestowed on the welfare of the ryots and for the general good of the estate. The Zemindar's retainers were of use in assisting to collect the revenue, but were of no use in actual warfare. They were a mere Oriental rabble, externally magnificent with the tawdry finery in which the Hindu mind takes delight; but they were of no service in an engagement, as exemplified by the army of Ananda Rázu at the battle of Condore, which proved rather a hindrance than a help to Colonel Forde.

The village communities remained in exactly the same condition as they had been in from time immemorial. Each village constituted in itself a perfect whole. Unheeding the changes which may have taken place in the government above them, the cultivators of the ground quietly continued their daily avocations. They yoked their bullocks to the plough, and followed them in their uneven course. They drew the scanty supply of water from the neighbouring stream or tank, and wrangled over the precious liquid. They cast their seed in the saturated soil, and transplanted the tender sprouts of the growing paddy. They gathered in the harvest, and tended their bullocks as they trod out the grain. The simple household routine went on as quietly and swiftly then as now. The women met at the village well, and joined in the petty gossip of the day. The only excitement occurred on the occasion of some feast in their own or in a neighbouring village, or of a journey to the festival at some sacred shrine. The village shopkeeper sat cross-legged behind his store, and offered loans at an extravagant rate of interest. The village scribe and accountant was employed in writing the accounts on palm leaves, in drawing up the simple documents and bonds executed by the ryots, and in assisting the village magistrate in his rude administration of justice under the spreading branches of the village tree, where all trials were held and all business was transacted. The rent was paid by the heads of the village in money or in kind, and the villagers were seldom troubled in the smooth course of their existence, except when the Zemindar's peons might make their appearance to demand more money on the occasion of some petty warfare or some extraordinarily magnificent ceremonial in their master's household.

The whole of the land was not under the Zemindars. Some of it was under the direct management of the Government. This was usually called the Havéli land. It consisted of the household lands of the Government, and was composed of districts in the vicinity of each capital town, which were originally resumed by the Mohammedans, and had been annexed to those towns for the supply of the garrisons and of the numerous civil and military establishments.*

During the Mohammedan rule in the Northern Circars, four courts of justice were established—one being stationed at Ellore and another at Rajahmundry, in which Kazis or Mussulman judges officiated, chiefly in criminal cases. The superior officers, such as

* Fifth Report, p. 220.

the Foujdars and Amildars, reserved to themselves the infliction of càpital punishment and the disposal of serious cases.*

Such was the condition of the great Northern Province, when it came under the English rule. The system of administration which was first adopted—namely, that under provincial Chiefs and Councils, did not prove satisfactory. They were ill adapted for carrying on efficiently the work which lay before them in their twofold character of superintending and executive officers. They had to superintend the commercial affairs of the East India Company, as well as to carry out the revenue and judicial administration of the country. They were utterly unequal to the task. Few of them were acquainted with the native character. Not one knew the native language. All entrusted the management of their affairs to their confidential advisers or "dubashes," as they were called, which was a fruitful source of peculation and misrule.

The Court of Directors, when they became aware of the evils of this system, were anxiously desirous to apply a satisfactory remedy. They were of opinion that a searching inquiry should immediately be made, and directed that a Commission, or, as they called it, a Committee of Circuit, should be appointed to make the necessary investigation. They gave instructions, therefore, that "a Committee of Circuit, to be composed of five members of the Council at Fort St. George, should be appointed to inquire into the state of the Northern Circars, by ascertaining, with all possible exactness, the produce of the country, the number of inhabitants, the state of the manufactures, the fortified places, the military strength of each Rajah, Zemindar, or landholder, the expense of his household and troops, and the means he had of defraying those expenses; the gross amount of the revenues, the articles from which they arose, the mode by which they were collected, and the charges of collection." The Court at the same time intimated that they did not desire to deprive the Zemindars of their revenue, but to ensure the collection of it without recourse to violence; and they expressed their hearty determination to protect the ryots from undue oppression and exaction.

A Committee was accordingly assembled on the receipt of these instructions from the Court of Directors. Soon after it had commenced its labours, however, it was abolished by the order of Sir Thomas Rumbold, the Governor of Madras. He directed the several

* Fifth Report, p. 230.

Zemindars, with whom the Committee was about to complete a settlement, to proceed to Madras, and to make the settlement directly with himself. Sir Thomas Rumbold has been most severely censured for his conduct in this and other respects; but by a collection of documents which has recently been published by his daughter in vindication of his memory, it has been proved that he was innocent of all the accusations which have been made against his character. He informed the Court of Directors that he considered the course he was adopting necessary, because the land-holders were endeavouring to mislead the Commissioners and to baffle their inquiries; and the Court declared themselves perfectly satisfied with the measures he had adopted.

Sir Thomas Rumbold afterwards resigned his appointment. Directly he had turned his back on the shores of India, the Committee of Circuit was reconstituted, and the members of it commenced their labours afresh. They forwarded to the Government of Madras their Report on the farms and Havéli lands dependent on Masulipatam from Rajahmundry on December 18, 1786, and that on the Zemindaris on February 15, 1787. The statements of this Commission must be accepted with some degree of reserve, because the estimate made by them of the value of the land and its probable revenue was, in a great measure, hypothetical, owing to the opposition received from the Provincial Councils, to the withholding of information by the Zemindars, the village authorities, and other interested persons, and to the ignorance of Telugu on the part of the Commissioners themselves. Both Reports, however, contain a full and valuable description of the District, and give a much better view of its condition than had previously been obtained, though in some respects the statistics are not entirely reliable. No immediate action, however, was taken on these Reports of the Committee of Circuit.

Between 1785 and 1790 there were several disturbances in the Zemindaris of Pólavaram and Gútála and in the adjacent hills, which required the interference of the military authorities before they could be effectually repressed. These Zemindaris were the most ancient in the Northern Circars. Together with the Taluk of Kottapilli, which is situated on the opposite side of the Godavery, they formerly belonged to a family of Reddis. The possessions of this family were once far more extensive, and consisted of several other estates besides Pólavaram and Gútála; but they lost their

Zemindari in a dispute with the Mohammedan Government, and these two estates only were restored to them.

A Zemindar of this family named Venkatapatiráyalu Dévu married two wives, the daughter of Bhúpati Dévu, Zemindar of Kottapilli, and a daughter of Shírabhúpati, Mansabdar of Rampa. He left two sons, the name of the elder being Jagarnáda Dévu, and that of the younger Mangápati Dévu. Jagarnáda Dévu had a son named Venkatarámala Dévu, who divided the Zemindary with his uncle Mangápati Dévu, keeping Pólavaram for himself and giving Gútála to his uncle. Mangápati Dévu had two sons, the elder of whom died early, and Lakshminaráyana Dévu, who succeeded him as Zemindar of Gútála. Venkatarámala Dévu died in 1772; and, as his only son, Jagarnáda Dévu, had died before him, he was succeeded by Mangápati Dévu, the eldest son of his cousin Lakshminaráyana Dévu, whom he had adopted. Lakshminaráyana Dévu died in 1780, leaving three sons, the above-mentioned Mangápati Dévu, Narasamma, and Vizayagópála Dévu. He was succeeded by his eldest son, whose title does not appear to have been in any respect disputed, and who thus became the possessor of both the estates of Pólavaram and Gútála.

In 1781, the Taluk of Kottapilli, which had for some time been severed from Pólavaram, and managed by the Dewan of the family, was re-annexed to it, and thus Mangápati Dévu came to be considered Zemindar of the whole; but being under age, his Dewan, Sítárámayya, was the person understood to be intrusted with the management and collection of the revenue.

Lakshminaráyana Dévu had two wives, one of whom was sister of Sítárámayya, and mother of his youngest son, Vizayagópála Dévu. Using his influence as Dewan, Sítárámayya succeeded in inducing the Chief and Council at Masulipatam to recommend a division of the estates; and Mr. Daniell, the Chief, wrote a letter to Government in 1782, showing that he had in some measure acquiesced in the separation of Gútála from Pólavaram, and stating that he had taken an obligation for the revenue of the former from Sítárámayya, and an obligation for that of the latter only from Mangápati Dévu. Kottapilli was at the same time separated again in order to make a provision for Narasamma, Lakshminaráyana Dévu's second son.

In 1785 it became necessary to send troops into the Zemindaris of Pólavaram and Gútála to quell a disturbance which had arisen. Sítárámayya had apparently died before that year; and Gúragamilli

Dásureddi, a hill Poligar, whose headquarters were at a fort named Nágavaram, about fifteen miles west of Gútála, attacked Gútála under the pretext of dissatisfaction at the behaviour of the managing Dewan, captured the fort, and took the young Rajah and his mother prisoners. At the request of the Chief and Council at Masulipatam, seven companies of sepoys, under the command of Captain Hugh Montgomery, entered the territory of Gútála, and Dásureddi, immediately he heard of their approach, conveyed the Rajah and his mother to Nágavaram. On the little force marching, however, as far as Anantapalli, on the way to Nágavaram, he returned to Gútála, still detaining his hostages in custody, and refusing to deliver up the management of their territory. Captain Montgomery's detachment had retired to Kovvúru, opposite Rajahmundry, on receiving Dásureddi's assurance that he would release his prisoners; but, as he still continued his contumacious conduct, an attack was made on the fort at Gútála, and Dásureddi was surrendered by one of his own adherents, and sent as a prisoner to Masulipatam. Two sepoys were wounded, and about eighty peons killed and wounded on both sides during the siege of Gútála. During this brief campaign, the town of Kottapilli was taken by a detachment sent by Captain Montgomery from Rajahmundry, and the country rescued from the usurpation of two persons named Kónéti Tammadu and Víramallu Kannayya, who had wrested it from the youthful Rajah.*

Similar disturbances occurred in the years 1786 and 1787, when the hill-people, who were generally understood to be the adherents of Dásureddi, were driven out of the Company's territories by a detachment of sepoys. But the jealousy between Mangápati Dévu and the mother of his youngest brother, Vizayagópála Dévu, still continued. The revenue of Pólavaram, however, was paid with as much punctuality as that of any other Zemindari, while that of Gútála fell into arrears—a circumstance which rendered it necessary to put the collections of the latter on some other footing. No measure appeared more advisable than placing the two estates under a single authority. Bávájі, Mangápati Dévu's Dewan, who by his skill in government had rendered himself worthy of such a trust, was nominated Dewan to the three brothers in December 1788. During the short period of his administration, Bávájі fulfilled the expectations which he had raised; but he died in August 1790. Nara-

* MS. Records.

samma and his brother, Vizayagópála Dévu, were at Masulipatam at the time of his death, together with the mother of the latter. Mangápati Dévu was also summoned thither, and, on his arrival, the three brothers, on the representation of the Chief and Council, agreed to nominate one Chatráti Pánakálu to be their joint Dewan, under the immediate authority of Mangápati Dévu.

An apparent reconciliation had taken place between Mangápatudu and his step-mother, and all the parties were permitted to return to their estates. The latter had, however, been dissimulating; and, on her return to Gútála, usurped all authority, and collected the revenue in her son's name. The commanding officer at Rajahmundry was directed to proceed to Gútála at once with all the troops at his disposal, to take the fort, and to compel Vizayagópála Dévu's mother to reside with the others at Pólavaram. Hearing of these preparations, she escaped to the hills, and by this step converted what had seemed to be merely a family dispute into a petty rebellion against the Government. As the detachment was considered to be insufficient for the service assigned it, a company of sepoys was sent from Ellore to reinforce it. Previous to its approach, the lady had returned to Gútála, and agreed to surrender one gate of the fort. The commanding officer still considered his force insufficient to justify him in proceeding to extremities; but the peons who guarded the fort deserted their mistress; and one evening, receiving intelligence that she had concealed sixty men in one of her apartments, he entered the fort, but assured her that no one should molest her, if she kept in seclusion. She opened the doors, however, of her own accord, dragged her son into the room where her followers were concealed, in which were two large open pots of gunpowder, and threatened to destroy herself and all who were near. On the officer prudently retiring, she was pacified, and afterwards surrendered quietly. She was taken to Masulipatam, and Mangápati Dévu was acknowledged Zemindar of the united estates of Gútála and Pólavaram, according to the recommendation of the Chief and Council.*

On the 20th of June 1785 instructions were received from the Governor in Council constituting Messrs. Davidson, Oakeley, Haliburton, and Mowbray, the first members of the Board of Revenue at Madras, and they were directed to report their proceedings to Government from time to time. In accordance with these instruc-

* MS. Records.

tions general reports of the Board's proceedings and of the state of the revenue under their charge were periodically forwarded to Government, which were transmitted to the Honourable Court of Directors. These reports contain a great deal of valuable information regarding the condition of the Northern Circars as well as the other provinces of the Madras Presidency.

On taking charge of the revenues of this Presidency, they found that those of the Northern Circars had been realized for some time past by settlements made with the Zemindars and Renters from year to year, and much irregularity had prevailed, since the Zemindars had been summoned to Madras in 1778, both in the accounts and in the payment of the revenue. No distinction had been made between the arrears and the current revenue. The payments had fallen back in such a manner that the amount due each year was not discharged till the succeeding year. Thus, exclusive of the old balances which appeared to the debit of each Zemindar, a year's revenue was always in arrear. The Board at once endeavoured to set this straight, and to clear the accounts from all perplexity and confusion. They directed that the debt of each Zemindar should be made up to the previous September, and the account carried to his account as "balance;" and that henceforward he should be regularly debited in a new account for his current revenue, as the *kists*, or instalments of revenue, became due.*

They also altered the system of settlement with the Zemindars. Being persuaded that the mode which had hitherto prevailed of making, or rather extending the settlement with the Zemindars from year to year was erroneous, they directed that henceforward a new adjustment for a term of three years should be adopted, commencing with Masulipatam. The Zemindars were directed to appear in person at that town, and Mr. Floyer, Chief of Masulipatam, aided by his Council, exerted himself heartily in carrying out the proposed settlement. A considerable portion of the old balance was included in this settlement, and 12½ per cent., which had been added to the total demand in 1778, but never collected, was fully established in proportion to the abilities of the respective Zemindars to bear this assessment. Many of the Zemindars fell considerably into arrears in paying their *kists*, and it was found necessary to arm the Chief and his Council with sufficient coercive authority to enable them to col-

* General Reports of the Board of Revenue to the Honourable the Governor in Council sent Home to the Court of Directors. Madras, 1871, vol. i. p. 10.

lect the arrears, stopping short, however, of sequestering the estates of the defaulters, which extremity was reserved by Government in their own hands.*

The violent storm and inundation of the sea which occurred at Coringa in May 1786, occasioned considerable damage to the country for several miles round. Mr. Westcott, one of the members of Council at Masulipatam, was deputed to make inquiry on the spot regarding the losses which were said to have been experienced by the Zemindars, whose estates were most exposed to the ravages of the cyclone. That gentleman submitted a report showing that considerable losses had been sustained in the Zemindaris of Peddapore, Rámachandrapuram, and Kóta. The Board of Revenue were of opinion, however, that, from the conditions of their tenure, the Zemindars of these estates were not entitled to any remission of revenue in consequence of such accidental losses; but, as they had suffered materially in their collections, an indulgence with regard to the time of paying their *kists* was extended to them.†

About this time the estate of Mogalturru, near Nursapore, was taken under management. Tirapati Rázu Gáru, the Zemindar of Mogalturru, had fallen very much into arrears, and the Board had recommended that his estate should be sequestrated in satisfaction of these arrears. The Government approved of this plan; but the Chief and Council at Masulipatam persuaded him to assign his Zemindari as security for the payment of the balance due from him as well as for his current engagements, and an instrument of this nature was executed with his freewill and consent. Mr Revell was appointed to take charge of the estate while it was under management, and Bhúpayya, the Zemindar's Dewan, was employed to assist him in perfecting the revenue arrangements within a reasonable period; and, on his being permitted to return to his estate, faithfully and punctually discharged all his obligations.‡

Great difficulty having been experienced in effecting a settlement with the various Zemindars, owing to the distance which they resided from Masulipatam, it was determined that it would be advisable to summon them all to that town in order that a satisfactory settlement might be made with them. The Chief and Council at Masulipatam had been consulted as to the advisability of a per-

* General Reports of the Board of Revenue to the Honourable the Governor in Council sent Home to the Court of Directors. Madras, 1871, vol. i. pp. 10, 16, 22.

† Ibid. p. 22.

‡ Ibid. pp. 30, 33, 51.

manent settlement being made with the Zemindars, about which the Court of Directors desired to have the fullest information to enable them to decide on its practicability. The Chief and Council were of opinion that the scheme was not yet ripe. They considered that great advantages might hereafter arise from such a permanent settlement; but that the time had not yet arrived for carrying it into effect. A more regular system must be introduced by degrees before a permanent one could be established, the authority of the Government not having yet penetrated to the interior business of the various Zemindaris. They suggested that, before it would be advisable to determine on a permanent settlement, it was necessary for the ryots of the Zemindaris to acquire a habit of considering themselves more immediately dependent on Government or its representatives than they had hitherto been; and that the authority of the Zemindar himself should be better limited and defined. Having thus expressed their sentiments with regard to the establishment of a permanent settlement at this time, the Chief and Council entered very fully into the subject of temporary settlements. An annual settlement, they observed, was liable to draw the Zemindars too often from their estates, and to dissolve that bond of union between the Company and themselves which they ought to respect. They considered that, while the engagements between the Company and the Zemindars lasted for a term of three or five years, the inconveniences of a permanent, or of too short a settlement, would both be avoided; and that the Government would then have the means of introducing such reforms from time to time as the conduct of the Zemindars or their own experience and observation might render necessary, which they were persuaded could only be done by degrees as the armed forces of the Zemindaris came to be reduced, the landed rights of the people composing them abolished, and the possessors brought to accustom themselves to a different mode of life. The Zemindars and their under-renters would be restrained by a settlement for a term of three or five years from oppression of the ryots and from other irregularities.

The Chief and Council, after carefully entering into the question of the capabilities of each Zemindari, came to the decision that each Zemindar, without exception, if otherwise clear and unencumbered with debt, could afford two-thirds of the gross revenue of his estate to Government; and that the remaining third of the gross revenue would be sufficient to enable him to defray all expenses incidental to the cultivation of his estate, the collection of the revenue, and the support of himself, his family, and his relations. The Chief and Council were accordingly authorized to conclude the settlement with the several Zemindars on the above-mentioned system for three or five years, as they should find it expedient.* The only exceptions made in the Godavery District were the Zemindari of Mogalturru, which was under assignment and had been rented, and that of Pittapore, the lease of which had not expired.

The Zemindari of Mogalturru was about this time annexed to the Company's dominions, the Rajah having died without issue. Since its assignment in 1787, Mr. Revell had been administering its affairs as Collector, and exercised his office under the control of the Chief and Council at Masulipatam. He was at this time compelled to proceed on leave to England owing to ill health, and Mr. Chamier was appointed Collector in his stead, but independent of the Chief and Council, and under the immediate superintendence of the Board of Revenue. Mr. Chamier did not retain the appointment long, being promoted to the Chiefship of Vizagapatam in December 1791.

In the month of January in that year an insurrection was raised in the Zemindari by one Jagga Rázu. A detachment of sepoys was sent against him, and a trivial engagement took place, in which a few lives were lost on the part of the insurgents. Jagga Rázu himself was severely wounded and taken prisoner, and subsequently died of his wounds. Peace was restored to the district, but it was considered advisable to station a company of sepoys at Mogalturru. The cause of this disturbance was attributed to the undue influence obtained by the principal renter, Bhúpayya, who not only withheld his own rents, to the great embarrassment of the Collector, but had gained such an ascendancy over all the other renters as to occasion a similar conduct on their part. The Rajah, Kaldandi Tirapati Rázu Gáru, died on the 28th of August 1791. Previous to his decease he had adopted a very distant relative as his successor; but, contrary to the policy which now prevails, the child was not permitted to succeed, and the estate of Mogalturru was annexed to the Company's dominions, and became a portion of the Government lands

* General Reports of the Board of Revenue to the Honourable the Government in Council sent Home to the Court of Directors. Madras, 1871, vol. i. pp. 19, 30, 56.

of Masulipatam.* This and the other Government lands were again placed directly under the Chief and Council.

A severe famine desolated the Northern Circars in 1791. Every alleviation was afforded by Government by the suspension of duties on grain and on every necessary of life. Those were not the days of political economy and free trade. The Collectors were exhorted to make every exertion to discover and distribute for general consumption the grain which had been hoarded by individuals for their private advantage. Many of the poorer classes perished from starvation. Great numbers emigrated to avoid the same fate, and the decrease in the population was enormous. Agricultural operations suffered in proportion. The Government directed that their share of the grain in the Government lands under Masulipatam should be reserved for the consumption of the sepoys; but the Collector of the Northern and Centre Divisions reported the impossibility of complying with their orders owing to the extreme distress.† The Government directed that the balance which was found after all the arrears of pensions due in the Zemindaris of Masulipatam had been paid, should be applied for the relief of the poor, who were suffering from the calamities of famine. The children of the poorer families were collected together, and fed at the public expense. As might naturally have been expected, the Zemindars fell into arrears in paying their instalments of rent. Large remissions were made by the Board and Government to assist them in this time of need; their leases were extended from three to five years, wherever the lower term had been fixed; but the Government were much displeased with the Chief and Council for their inability to ascertain the exact state of the balances, and the extent to which the famine had affected the Zemindars, and this proved incapacity materially tended to smooth the way for the change of system which was then impending. The effect of the famine on the people was terrific, it was computed that one-fourth either emigrated or fell victims to want.‡

The balances due by the various Zemindars continued to be very heavy, and sufficient exertions were not made by the Chief and Council to collect them. Indeed, they openly confessed their inability to comply with the orders of the Board of Revenue and of Government to ascertain the amount of loss sustained by each Zemindar from the recent failure of the crops. Acknowledging the

* Ibid., vol. ii. pp. 81, 95, 106, 114, 127, 143. † Ibid., vol. ii. pp. 130, 145.
‡ Ibid., vol. ii. p. 143; vol. iii. pp. 2, 22, 37, 53, 73.

letter from the Board requiring them to transmit a list of the balances, with the reductions which they proposed to allow, the Chief and Council replied that this could not well be done before they found what terms the Zemindars were likely to be brought to. They vaguely thought that some Zemindaris must have suffered more than others, yet, as they had no authentic account of the losses actually sustained by each, they considered it impossible to discriminate between them in such a manner as would be thought just and impartial. The granting a greater remission to one Zemindar than to others would be the cause of very great umbrage and discontent; and, therefore, they were of opinion that an equal proportion of the outstanding balances should be granted to all the Zemindars north of the Kistna, which would be likely to occasion less discontent than any other mode of deciding the question. They proposed that a remission of one-fifth of the balances should be granted, which would prove satisfactory to all the Zemindars, and enable them to come to terms sooner than could otherwise be expected. Though not quite satisfied with this arrangement, and with the manifest supineness of the Chief and Council, the Board and Government gave their permission for one-fifth of the balances being remitted, on the understanding that the payments were to be secured before the Zemindars quitted Masulipatam, where they had been assembled for this purpose.

The Zemindars of Kóta, Rámachandrapuram, Pólavaram, Gútála, and Kottapilli, made satisfactory arrangements for the liquidation of the arrears due from them; but the Zemindars of Peddapore and Pittapore were much more difficult to deal with. The former would not consent to pay his arrears, until a threat of sequestrating his estate had been uttered by the Government, and preparations had been made to carry it into effect. The Chief and Council of Masulipatam evaded the orders from Madras, and made no secret of their endeavours to screen the delinquents from the consequences of their default. The Board animadverted with very strong, but just, severity on the backwardness and inertness of the Chief and Council. They entertained a deep conviction, they wrote, that "the protraction of the payments on the part of the Zemindars had been greatly owing to the want of proper energy and exertion in the subordinate executive authority, and that without the most decided conduct on their part, at the proper season of collection, the Company could have no adequate security for the due realization of their revenue. It is universally allowed that, to permit a Zemindar to retain in his hands collections which it is known must be made from the country, is only throwing in his way a temptation to dissipation and extravagance; and, while vague excuses are admitted in lieu of payment, it is not to be supposed he will feel the due observance of his public engagements an act requiring his serious attention. It was to eradicate the baneful effects of this ruinous system that we earnestly called on the Chief and Council to use their utmost endeavours to impress on the minds of the Zemindars the indispensable necessity of punctuality in the payment of their kists; but so far from insisting upon the regular discharge of the current revenue, we did not find, upon a reference to their Proceedings, that a single requisition had been made in writing to any Zemindar, nor any minute or remark contained in their consultations, no report of difficulties in their correspondence with us, nor any measures proposed even to obtain security for the current revenue within any reasonable period." The Board added that, if the conduct of the Chief and Council should not appear to them completely satisfactory by a fixed resolution in future to enforce the orders of Government, they would feel it incumbent on them to recommend to Government their removal from their appointments.* The above statement is given to show the inefficiency of the system of revenue administration then prevailing. The days of the Chiefs and Provincial Councils were numbered. After the careful inquiry instituted into the condition of the country by the Committee of Circuit, the Government came to the decision of abolishing them, and of dividing the country into Collectorates, the Collectors being directly responsible to the Board of Revenue at Madras. In carrying out this measure, the Government were exceedingly anxious to impress upon the Zemindars and on the people that their sole desire was their welfare, and to soothe any irritation or alarm which might be felt at the introduction of the new régime.

* General Reports of the Board of Revenue to the Hon. the Governor in Council, sent Home to the Court of Directors. Madras, 1871, vol. iii. p. 135.

CHAPTER XIV.

THE FIRST COLLECTORATES.

DIVISION OF THE NORTHERN CIRCARS INTO COLLECTORATES—FIRST DIVISION OF MASULIPATAM—THE ZEMINDARIS OF PEDDAPORE AND PITTAPORE—SECOND DIVISION—INCURSION OF BHŮPAYYA—THIRD DIVISION—DISTURBANCES IN PÓLAVARAM.

THE new system came into operation at the close of 1794. The Provincial Councils, which had continually been brought into collision with the Board of Revenue, were abolished, and Collectors were appointed throughout the Northern Circars. The present Godavery District includes what were then called the First, Second, and Third Divisions of the Masulipatam District. A small portion of the Second and Third Divisions are, perhaps, included now in the Kistna District. The First Division comprised the large Zemindaris of Peddapore and Pittapore, and extended as far as the Godavery on the south. The Collector's headquarters were at Cocanada. Mr. Matthew Tuder was appointed; but, as he died soon after his appointment, Mr. Snodgrass was really the first Collector. The Second Division comprised Undi, Tanuku, Nursapore, and all the territory formerly belonging to the Zemindari of Mogalturru. The Collector's headquarters were at the town of Mogalturru. Mr. Gambier was the first Collector. The Third Division comprised the Central Delta, Rámachandrapuram, the former Government villages near Rajahmundry, and Kórukonda, Kottapilli, Pólavaram, Gútála, and all the territory on either side of the upper part of the Godavery, extending on the west as far as Nuzvídu. The Collector's headquarters were at Rajahmundry. Mr. Branfill was the first Collector. It is proposed to give an abstract of the chief events, principally from a revenue point of view, in each of these divisions, until the introduction of the Permanent Settlement.

After the arrangements made for the liquidation of his arrears of revenue, little was heard of Jaggapati Rázu Gáru, Zemindar of Peddapore. He died in October 1797, and was succeeded by his son, Ráya Jaggapati Rázu Gáru, whom the Board of Revenue reported as in every way qualified for his high position. The Court of Directors had determined that the Zemindars under Masulipatam should be assessed at two-thirds of their gross revenue. The Board of Revenue determined, therefore, to demand that rate from the new Zemindar, calculated on the valuation of the Zemindari made by the Committee of Circuit, which they had every reason to believe had been made on a very moderate estimate. This raised the revenue to be demanded from the Zemindar from 160,000 M. pagodas to 176,935 pagodas. The document of investiture was at the same time transmitted to the Collector to be delivered to the Rajah. The Zemindar resisted this increase, and he was supported by Mr. Ince, who had succeeded Mr. Snodgrass as Collector in 1797. The reasons given by the Collector for doubting the propriety of demanding this increase were, the floods which had been occasioned by a peculiarly high fresh and overflow of the Godavery this year, and "the uncommon languor which had prevailed during the past three years in every branch of commerce." The Board of Revenue did not consider that either of these reasons was adequate. The loss occasioned by the inundation from the river was temporary, whereas there was every probability that the settlement would be prolonged for an indefinite period. While, with reference to the stagnation of trade, large advances had been made from the Collector's treasury at Cocanada to the Commercial Department during the past three years, and a very great part of the trade occasioned thereby must have been centred in the Peddapore country, where less loss must have been suffered by diminution in foreign trade than in any other part of the coast. The Government, being convinced of the justice and moderation of the proposed assessment, approved of the opinion on the matter pronounced by the Board; and directed that the Cowle should again be offered to the Zemin dar, who, it was ascertained, was under sinister influence, and that, if it were again rejected, his estate should be sequestrated without further reference to them. The youthful Zemindar had, however, acquiesced in the proposed arrangements, and agreed to accept the Cowle, before this decision was announced. With reference to this matter, the Board of Revenue thought it right to express their opinion that Ráya Jaggapati Rázu's consent would have been immediate, if the Collector had exerted himself as he ought to remove the improper influence by which the Zemindar had been actuated. As the realization of the revenue greatly depended on the firm and vigilant attention of the Collector, they reminded him of the important charge with which he was entrusted, and earnestly recommended him to bestow the most scrupulous attention in order to guard the public interests from suffering by the arts and procrastinating disposition too generally evinced by the Zemindars. These could not be more effectually checked, they observed, than by making himself completely master of their resources, by immediately resisting every attempt to delay the regular payment of their instalments of rent, and by decidedly rejecting every demand for remission, except in cases of the most obvious necessity, which never could arise but from extraordinary calamity.

The other large Zemindari in the First Division was Pittapore. But little of consequence took place in this estate during the period under review. It has already been stated that, on the accession ot the youthful Rajah, a manager was appointed, who was held responsible for the payment of the revenue. Some little trouble regarding this was experienced, and the growing crops were at one time attached; but eventually all the kists were paid, the unusual indulgence being granted of grain being received in lieu of cash payments, any deficiency in the price of the grain being deducted. In September 1799, Row Venkayya, the manager, died, and it was considered advisable that no one should be appointed in his room. Row Venkata Row, the manager's son, refused to be answerable for his father's rent, and the unexpired portion of the lease was advertised for sale, and he was informed that any difference which might arise in the offer made for it and the original rent would be considered as payable by him to the Zemindar. The renters, who had entered into separate agreements for paying their rents into the Collector's treasury, were individually considered responsible for the amounts due by them; and, therefore, the settlement then existing between the Zemindar and the Government was considered quite sufficient for the realization of the revenue without the appointment of a new manager and security taken from him. At the same time the Collector was desired to impress on Níládri Row Gáru, the youthful Zemindar, and on his relations who were in attendance on him, how much his own interest and future welfare would be concerned in seeing the rents regularly discharged, and in acquiring a complete knowledge of the affairs of his extensive estate.*

The greater part of the Second Division had been leased to two wealthy individuals named Bhúpayya and Venkataráma Rázu, who had failed to pay their rent, although it was proved, on careful inquiry, that they had collected more than sufficient to meet it. They were deprived of their farms, and all their authority in the the country suspended. As they still continued refractory, they were summoned to Madras, in order that they might make their representations in person to the Board of Revenue and to Government, and that the former might deal directly with them. After a long inquiry, the ultimate decision was, that they were to be placed in confinement at Conjeveram until they should pay the rent which was due from them. The conduct of these men and their total disregard of their public engagements by withholding all payments, notwithstanding the ample collections which they had made, deprived them of all sympathy and indulgence.

The removal of Bhúpayya and Venkataráma Rázu to Conjeveram, where they were to remain under charge of the Collector of the Jaghire, was delayed for a short time, pending advices from the Collector of the Second Division, showing the exact amount due from them. Meanwhile, a careful plan had been prepared for their flight from Madras. The Naik of the military guard set over them had probably been bribed, and at first no trace of their places of concealment could be found. The care and deliberation with which their flight had been arranged are shown by the fact that their families left Mogalturru on the very same night that they escaped from Madras. At length intelligence was received from the Collector that their families had arrived at Bhadráchalam, and that they had passed the boundary of the Company's possessions, and taken refuge in the territory of the Nizam.

The Collector was apprehensive that the object of these men was to invade the Mogalturru District, and commit depredations there. He consequently applied to the comanding officer for a force sufficient for its protection; but the exigencies of the service prevented any adequate arrangements being made. Mr. Gambier continued to keep a watchful eye on the conduct of the parties, under the full

* General Reports of the Board of Revenue to the Honourable the Governor in Council, sent Home to the Court of Directors. Madras, 1872, vol. v. pp. 1, 27, 49, 110.

impression that they would ere long make an incursion into his District; and from the reports made to him of their collecting armed men, countenanced and assisted, it would appear, by the Zemindar of Bhadráchalam and the Nizam's Amildar at Kammamet, no doubt remained that they intended to enter Mogalturru with a body of armed peons for the purpose of exacting satisfaction. On July 15, 1795, Bhúpayya carried his threatened incursion into execution. With 2000 armed peons he crossed the hills from the Nizam's territory, and penetrated as far as Mogalturru, having encamped at Yarnagúdem and Attili on the way. He experienced no opposition at first, and marched with such rapidity that he very nearly surprised the Collector in his house. The short intimation of his advance received by Mr. Gambier only allowed of his collecting the few sepoys and peons immediately about him, to guard against the attempt to seize his person, and to afford protection to the public servants and records of the station. On the near approach of Bhúpayya with a large party armed with matchlocks and with pikes, a distant firing took place between them and the sepoys, by which three of the latter were wounded. This petty skirmishing continued for two or three hours, when Bhúpayya sent a messenger to express his desire of making a representation; and, as Mr. Gambier had not sufficient force to repel the attack, there was no alternative but to comply with his request. His representation was consequently received, and, on a promise that it should be forwarded to the Board of Revenue, Bhúpayya and his followers withdrew, and soon afterwards returned to Bhadráchalam. To show that their object was simply to obtain what they considered just, and not for rapine and revenge, the Collector reported that not one of the villages through which they passed, either in coming or in returning, was plundered.

On receipt of the intelligence that Bhúpayya was proceeding with so much expedition to Mogalturru, the Collector repeated his application to the commanding officer, in the most urgent terms, for military aid, which was in some degree afforded, though it did not arrive in time for the purpose required. It was felt that the means of defence at the disposal of the Collector were totally inadequate, and that it was in the highest degree unadvisable that the country should be left unprotected and exposed to the sudden incursion of men who were able to raise a sufficient body of men to insist on demanding what they considered their rights by force of arms. A sufficient guard of sepoys was now afforded the Collector; troops were stationed at Duvva; and confidence was restored to the inhabitants, who were deserting their villages from fear of another incursion by Bhúpayya. A *Sibbandi*, or Revenue, Corps, 800 strong, was ordered to be raised at once, and Lieutenant Bowness was appointed to the command. It was divided into several companies, of which three were employed in this Division. It was reduced in number, however, after the apprehension which had called it into existence had passed away. The Government, on receiving Bhúpayya's representations and proposals, at once rejected them as totally inadmissible, especially as they had been made when he was in arms against the Company's authority. The Resident at Hyderabad was directed to point out in the most forcible manner to his Highness the Nizam, the unwarrantable conduct of the Zemindar of Bhadráchalam, and of his Amildar at Kammamet, and the great inconvenience occasioned by the harbour which they had afforded to refractory persons fleeing to them for protection from the Company's territories. These representations, as might have been expected, were of no avail. Bhúpayya and Venkataráma Rázu still received shelter at Bhadráchalam—orders which were issued from the Nizam's court having proved of no effect; but they attempted no further incursions into the Mogalturru Division. Two years afterwards, Mr Gambier received authentic information that they had both died; and the detachment of regular sepoys stationed at Duvva returned to its headquarters at Ellore, and the Revenue Corps was considerably reduced.*

The Collector of the Third Division at Rajahmundry had also been obliged to demand more military assistance during the above period, Bhúpayya and his followers having passed through his Division. There were, of course, continual rumours of coming invasion. In the September after Bhúpayya's raid into Mogalturru, some of his peons attacked and plundered Chágallu, not far from Rajahmundry, but on the opposite side of the river, and they were dispersed by the detachment of sepoys stationed at Kovvúru. Troops were also stationed at Anantapalli, further on in the Ellore road, so that the access to Mogalturru was completely covered. The Collector of the Third Division demanded during this period a

* General Reports of the Board of Revenue to the Honourable the Governor in Council, sent Home to the Court of Directors. Madras, 1872, vol. iv. pp. 6, 38, 52, 84; vol. v. p. 1. Also MS. Records.

detachment of sepoys to accompany him, whenever he went out into the District.*

After these two renters had been dismissed, Mr. Gambier was enjoined to use his best endeavours to rent the villages under his charge to the head inhabitants and others. He succeeded in thus renting the villages in six out of the eight Taluks in his Division for Faslis 1204 and 1205. The lands in the two omitted Taluks, namely, Undi and Kaldindi, were not so advantageously situated, being at some distance from the Godavery, and he was obliged to keep them under his own immediate management, as he was unable to induce the inhabitants to take them on rent. Among other means of improving these Taluks, he strongly recommended the repair of a channel leading into Undi from the Godavery, which he considered would yield a supply of water considerably to benefit the low-lying lands. Nine hundred pagodas was the estimated expense. The Government sanctioned this expenditure, and the Collector was requested to avail himself in this matter of the professional advice of Mr. Topping, who must then have been in the neighbourhood.†

At the expiration of the leases already granted for two years, the Board of Revenue exhorted Mr. Gambier in the strongest terms to spare no pains or exertion to induce the inhabitants to come forward with offers for their own villages for a term of years. They had desired all Collectors, on the occasion of the change of system, to keep in view their wish that on all occasions the inhabitants were, by every reasonable encouragement, to be induced to rent their own villages in preference to any other mode of management. The Collector succeeded in renting the whole of the Mogalturru and Nursapore Districts for four years, with the exception of fifty-five villages. Although he had not been able fully to introduce the rent of single villages, yet it was hoped that what had been done would lead to the adoption of that system.

Mr. Gambier died in June 1799, and was succeeded by Mr. S. Skinner, who received early promotion on account of his diligence in acquiring Telugu, evidently a rare accomplishment in those days. Very soon after he joined the Division, he went out into the district to examine the state of the country and of the people. He found that the crops had been seriously injured by heavy and

* MS. Records.

† General Reports of the Board of Revenue to the Honourable the Governor in Council, sent Home to the Court of Directors. Madras, 1872, vol. iv. pp. 7, 38, 54, 84, 92.

unseasonable rains which fell at the end of the year, and completely destroyed all the crops that had been cut. These unusual rains continued in January and February, and raised the loss to the rank of a calamity. In consequence of this a considerable deficiency of revenue was experienced. The Collector proceeded into the district while the grain was being cut, and moved about from place to place as he considered necessary, for the sake of observing accurately the extent of the harvest, and he felt that if he had exacted more than he did, he would have destroyed all hopes of the cultivation of the succeeding year, and would have put out of the power of the people to liquidate at a future period any part of the arrears due from them. Large arrears were left unpaid; and an advance of 5500 star pagodas for cultivation, and of 2200 pagodas for the repair of tanks was sanctioned.

In the year 1798 there was another petty disturbance both in this and in the Third Division. Kaldindi Chinna Timmarázu, who was a revenue defaulter, and had fled the country with Bhúpayya in 1795, invaded this Division from the Nizam's territories with a body of from 200 to 300 men armed with pikes. He penetrated as far as Undi. There he attacked the public office, and then proceeded to the house of Mudukrishna Mudeliar, the Tanedar. It was night. The confusion and excitement was great. The glare and smoke from the torches added to the confusion, as Timmarázu entered the court-yard with his followers, and demanded that the Tanedar should be delivered up. The Tanedar's wife issued from her private apartments, where he had taken refuge, and entreated Timmarázu, with cries and tears, not to put him to death. Timmarázu, laying his hand on her head, solemnly swore that her husband's life should be spared if he would come out unarmed. On hearing this assurance, the Tanedar surrendered himself without any weapons in his hand, embraced Timmarázu, and besought him not to kill him, because he had many children. "Well!" cried Timmarázu to his followers; "why do you look at me, my men?" He had no sooner said this, than they rushed on the helpless Tanedar and stabbed him in the stomach. One sepoy was killed and another mortally wounded, and several people were slightly wounded in this attack.*

When more troops had been collected in various parts of the Second and Third Divisions, Timmarázu and his followers made good their retreat into the Nizam's territories. There Dámera Shá-

* MS. Records.

yanna Row, one of the Zemindars of the Bhadráchalam country, apprehended Timmarázu Subbayya, one of the principal insurgents, and three others, and sent them under a guard to Masulipatam. Friendly intercourse was thus opened with this Zemindar, and every inducement was held out for him to apprehend the chief offender; but without success, and Timmarázu afterwards helped to instigate and joined in the more serious rebellion of Mangápati Dévu, the Zemindar of Pólavaram, which will subsequently be related.*

Mr. Benjamin Branfill, the Collector of the Third Division, commenced his administration with great vigour and zeal. In exerting himself to carry into effect the instructions contained in the Board of Revenue's circular of the 8th of November 1794, he reported that the Zemindars, instead of assisting him, had thrown every impediment in the way of his endeavouring to prosecute his inquiries. He pointed out that they had grossly imposed on Government, by representing losses during the time of the late scarcity which they had never suffered. He made it appear, on the contrary, that their receipts during that period were supposed even to have exceeded former years; and it seemed manifest that such excess had arisen from misconduct and disobedience, particularly in levying duties on grain, in that season of extreme distress and of general calamity, in opposition to the repeated orders of Government. The Collector further represented that the Zemindars were generally most improvident in their mode of life, and had continued the injurious practice of anticipating their rents. Some, with a view to keep a knowledge of their resources and expenditure from the inspection of the Government, had destroyed all the village accounts immediately on concluding the final collection of the year.

The Collector of the Third Division experienced most anxiety and trouble from the Zemindar of Pólavaram and Gútála. The arrangements which were made regarding the affairs of these Zemindaris, consequent on their distracted condition owing to family disputes, have already been related. It had been considered advisable to place all the three estates of Pólavaram, Gútála, and Kottapilli under the eldest brother, Mangápati Dévu; and the youngest brother, Vizayagópála Dévu, had been detained at Masulipatam since the settlement of the dispute. Mr. Branfill found that the conduct of the ruling Zemindar was so very reprehensible in withholding the accounts of his estate, and in persistently failing to liquidate the

* General Reports of the Board of Revenue, vol. vi. p. 76.

balances due from him, that the Board of Revenue directed him, if no other means should appear adequate to obtain the accounts and to secure the payment of the revenue, to apprehend the person of the Zemindar in such a manner as might appear advisable.

In noticing the refractory conduct of this Zemindar, the Collector submitted a proposal for dividing the Zemindari again, and re-establishing the authority of the younger brother in Gútála. As, however, the estates had been united under Mangápati Dévu after mature consideration, and the Court of Directors had approved of this measure, Mr. Branfill's proposal was not entertained. Attention was drawn to the case of the younger brother Vizayagópála Dévu; and, as the Collector of the Fifth Division reported most favourably on his conduct during the time he had been under surveillance at Masulipatam, and as he appeared to have been too young to have taken an active part in the transactions which occasioned his being sent there, the Board directed that measures should be taken for his release. They sent instructions to Mr. Branfill to select a proper place for his residence and that of his family immediately attached to him, but as far removed from Pólavaram as he might consider necessary. He was accordingly escorted to Rajahmundry, where he was permitted to reside. The allowance of 100 pagodas a month, which had hitherto been given him, was continued, and every precaution was taken to prevent the hazard of intrigues in the Gútála Zemindari by a renewal of dissensions between the parties who might be disposed to create rivalry between the brothers.

Mangápati Dévu's conduct continued to be most unsatisfactory. He refused to fulfil his engagements, and a large balance having again become due, the Collector was desired to lose no time in securing his person, which was effected without the slightest disturbance. He was also directed to take the most effectual measures for the security of the crops, and for realizing the current revenue from the country, unless the Zemindar could be induced to make a satisfactory arrangement for the immediate payment of the balance due. The Collector again urged the necessity for dividing the estates, and even submitted proposals made to him by Vizayagópála Dévu in the event of his being placed in possession; but the Government would not listen to his suggestions, and directed that the estates should be continued under sequestration, until all demands on them should be cleared off. On receipt of these orders, Mangápati Dévu made a proposal to pay the sum of 16,000 pagodas on being released from confinement, to give ample security for the payment of the current revenue as it fell due, and to discharge the old balance in two years. This proposal was accepted; but the Government ordered that, in consideration of Mangápati Dévu's character, and the little dependence to be placed on his promises, he was to be told that, if regardless of this further proof of the lenity and indulgence of the Company's Government, he should swerve from his present engagements, they would be under the indispensable necessity of finally sequestering his Zemindari.

At this time the younger brother, Vizayagópála Dévu, fled from Rajahmundry. He was himself a pleasing and amiable youth, and the Collector had every confidence in him, and, even after his flight, continued to feel a kindly interest in him and to rely on his good intentions. He had evidently been persuaded into this overt act of disaffection by the evil counsel of his advisers. He fled in the first instance to Rampa, where, however, he would not yield to the solicitations of the people to create disturbances and to attack the Company's territory. He subsequently took refuge with Lingáreddi, one of the hill chiefs, who, with their Koi followers, have frequently occasioned trouble. Lingáreddi's territory was on the eastern bank of the Godavery, above Pólavaram and nearer the Gorge. It was nominally dependent on the Zemindar of Pólavaram; but this dependence was merely nominal, as he paid no revenue for it, and acted as he pleased in regard to its internal management. It was said to be worth 1500 or 2000 pagodas a-year, and formerly Lingáreddi used to pay to the Zemindar a tribute of 100 pagodas, but of late years he had refused to pay even that small sum, and it was not without difficulty he was kept quiet. The Collector continued to entertain a high opinion of Vizayagópála Dévu, even after his flight, and after making overtures to him, wrote in his favour to the authorities at Madras. The Board of Revenue, acting in communication with Government, agreed to extend the period for leniency which they had limited, and instructed Mr. Branfill to send further conciliatory messages to him, promising him pardon and protection in consideration of his youth and inexperience, and warning him of the fatal consequences which were likely to ensue in case of continued contumacy. A little later on, Vizayagópála Dévu was drawn into rebellion by the persuasion of his host and Kaldindi Timmarázu, who had joined them, and the whole combined party plundered two villages in the Pólavaram Zemindari. A fresh *fitúri*, as it is called in the District, or petty insurrection, had begun, and the military had to be called out.

The Zemindar of Pólavaram took advantage of the opportunity occasioned by his brother's escape to claim indulgence with regard to the payment of his balances. These had again accumulated to a considerable extent, owing to his own negligence. Another serious warning was made to him on the subject, and his request for indulgence was peremptorily refused. This refusal and the accompanying expostulation elicited from him a promise of payment. His submission was merely pretence. His conduct soon became so refractory and turbulent that the aid of the military had to be called for against him, as well as against his brother and Lingáreddi. They had evidently made common cause with each other. The ostensible reason for Mangápati Dévu's rebellious conduct was to enforce an acquiescence in the exorbitant claim for remission extending to 52,580 pagodas. He declined obeying a summons which the Collector had issued requiring his attendance at Rajahmundry, and his object was evidently to intimidate the Government into granting him this unjustifiable remission by threats of rebellion.

The Collector felt that it was necessary to make adequate arrangements against insurrection, as he was certain that, the instant Mangápati Dévu should be informed that his proposals had been rejected, he would at once commence depredations in the neighbouring territory of the Company, or would return an evasive answer for the purpose of gaining time until he could collect a sufficient body of peons for that object. He, therefore, made every exertion that lay in his power to collect sufficient troops, not only to protect the country, but to act efficiently, if necessary, before the final orders of Government were made known to the Zemindar. He requested the permission of the officer commanding the Northern Division of the Army to detain a detachment which was passing through Rajahmundry on its way to Masulipatam, so that he might be ready to act in case the Zemindar should have discovered that his terms had not been accepted, and should commence depredations, and might be in readiness to join the troops, if coercive measures should be determined upon. All the necessary preparations having been made, the Board of Revenue proposed and the Government agreed that the Zemindar should be informed that his proposition was inadmissible, and that to admit it would be to sanction not only the waste of public revenue at the pleasure of a Zemindar.

but the propriety of resistance to the orders of Government. They were of opinion that a remission of 1800 pagodas was as much as ought to be granted for the past, and that an adjustment of the remaining balance should be required.

During the negotiations consequent on these instructions, the Zemindar had been collecting men and arms to enable him to make a successful resistance to them. All the efforts of Mr. Branfill to induce him to accede to them and to return to his allegiance to the Company, were unsuccessful. The military force which had now been collected was ready for action. It was under the command of Colonel Gardiner. Hopes were entertained that a rapid dash at the commencement would bring hostilities to a speedy conclusion; and, therefore, a plan was concerted, by which it was believed the fort of Pólavaram would be captured, and the Zemindar's person secured. The fort was taken after a brief resistance by the Zemindar's peons, during which several sepoys were killed or wounded. The Zemindar had, however, fled, and the principal object of the siege was left unfulfilled. The fort was destroyed.

On receiving intelligence of the capture of Pólavaram, the Government forwarded a proclamation to the Collector for publication throughout the District. In this document the rebellious conduct of Mangápati Dévu, the lenity of Government in the measures adopted towards him, and the audacity of his opposing the Company's troops were pointed out. A reward of 10,000 rupees was offered for his apprehension and delivery to the authorities; and, at the same time, the Zemindar had an opportunity afforded him, by unconditional surrender, of throwing himself on the mercy of Government. In the event of his not availing himself of this indulgence, the inhabitants of the neighbouring districts were warned to hold no communication with him, and not to aid him in any respect, either by taking up arms or attaching themselves to his person or cause, as such conduct would subject them to trial before a military tribunal. The Zemindari of Pólavaram and the neighbouring districts were thus placed under martial law. A free pardon was offered in this proclamation to Vizayagópála Dévu, on condition of his surrender within a given period.

As soon as he heard of the preparations made against him, Mangápati Dévu fled to the Nizam's territories, whence he returned when he thought the coast was clear. Directly information was received of his return, the Collector again concerted a plan with the officer commanding the Northern Division of the Madras army, with the object of securing the Zemindar's person, and thus ending the anticipated campaign by one stroke. The difficult nature of the hilly country to be traversed, and the celerity with which information of the movement of troops is conveyed in that region, render such an operation nearly impossible. A reinforcement of three companies of sepoys, under Captain Wahab, was ordered to proceed for this purpose to Ganapavaram, a village thirty-four miles nearly due west from Pólavaram. The sepoys arrived there on August 11, 1800. The Collector, accompanied by Colonel Smith, repaired thither on the following day, and a council of war was held. It was then agreed that Captain Wahab's detachment should proceed on the morning of the 18th, by the route of Nágavaram, to Chiruváka, the village where the Zemindar had taken up his residence, and that Colonel Smith, with the troops from Pólavaram, should take the route of Kondrakóta on the same day, so that both parties might reach the place appointed nearly at the same time. As might have been expected, this manœuvre was unsuccessful. The two detachments met at the appointed place and at the appointed time; but, though the strictest search was made for the Zemindar, he could nowhere be found. Though every exertion was made to ascertain his retreat, no tidings could be obtained of him, and it was supposed that he had fled across the river into the Rampa territory upon hearing that the troops were in search of him. The detachments on their way to Chiruváka did not meet with any opposition; but the one from Pólavaram was attacked on its return by a large body of peons belonging to Lingáreddi and the other hill chiefs. They were speedily dispersed. An officer and a sepoy were wounded—the former slightly, with an arrow; the latter dangerously.

Previous to their departure from Pólavaram, the Collector had requested Colonel Smith to destroy Lingáreddi's villages. This was done, but all efforts to secure some of his followers were ineffectual. During his brief stay at Ganapavaram, the Collector prevailed on Munireddi, the principal hill chieftain in that quarter, not only to accept a lease from the Company, but also to take an active part against the Zemindar. He showed his friendliness and zeal by conducting Captain Wahab's detachment across the hills, by a mountain track known to few besides himself, to Chiruváka, and by giving what assistance he was able with the peons under his command.

Overtures were also made to Lingáreddi, and two letters were addressed to him on the subject of his disaffection; but he took no notice of them, and treated them with the most contemptuous indifference. He apparently never assigned any reason for having so suddenly broken his engagements with the Company.

In order to keep the inhabitants of Rampa in check, a company of sepoys was stationed at Kottapilli, and another at Indigupéta. A party of hill people attacked the latter, which was under the command of Lieutenant Macdonald, on the night of the 28th of August. They were soon dispersed, but not before one of the sepoys was mortally wounded. On the 31st, Pandu Dora, the chief of the insurgents in Rampa, called by the Collector "the Rumpah Head Peon," accompanied by three or four hundred men armed with various weapons, advanced to Purushottapatnam, which was directly opposite Pólavaram and within sight of the troops stationed there, and seized the boats and the people belonging to them who were on that side the river, so as to cut off all communication.

It was decided by the Right Honourable the Governor in Council, that the 1st Battalion of the 9th Regiment, which had been detained on its way and sent to Pólavaram, should continue its march to Ganjam, and that Captain O'Reilly, with four companies of the 2d Battalion of the 8th Regiment was to relieve it. The Collector, hearing of this, wrote a strong remonstrance to the officer commanding the Division, pointing out that the country was in a much worse state of disquietude than it had been since the commencement of the disturbance. Besides the active hostility in the territory of Rampa on the east side of the river, he had discovered a conspiracy in Pólavaram itself, notwithstanding the presence of the troops. The Collector took on himself, therefore, to request Colonel Smith to postpone his departure for Ganjam until he could be relieved by the arrival of Captain O'Reilly's detachment, as it was necessary for the defence of the country and for the protection of the peaceably inclined inhabitants not to leave the place unguarded.

Vizayagópála Dévu had surrendered himself to the officer commanding at Ganapavaram. He stated that Mangápati Dévu had entered into correspondence with him and his other brother, Narashima Dévu, who had consented to join him, and had proposed that all three brothers should combine and create disturbances in the Pólavaram estate, by which course Mangápati Dévu hoped to have it restored to him. Vizayagópála Dévu was at the time in the Rékapalli country, and a few days afterwards he entered the Company's territories and surrendered himself. The Collector reported that he appeared to be sincerely penitent for the part which he had been playing in the disturbances, which he ascribed entirely to evil advisers. The third brother, Reddi Narashima Dévu, had been captured by a detachment sent from Pólavaram.

While Mr. Branfill was at Pólavaram, he entered fully into the subject of the uncollected revenue of Fasli 1209, and formed a settlement for Fasli 1210. The latter amounted to 42,698 pagodas. On the state of the villages comprising this estate, he made the following observations, which clearly show that it was a very fertile and naturally prosperous Zemindari, and might have proved a great source of profit to the Zemindar, if he had been well advised and prudently inclined. "Their produce of late years," the Collector wrote, "has very much decreased, for which many reasons can be assigned—the Zemindar's total neglect of his concerns, his injudicious choice of people to manage for him, insufficient attention paid to the state of tanks and water-courses, not a single pagoda advanced, but principally the oppressive mode of forestalling his revenues, which obliged the inhabitants to borrow money at a high interest to pay their kists; but notwithstanding the present unfavourable appearance of these countries, I am convinced they would in a short time, with attention and good management, yield the full amount of the Committee's valuation, the soil being remarkably fertile." The Board of Revenue regarded the settlement made by Mr. Branfill as that of a distracted country whose actual resources could not be properly ascertained, and whose affairs could not be regulated until the Zemindar himself was secured and his influence eradicated.* The estate was given to a cousin named Reddi Lakshminaráyana Dévu, with whom the permanent settlement was made.

* General Reports of the Board of Revenue, vol. iv. pp. 85, 150; vol. v. pp. 2, 54, 111; vol. vi. pp. 10, 78. Also MS. Records. Three battalions of volunteers from Bengal, under Colonel Gardiner, who was a Bengal officer, were employed in this campaign. They had volunteered for service in the war against Tippoo Sultan, and had been engaged in Mysore after the fall of Seringapatam; and they received the warmest thanks both of the Government of Madras and of the Governor-General for their services in Mysore and at Pólavaram. Government Order, May 12, 1800. Government Order of Governor-General in Council, August 6, 1800. Madras Gazette, August 23, 1800. East India Military Calendar, vol. ii. p. 303; vol. iii. p. 295.

CHAPTER XV.

THE PERMANENT SETTLEMENT.

NEGOTIATIONS REGARDING THE INTRODUCTION OF THE PERMANENT SETTLEMENT—APPOINTMENT OF A SPECIAL COMMISSION—INTRODUCTION OF THE SYSTEM INTO THIS DISTRICT—LIST OF THE ESTATES AT THAT TIME—WORKING OF THE SYSTEM—DECLINE OF THE ZEMINDARIS AND PROPRIETARY ESTATES—TOUR OF SIR THOMAS MUNRO—THE GREAT FAMINE—DETERIORATION OF THE DISTRICT—SIR HENRY MONTGOMERY'S COMMISSION.

THE Permanent Settlement was introduced into the Rajahmundry District in 1802-3. This system had been adopted in Bengal in 1793 under Lord Cornwallis, and the Court of Directors were so fully satisfied of its excellence that they had for some time been anxious to see it introduced into all the possessions belonging to the East India Company. The Committee of Circuit was instituted with a view to the ultimate adoption of a similar system; and the delay in the introduction of it into the Northern Circars was occasioned by the imperfect manner in which the authority of the Company had been established there, the failure of the local authorities in acquiring the requisite revenue knowledge, and the want of legislative power sufficient to authorize the introduction of courts of justice. When the Court of Directors authorized the abolition of the Provincial Councils, they clearly stated their desire to see this system ultimately established throughout the whole of the territories of Fort St. George. Being thoroughly sensible of the propriety and expediency of the late revenue and judicial regulations in Bengal, they directed the Madras Government to consider the expediency of adopting similar plans for the Northern Circars. Should that Government be of opinion, after mature deliberation, that the Bengal arrangements might be extended with equal promise of general advantage to the districts under their superintendence, the Court confided in their wisdom and discretion to carry the same into effect, by such decrees and in such manner, and at such times, as local circumstances appeared to warrant.*

* Letter from the Court to the Madras Government, dated April 21, 1795.

The Government of Madras, while admitting the advisability of introducing the Bengal system, were of opinion that the fitting time for it had not yet arrived. But the matter was not suffered to drop. In 1798 Lord Wellesley, when Governor-General, directed the Government of Madras to make a full and complete inquiry into the actual condition of the public service in every branch, in consequence of the pecuniary distress of that Presidency which had been reported to him, in order that whatever reforms might be found needful should immediately be applied. At the same time it was stated to be the wish of the Supreme Government, that, with this reform of the civil establishment, the introduction of the Bengal system of revenue and judicature should be made. In accordance with these instructions a Committee was immediately appointed to consider the revision and reform of the Civil Service, and the Board of Revenue were requested to make preparations for the introduction of the new system as soon as practicable.* In September 1799, they sent in to the Government an elaborate Report on the subject. They were of opinion that the new system might be applied at once to the Northern Circars; but there was one particular, in which the territories under the two Governments materially differed, and they proceeded to make suggestions by which that difference might be met. In Bengal nearly the whole country was in the hands of Zemindars at the time of the Permanent Settlement, and there was consequently no great difficulty in applying it to them; but in the Northern Circars, a very large portion of the land was not in possession of Zemindars, but was under the immediate management of the Company. It was necessary, therefore, to determine how these lands could be brought under the settlement. The Board of Revenue recommended that they should be formed into estates, or "mootahs," as they were called, yielding a revenue from 1000 to 5000 pagodas a year each, and that these estates should be sold or granted to individuals who should be called Proprietors. The Government of Madras at once gave permission to the Board to prepare the way for carrying into effect a permanent settlement of the lands on the principles they had enunciated. The Board of Revenue, on the receipt of this authority, issued a long letter of instructions to the several Collectors, explaining the principle of the intended settlement, and requesting them to obtain the best information they could, in order most effectually to carry out the wishes of Government.

* General Reports of the Board of Revenue, vol. v.. 104; vi. pp. 70, 145.

The Collectors were informed that the Madras Government were fully convinced that the public prosperity and welfare of the country absolutely required the introduction of the new system, and they were requested to use every exertion to have it introduced in the best possible manner.*

In expressing his approval of these arrangements, the Governor-General distinctly informed the Government of Madras that the acknowledgment of a proprietary right in the Zemindars who were then in possession, or in the Proprietors who were about to be created, was not to be allowed in any respect to affect the rights of the ryots or others who had hitherto been, in any way, subject to the authority of the Zemindars or other landholders; nor was it to be understood as preventing the Government from passing any laws which might be considered expedient for the protection of the ryots.

The Court of Directors also gave their full approval to the scheme. In bestowing on the Madras Government power to proceed in carrying into execution the plans which had received their approval, they added that "there was one material circumstance to be attended to in the conduct of this important measure, namely, that any attempt to introduce a regular system of order would be idle and nugatory, till the minds of the people were prepared to feel the importance of the benefits they were about to receive. The first object, therefore, was to establish the authority of the Government itself in the different Zemindaris before they were invited to participate in the advantages to be conferred on them, and this could never be done till the spirit of rebellion and insubordination which was so conspicuous in the Northern Circars was suppressed. It was of the first importance to the attainment of that object, that all subordinate military establishments should be annihilated within the limits then subject to the dominion of the Company; and that the countries to which this observation applied must be brought to such a state of subjection as to acknowledge and submit to the principle that, as they must be indebted to the beneficence and wisdom of the British Government for every advantage they were to receive, so, in like manner, they must feel indebted solely to its protection for the continuance and enjoyment of them."†

In the following year a special Commission was appointed by the Madras Government to consider as to the most appropriate manner in which the principles of the new system were to be carried into

* Circular Instructions to Collectors, dated October 15, 1799.

† Fifth Report, p. 309.

effect, and to apply them to those districts which were considered to be ready for its introduction. This Commission merely remained in existence long enough to perform the special duties for which it was created. The Zemindaris in the Rajahmundry District, to which the Permanent Settlement was first extended, were the two large estates of Peddapore and Pittapore.

The estates of the Zemindars who were already in possession were confirmed to them in perpetuity. The Government lands were divided into estates of convenient size, yielding from 1000 to 5000 star pagodas annual revenue, and these were sold at public auction to the highest bidders, subject to the terms of the permanent Zemindari tenure. The assessment on each Zemindari was fixed exclusively of the revenue derived from all extra sources, such as the abkari, salt, and sayer; and the general standard by which the land-rent to be paid by the Zemindars was regulated was mostly two-thirds of the average gross collections of preceding years, varying from eight years to thirteen, as the accounts could be found—one-third of these assets being remitted as compensation to the Zemindars for the charges of the management of their estates and for their own maintenance. In this average only the culturable land belonging to Government was included.*

At the time of the Permanent Settlement, the Rajahmundry District consisted of thirteen ancient Zemindaris, together with the possessions of the Kaldindi (the Zemindari of Mogalturru) and of the Mandapáti families, which had been held under the direct management of the Government since their voluntary cession. There were forty-nine Government villages. The Zemindari of Mogalturru, the possessions of the Mandapáti family, and the Government villages were divided into twenty-six estates, and the permanent revenue fixed on them were in most cases but little short of the assets, and in many cases equal to them or exceeding them. These estates were sold in 1803, and the purchasers were called Proprietors. They were allowed for the first ten years of their occupancy a temporary abatement of the fixed demand. The amount realized by the sale of these estates was 331,947 rupees. The village of Uppáda was at this time transferred to Rajahmundry from the Vizagapatam District. The following Statement shows the names of the Zemindaris and Proprietary Estates at this time, the names of the owners or purchasers, the estimated assets, and the permanent assessment then imposed on each.

* Sir Henry Montgomery's Report, § 6. Fifth Report, p. 313.

Names of the Estates.	Names of the Owners or Purchasers.	Assets.	Assessment.
Ancient Zemindaris—		Rs.	Rs.
1. Peddapore . . .	Vatsváya Ráya Jaggapati Rázu	994,623	667,817
2. Pittapore . . .	Row Venkataniládri Row . .	392,182	258,979
3. Pólavaram . . .	Reddi Lakshminaráyana Dévu	199,853	105,700
4. Kóta Rámachendrapuram . .	C. Jaggannádha Rázu . . .	178,902	124,596
5. Vógayyammapóta	V. Sómappa	13,121	8,750
6. Velampálem . .	A. Krishnabrahmáji . . .	16,170	16,408
7. Venkatáyapálem	Mirza Usaf Sahib	2,201	1,946
8. Vella	Mir Mohammed Ibrahim Kási	2,156	1,445
9. Telakacherla . .	U. Jógi Jaggannádha Rázu .	3,426	1,925
10. Jálimúdi . . .	J. Bhanóji Ráma Row . . .	399	287
11. Panangipalli . .	S. Venkayya	1,179	854
12. Undéshwarapuram	G. Venkatanarasu	924	637
13. Mukkámala . .	D. Venkatapati Sómayáji . .	588	133
14. Vilasa and Jánupalli	J. Rámóji Bhánu	3,013	2,439
15. Bantumilli . .	G. Venkatarámanna . . .	306	240
		1,809,043	1,192,156
Proprietary Estates—			
1. Rajahmundry	Mirza Rája Púsapáti Nárayana Gajapati Rázu Bahadur, Zemindar of Vizianagaram .	14,875	12,456
2. Penumadam .		33,824	30,019
3. Kovvúru . .		33,936	33,568
4. Perúru . . .		21,000	20,520
5. Cheyyóru . .		24,577	25,249
6. Viravásaram .		45,237	39,795
7. Káza . . .		38,552	34,937
8. Mogalturru .		47,229	51,082
9. Gunupúdi . .		29,351	35,455
10. Undi . . .		36,848	41,720
11. Sakhinótipalli		16,268	21,668
12. Bendamúrlanka		8,134	8,134
13. Nágampalli .	Rája Vatsaváya Ráya Jaggapati Rázu Bahadur, Zemindar of Peddapore	16,033	15,372
14. Kápavaram .		16,499	16,191
15. Murári . .		18,634	18,277
16. Raghadévapuram . . .		22,925	20,961
17. Doddipatla .		39,354	37,642
18. Penugonda .	Anapindi Ammanna . . .	47,183	44,128
19. Amalápuram .		25,798	21,987
20. Tanuku . .		35,399	33,481
21. Átsanta . .	Kócharlakóta Venkata Rázu .	48,562	46,816
22. Bondáda . .		18,410	27,181
23. Siddhántam . .	K. Narasa Rázu	27,986	26,274
24. Attili	S. Venkatáchalam	49,906	48,111
25. Duvva	Venkatanarasimha Appa Row	24,650	22,466
26. Nilapalli . . .	T. Káma Rázu	8,743	8,743
		749,913	742,173
27. Uppáda	Mirza Rája Púsapáti Gajapati Rázu Bahadur, Zemindar of Vizayanagaram	1,998	1,800

It should be observed that many of the above-mentioned estates were merely single villages which were bestowed on the families who were then in possession, and granted to them on favourable tenures.

The Zemindaris of Peddapore, Pittapore, and Pólavaram contained respectively 372, 128, and 128 villages each. The united estate of Kóta Rámachendrapuram contained 66 villages. Besides these there were the hilly and thinly-populated estates of Rampa, Tótapalli, and Jaddangi, comprising 338, 103, and 88 villages. The owners of these estates were called Mansabdars. Their influence was small, their revenues trifling, and the value of their possessions inconsiderable. The estates of Tótapalli and Jaddangi were formerly held on a kind of feudal tenure from the Zemindar of Peddapore, to whose possessions they formed a kind of appanage, and on whose behalf they were bound to provide an armed force to repel incursions from the hills, and to assist the Zemindar, whenever the services of their wild military establishment of peons were required. These three estates do not appear to have been brought under the system of the Permanent Settlement like the other parts of the District. The materials for such a settlement could have been obtained with only the greatest difficulty, and, perhaps, could not have been obtained at all. The Rampa estate is particularly wild and jungly, and though containing so many villages, yet, if half a dozen in the plains are excepted, the revenue derived from them did not average more than two or three rupees a year from each.* The two small estates named last on the list of the ancient Zemindaris were subsequently added to the number, and made the total fifteen. They consisted of three villages which were afterwards ascertained to have been surreptitiously enjoyed as *inam*, or rent-free land, by members of the Jillella and Gámóji Mazumdar families. A fixed assessment was imposed on them in Faslis 1233, 1237, and 1240, and they were from that time classed among the ancient Zemindaris.†

The Permanent Assessment did not prove a success in the Rajahmundry District. The causes of the failure were different in the two different kinds of estates which were at this time created. The ancient Zemindari estates deteriorated principally from the inherent defects of the system itself, and from the incapacity of those by whom they were managed. It was at first imagined that the assessment which was originally imposed on them was too high, and that,

* Mr. R. E. Master's Report on the Settlement of the Central and Eastern Deltas, § 10.

† Sir H. Montgomery's Report, § 5.

as sufficient had not been left for the maintenance of the owners and their families and dependents, they were reduced to ruin. Such was not, however, the case. The assessment was comparatively moderate. The most lightly assessed Zemindari was the first to fail.

It would be of little practical use to trace the manner in which these Zemindaris gradually became divided and subdivided, until but small portions of them remained in the possession of the original owners. It will be sufficient to quote the graphic and forcible description of the downward tendency of the system of selling estates for arrears of revenue given by Mr. Robertson, a former Collector of the District. "The measure of resorting to a sale of defaulters' lands as regards this District," wrote that gentleman in 1819, only seventeen years after the introduction of the Permanent Settlement, "failed in a great degree to secure the object intended. A reference to the list of sales will show that estates once exposed to public auction seldom remain any length of time in the possession of the first purchaser. After repeated changes many of them lapse to Government with large outstanding balances for want of bidders, and such, I apprehend, will ultimately be the fate of the remainder. The reasons appear to me obvious. The original possessor of an estate of this description has usually exhausted its resources before he gives it up. The new proprietor, not aware of its actual condition, pays a considerable premium for his purchase, in expectation of immediate profits. On taking possession he learns his disappointment. The measures to be adopted in such a state of affairs requiring both trouble and heavy expenses for repairs, &c., he is unwilling and unable to undertake them. Nevertheless, attempts leading to much oppression are made to extract a revenue which, under such circumstances, cannot be realized. As matters thenceforward become worse, some individuals are fortunate enough to shift the responsibility to others by a timely transfer. The next process is subdividing the estate, and transferring the better portions of it to raise loans. Meantime the arrears are progressively accumulating, and, to relieve himself of his embarrassments, the Proprietor at length resorts to a collusive transfer in the name of some ignorant or needy dependent. Persons are readily found to lend themselves for this purpose, who, when the day of reckoning arrives, either fly the District, or, if apprehended, suffer some years' imprisonment in the Zillah Jail, and the balances due to the Government become desperate." *

* Sir H. Montgomery's Report, § 25.

The downfal of the Proprietary Estates was equally rapid and equally sad. The above description applies to them also. The twenty-six estates of this kind remained in their entirety only for a very short time. They were very much over-assessed, and they were not able to bear the burden thus imposed on them; and, in addition to this evil, the Proprietors too frequently followed the example of the Zemindars, and imitated their habits of living, and their affectation of princely pomp. In 1843 the Special Commissioner wrote: "When it is remembered that the assessment on the Proprietary Estates equalled, and sometimes exceeded, the ascertained assets, it is not surprising that nearly the whole of them, after divisions and subdivisions, sale and resale, both publicly and privately, have long since reverted to Government, and have changed their denomination to Government Estates; and that of the few still classed under the head of Proprietary Estates, the small proportion of one-fourth only are now actually so held, the rest being either attached for balances which must bring them to speedy sale, or, after several years of minority management, proposed, as a relief to their possessors, for surrender to Government."*

For ten years after the introduction of the Permanent Settlement, there were no lands under the immediate management of the Collector, for the whole District having been divided into private estates, there were no rents due direct to Government. The first lapse occurred in 1813-14. One of the estates was sold for arrears of revenue, and, being purchased on behalf of Government, became what was called a Government Estate. The Collector was instructed to rent the villages to the head inhabitants. The brief statement given below will show the rapid manner in which the various estates, both Proprietary and Zemindari, fell into the direct possession of Government. The former were the first to fail: the latter continued much longer in the possession of their original owners.†

Year.	No. of villages under Government.
1813	10
1817	59
1820	133
1832	150
1840	361
1844	580
1851	876

* Sir H. Montgomery's Report, § 17.

† Mr. Master's Report on the Western Delta, paragraphs 8, 13.

During the latter half of the year 1822, Sir Thomas Munro, then Governor of Madras, made a tour through the Northern Circars and Nellore. His principal object in this journey was, not so much to learn anything new regarding these the oldest possessions of the Company, as, from personal communication with the local authorities and the Zemindars and chief inhabitants, to ascertain the general condition of the people, the political state of the country, the main causes which had led to the frequent disturbances of its tranquillity, and the means most likely to remedy the disorder.

"Although the Circars," he wrote in an excellent Minute, "are our earliest possessions, there are none, perhaps, of which we have so little accurate knowledge in everything that regards the condition of the people. Little or nothing has been added to the information given forty years ago by the Committee of Circuit. By being so much nearer to the time of the conquest of these districts, they had the advantage of communicating with many of the local officers and inhabitants who had lived under the native Government, and they had thereby a better opportunity than we now have of ascertaining what had then been the rights of the different classes of the people, and the rules and customs by which the public revenue was secured.

"The plans of the Committee of Circuit might in general have been adopted with great advantage, but nothing was done upon them. The Chiefs and Councils were abolished, and Collectors appointed in their room in 1794; but the same system of revenue continued with little alteration until the introduction of the Permanent Settlement. The want of sufficient information caused this settlement to be unequal. This would have been of less consequence, had it not in many places been too high, which will make most of the new estates, and probably some of the old Zemindaris, revert hereafter to Government. We have left ourselves in the Circars with so few means of acquiring information, that it is not easy to say, after a trial of twenty years, whether the effect of the Permanent Settlement has been beneficial or otherwise to the country. It has been favourable to the cultivation of estates whose assessment is moderate, and whose proprietors are active; but it has not improved the condition of the ryots generally, and has certainly rendered it worse than before in all those villages which have come back to Government with diminished resources. It has not been favourable to the Karnams and village servants, because the landholders have displaced many and deprived others of their just dues. It has not been favourable to Inamdars, a great number of whom have been ejected from their inams without any authority whatever, and their lands converted to the use of the Zemindar or Proprietor without paying any revenue to Government; and it has been unfavourable to all the old Zemindars by making their lands liable to sale for private debts, by exposing them to frequent lawsuits, and by stripping them of the greatest part of their possessions, as in the case of the Rajah of Pittapore; and it has also been unfavourable to the authority of Government, and to the efficiency of the Collectors and Magistrates.

"The weakness of the authority of Government in the Circars is owing to our restoring the estates of the petty Zemindars, who had been subdued, contrary to the opinion of the Committee of Circuit; to our erecting by the Permanent Settlement a new set of Proprietary Zemindars; to our not reserving a single village in which we could have direct control over the ryots; and to our transferring to these Proprietors the Karnams, who are the source of all our information. In an open country long under the immediate authority of Government, the Permanent Settlement, though it tends to conceal the real state of the country, does not seriously affect the public authority by encouraging resistance or rebellion; but in mountainous and unhealthy districts, like the Northern Circars, the greater part of which have long been in the hands of a number of petty rajahs, some claiming independence, and all constantly ready to withhold their tribute, and to raise disturbance whenever they see a favourable opportunity, the Permanent Settlement has the effect of weakening the authority of Government over the whole province, and of rendering the establishment of security and good order more difficult than before. When we received the Circars from the Nizam, a considerable portion of them was Circar land in the hands of the officers of Government, and was generally composed of the most fertile and populous tracts along the sea-coast. By having direct authority over a great population and over the most unhealthy part of the community, the influence of Government increased daily, both over its own districts, and those of the petty rajahs, and would in time have become sufficient, without the aid of military force, to have ensured obedience and tranquillity; but by creating new Zemindars and Proprietors, and divesting ourselves of the Circar lands, from the immediate possession of which our influence almost entirely arose, we have placed the prospect of the establishment of subordination and good order among the petty rajahships at a greater distance than ever. We are much more powerful now than in 1784; but we are not now so able to establish the authority of Government over them as then, because at that time a considerable part of the country was Circar land; but now we have made over the Circar lands to new Zemindars, and restored all the reduced rajahs. . . . Our system in the Circars is one of forbearance, and we are obliged to connive at irregularities which would not be tolerated in other provinces, lest we should be compelled to use force, and involve ourselves in a petty warfare against banditti, in a pestilential climate among hills and jungles.

"The affairs of the Circars can never be well administered, nor the great body of the people protected against oppression, nor the country be secured from disturbance and the incursions of plunderers, until our Government becomes more respected in those provinces than it is at present. The system which has already been adopted there renders the speedy introduction of any great or general improvement quite impracticable; but much may be done, in time, by pursuing steadily measures calculated to give the Government more weight in the country, and more direct intercourse with and control over the people. No Zemindari once forfeited for rebellion should ever be restored, whatever temporary evil the retention of it might occasion. All estates falling in should invariably be kept and annexed to the Circar lands. The gradual extension of the Circar lands should be our main object, because it is by having the direct possession and management of landed property that we can best protect the ryots, grant them remission of rent, assist them in agricultural improvements, and attach them to our Government. The extension of the Circar lands gives us also a great influence over all the military classes residing upon them, as we have thereby the power of granting them indulgences in rent, and other matters, in their several villages. Were the open country all Circar land, we should have little difficulty in raising peons whenever it was necessary, sufficient to quell any disturbance among the Zemindaris, with little or no aid from regular troops; but, while the open country is in the hands of either old or new Zemindars, the peons raised in the villages will never act cordially in our service, nor be deserving of any condence, because we have no patronage in their villages, and do nothing for them or their families, while the Proprietor or Zemindar of the village, if he be secretly adverse to the cause in which they are employed, can do them much serious injury in various ways. When the open country becomes Circar land, a strong and just Government acts silently on the people, and through them upon those of the neighbouring hill Zemindaris. The better class of traders and cultivators in both districts find that their interest is promoted by the tranquillity of the country. Their influence gradually extends to the leading men of the Zemindari, and to the rajah and his military followers, and discourages them from raising disturbances; and these men, when they see that the body of the people is against them, and that the Government is strong, remain quiet, and in time lose their turbulent and predatory habits.

"One point which requires some arrangement in order to promote the continuance of tranquillity in the Circars, is the securing to the ancient rajahs the possession of their old hereditary domains. This subject has been long before the Board, and all that is wanted might be accomplished by passing a Regulation placing these domains on the same footing as they were previous to the introduction of the judicial system, by which they will be exempted from sequestration on account of any private debt which may hereafter be contracted. The object of this measure is not only to save the families of the old Zemindars from ruin, but to save ourselves from being forced into hostilities in order to support the claims of money-lenders. The Zemindars, but more especially those of the hill districts, will often submit peaceably to the resumption of the Zemindari by Government, when they will oppose by arms its transfer to a merchant or soucar. They are not dishonoured, they think, by their possessions falling into the hands of Government; but they consider themselves as disgraced by seeing the abodes of their ancestors become the property of a low trader. As the Regulations now stand, we must, whenever a soucar obtains a decree against a Zemindar for a part or the whole of the Zemindari, on account of a debt, support him by force both in getting and maintaining possession of it; and hence we are every day liable to be dragged into a petty warfare among unhealthy hills, where an enemy is hardly ever seen, when numbers of valuable lives are lost from the climate, and when we often lose, but never gain, reputation. We have hostilities enough on account of public objects, and it is undoubtedly our duty to adopt such measures as may remove the necessity for our being obliged to have recourse to them in support of private speculations.

"On the whole it appears to me that, in order to render the local administration of the Circars gradually more efficient, it will be advisable to restore no lands which have once reverted to Government; to improve the establishment of the Collectors; to pass a Regulation for securing to the ancient Zemindars their hereditary domains; and to pass a Regulation for enabling the Collectors either to restore or to assess such inams as have been resumed without authority since the Permanent Settlement, according as they may have been held under valid titles or otherwise."*

But little occurred during the next few years to disturb the uneventful history of this District. The condition of the people was unhappily deteriorating, owing to a combination of causes which will hereafter be considered. Several seasons unfavourable to agriculture succeeded each other; but the most calamitous season, perhaps, that has ever been experienced in the Northern Circars was that of 1833. It is generally known by the name of the Great Famine; and so deeply did the remembrance of it enter into the hearts of the people that it became a marked era from which they were accustomed to reckon dates. I have frequently asked a man his age, and he has been unable to state it; but he was quite ready to answer the question, "How old were you at the time of the Great Famine?" There had been too much rain in the previous year, and in May 1832 there was a most destructive hurricane, which did an immense deal of damage to the crops and destroyed a good number of cattle. The famine was so very severe that private benevolence and the contributions freely and cheerfully rendered by the wealthier European and native inhabitants of the District were quite inadequate to stem the tide of misery and want. Mr. Crawley, the Collector, was consequently obliged to make an application for a grant from Government to enable him to relieve the pressing wants of the poor, particularly of the women and children. From March to the end of July he was able to procure food for about 5000 starving, destitute people a-day through the liberality of private individuals; but he was obliged to apply to Government for assistance from the State to mitigate in some degree the existing misery. He stated that he had deferred making this requisition till he was absolutely obliged, because he would infinitely prefer relying

* Selection of Papers from the Records at the India House relating to the Revenue, Police, and Civil and Criminal Justice under the Company's Government in India. Vol. iii. p. 566. 1826.

on private subscriptions to requesting a grant of public money. He asked only for the modest sum of 600 to 800 rupees.*

The famine was not quite so grievous in the Rajahmundry District as it was in the neighbouring District of Guntoor, but it was very bad. The hurricane in the previous year had destroyed much of the crops, which had thus no chance of recovery. The rain having also failed in the western parts of India, the usual freshes in the Godavery were deficient, and cut off the supply which was expected by the cultivators who dwelt near its banks. A partial rise early in the season induced them to commence agricultural operations, but this merely tended to delude them, and to frustrate the hopes which had been excited.† The crushing misery which gradually came upon the people and slowly destroyed them was appalling. As it increased from day to day, thousands emigrated to Madras and to other more fortunate Districts. A stream of pilgrims flowed night and day towards the south. Madras being the seat of Government, thousands repaired thither with the remnants of their household possessions, and with the children and dependants who had not died upon the road. In many cases the famishing parents sold their little perishing daughters to men who carried them off to Hyderabad. The great northern road soon became one long graveyard. It was often most difficult to distinguish between the dying and the dead. It was directed that no one should be relieved at the public expense, without undergoing the ordeal of working for this relief. Many of the better castes considered this worse than death, and refused to undergo the indignity of digging tanks, the work which was usually selected. Others accepted with shame the relief which was accompanied by such terms; and tenderly-nurtured women and high-born men were seen working at this manual labour under the direction of native overseers, while some decided to starve rather than submit to such degradation.

The pressure of hunger made men lose all regard for others and thought for the rights of property. It became impossible to transport grain without the protection of armed escorts. When they heard of the approach of grain merchants with a convoy of food, the villagers would turn out *en masse*, and strive to obtain possession of the grain by force. The usual routine of village life was most melancholy. During the day men could be seen prowling about the

* Letter to the Chief Secretary to Government, dated August 13, 1833.

† Also MS. Records.

streets picking up anything edible, even from the most defiled sources, and at night women would go to the village well, and watch the water drop slowly into their brazen vessels, every drop being carefully prized and cherished. "Deeds of violence," writes one who was evidently an eyewitness of these sad scenes, "could not be altogether suppressed; yet, on the whole, it was marvellous with what patience and submission this long period of calamity was endured—such pining want; such personal anguish; cattle dying from thirst in the fields; the little heirlooms of jewels and silver and golden ornaments parted with; the wail of famishing children; and yet no *jacquerie*, no fanatical outbursts against their rulers, in whose truth they still trusted." *

Happily this time of famine did not extend beyond a year, as is frequently the case in India. The two following seasons were favourable; but there was a general failure of the rains in the years 1836, 1837, and 1838, culminating in the latter year in distress which fell very little short of famine.† In 1839 the District was visited by another severe cyclone, which was more destructive than any that had occurred since that of May 1788. The seasons which followed were poor and unfavourable for cultivation, and this succession of unfavourable weather and scanty rains tended considerably to impoverish the District.

The cyclone of 1839 raged all along the coast from Vizagapatam to Nursapore, and its ravages extended so far inland as Rajahmundry. It was, however, most destructive near the coast. It was accompanied by a tidal wave, which burst upon the shore, and caused an inundation at Cocanada and Coringa. The shipping were driven on shore, some of the wrecked vessels being carried, it is said, four miles inland. The loss of life was very great. Very many of the native houses at Samulcotta were blown down; all the European houses except two were unroofed; and, even in Rajahmundry, some of the houses were nearly dismantled by the violence of the storm. The destruction of property was very great. The merchants' storehouses at Coringa and Injaram were ruined; cattle and crops were destroyed; large tracts of land were rendered unfit for cultivation by the overflow of salt water; the tanks were filled and spoiled by the same cause; and the wells were filled with brackish and undrinkable water for some miles inland. It was, in fact, a

* From a letter to the "Times," by E. L. K., in January 1874.

† Sir Henry Montgomery's Report, § 30.

similar, though not so destructive, a visitation as that which desolated Masulipatam just a quarter of a century afterwards.*

Before proceeding farther it is necessary to mention a tragic èvent which took place on April 26, 1843, while the Collector was engaged in conducting the annual Settlement at Amalápuram. Hussain Beg, a peon belonging to the Zillah Court, had served a summons on the village Munsiff or Magistrate of Amalápuram, and the Collector had informed him that the Munsiff should attend the Court, when he could be spared from the duties on which he was then engaged. Vexed and annoyed at this delay, the peon vented his irritation by stabbing Gázavilli Narasinga Row, the Collector's Head Sherishtadar, as he was leaving the Collector's presence and returning to his lodgings for the night. The Sherishtadar was wounded in the right side, and died after lingering two days in great pain. This act was apparently the result of momentary vexation on the part of the peon, for there appears to have been no previous malice. The deceased Sherishtadar was highly respected.†

The recent unfavourable seasons, besides the imperfect administration under the Permanent Settlement, had so impoverished the people, and had consequently so deteriorated the revenue of the District, that the attention of Government was aroused. They determined, after a careful consideration of the facts of the case, to send a special Commissioner to make minute inquiries on the spot into the causes of the decline of the revenue, and into the general condition of the people. Sir Henry Montgomery, Bart., afterwards Member of the Council of the Secretary of State for India, and now of Her Majesty's Privy Council, was appointed to perform this delicate and difficult duty. The Collector, instead of cordially co-operating with the Commissioner, did all that lay in his power to place obstacles in the way of his obtaining information and prosecuting his inquiries, so that the Government considered it advisable to remove the Collector from the District, and to authorize Sir Henry Montgomery for a time to perform his duties in addition to those of Commissioner.‡ After some months of careful and patient inquiry, he submitted to the Government a full and exhaustive Report, in which he discussed the causes of the deterioration of the revenue and of the general condition of the people, and stated the remedial measures which he recommended. The principal causes which he assigned

* Letters from Madras, by a Lady. London, Murray, p. 144. † MS. Records.

‡ Extract from Minutes of Consultation, No 852, dated August 11, 1843.

were the succession of adverse seasons, the decrease in the population, the exceptionally low price of grain, the neglect of works of irrigation, the inefficiency and corruption of the village revenue authorities, the extravagance of the Zemindars, and their mismanagement of their estates. A few remarks on each of these points taken from the Commissioner's Report will clearly show the lamentable state to which the District had then been reduced.

During the twelve years preceding the inquiry, five had been marked by peculiar distress, and three seasons had been most unfavourable. The country had partly recovered from the effects of the disastrous years 1831–32 and 1832–33, when the three unfavourable years, 1835–36, 1836–37, and 1837–38, were followed by the calamities of 1838–39 and 1839–40, and by the almost equally calamitous season of 1840–41. It could not be doubted that a series of such adverse seasons had considerably affected the resources of the District, and that the rapid decline of revenue was mainly attributable to this cause.

The decrease in the population had been very considerable. The only statistics which could then be obtained on this point are given below for the sake of comparison with the more reliable statistics of the present time.

Years.	Population.
1821–22	738,308
1826–27	654,260
1830–31	695,016
1838–39	570,481
1839–40	543,446
1840–41	533,836
1841–42	546,809
1842–43	561,041

It may be stated, in passing, that the highest figure here given is much less than half of the population of the District according to the census of 1871. The abolition of the Government factories, causing the emigration of the weavers who had hitherto been dependent on them, and the successive unfavourable seasons, appear to have been the cause of this decrease.

The prices of agricultural produce commenced to decline in 1827. Except in years of extreme scarcity, they continued very low, until, in the year preceding the inquiry, they had attained a very low ebb indeed. This depreciation in the value of their produce affected the means of the cultivators, and materially aided in the depression of the revenue.

It has already been stated in the account of the construction of the Annicut, that Sir Henry Montgomery pointedly drew the attention of Government to the want of proper irrigation works in the District. This was one of the remediable causes which led to the impoverishment of the people. "My own impression," he wrote, "leads to the opinion that much may be done with the Godavery, both in improving the means of cultivation in adverse seasons when local rains fail, and in counteracting the ill effects which follow an over-abundance; but whatever works of a general nature are undertaken, they must be accompanied by a more extensive and efficient supervision of the repairs of those subsidiary works on which the efficiency of the greater so much depends. It is impossible to traverse this District without observing the neglected state of minor works of irrigation, extending to the village channels of supply and drainage and the embankments of fields, and not to deplore the apathy of the people, who, while they are loud in their complaints of the little that has been done by Government towards the maintenance in efficiency of the existing works, have disregarded their own interest in not preserving those under their immediate control." The present condition of the District in this respect contrasts most favourably with that of the time to which reference is now made.

Not bringing to the credit of Government the full collections made from the ryots was another fertile source of the decrease of revenue in the villages belonging to Government. The village expenses amounted to 9¼ per cent. of the collections, and out of them large sums were paid to the Government officials. But the principal cause was stated to be the inefficiency of the management of their estates by the Zemindars and Proprietors. No fixed principle was adopted. In some parts the practice of renting villages annually or for a term of years existed, preference being given to such proposals as ensured the highest amount of rent, and afforded security for its punctual payment, with little regard to the class of persons proposing, and with no reference to the influence rack-rents would have on the future resources of the village and on the condition of the ryots. The villages were held under various tenures, and little endeavour was made to secure the welfare of the cultivators themselves.

Few of the Zemindars interested themselves in the management of their estates. They intrusted everything to the care of their ministers, whose policy it was to make the Zemindars entirely dependent on them, and to prevent them from interfering in the administration. There was no system of management. The only object was to extract from the ryots the utmost possible amount of revenue. In adverse seasons all that could be taken of the ryots' produce was claimed on the part of the Zemindar, and the demand purposely exceeded the means of the ryots in ordinary seasons. The deficiency of bad seasons was made good in favourable seasons, so that, in either case, the ryot was left merely a bare subsistence. The Proprietors of the new estates, which were created on the introduction of the Permanent Settlement, followed the example set them by the ancient Zemindars, and copied their affectation of regal pomp. Their estates were put up to sale in satisfaction of arrears of revenue after they had thus drained their resources, and passed into the hands of fresh speculators, who followed the same course. The realization of the Government revenue was for a time secured by these means; but the ultimate impoverishment of the country was thus gradually advancing.

The system of the Permanent Settlement had proved a failure. The causes of this failure were the inherent defects of the system itself, and the incapacity of the persons on whom the administration of the system devolved. The Board of Revenue, in their comments on the Commissioner's Report, remarked that "the system, besides involving the principle of intermediate agency, injurious in any form however modified, presents the anomalous aspect of two proprietors—the ryot virtually so, and the Zemindar proprietor by creation. The ryot occupies the most important place in the fiscal system of India. He is the source whence all rent is drawn; but his position was affected, and his importance destroyed, by the power and rights acquired by the Zemindar. The two interests, it is obvious, cannot coexist. The Zemindar and ryot are placed in a position of antagonism, and one or other must yield. As rent is entirely drawn from the ryot, it does not require any lengthened argument to show that, where the ryot is obliged to yield, the sources whence revenue is drawn become impaired. The Board are of opinion that this fundamental defect in the Permanent Settlement has been the main cause of the decay of the revenue in the Northern Circars."

The Commissioner strongly recommended that a careful and

judicious assessment, based on a regular survey of the District, should be carried out as the most effectual remedy for the evils of the revenue administration. Meanwhile, he considered that the system of renting villages to the inhabitants themselves, denominated "joint rents," ought to be adopted in all Government lands, as the system best adapted for the welfare of the people and for the security of the Government revenue. He was of opinion that it afforded encouragement to the improvement and extension of cultivation, protection to the poorer ryots so far as their interests were involved in those of the richer cultivators, and it relieved all from the obnoxious interference of the Government officials at the time of cultivation and of harvest. Under this system a certain amount was demanded as the rent of each village, the arrangement being made with the village authorities, and the ryots being jointly responsible for the payment of it. The Government approved of this proposal, and directed that the system which the Commissioner had so strongly recommended should at once be introduced, until a regular survey and settlement could be carried out.

The Commissioner recommended that the greatest leniency and kindness should be shown towards all those Zemindars whose estates had been sequestrated for arrears of revenue, or forfeited from the same cause. The Zemindars of Rámachandrapuram and of Kóta were deeply involved in private debts in addition to the large revenue arrears against them. Both of these estates were sold, and yearly allowances granted to the owners. The Zemindari of Peddapore had long been dismembered. The Zemindar, however, retained a portion of it called the Kottám Estate, from which he derived an income sufficient to support him in dignity and affluence. The representative of the family is still in possession of this estate. The Government adhered to the principle advocated by Sir Thomas Munro, that all estates falling in should invariably be kept, and annexed to the Government lands. It was considered that the policy of restoring these estates to the Zemindars was incompatible with the interests of the agricultural classes. "The proposition," the Board of Revenue remarked, "involves the perpetuation of Zemindari influence and agency, the destructive effects of which are now fresh under review, and the mass of the people will be left without the power of attaining independence and proprietary consequence. Nor would the proposition benefit the families. Ultimately they will again find themselves in the same position as at present, because the operation of the same causes must terminate in producing the same effects. Considerations of the revenue and of the ryot are unfavourable to any further experiments. They desired, however, that the greatest kindness and consideration should be shown to the families of those whose estates had been sold for arrears of revenue contracted by their own extravagance and laxity of administration." *

In bringing to a close this abstract of Sir Henry Montgomery's able and interesting Report, a brief comparison between the state of the District then and its present more flourishing condition is unavoidable. There cannot be a shadow of doubt that the Permanent Settlement as introduced into this District at the commencement of the century was a decided failure. It was ill adapted to the wants of the people, and it was most injudiciously administered. The ancient Zemindars and the new Proprietors alike were unthrifty, improvident, and totally unfitted for the transaction of business. They allowed the payment of their rents to Government to fall into arrears, and they neglected the best interests of the ryots, upon whom they really depended for their support. Under this system the population decreased, the revenue diminished, and the people were reduced to poverty and distress. Since that time the population has been more than doubled; important works of irrigation have been constructed; a regular survey and settlement have been undertaken; the revenue has very much increased; commerce has been greatly extended; the condition of the cultivating classes has been considerably improved; the Zemindars themselves have benefited in every way; and the people in general are happy, prosperous, and contented.

* Sir Henry Montgomery's Report, dated March 18, 1844. Proceedings of the Board of Revenue, dated July 14, 1845. Extract from Minutes of Consultation of the Madras Government, Revenue Department, No. 432, dated April 14, 1846.

CHAPTER XVI.

RECENT HISTORY.

APPOINTMENT OF THE COMMISSIONER OF THE NORTHERN CIRCARS—UNFAVOURABLE SEASON—THE GREAT MILITARY MUTINY IN THE NORTH—SUBBAREDDI'S REBELLION—SIR CHARLES TREVELYAN'S VISIT TO THE DISTRICT—RE-ARRANGEMENT OF THE BOUNDARY BETWEEN RAJAHMUNDRY AND MASULIPATAM—REDISTRIBUTION OF THE CIVIL JURISDICTION—JUDICIAL ARRANGEMENTS—MUNICIPALITIES—LOCAL FUNDS—INTRODUCTION OF THE MOFUSSIL POLICE.

THE deplorable condition in which Sir Henry Montgomery found the District of Rajahmundry was not peculiar to it. Guntoor was just as bad; and in 1844, Mr., now Sir Walter, Elliot was deputed to make a similar inquiry there. His attention was specially directed to the causes of the decay of the revenue, to the condition of the Zemindars, whose estates were all under sequestration for arrears, and to the preparation of a plan for the survey of the land and the revision of the settlement. His report on the last measure was deferred for consideration until the scheme for the general survey of the whole Presidency was organized. On receiving his general report, which was subsequently submitted, the Court of Directors were of opinion that a most searching investigation into the condition of the whole Northern Circars was necessary. In order to secure the vigorous and energetic action which such an investigation demanded, they considered it advisable to place the province under the immediate charge of one of the members of the Board of Revenue as Special Commissioner, who was to exercise the full powers of the Board, and to correspond direct with Government. Mr. Elliot was appointed the first Commissioner of the Northern Circars in 1849. His principal duty was to carry out the measures of reform which had been inaugurated by Sir Henry Montgomery and himself. His particular attention was directed towards the district of Masulipatam; but the other districts also were entirely under his jurisdiction in all revenue matters. In 1854 Mr. Elliot was appointed to a seat in the Council at Madras, and Mr. Goldingham, then senior member of the Board of Revenue, was appointed by the Madras Government to succeed him. The Court of Directors, however, were of opinion that the temporary expedient of a Special Commissioner being appointed to exercise in the Northern Circars the full powers of the Board of Revenue, ought to cease, the object for which it had been adopted having been sufficiently attained. They directed, therefore, that the province should again be brought under the ordinary superintendence, and their orders were carried into effect in the following year.*

With some deficiency in non-irrigated lands from a failure in the periodical rains, the season of 1855–56 was, on the whole, favourable, and the District prosperous. The produce was comparatively abundant; but large exportations of rice and oil seeds to Europe kept up the rapidly increasing prices of every kind of provision. There was, however, a decrease in the revenue of 22,898 rupees, the land revenue being less by 52,422 rupees, while there was an increase in the revenue from other and various sources of 29,524 rupees.

The season of 1857–58 was most unfavourable. Scarcity and dearness of food pressed heavily on the people, and the poorer classes were deprived of a profitable means of employment by the stoppage of all public works. The early rains of the south-west monsoon, on which the dry-grain cultivation depends, were scanty; and, when the heavier rains of the north-east monsoon commenced, the whole rainfall seemed to have been concentrated into one violent burst, which discharged in the space of a few days such a volume of water that it proved too great to be confined in the ordinary channels and reservoirs, which were extensively injured by this excessive supply.

The Annicut was breached during the year; but, fortunately, this accident occurred just when the rice crops were mature. Some loss was experienced, especially by the cultivators of sugar-cane; but the breach was closed in time to prevent more serious consequences. The breach occurred in the Maddúru branch of the Annicut. It was closed in a temporary manner within six weeks from the time of its occurrence. The total cost of repairing it was

* Despatches from the Court of Directors to the Government of Madras, dated January 31, 1849, and December 6, 1854.

estimated at 90,000 rupees, being about 10 per cent. of the first cost of the work.*

The difficulty of procuring labour was at this time keenly felt. The improvements which had been so extensively made in the District for many years had their natural effect on the labour market. The great extension of cultivation throughout the Delta, and the increased facilities for transport had so reduced the available number of labourers, that the Department of Public Works was unable to obtain the supply which it formerly could command with ease; and, notwithstanding that the departmental rate of wages had been raised fully 30 per cent., serious difficulty was encountered, and the rate demanded continued to rise.

This year was, however, marked by far more serious occurrences than an adverse season and increased prices. The anxiety felt throughout Southern India, on account of the great military mutiny in the North, was felt in full proportion in this District, although there were few parts of India quieter during that perilous period. Some apprehension was experienced during the Mohurrum, which that year took place in August, while the result of the deadly struggle in the North-West Provinces was undecided. Delhi was still untaken, and Lucknow unrelieved. Though a good deal of sedition was preached by wandering mendicants, the people, especially the Hindus, were perfectly peaceful and loyal.

A petty disturbance took place in the hills to the north of the Yarnagúdem and Tádimalla Taluks, as they were then called. It originated in matters connected with a private dispute between some of the Reddis, or petty hill chiefs; but, as the principal person concerned informed me, when, after his apprehension, he was placed upon his trial before me, it was fomented and increased by the lamentable tidings from the North. Putting his hands together in the attitude of submission, he said, "May I be permitted to speak? I heard that Nana Sahib was advancing with his victorious army, and that whosoever did most against the English would be rewarded most."

Kárukonda Subbáreddi was the head man of Koratúru, a village on the Godavery not far from the Gorge. He had been anxious to obtain a certain rich widow in marriage for his son; but, hearing that she had become the concubine of Sunkaraswámi, the

* Administration Report for 1857-58, pp. 5, 6, 32.

village munsiff or magistrate of Buttayagúdem, he attempted with a large body of his Koi followers to carry her off by force from his protection. Failing in the immediate object of his raid, he plundered the village, and retreated with a quantity of booty and cattle to the village of the widow's late husband, where he was reinforced by other Reddis with a considerable number of followers.

The Acting Head-Assistant Magistrate, hearing of these events, hastened from Rajahmundry to the scene of action. Taking with him sixty or seventy peons and the Tahsildar of the Taluk, he went to the plundered village, where he made his headquarters. He advanced to the position taken up by the marauders, who did not await his arrival. Having made a few prisoners, he returned with them to Buttayagúdem, where he passed the night. Early next morning he found that his small party was surrounded by an overwhelming number of hill-men under Subbáreddi and his son, armed with matchlocks and bows and arrows. The peons with him failed to stand their ground. He was consequently compelled to release his prisoner, to surrender the recovered property, and finally to retreat. Sunkaraswámi was carried off by the insurgents, and was taken to the hills, where he was murdered.

Directly these events were reported to the Collector, two companies of the Sappers and Miners were sent from Dowlaishweram to Yarnagúdem. The Acting Joint Magistrate soon afterwards joined them and assumed the civil charge of the party, while Captain Rose commanded the military detachment. Directly arrangements had been made, the party advanced into the hills. Information was received that some of the principal insurgents had taken up their quarters in the dilapidated fort at Nágavaram, and a forced march was made thither from Yarnagúdem, in the hopes of surrounding the place before they could make their escape. They heard of the approach of the detachment, however, and absconded by secret paths known only to themselves. On the entrance of the military about ten o'clock at night, the fort was found entirely deserted.

The only place where the insurgents attempted to make a stand was Jílagamilli. This village is situated at the top of a steep ascent by a mountain stream. The inhabitants had raised a stockade, and, as the sepoys ascended the hill, the insurgents fired at them from behind their defences. They abandoned them, however, without further resistance, and fled to a plain behind the village, which was flanked on two sides by the jungle, and on the third by a field of Indian corn. Directly the sepoys made their appearance, they were assailed by arrows and a few shots from matchlocks, and the enemy immediately fled into the jungle. During the remainder of the campaign in the hills, the enemy was scarcely seen. Every now and then a matchlock was discharged from behind a rock or a bush; but the person who fired it was generally hidden. The rule followed was that no retaliation was made, except in the few instances in which a sepoy or a camp-follower was wounded by some unseen or distant opponent, and then the nearest village was burnt down as an example and a warning. All these villages had, of course, been deserted. A few prisoners were captured. After this harassing pursuit had been continued for a fortnight in a most unhealthy country, the troops were withdrawn. Almost all employed on this service were attacked with jungle fever, which, in a few instances, proved fatal.

The campaign was continued by a Sibbandi or Revenue Corps, which was embodied for that purpose, and placed under the command of Captain Alleyne F. F. Bloomfield. Subbáreddi and seven other ringleaders were captured, and were sentenced to suffer capital punishment by the Session Judge, acting as Commissioner under Act XIV of 1857. Subbáreddi and Korla Sítárámayya, who had been proved to have been one of the most active and desperate of the leaders in the rebellion, having been convicted of participation in Sunkaraswámi's murder, as well as the murder of another, were executed at Buttayagúdem, the scene of their crime, on October 7, 1858. Korla Venkata Subbáreddi, half-brother of Sítárámayya, also an active leader, and Guruguntla Kommireddi, who had assisted in the murder of Sunkaraswámi, were hanged at Pólavaram on the same day. On the same occasion Kárukonda Tammireddi, Subbáreddi's brother, was executed at Tútigunta. He had joined in the rebellion, and had, with his own hand, shot a man who was conveying a message from the camp of the officer commanding the corps.*

No attempt besides this comparatively insignificant rebellion was made to disturb the public peace. The District remained perfectly tranquil throughout the remainder of that trying time, and nothing worthy of particular note occurred. The Royal Proclamation, announcing that her most gracious Majesty the Queen had been

* Administration Report for 1857–58, p. 83. District Gazette for 1858, p. 210.

pleased to assume the direct government of her Indian dominions, was publicly read on November 1, 1858, in the presence of large and respectful crowds, at all the larger towns—namely, Rajahmundry, Cocanada, and Nursapore.

In September 1859, Sir Charles Trevelyan, then Governor of Madras, paid an official visit to the District. He bestowed particular attention on all its principal requirements. The improvement of the town and port of Cocanada, the complete development of the system of the works of irrigation, the plans for opening up the navigation of the Godavery, the settlement of the assessment on the newly irrigated tracts of land, were the subjects which principally engaged his attention. The interesting minute in which his observations were recorded, has been referred to in other portions of this volume.

One of the results of Sir Charles Trevelyan's visit was the re-arrangement of the Rajahmundry and the Masulipatam Districts. The boundary between them had hitherto been inconveniently irregular. They completely interlaced each other. Patches of the latter district were to be found so entirely surrounded by portions of the former that they appeared in the old maps of Rajahmundry like islands. The Masulipatam district extended to the very banks of the Godavery, while the Sub-Collector of Rajahmundry, when travelling from Nursapore to the north of his division, had to pass through large tracts of Masulipatam. The greatest inconvenience, however, arose with reference to the irrigation works. The deltas of the Godavery and the Kistna were under separate jurisdiction in the Department of Public Works; but, the revenue jurisdiction being different, each of the two District Engineers had to deal with two Collectors. It was, therefore, considered advisable that each of the two complete systems of works should be placed under only one set of authorities, both in the Revenue and in the Public Works Departments. Three proposals were made for the satisfactory re-arrangement of the boundary. It was eventually decided that the three districts—Rajahmundry, Masulipatam, and Guntoor—should be divided into two. The boundary between them was to follow the course of the Upputéru and Tamaléru rivers. The names of the two districts were to be respectively the Godavery and the Kistna, after the noble river in each. The change, however, was to be effected without dividing villages. In every case where a village was divided by the boundary stream, the whole village was to belong to the district on the side of which its greater part was situated. The headquarters of the Collector and of the Sub-Collector of the Godavery District were to remain at Cocanada and Nursapore, while that of the Head-Assistant was to be Rajahmundry. These arrangements came into operation from December 16, 1859.*

While describing this very desirable redistribution of the District, it will be convenient to mention here the arrangements which were subsequently made for the Sub-Collector's Division and the Head Assistant-Collector's charge. When the Collectorate of Rajahmundry was originally formed, the whole country was held under Zemindari tenure, and the services of the Collector were only occasionally demanded for the internal management of the estates. As time went on, however, several of these estates, as already stated, lapsed or were sold for arrears of revenue and purchased for Government. The duties of the Collector thus became more and more onerous, until they exceeded the power of one official adequately to perform. The Court of Directors had their attention directed to the arduous duties of the Collector in this District, and as early as 1833 expressed their opinion that the suggestion to select an experienced Head Assistant-Collector from a ryotwary district, and place the Government villages in Rajahmundry under his management, was worthy of consideration; and Sir Henry Montgomery, in his Report on the District ten years later, strongly recommended the appointment of a Subordinate Collector to assist the Collector in his labours. He recommended that he should be stationed somewhere in the Taluks to the south and west of the Godavery. The Governor in Council accordingly appointed a Sub-Collector in the Rajahmundry District, with the necessary establishment, and his headquarters were fixed at Nursapore. The Taluks to the west of the Godavery, from Yarnagúdem and Tádimalla in the north to Nursapore in the south, were placed under him. This gave him a long and rather irregular range, the irregularity of which was augmented by the interlacing of the Masulipatam district; but the most populous and the most fertile Taluks were in the south, from which there was easy access to Nursapore. At one time the Sub-Division of Rajahmundry was, perhaps, the most important in the whole Presidency of Madras. The people were wealthy and prosperous;

* Proceedings of the Madras Government, Revenue Department, November 4 and December 3, 1859. District Gazette, December 12, 1859.

the Delta Taluks were freely irrigated from the Annicut; the land was as fertile as any in Southern India, with the exception, perhaps, of Tanjore; the new survey and assessment were early carried out there; and a new and most interesting scheme of popular education was established and efficiently carried out: and yet, during the ten most important years in the history of the Sub-Division, owing to the exigencies of the service, and to the particular period of their service when Sub-Collectors are usually promoted, there were no less than nine officers appointed to it.*

Mr. Henry Forbes, the first Sub-Collector, resided a great deal at Dowlaishweram and Rajahmundry. Subsequently a house near the bank of the Godavery, at Madapollam, a suburb of Nursapore, was inhabited by the Sub-Collector; and, as there was no building in the town available for his office, this was usually held in a bungalow not far from his residence and in his own grounds. During a correspondence which took place in 1866 regarding the site of a new office, the suggestion appears to have been first made as to the advisability of removing the Sub-Collector's headquarters from Nursapore.† The original proposition made in reply to the suggestion of Government on this point was, that a general change should be made, the Collector's headquarters being transferred to Rajahmundry, with charge of the Rajahmundry, Peddapore, and Yarnagúdem Taluks; the Sub-Collector's station being Cocanada, with charge of the Taluks of Rámachandrapuram and Amalápuram; the Head Assistant-Collector going to Ellore, with charge of Ellore and Tanuku; and the Deputy-Collector for general duties being stationed at Nursapore, with charge of the Taluks of Nursapore and Undi, instead of remaining at Ellore, where he had been stationed since the office of Deputy-Collector was created.‡ It was finally arranged that the Collector should still remain at Cocanada, where his presence was required more than at Rajahmundry, in consequence of the numerous interests and continual cases demanding his personal intervention in that populous and increasingly flourishing port. The Sub-Collector was stationed at Rajahmundry; the Head Assistant-Collector at Ellore; and the Deputy Collector at Nursapore.‖

* Sir Henry Montgomery's Report, §§ 83-85. Government Order, March 3, 1846, No. 153.

† Government Order, No. 2979, Miscellaneous, dated November 3, 1866.

‡ Collector to Secretary to the Board of Revenue, January 8, 1867. Government Order, No. 1840, Miscellaneous, August 8, 1867.

‖ Government Order, No. 2639, dated November 7, 1867.

The Taluks under the charge of these officers respectively had in this new arrangement been apparently allotted more according to the population and the amount of revenue derivable from each than from any other consideration. It was soon discovered that, in reality, the Head Assistant-Collector had more work and a more important charge than the Sub-Collector; and, on a reference being made to the Acting Collector and Magistrate whether the practice of referring some of the magisterial work of the District to the Principal Sudder Amin could not be avoided, he suggested a fresh arrangement of the revenue charges as well. It was shown that the 2058 square miles which were set down as the area of the Rajahmundry Taluk, when it was placed under the Sub-Collector, included the hills of Rampa, a tract of country very sparsely populated and yielding no revenue at all. Three hundred miles of almost uninhabited hills were included in the Taluk of Yarnagúdem. Excluding these tracts of country, the remainder of the portion allotted to the Sub-Collector was the worst cultivated and most thinly peopled part of the District. With regard to the revenue the disproportion was just as great. There were numerous small Zemindaris in the Sub-Division, the payment for which to Government contributed to swell the amount of the revenue. The collection of this, of the abkarry, and of the stamp revenue, gave but little trouble to the offices either of the Sub-Collector or of the Tahsildars; and, when these items were eliminated, the land revenue, ryotwary and miscellaneous, hardly exceeded four lacs of rupees, whereas in the Head Assistant-Collector's division it was between six and seven lacs, and in the Deputy-Collector's nearly ten. In the Principal Division at that time the land revenue under the same heads amounted to upwards of fourteen lacs of rupees, a charge which the Collector was unable to perform efficiently in conjunction with his various other onerous duties. In accordance with the Acting Collector's proposal, the Government finally decided that the Sub-Collector, while still continuing to reside at Rajahmundry, should have charge of the Taluks of Rajahmundry, Amalápuram, and Rámachandrapuram; that the Head Assistant-Collector's division should consist of Ellore, Yarnagúdem, and Tanuku, with his headquarters at Ellore; and that the Deputy-Collector should remain in the charge already assigned to him, namely, the Taluks of Bhímavaram and Nursapore. The effect of this re-distribution of Taluks was to give the Sub-Collector a charge more in proportion to his position in the service and to the extent of his office establishment than he had lately possessed, while, at the same time, it relieved the Collector of the immediate charge of two heavy Taluks at some distance from his head-quarters, and enabled him, with the aid of an experienced Assistant, to take up the magisterial work hitherto performed by the Principal Sudder Amin, or, as he is now called, the Subordinate Judge.*

While mention is being made of the executive and administrative arrangements, a good opportunity is afforded of stating the judicial arrangements. A Court of Adawlut or of Justice was established at Rajahmundry in 1802 at the time of the introduction of the Permanent Settlement. It was subordinate to the Provincial Court at Masulipatam, the judges of which used to come on circuit, from time to time, for the purpose of holding the criminal sessions. In 1827 Auxiliary Courts were established, and native judges with extensive authority were appointed. In 1836 these judges received the designation of Principal Sudder Amin. In 1843 further changes were made. The Provincial and Zillah Courts were abolished, and Civil and Subordinate Courts were created in their stead. A Civil and Session Court and a Subordinate Court were established at Rajahmundry. The latter was abolished in 1859; but, as in all other districts, the title was transferred to the Principal Sudder Amin, in 1873, in which year the chief court in the District was designated the District and Session Court.

The system of trial by jury in certain cases of offences against property was, in the year 1861, introduced under the Code of Criminal Procedure. It was introduced into only seven districts, of which Rajahmundry was one. After the experience of the new system for a few years, the High Court of Judicature at Madras, recorded their opinion that it had, on the whole, worked favourably, though this was partly attributable to the fact of the careful selection of the offences to which it was made applicable.

Inferior native courts were created in 1802. Native commissioners were appointed to hear and decide all civil causes that might arise for sums of money not exceeding 80 rupees. A few years later they received the designation of District Munsiffs, which title they still bear, though their powers have since been very con-

* Government Order, Revenue Department, No. 192, dated February 16, 1872. Letter from Acting Collector, No. 3, dated January 6, 1872.

siderably increased. There are six District Munsiffs' Courts, which are situated at Rajahmundry, Cocanada, Peddapore, Nursapore, Amalápuram, and Ellore. A second Subordinate Court was established in 1874, and located at Cocanada.

The principal feature which has, perhaps, characterized the administration of India during the last few years, is the introduction into the provinces of the principles of local government. The Godavery District has had its full share in this salutary movement. An organized and systematic effort was made, about the year 1862, for the sanitary improvement of the town of Cocanada. This movement was attended with a considerable degree of success. Influential merchants, both European and Native, were members of the local committee, of which the Collector and other Government officials were *ex officio* members. Subscriptions were raised, and certain cesses voted, by which, aided by Government grants equal to the amount collected, many sanitary improvements were effected. The Government at the time regarded this movement with much satisfaction, looking upon it as a more promising symptom of self-government than the adoption of the Municipal Act, which was then merely permissive, would have been. It lasted, however, only two years, when it was merged in the general scheme involved in the universal adoption of the Municipal Act.*

In 1866 municipalities were instituted in most of the large towns throughout the Presidency of Madras, under Act X of 1865 (Madras). They were intended to provide for the police, the conservancy, and the general improvement of the towns. In a few places some opposition was experienced; but wherever the objects for which the Act was passed were carefully explained, and the introduction of it effected in a judicious manner, the interest of the native Commissioners was aroused, and the provisions of the Act carried out with much heartiness. The towns into which it was introduced in this District were Cocanada, Rajahmundry, and Ellore.

The principle on which this measure was founded was soon extended further. The origin of the local funds scheme, which has of late years assumed proportions of considerable magnitude, was comparatively humble. It is stated in the Administration Report for 1858-59 that funds for the construction, repair, and maintenance of minor roads, with the bridges and other works

* Administration Report for 1865-66.

connected with them, had been established in sixteen districts. They consisted of the proceeds of ferry rents and tolls, road cesses, interest on funded capital, and sundry miscellaneous items. These funds, it was stated, had proved of great utility in districts where they had been thoroughly established, particularly in South Arcot, Malabar, and Canara. A network of cross-roads was constructed, and provision made for their proper maintenance after completion. Thus, while the trunk roads were made and maintained by the State out of the imperial funds, the minor communications, without which the imperial lines would lose much of their utility, were constructed from these local funds. The Local Fund in each District was entrusted to the Collector and the Engineer, who together determined the works to be undertaken each year, subject to the concurrence of the Chief Engineer in regard to masonry and timber works likely to cost more than 2500 rupees.* The commencement in this District was gradual, the first receipts being very small, and those for the second year only 335.† The receipts for 1859–60 were 242. Those for 1860–61 only 47. In 1861–62, 1221.

The Local Fund was levied for some years, but it speedily degenerated into a District Road Fund, which was subsequently consolidated by a legislative measure, known by the title of the District Road Cess Act. This enactment increased the income by 93 per cent., and enabled the Government to undertake the repair of roads and other public works connected with all the lines which were not strictly imperial.‡ But in 1871 the whole scheme was elaborated into a wider and more extensive plan for local self-government by the passing of the Local Funds Act (Act IV. of 1871). The District was divided under this new measure into two Local Fund Circles. Each Circle had a Local Fund Board, presided over by the Collector, which administered the funds entrusted to it under the supervision of the Board of Revenue and Government. No part of the income of one Circle could be expended in the other without the express sanction of Government. The funds were raised by a tax of nine pies in the rupee on the rent value of land, by tolls on carriages and animals where Government allowed toll-gates, as at Rajahmundry, and by a house-tax, which was levied in unions or group of villages where Local Fund

* Administration Report for 1858–59, p. 250.

† Ibid., 1859–60, p. 20.

‡ Ibid., 1867–68, p. 40.

schools were established. The funds were spent on three classes of objects—on roads and other communications, on education, and on hospitals, medicine, and sanitation. The following short statement will show the rapid manner in which the finances of the Local Funds have increased of late years :—

Years.	Rupees.
1863-64	30,389
1864-65	51,802
1865-66	46,107
1866-67	53,069
1867-68	216,246
1868-69	368,280
1869-70	479,950
1870-71	447,528

The new organization of the Mofussil Police was introduced into this District in 1861-62. At first it was necessarily rather incomplete. In the first year of its introduction, seven out of the thirteen Taluks were occupied, and 971 men enlisted out of a force estimated at 1502. The Sibbandi Corps which was raised at the time of Subbáreddi's disturbance, was reduced in number and amalgamated with the Police, and the remnant was maintained as an armed reserve in full military efficiency. Its original strength was 237, and it was reduced to 118. Captain A. F. F. Bloomfield was appointed Superintendent of the District, and Lieutenant Robertson Assistant-Superintendent. They had both been officers of the Sibbandi Corps. The whole system was fully carried out in the following year, and the constabulary organized.*

The services of the new Police were soon required. The Zemindari of Rampa became the scene of disturbance in 1862, and as had frequently been the case, the disturbance was caused by action taken by the Mansabdar. He had been long resident in the low country because of the detestation in which he was held by the people; but he now attempted to return, and take up his abode in his own Zemindari. This occasioned such irritation that he had to return more speedily than he went. The insurrection rapidly spread. A strong force of police was marched into the hills, they took all the stockades, which the people had erected, and soon reduced the malcontents to order and submission. The

* Administration Report for 1861-62, p. 11.

law then took its course, and the principal instigators of these disturbances were tried and transported. The country was permanently occupied by the Police, and a village police formed. The men suffered very much in health. Nearly the whole body employed in this insalubrious country passed through hospital, and many died. Both the European officers broke down, after having gallantly performed all that was required.* The whole force suffered very much from fever after the occupation of the Zemindari; and the wise measure was accordingly adopted of recruiting from the hill people themselves for service in that part of the country.

* Administration Report for 1862–63, p. 21; for 1863–64, p. 18.

CHAPTER XVII.

THE REVENUE SURVEY AND SETTLEMENT.

PROPOSALS FOR A REGULAR SURVEY—ADOPTION OF THE SYSTEM OF JOINT RENTS—DESCRIPTION OF THE VARIOUS REVENUE SYSTEMS—THE VÍSABADI SYSTEM—THE SHARING SYSTEM—THE PRACTICE OF CHALLENGING—OPINION OF THE SPECIAL COMMISSIONER—DESCRIPTION OF JOINT RENTS—COMMENCEMENT AND PROSECUTION OF THE REGULAR SURVEY AND ASSESSMENT—CONCLUDING REMARKS.

IT has been stated that both Sir Henry Montgomery in his Report on the condition of this District, and Mr. Elliot in his Report on Guntoor, strongly advocated the introduction of a complete survey and settlement of the Government lands. A scheme for organizing a general survey throughout the Presidency of Madras had been for some time under consideration, and it was at this juncture about to be commenced. Before noticing its operations in this District, it will be advisable to give a brief account of the various revenue systems which had, from time to time, been adopted. The system of Joint Rents was the one most general at this period. It was, however, intended to be only a temporary expedient. From the very first the object of the Court of Directors was to place the revenue management of the Northern Circars on a sound basis at the earliest opportunity, and they fully intended that all the Government lands should eventually be placed under the Ryotwary system. The Joint Rents were, in fact, only preparatory to the anticipated Survey and Settlement.*

The several revenue systems cannot be better described than by Mr. R. E. Master in his admirable Report on the Settlement of the Western Delta, and I have, therefore, taken the liberty of freely using

* Extract from Minutes of Consultation, March 3, 1849. Revenue Department, No. 310. Administration Report for 1855-56, p. 23.

his remarks on this subject. The most ancient revenue system in the country was the "*Ásará*" or division of the produce; but in the Government estates, as well as in many Zemindaris, this was often effected through the intervention of a renter. The system is thus described by the Committee of Circuit:—"The ancient established custom among the Hindus of collecting the revenue was by a division of the crop. At present, several different modes are adopted, as suits the interest or pleasure of the Zemindars. In the Rajahmundry Circar, and in part of Ellore, the shist is generally established, particularly in the more fertile soils producing paddy. In the other parts of the Ellore and Mustafanagar Circars, a division of the crop according to the fertility of the soil, after the usual deductions for charity and village servants, is still the practice, and in all the three Circars, lands producing dry grains (excepting Indian corn), tobacco, cotton, betel, betel-nut, sugar-cane, oil seeds, palmyra, and fruit-trees, and garden grounds, are generally let by 'Bilmakta.' It is the usual practice of the Zemindars in collecting the revenue, to divide it into four kists—the first is taken in June, the second in September, the third in December, and the great kist in February, so that the whole is received by the end of the harvest. The other taxes which do not depend on the crop are not levied at any particular season.

"The usual nominal shares allowed the cultivator are, of paddy, eight, ten, and twelve tooms in twenty. The fixed cultivators receive the first proportion. Brahmins, Rachawars, strangers, and those favoured by the Zemindars, are allowed ten and twelve tooms. Dry grains ought to be equally divided between the Zemindar and the ryot.

"Were the cultivators to receive even the first proportion of eight tooms, without deduction, they would be amply repaid for their labour; but, from the information of many of the inhabitants on this subject, as well as by an inspection of their accounts, we find the shares seldom exceed a fourth or fifth part of the produce. Even with these proportions, the lands of the Zemindars are better cultivated than the farms immediately dependent on the Company. The natives in the Zemindaris have no security for their property or right in the soil. Their only refuge in cases of oppression is in the Zemindar, whose interest it is to give them protection; but in cases that affect the Zemindars themselves, they have no other resource than in the Chief in Council, but the timidity of the natives, were they certain of procuring redress, will be always an obstacle to their applying for justice to that quarter." *

In a letter to the Collector of the First Division of the Rajahmundry Circar, dated November 8, 1794, the Board of Revenue recommended as a principle to be uniformly kept in view, that, when any lands fell under the immediate management of Government, the inhabitants should be encouraged to rent their own village in preference to any other mode of management, and that, if possible, the lands of a village should be divided into several farms, to be let out to the more wealthy ryots. It was hoped that by this means individual property might be extended, the improvement and prosperity of the country secured, and that the ryots, by holding their farms immediately from Government, would become more independent, and be screened from the vexatious exactions to which they had hitherto been subjected by the intermediate renters and their dependents. It was not anticipated that the ryots would at first relish the change, as, holding their lands direct from Government, they would have to meet their engagements with punctuality; but it was hoped that they might be gradually brought to see the advantages to be derived from the protection of Government, and from the certainty that the demand would not be enhanced beyond the fixed rent. Joint responsibility was the principle of the rents thus ordered, for the Board go on to say, "the only security required is the inhabitants of each village becoming jointly and severally bound for the rent of Government."

As the whole of the Government lands were formed into Proprietary Estates at the introduction of the Permanent Settlement, the rents held direct from Government necessarily ceased, and for ten years there were no lands under the immediate management of the Collector. At the end of that time, the first Proprietary Estate failed, and became a Government estate, and the Collector was instructed to rent out the villages to the principal inhabitants.

The renting system was not long continued, and, in June 1817, the Board issued instructions for the introduction of the "Vísabadi" and "Ásará" systems. When the latter mode of settlement was adopted, the ryots were to be induced to take the Government share of the crop at a fair valuation, either agreed upon beforehand, or just before the harvest. The settlement, in either case, was to be

* The Committee of Circuit's Report on Zemindaris, 1787, § 40.

made with the resident ryots of the village, and it was only in the event of the ryots refusing to come to reasonable terms, that the Collector was authorized to rent the village.

In March 1825, Mr. Kindersley, in reporting on the settlement of the Government estates for Fasli 1234 (1824–25), explained fully the Vísabadi and Ásará systems, which had by that time entirely replaced the village rents, the former being usually confined to dry, and the latter to wet lands. The Vísabadi, which was a division of the gross assessment upon the entire lands of the village of each ryot, was of two kinds, annual and for a term of years. Under the former, the ryots generally retained the same lands; but the assessment on them was revised every year, the revision being made by the ryots themselves, and, to ensure its impartiality, the peculiar practice of "challenging" was introduced. Under this system, any ryot who considered that his own holding was over-assessed, and that of his neighbour under-assessed, demanded that the latter should be made over to him at an increased rate, which he named. If the ryot in possession consented to pay the enhanced rate, he could retain the land, and in that case, a proportionate reduction was made in the assessment of the land held by the complaining party. If the ryot in possession refused to agree to the enhanced demand, he was compelled to give up the land to the complaining party, who undertook it on the higher terms. The evil effects of the challenging system were self-evident. It necessarily tended to deter wealthy ryots from incurring expense in improving inferior land, as they had no certainty of possession, and were always liable to be ousted, as soon as they had, by their labour and capital, rendered any particular field productive.

It is curious that the practice should have been retained even after the Vísabadi system was abandoned, and it is only in comparatively recent times that it was finally abolished. Mr. Prendergast, the Collector, in writing to the Commissioner of the Northern Circars on March 5, 1850, considered that, although the practice had obvious disadvantages, it was quite in unison with the feelings of the people, that, when difficulties arose, it was the only method of doing strict justice and putting a stop to violent disputes, and that it was an essential part of the existing system. Under the Vísabadi for a term of years, the lands were exchanged, and the assessment revised every few years, according to the custom in each particular village

The *Ksará*, or sharing system, was simply the conversion into money of the Government share of the crop, as ascertained by estimate or by the actual measurement of the grain. This system is said to have been almost universal in wet lands. It is surprising that greater efforts should not have been made to get rid of it, for certainly no system, better calculated to defraud the Government of its just dues, could well be devised. The Government share was at the mercy of those who conducted the measurement; and, although the operations of these men were nominally checked by three separate estimates of the produce made by the various revenue officials, it is not difficult to understand that, practically, such checks could be of little use. The supposed share of the Government was one-half, the ryot enjoying the other half, but Mr. Anstey mentioned, in writing to the Board of Revenue in 1828, that where the ryot was of the Brahmin or of the Rajah caste, he was allowed a little more, in consideration of his being unable to cultivate himself, and being obliged to employ labourers.

Although in the Vísabadi villages, the settlement was an individual one, it appears to have been the practice, in addition to the individual agreements, to take an agreement, signed by all the ryots, in which they bound themselves to be jointly answerable for the due payment of the assessment imposed on the village: thus, in fact, the Vísabadi system was converted into the Joint Rent system. The practice was disapproved of by the Board of Revenue, who, so early as 1828, expressed their opinion that it tended to repress industry and improvement, and enabled the more powerful ryots to procure a favourable assessment of their own land at the expense of their poorer neighbours.

In 1830, Mr. Crawley, who was then the Collector, proposed to revert to the renting system, and submitted various offers to the Board of Revenue for sanction. In reply, the Board disapproved of the proposal, on the ground that the offers made were very slightly in excess of the average collections under the direct management of the Government, and that it was not desirable to incur the risk of having the villages returned on the hands of the Government in a deteriorated state at the expiration of the rents, or of the lands of the neighbouring villages, under direct management, being thrown out of cultivation, by the withdrawal of the ryots to the rented villages.

Each Collector concurred with his predecessor in condemning the revenue system in force in the District; and, from time to time, efforts were made to remedy its defects, but, for a lengthened period, no real reforms were initiated. Mr. Lewin, in 1834 reported that the Vísabadi demand was regulated by a discretional assessment, based on a system of estimates of the gross produce, thus introducing the Ásará principle into the Vísabadi villages. He also stated that the demand was fixed at as high a rate as it was supposed the ryots would pay, and that it was frequently raised at the Jummabandi, or the time of settlement, without any apparent reason. In 1839, the Government authorized the abolition of the distinction between rich and poor ryots, the discontinuance of the estimates of produce, and of remissions, except in special cases. Freedom of cultivation was to be granted, and the renting of villages to the resident ryots allowed. These rules, though authorized, do not appear to have been carried out.

Sir Henry Montgomery, when employed as Special Commissioner in the District, strongly recommended that a general Survey and Settlement should be undertaken; and that the revenue should thus be placed on a sound and reliable basis. Such a measure had frequently been proposed. The following extract from his Report clearly shows the different attempts which had been made towards that object, and the system he considered it most advisable to adopt, pending its introduction:—"As the most effectual remedy for the evils of the revenue system of management prevailing in this District, the different Collectors of Rajahmundry have recommended an assessment based on a regular Survey, and the Board of Revenue, the Government, and the Court of Directors have frequently expressed their concurrence in this opinion. In 1818, the accounts of the experimental survey, undertaken by Mr. Smalley, were submitted to the Board of Revenue, but were not approved. In 1821, Mr. Robertson's experiment was sent for scrutiny, but not confirmed. In 1841, the accounts of the survey and assessment of two villages were rendered by Mr. Smith, and are still under consideration. Until some plan of proceeding in this important undertaking meets with approbation, or is distinctly laid down for the guidance of the Collector who is to carry it out, nothing further can be done towards its accomplishment. In the meantime, the system of renting villages to the inhabitant villagers, denominated 'joint-rents,' seems to me the best adapted for the welfare of the people and for the security of the Government revenue. It affords encouragement to improvement and to extension of cultivation, protection to the poorer ryots, so far as their interests are mixed up with those of the richer ryots, and it relieves all from the obnoxious interference of the Government servants at the time of cultivation and harvest."*

The recommendations of the Commissioner were approved by the Board of Revenue, the Government, and the Court of Directors, and the system of joint-rents was ordered to be generally introduced. It was avowedly only a temporary expedient, the ultimate Survey and Assessment of the District looming in the distance. The temporary expedient lasted, however, fifteen years.

The two great principles of the joint-renting system were joint and several responsibility for the entire demand, and the non-interference of the Government officials when once the demand had been fixed. Neither of these principles was really carried out. The engagement of joint responsibility existed, it is true, and the stipulation was invariably inserted in the agreement taken from the villagers; but it was very rarely, if ever, acted on, and for many years there was the same interference on the part of the subordinate Revenue Officers in arranging the estimate of the probable assessment, in extending the cultivation, introducing new ryots, preventing the ryots from making away with their produce before paying their instalments of revenue, that there had been under the Vísabadi and Ásará systems. Mr. G. N. Taylor, formerly Sub-Collector of Rajahmundry, in a pamphlet published in 1854, thus explains the leading principles of the joint-rent, and the impossibility of fully carrying the theory of the system into practice :—

"It was laid down as a fundamental rule that the whole body of cultivators were to be held jointly and severally responsible for the payment of the entire rent of the village, that the rents were to be annual and the amount moderately fixed, that all the details were to be adjusted by the villagers themselves, that unnecessary village expenses and extra cesses of all kinds were to be swept away, and that remissions were unnecessary, and not to be granted except in extraordinary cases. It will be seen in the sequel how far these principles have been adhered to, and to what extent the welfare of

* Sir H. Montgomery's Report, § 76.

the people has been promoted by an arrangement devised for their especial benefit.

"Under the present system, the period of the joint village rent is restricted, except under peculiar circumstances, to one year. The settlement is, therefore, annual, as in the Ryotwary Districts, but the demand is even more fluctuating and uncertain. Proposals are taken from the villagers for the rent of the ensuing year, during the Jummabandi of the current Fasli, the amount being, in the first instance, determined by the Collector or Settling Officer. In point of fact, the fixing of this demand forms the chief item of work during the annual tour; for the Revenue Officer is guided in the matter by his knowledge of the real condition of the village, past and present, and all the details which are necessary to enable him to make the settlement for the current year, assist him in forming a judgment of what the village will bear for the next. The determining of the demand for the coming Fasli thus early in the year is obviously to the advantage of the ryot; it allows him time to look before him; knowing the amount assessed upon the whole village, he can calculate the quota or percentage of increase which will fall to his share, and with some sort of feeling of security that the holding will remain his own for another year at any rate, he prepares the ground for fresh tillage as soon as this year's crops are off, and is thus encouraged to enter upon those expensive agricultural operations, which are necessary for the improvement of his land.

"The demand having thus been fixed by the Settling Officer, after a careful scrutiny of all the sources of information at his disposal, *i.e.*, a comparison of past collections, the extent of former and present cultivation, the number and circumstances of the ryots and the general condition of the village, it should remain to the villagers to adjust the details among themselves. Nominally, each individual ryot is responsible for the aggregate assessment, his consent having been obtained to the written agreement presented to the Revenue Officer by the headmen of the village; nominally, his assent has been cheerfully given; and, nominally, the villagers proceed to make a distribution of the land and shist. The theory of the joint-rent system is admirable. It supposes a fair rent payable by the collective village community, an engagement alike advantageous to themselves and to the Government; it ignores any approach to discontent on the part of the renters; it professes absence of interference on the part of native officials; it looks for justice in place of oppression; it understands an equitable distribution of land and assessment by the heads of villages, to whom all internal arrangements are entrusted, and provides for the punctual discharge of each instalment of the rent by certain imposed penalties. Practically, however, much of this is a delusion. It has been found inexpedient, and, in fact, impossible, with any show of justice to collect by extra collections from the general body, deficiencies on the part of individuals, and although the stipulation still exists and is held *in terrorem* over the people, it is rarely resorted to. Were the headmen alone made answerable for the public demand, it would undoubtedly be their interest to make a fair distribution of the lands of their village, so as to ensure the realization of each man's quota; but, as the responsibility is general, so also is the indifference to a neighbour's welfare, and the better class of ryot looks after himself, and cares little for his poorer brother. The influential members of the community are not bound by common ties to the poor class of cultivators, being of different castes, and regarding them rather as a dead weight upon the village than as contributors to the common weal, they not only afford them no assistance, but are the very persons who inflict injustice, which it ought to be their province to prevent. The real responsibility then lies at the door of the Government Officer, and it is he who virtually fixes the rent of a village.

"The rent having been determined by the Revenue Officer, and the villagers persuaded to accede to the terms in the manner above described, there follows what is called the 'Amarakam,' or apportioning of land and shist, which, according to one of the fundamental principles of the joint-rent, should be arranged by the renters themselves. The controlling revenue authority, who fixes the collective demand, is supposed to be relieved of the adjustment of details. Accordingly, it has been the practice, after accepting the proposals of the 50 or 100 villages of a Taluk during the Jummabandi of the current year, to leave the people to distribute their individual holdings among themselves. But this is only the theory, as I have before explained; in practice it is not so. The period allowed for this apportionment of the land and shist of the village has hitherto been, as in Ryotwary Districts, from the Jummabandi, which usually terminates in March or April, till September. The village Munsiff and other influential ryots called Pettanadars, who are Government servants and receive emoluments for their services, are expected to effect this without the aid of the Taluk authorities. But first a Peon, then a Samutdar, and afterwards the Tahsildar, are successively called to their aid, and the matter is not finally arranged without constant reference to the European Officer, whose authority is necessary to adjust disputes and differences."

The deviations from the sanctioned principles of the joint-rents attracted the attention of the Commissioner for the Northern Circars, and in his proceedings of February 11, 1854, he laid down the following rules to be strictly attended to in future :—

(1.) The joint demand to be formed in strict accordance with the existing means of the village, and so moderate as to allow of improvements being undertaken, and of the observance of periodical fallows.

(2.) The "beriz," or gross assessment of the village, having been once determined, to be considered a certain demand, or if liable to be increased, the conditions to be understood and recognized by the ryots.

(3.) No settlement to be valid unless every individual member of the joint settlement has signified his assent to the "Amarakam," in presence of the Collector or Settling Officer.

(4.) The interference of the Revenue Officers with the details of the "Amarakam" to be prohibited.

(5.) The right of "challenging" to be abolished.

(6.) Temporary establishments for carrying out the interference with the ryots' proceedings to be discontinued.

(7.) The issue of "Takávi," or advances to the ryots to enable them to purchase seed and stock, to cease.

(8.) The settlement of the lanka lands to be revised.

(9.) The "Kistbandi," or settlement of payment by instalments, to be relaxed.

(10.) Ryotwar receipts to be granted by the Karnams or village accountants.

(11.) Village accounts to be remodelled.

The greater number of these rules were carried out; but it is doubtful whether it was practicable to enforce all of them, particularly the provision forbidding the interference of the Revenue Officers with the "Amarakam."

The final orders of Government on Sir Henry Montgomery's Report were not passed till April, 1846, as soon as possible after which the system of joint-rents was introduced generally, and, as a rule, it was followed until the introduction of the present Settlement.*

Rajahmundry was one of the districts in which the important works of the Revenue Survey and Settlement were commenced. In accordance with the orders of the Court of Directors for the general survey of the whole of the Presidency of Madras, a Director of Revenue Settlement was appointed in the year 1858, with two deputies and an efficient establishment. The Settlement on the revision of assessment, which has proceeded hand in hand with the Survey, was from the commencement intended to be Ryotwary.† The organization of the establishment of the Survey was afterwards completed. Four parties were employed on the scientific survey and mapping of the country, the result of their labours being connected by triangulation with the great Trigonometrical Survey; and four other parties were also organized to perform the preliminary operations of demarcation to facilitate the labours of the surveying branch, and the subsequent duties of classification of the soil and assessment of the Government demand. The survey in the north was commenced in those parts of the Rajahmundry and Masulipatam Districts, which then included the Western Delta of the Godavery. During the first year 66,490 acres were surveyed in the former district, and 14,400 in the latter.

On the other branch, which was more immediately under the Director of Revenue Settlement, devolved the duties of demarcation, classification, and assessment of the land, thus partly preceding and partly following those of the Survey branch. One of the newly organized parties began work in the Rajahmundry District, the headquarters for the time being of the Deputy-Director, Mr. R. E. Master, as well as Captain Priestley of the Survey Department, being Nursapore. The work commenced in May 1858. Up to the end of the official year 416 villages, containing 835 square miles, were demarcated, and 237 villages classified.

During the year 1859-60 both the Settlement and Survey were actively carried on. The Settlement party first completed the work allotted to it in the Delta, and gradually extended it to the whole District. The demarcation of the lands and the classification of

* Report on the Survey and Settlement of the Western Deltas, by Mr. R. E. Master, being Selections from the Records of the Madras Government, No. xxii., p. 7.

† Administration Report for 1857-58, p. 14.

them for assessment were completed in 1860. The progress of the Survey party was not quite so rapid. The training of the men employed took longer, and, moreover, attacks of disease impeded the work. It was, however, considered so essential to hasten the work in the Godavery District, because of the irrigation works which had materially increased the power of production in the soil, that the strength of the party was raised, and every effort was made to press the work forward to the utmost possible extent.

It was, of course, one of the most pressing questions in connection with the increase of irrigation, and the proportionate increase of cultivation, in what manner the State could reap the advantage in an increase of revenue. This question was carefully considered at this time, as the operation of the Settlement and Survey parties were drawing to a conclusion, and it became necessary to bring them to a practical issue. It was decided that, on the whole, the best mode of levying an assessment for the increased advantages of the land under irrigation was by levying a general water-rate per acre for irrigation in addition to the land assessment.* The present rates were determined on after careful thought and frequent revision. All former rates have been superseded by these, which have been tested by experience, and by the suggestion and advice of the Collectors, who had watched the working of the rules in actual practice.

Rules for levying Water-Rate in the Kistna and Godavery Deltas.†

RULE I.

The water-rates charged for irrigation in the Godavery and Kistna Deltas are as follow:—

1. For a single *wet* crop, Rs. 4 an acre.

2. For a second *wet* crop on irrigated land, Rs. 4 an acre, provided that the cultivator may compound for irrigation for two crops for a term of years not less than five, for Rs. 6-8-0 an acre.

N.B.—A second crop is a crop grown on land on which a first crop has been grown in the same Fasli.

3. For a second *dry* crop on irrigated land, Rs. 2 an acre, except where the land-holder has compounded under Clause 2.

4. For sugar-cane, betel, plantains, and other garden-produce, remaining on the ground for the time of two crops, Rs. 8 an acre,

* Administration Report for 1859-60, p. 25.

† These Rules came into force on the 1st July 1873.

provided that the cultivator may compound for a term of years not less than five, for Rs. 6-8-0 an acre.

5. For a dry crop grown on land for which irrigation has never been supplied, or, having been once supplied, has been since discontinued under Rule III., Rs. 2 an acre, whether the crop be a first or a second crop. These rates shall be paid according to the Kistbundy of the district.

6. Ryots taking water for a portion of a field will be charged on the whole, unless the sub-division and irrigation of a particular portion has been previously sanctioned by the Collector.

7. When the water used for irrigation cannot be obtained without raising it by baling or mechanical contrivances, a deduction of one-fourth of the water-rate will be made.

Rule II.

1. Cultivators will be allowed to take or refuse irrigation for *wet* crops every year, on condition that a formal application, specifying the number and extent of the fields for which irrigation is sought or declined, be made to the head of the village, and, after registry by the Karnam, be sent to the Tahsildar up to the following dates:—

Applications for irrigation to be supplied—

(*a.*) For a first crop, 30th June.

(*b.*) For a second crop, 30th November.

Applications for irrigation to be discontinued, 31st March.

2. When water is required for *dry* crops under Rule I., Clause 5, the application may be made at any time.

3. When water is not available for all applicants, applications will ordinarily be admitted in the following order:—

(*a.*) To applicants for water for two crops or one of sugar-cane, &c.

(*b.*) To those who have received water longest, preference being given to those whose lands lie nearest the head of the channels.

4. In the case of all applications for irrigation to be supplied, water being available, and of all applications for irrigation to be discontinued, the Tahsildar will admit the application, endorse it to that effect, and give it back to the Karnam for delivery to the applicant.

5. Printed forms of these applications will be kept in stock by the Karnam.

6. A register of applications, showing whether they have been admitted or rejected, will be kept both by the Tahsildar and the Karnam.

7. The Tahsildar will send extracts from his register to the range officer every week. The Karnam's register will be kept open to inspection by the villagers.

Rule III.

When land has once been irrigated as *wet* land, it will be described as such in the accounts, and will be supplied with water, and remain liable to the water-rate (water being available) until a formal application for the irrigation to be discontinued has been made and admitted in the manner prescribed in Rule II.

Rule IV.

Application for water for *dry* crops grown on *dry* land, *i.e.*, land for which irrigation has never been supplied, or, having been once supplied, has been since discontinued under Rule III., may be made at any time to the Karnam, who will send one copy to the Delta Gumasta or Overseer, and one to the Tahsildar.

Rule V.

When water is taken for land not previously irrigated before a formal application for it has been made, as prescribed in Rules II. and IV., a water-rate, equal to one-and-a-half times the rate chargeable according to Rule I., will be rigidly exacted, and if no application is made, or there is reason to suspect that the cultivator meant to evade payment, the rate charged shall be double that prescribed in Rule I.

Rule VI.

Zemindars and Inamdars will be allowed to compound for fixed yearly payments, or according to the quantity of water supplied. When no such composition is made, the cultivators will be subject in all respects to the rules; but the applications referred to in Rule II. will be sent to the Deputy-Tahsildar in charge of the Zemindari.

Rule VII.

No water-rate will be levied for a single crop on lands in Inams and Zemindaris which have been determined by the Collector under the orders of the Board of Revenue to be entitled to irrigation from before the time the Annicut was built as "mamool wet" lands.

Rule VIII.

Water will be granted free of charge on application to the Department Public Works officers, through the Collector, for flooding lands made barren by "Tsaudu" (that is, salt efflorescence or brackishness), whenever a sufficient supply of water is available, for a period not exceeding two years, provided that, if a crop or crops are raised on the land during this period, half the usual water-rate will be charged.

Rule IX.

Anything in foregoing rules notwithstanding, Government reserve to themselves the full right, with or without reason given, to discontinue, either temporarily or permanently, the supply of water for irrigation.*

Rules for the Charge of Water-Rate on Dry Lands irrigated in Upland Taluks.

It should be borne in mind that these rates are intended for Upland villages only. The above rules are for the Annicut irrigation.

1. All dry lands temporarily cultivated with wet crops shall, in lieu of any other system now in force, pay a fixed water-rate at the following rates per acre, irrespective of the source from whence the water may be derived. When water is raised by mechanical contrivances, the rate will be reduced by one-fourth.

Standard Rates.

Water-rate for a single wet crop raised on dry land, per acre, Rs. 4.

Second crop on the same land, per acre, Rs. 2.

* Proceedings of the Madras Government, Revenue Department, 16th June 1873.

For sugar-cane, betel, cocoa-nuts, plantains, &c., requiring water longer than an ordinary wet crop, per acre, Rs. 6.

For dry crops watered, whether first or second crop, per acre, Rs. 2.

2. As a rule, the entire Survey number will be charged with water-rate, but where the fields are large, it will be at the discretion of the Settling Officer at Jamabandi to charge only for the area actually irrigated. Nothing less than one acre to be charged, and fractional parts to be charged as one acre.

3. The Collector has power to impose prohibitory rates whenever water is taken without permission.

4. The above rules are applicable to all Government sources of irrigation, the supply in which is at all regular and to be depended on. Simple jungle streams, which only receive a casual supply, may still be utilized without charge.

5. No Government water is to be taken under these rules without the express sanction of the head of the village, or of the Department Public Works Officer, when the works are in charge of that Department, who will make a special report on the subject to the Tahsildars *immediately on granting permission.*

N.B.—These rules do not apply to a second crop raised on wet land, for which the usual charge (generally half the first crop assessment) will be made.

The demarcation and classification were completed in the year 1860–61. The field measurements were completed during the year 1861–62, and the settlement was introduced, and its nature and principles explained to the ryots individually in 154 out of 240 Government villages in the Taluks of the Western Delta. It came into actual operation in those Taluks on July 1, 1862.

The results of this Settlement were not immediately satisfactory. The actual demand for Fasli 1272 (1862–63) was less than the joint-rents of the preceding year by about 21,000 rupees, owing to the new assessment being, in many instances, gradually imposed. Land assessed at 66,000 rupees was, however, newly taken up by the ryots, and the full assessment to be eventually imposed on the area then occupied, was much in excess of the joint-rents above-mentioned.* The Settlement was introduced into the Central and Eastern Deltas, and into most of the upland Taluks of the District

* Administration Report for 1862–63, p. 56.

in the year 1865–66; and, in the following year, it was announced that the whole of the District had been brought under the new Revenue arrangements.*

I have thus endeavoured to give a succinct and accurate account of this flourishing District. I have related the history of the portion of Southern India in which it is situated, so far only as it refers to the District itself, leaving untouched all that more intimately concerns the adjoining districts; and I have attempted to bring into one focus the scattered and obscure rays of the early history of the kingdoms and of the governments with which it was once immediately connected. The peaceable and pastoral people inhabiting the fertile maritime plain which skirts the western shore of the Bay of Bengal, have lived successively under the rule of their own native Rajahs and Reddis, under the growth of Brahminism, the fascination of Buddhism, and the revival of Brahminical power, under the dominion of the conquering Rajahs of Orissa, under the distracted government of the Mohammedans, under the brief rule of the French, and under the more stable administration of the English Government. Through all these changes they passed comparatively unchanged; but their present condition is incomparably superior to anything they had ever before enjoyed. The hill tribes and the people living in the upland Taluks bordering on the hills have been less peaceful; but, whatever disturbances may have occurred, they have generally been occasioned by discontented chiefs, who have taken refuge in the fastnesses and forests of the mountains, for the purpose of escaping the payment of tribute, or evading the execution of the law.

The annals of this District, since it came under the English Government, form a varied record of temporary depression and subsequent improvement. At the commencement of our rule, it constituted a portion of a neglected province; and, at one time, it was, from various causes, brought into a state of extreme impoverishment and distress. It was desolated by famine, and misgoverned by the numerous land-owners and their advisers. Since the introduction, however, of the admirable system of irrigation which, in a previous chapter, I have endeavoured to describe, it has brightened and revived. Famine is unknown. The people are prosperous and

* Administration Report for 1865–66, p. 37, and for 1866–67, p. 39.

contented. It is the garden of the great Northern Province. Its revenue, instead of being reduced, as it once was, to the verge of bankruptcy, is more elastic than it has ever been; its population has more than doubled; the material prosperity of its inhabitants is proved by their being better fed, better clothed, and better educated than formerly; its commerce has flourished, and its trade has developed to a marvellous degree; and it may confidently be asserted that it is in as peaceful, happy, and prosperous condition as any part of Her Imperial Majesty's dominions.

TABLES.

No. 1.—STATEMENT showing the Number of Villages and Hamlets in the Godavery District as they stood in Fasli 1281 (or official year 1871–72).

TALUKS.	Area in Square Miles.	GOVERNMENT.				ZEMINDARI.				INAM.				TOTAL.					
		Inhabited.		Uninhabited.		Inhabited.		Uninhabited.		Inhabited.		Uninhabited.		Inhabited.		Uninhabited.		Total.	
		No. of Villages.	No. of Hamlets.	No. of Villages.	No. of Hamlets.	No. of Villages.	No. of Hamlets.	No. of Villages.	No. of Hamlets.	No. of Villages.	No. of Hamlets.	No. of Villages.	No. of Hamlets.	No. of Villages.	No. of Hamlets.	No. of Villages.	No. of Hamlets.	No. of Villages.	No. of Hamlets.
1.	2.	3.	4.	5.	6.	7.	8.	9.	10.	11.	12.	13.	14.	15.	16.	17.	18.	19.	20.
Peddapore	505	131	15	25	...	52	10	2	...	2	...	1	...	185	25	28	...	213	25
Rámachandrapuram	507	131	46	...	...	28	12	...	...	4	...	...	...	163	58	...	...	163	58
Amalápuram	437	114	96	...	...	47	49	...	...	11	...	...	...	172	145	...	...	172	145
Rajahmundry	2,058	86	67	8	2	369	62	...	...	6	...	...	...	461	129	8	2	469	131
Tanuku	366½	86	38	2	...	62	9	3	...	24	1	3	...	172	48	8	...	180	48
Ellore	729	81	51	11	18	92	36	8	21	44	14	14	2	217	101	33	41	250	142
Yarnagúdem	1,249½	84	129	10	72	86	170	6	88	15	8	2	...	185	307	18	160	203	467
Nursapore	450	120	62	...	...	13	4	...	...	6	...	...	...	139	66	...	...	139	66
Bhimavaram	416	86	15	2	...	51	...	6	...	3	...	...	...	140	15	8	...	148	15
Coringa	66	...	...	...	...	10	23	...	...	...	...	...	...	10	23	...	...	10	23
Cocanada	331 (Cocanada and Pittapore)	2	...	...	...	50	38	..	...	...	...	...	...	52	38	...	...	52	38
Pittapore		...	...	...	...	65	31	1	1	...	...	...	...	65	31	1	1	66	32
Tuni	419	...	...	...	...	121	52	16	...	...	...	...	...	121	52	16	...	137	52
Total	7,534*	921	519	58	92	1,046	496	42	110	115	23	20	2	2,082	1,038	120	204	2,202	1,242

N.B.—The statistics contained in the Appendix are given on the authority of the Collector of the District.

* This area is given on the authority of the Collector, and differs from that given in the previous text as extracted from the Census Report.

No. 2.—STATEMENT of Population, arranged with reference to Caste, according to the Census of 1871.

Nationality.	Caste.	Population.		
		Males.	Females.	Total.
Hindus	Brahmins (Priests)	45,030	45,792	90,822
	Kshatriyas (Warriors)	21,069	20,360	41,429
	Chetties (Traders)	20,408	19,840	40,248
	Vellálars (Agriculturists)	250,128	248,245	498,373
	Idaiyars (Shepherds)	29,858	28,951	58,809
	Kammálan (Artisans)	15,692	15,043	30,735
	Kanakkan (Writers)	2,080	2,003	4,083
	Kaikalar (Weavers)	33,363	32,542	65,905
	Vannian (Labourers and Cultivators)	19,443	20,814	40,257
	Kusavan (Potters)	5,682	5,416	11,098
	Sátáni (Mixed Castes)	7,060	7,337	14,397
	Sembadavan (Fishermen and Hunters)	3,505	3,093	6,598
	Shánán (Toddy Drawers)	84,114	81,719	165,833
	Ambattan (Barbers)	8,353	8,150	16,503
	Vannán (Washermen)	19,539	19,285	38,824
	Others	30,413	29,575	59,988
	Pariahs	189,557	183,131	372,688
	Total	785,294	771,296	1,556,590
Mohammedans	Labbays	19	18	37
	Mapilas	...	...	...
	Arabs	2	...	2
	Sheiks	9,535	9,596	19,131
	Syuds	1,360	1,318	2,678
	Pathans	832	797	1,629
	Moghuls	479	514	993
	Other Mohammedans	5,436	5,267	10,703
	Total	17,663	17,510	35,173
Europeans		252	199	451
Eurasians		202	183	385
Others		192	148	340
	Total	646	530	1,176
	Grand Total	803,603	789,336	1,592,939

N. B.—It may be observed that, for the sake of uniformity with the other Manuals, the headings in some of the Tables are in Tamil, instead of in Telugu, the language of the District. The number of native Christians is 585.

No. 2 (A).—STATEMENT showing the Male Population, arranged with Reference to Occupation, according to the Census of 1871.

Major Headings.	Minor Headings.	No. of Males Employed.
Professional . . .	Government Service . .	4,089
	Military	1,067
	Learned Professions . .	1,237
	Minor do. . .	4,939
Domestic	Personal Service . . .	32,796
Commercial . . .	Traders	31,995
	Conveyors	2,218
Agricultural . . .	Cultivators	267,789
Industrial	Dress	31,318
	Food	20,657
	Metal	6,601
	Construction	3,139
	Books	81
	Household Goods . . .	3,779
	Combustibles	728
Indefinite and Non-Productive . .	Labourers	96,867
	Property	23,401
	Unproductive	5,207
	Others	4,667
	Total . .	542,575

No. 2 (B).—STATEMENT showing the Number of Houses, Population, and Cattle in each Taluk.

TALUKS.	NUMBER OF HOUSES.					POPULATION.			AGRICULTURAL STOCK.						
	Terraced	Tiled.	Thatched.	Unspecified.	Total.	Males.	Females.	Total.	Tilling Cattle.	Cows.	She-Buffaloes.	Sheep.	Ploughs	Horses.	Ponies.
Amalápuram	87	2,393	41,237	661	44,378	105,045	101,840	206,885	20,569	6,467	3,875	1,948	10,343	Not known.	Not known.
Nursapore	15	5,072	33,555	147	38,789	89,768	88,108	177,876	26,153	8,502	4,434	4,310	13,044		
Bhimavaram	5	1,068	19,864	332	21,269	46,342	46,115	92,457	16,789	5,888	2,539	1,612	8,626		
Cocanada	58	606	15,402	76	16,142	34,128	32,816	66,944	43	15	16	...	12		
Ellore	9	2,422	35,165	150	37,746	70,577	66,298	136,875	17,250	10,610	6,578	11,931	8,061		
Rajahmundry	31	2,625	31,640	238	34,534	66,255	62,646	128,901	13,586	7,520	4,002	3,959	5,111		
Pittapore	48	270	21,780	15	22,041	39,232	40,374	79,606	...	...	...	...	...		
Coringa	12	666	5,956	1	6,635	11,807	13,109	24,916	...	...	...	...	...		
Tanuku	15	1,796	33,113	122	35,046	83,757	83,734	167,491	17,109	8,247	4,756	2,926	8,185		
Peddapore	43	654	31,847	7	32,551	55,388	56,101	111,489	13,825	6,231	3,274	3,337	6,107		
Rámachandrapuram	10	2,729	41,736	193	44,668	102,136	101,447	203,583	33,339	9,371	8,039	1,926	15,618		
Yarnagúdem	4	830	40,564	3	41,401	72,866	72,849	145,715	16,418	11,227	8,105	12,382	7,492		
Tuni	30	286	14,195	1	14,512	26,302	23,899	50,201	...	...	...	...	...		
Total	367	21,417	365,982	1,946	389,712	803,603	789,336	1,592,939	175,181	74,078	45,618	44,331	82,599		

No. 3.—Statement of Rent Roll for Fasli 1284 (1874–75).

Puttas.	Single Puttas.		Joint Puttas.		Total Puttas.	
	No.	Assessment.	No.	Assessment.	No.	Assessment.
		Rupees.		Rupees.		Rupees.
Below 10 Rupees	14,338	72,759	3,313	16,821	17,651	89,580
Above 10 Rupees, but below 30 Rupees	15,458	2,90,008	3,784	72,284	19,242	3,62,292
,, 30 ,, 50 ,,	6,962	2,74,506	1,540	59,820	8,502	3,34,326
,, 50 ,, 100 ,,	6,496	4,49,944	1,284	88,623	7,780	5,38,567
,, 100 ,, 250 ,,	3,731	5,57,526	718	1,01,530	4,449	6,59,056
,, 250 ,, 500 ,,	548	1,83,204	129	42,423	677	2,25,627
,, 500 ,, 1000 ,,	112	72,589	30	18,713	142	91,302
Upwards of 1000 Rupees	22	28,697	10	16,164	32	44,861
Total	47,667	19,29,233	10,808	4,16,378	58,475	23,45,611

No. 4.—STATEMENT showing the different Sources of Irrigation belonging to Government.

TALUKS.	TANKS.			CHANNELS.			ANNICUTS.		
	Number of Tanks.	Average Extent of Cultivation within the last Five Years.	Assessment, including all Charges for Water, &c.	Number of Channels.	Average Extent of Cultivation within the last Five Years.	Assessment, including all Charges for Water, &c.	Number of Annicut Channels.	Average Extent of Cultivation within the last Five Years.	Assessment, including all Charges for Water, &c.
		Acres.	Rupees.		Acres.	Rupees.		Acres.	Rupees.
Collector's Division—									
Peddapore	476	12,899	39,696	42	5,137	42,195	...	...	...
Cocanada	...	...	...	...	...	...	3	17,024	17,019
Coringa	...	...	...	...	...	...	3	2,463	5,729
Sub-Collector's Division—									
Rámachandrapuram	82	1,503	9,911	...	...	...	6	1,22,456	6,50,996
Amalápuram	...	...	...	...	...	...	5	58,972	2,69,013
Rajahmundry	457	10,833	4,44,777	17	621	3,287	4	1,206	4,499
Head Assistant Collector's Division—									
Tanuku	24	173	345	...	...	...	8	87,415	4,03,209
Ellore	267	7,092	16,933	2	20	45	2	30,202	1,17,579
Yarnagúdem	111	4,068	9,951	9	770	1,945	1	1,617	5,665
General Duty Deputy Collector's Division—									
Nursapore	...	...	...	...	...	...	4	83,727	4,60,387
Bhímavaram	...	...	...	...	...	...	6	1,20,115	4,04,192

No. 5.—STATEMENT showing the Rainfall for a Series of Ten Years.

Faslis.	Official Years.	July.	August.	September.	October.	November.	December.	January.	February.	March.	April.	May.	June.	Total.
		Inches.	Inches.	Inches.	Inches.	Inches.	Inches.	Inches.	Inches.	Inches.	Inches.	Inches.	Inches.	Inches.
1275	1865–66	3·41	10·42	7·49	1·26	0·98	0·15	...	0·13	...	2·12	3·43	0·81	30·20
1276	1866–67	6·75	6·43	3·61	8·59	0·80	0·4	1·95	0·8	0·7	0·42	1·20	2·97	32·91
1277	1867–68	4·18	6·3	5·14	8·13	0·72	0·15	...	...	0·5	0·61	0·75	9·62	35·38
1278	1868–69	8·11	3·75	4·30	1·5	0·12	...	0·5	0·3	0·62	0·29	0·74	6·76	25·72
1279	1869–70	4·96	2·94	6·77	6·36	1·24	0·37	1·13	...	0·22	0·45	0·36	5·68	30·45
1280	1870–71	4·88	2·81	11·68	17·16	1·27	...	0·57	0·99	1·66	0·68	3·45	3·59	49·14
1281	1871–72	7·56	4·16	5·25	1·59	3·56	0·29	...	0·10	...	0·60	1·35	6·33	27·79
1282	1872–73	6·0	8·3	9·42	12·0	1·82	2·25	...	0·10	...	1·30	1·40	1·38	42·70
1283	1873–74	7·05	4·45	7·87	26·53	0·70	...	0·20	...	0·60	0·48	3·50	4·73	56·11
1284	1874–75	7·33	3·49	8·99	11·70	1·50	0·70	1·37	0·78	0·19	0·65	2·79	2·86	42·35

No. 6.—Statement showing the Prices of Grain for a Series of Ten Years.

Faslis.	Official Years.	Rice, 1st sort, per garce.	Rice, 2nd sort.	Paddy, 1st sort.	Paddy, 2nd sort.	Cholum.	Cumboo.	Raggy.	Varagu.	Horse Gram.	Ulundu.	Wheat.	Salt.
		Rupees.	Rupees.	Rupees.	Rupees.	Rupees.	Rupees.	Rupees.	Rupees.	Rupees.	Rupees.	Rupees.	Rupees.
1275	1865–66	319	300	144	135	175	149	167	141	198	388	633	262
1276	1866–67	361	334	162	153	193	160	184	158	260	402	630	250
1277	1867–68	209	195	94	88	109	86	101	95	118	291	319	245
1278	1868–69	265	245	124	114	136	113	129	120	158	361	449	244
1279	1869–70	282	259	129	117	141	109	133	125	203	341	549	268
1280	1870–71	228	210	101	94	118	96	109	107	150	260	475	279
1281	1871–72	276	253	127	117	135	109	121	102	157	195	396	279
1282	1872–73	268	246	122	113	153	124	129	114	213	227	418	278
1283	1873–74	265	244	116	109	140	123	124	109	159	230	405	275
1284	1874–75	248	233	112	102	122	113	114	110	133	245	398	268

No. 7.—STATEMENT showing the Particulars of Cultivation of Land and Land Revenue for a series of Ten Years.

Years.		Ryotwary.								
		Area Occupied.						Add Second Crop, and Additional Assessment.	Charge for Water.	Total Assessment.
		Dry.		Wet.		Total.				
Official.	Fasli.	Extent.	Assessment.	Extent.	Assessment.	Extent.	Assessment.			
1.	2.	3.	4.	5.	6.	7.	8.	9.	10.	11.
		Acres.	Rupees.	Acres.	Rupees.	Acres.	Rupees.	Rupees.	Rupees.	Rupees.
1864–65	1274	371,448	10,17,315	*202,111	*6,61,567	573,559	16,78,882	...	†5,70,305	22,49,187
1865–66	1275	230,537	8,50,838	*359,160	*9,28,441	589,697	17,79,279	...	†8,42,998	26,22,277
1866–67	1276	382,975	6,46,997	223,656	6,40,855	606,631	12,87,852	‡1,135	7,82,904	20,71,891
1867–68	1277	458,180	7,44,510	217,176	6,14,485	675,356	13,58,995	‡1,740	8,51,100	22,11,835
1868–69	1278	438,505	7,26,543	224,657	6,43,667	663,162	13,70,210	‡1,746	8,17,005	21,88,961
1869–70	1279	456,066	7,41,835	251,135	6,96,642	707,201	14,38,477	‡2,074	9,30,584	23,71,135
1870–71	1280	460,878	7,42,587	262,806	7,23,598	723,684	14,66,185	‡2,195	9,90,144	24,58,524
1871–72	1281	440,936	7,02,113	263,345	7,23,914	704,281	14,26,027	‡1,121	9,41,633	23,68,781
1872–73	1282	448,719	7,04,527	275,477	7,47,747	724,196	14,52,274	§19,888	9,47,478	24,19,640
1873–74	1283	421,413	6,78,118	299,939	7,82,565	721,352	14,60,683	¶13,479	9,65,999	24,40,161

* Including garden land, and assessment thereon. † Including additional assessment. ‡ Additional assessment only. § Second crop, and additional assessment. ¶ Second crop, assessment only.

RYOTWARY.				Revenue from Permanently Settled Estates.	Jodi on Shotriam Villages.	Total Land Revenue Demand.	Arrears of previous Years.	Total Demand for the Year.	Gross Collections, including Current, Arrears, and Remissions.	Balance at end of Fasli or Year.
Deduct Remissions.	Remainder.	Add Miscellaneous Items.	Total Ryotwary Demand.							
12.	13.	14.	15.	16.	17.	18.	19.	20.	21.	22.
Rupees.	Rupees.	Rupees.	Rupees.	Rupees.	Rupees.	Rupees.	Rupees.	Rupees.	Rupees.	Rupees.
42,679	22,06,508	7,28,977	29,35,485	7,37,781	24,363	36,97,629	2,93,947	39,91,576	38,46,035	1,45,541
31,766	25,90,511	8,09,536	34,00,047	7,37,016	30,215	41,67,278	5,01,164	46,68,442	45,74,414	94,028
29,550	20,42,341	10,26,959	30,69,300	7,36,926	31,531	38,37,757	4,17,665	42,55,422	41,54,369	1,01,053
45,452	21,66,383	10,50,264	32,16,647	7,37,667	30,335	39,84,649	4,30,592	44,15,241	42,98,521	1,16,720
84,000	21,04,961	9,63,660	30,68,621	7,37,667	30,339	38,36,627	4,64,094	43,00,721	41,13,514	1,87,207
61,613	23,09,522	10,20,110	33,29,632	7,37,056	30,358	40,97,046	4,69,107	45,66,153	44,44,890	1,21,263
48,456	24,10,068	10,45,401	34,55,469	7,37,056	30,378	42,22,903	4,83,614	47,06,514	45,38,360	1,68,154
73,515	22,95,266	9,37,143	32,32,409	7,37,056	30,621	40,00,086	5,92,574	45,92,660	44,55,565	1,37,095
54,000	23,65,640	9,62,699	33,28,339	7,36,996	30,292	40,95,627	3,49,430	44,45,057	42,51,248	1,93,809
71,238	23,68,923	10,34,835	34,03,758	7,40,328	30,317	41,74,403	4,64,042	46,38,445	44,74,047	1,64,398

NOTE.—The figures showing the extent of land under occupation represent the total holdings by the Ryots with the assessment bearing thereon, and are supposed to include the land under irrigation. Column 23 shows the balance at the end of each year, after taking into account the subsequent collections up to July in each year; and, by deducting this column from column 21, the gross collections are arrived at, including current and arrears, which will explain the difference between the figures under this heading with those showing collections in each year, as rendered in the Board of Revenue's Returns received from Madras. The area of Zemindari lands cannot be accurately ascertained.

No. 7 (A).—Agricultural Statistics, Acreage of Crops, &c., in Government and Inam lands, for Fasli 1284, or Official Year 1874-75.

No.	Taluka.	Population.	Whether Government or Inam.	Area in Acres.	Total Acres held in Holding.
	1.	2.	3.	4.	5.
1.	Peddapore	111,489	Government	100,679	85,737 88
	Do.	...	Inam	24,070	24,070 ...
2.	Bhadráchalam	...	Government	1,555	1,555 ...
3.	Cocanada	66,944	Government	524	524 ...
	Do.	...	Inam	86	86 ...
4.	Coringa	24,916	Government	235	2 41
5.	Pittapore	79,606	Government	21	20 92
6.	Rámachandrapuram	203,583	Government	117,263	112,145 84
	Do.	...	Inam	65,388	65,388 ...
7.	Amalápuram	206,885	Government	95,396	68,252 28
	Do.	...	Inam	65,932	65,932 ...
8.	Rajahmundry	128,901	Government	138,493	107,091 74
	Do.	...	Inam	33,952	33,952 ...
9.	Tanuku	167,491	Government	81,241	74,611 88
	Do.	...	Inam	40,798	40,798 ...
10.	Ellore	136,875	Government	184,021	97,532 41
	Do.	...	Inam	11,426	11,426 ...
11.	Yarnagúdem	145,715	Government	166,964	115,389 17
	Do.	...	Inam	33,329	33,329 ...
12.	Nursapore	177,876	Government	124,036	93,754 17
	Do.	...	Inam	57,123	57,123 ...
13.	Bhimavaram	92,457	Government	81,488	67,643 52
	Do.	...	Inam	25,897	25,897 ...
14.	Tuni	50,201	Government	...	...
...	Do.	...	Inam	25,897	25,897 ...
			Government	1,092,276	824,261 22
			Inam	358,001	358,001 ...
			Total	1,450,277	1,182,262 22

N.B.—The Telugu and the botanical names of the various products mentioned in these tables will be given on a subsequent page.

No. 7 (A).—Agricultural Statistics, &c.—*Continued.*

No.	No. of Acres under Crop and Fallow.			Food Grains.			
	Whereof under			Rice.			Cholum.
	Food Grains.	Other Products.	Fallow and Waste.	One Crop Irrigated.	Second Crop do.	Unirrigated.	
	6.	7.	8.	9.	10.	11.	12.
1.	30,466 4	15,247 17	40,024 67	15,201 95	71 2	1,244 55	1,346 30
	10,322 93	4,491 10	9,245 97	6,545 80	8 45	335 15	89 44
2.	1,431 ...	124 ...	...	...	...	241 ...	980 ...
3.	107 99	...	416 1	107 99	...	...	...
	52 37	...	33 63	52 37	...	...	...
4.	... 43	...	1 98	... 43	...	...	...
5.	20 92	...	...	20 92	...	...	...
6.	78,876 61	14,293 15	18,976 8	58,350 77	26 65	18,470 60	1,089 65
	52,393 2	5,680 5	7,314 93	36,061 45	2 61	14,970 90	871 36
7.	43,812 78	13,234 65	11,204 85	24,888 22	5 74	9,319 9	3,660 67
	39,682 5	16,209 36	10,040 59	19,595 65	6 40	10,856 77	4,093 92
8.	27,805 71	18,205 37	61,080 66	9,113 65	...	5,218 3	3,567 6
	12,642 33	6,964 13	14,345 54	5,928 10	...	2,518 23	1,579 23
9.	51,357 25	11,160 96	12,093 67	38,606 48	... 34	8,647 51	3,617 61
	28,429 49	5,528 74	6,830 77	21,176 72	...	4,954 82	2,047 88
10.	52,946 31	10,464 40	34,121 70	32,100 30	...	1,580 69	16,966 39
	4,150 11	1,422 82	5,853 7	2,146 32	...	31 53	1,839 73
11.	30,267 48	30,873 33	54,248 36	3,563 6	197 10	2,304 32	19,843 67
	12,695 17	7,815 34	12,818 49	1,664 1	...	1,712 94	9,312 91
12.	58,937 66	14,186 63	20,629 88	41,159 76	12 3	8,385 5	924 64
	33,246 2	6,490 76	17,386 22	27,110 49	1 9	3,577 21	206 61
13.	53,618 21	2,274 58	11,750 73	49,227 89	21 82	3,418 23	52 51
	20,366 22	374 32	5,056 46	19,030 32	...	1,091 87	4 7
14.	...	...	...	...	...	...	...
...	20,366 22	374 32	5,056 46	19,030 32	...	1,091 87	4 7
	429,648 39	130,064 24	264,548 52	272,291 42	334 70	58,829 7	52,048 50
	213,989 71	54,976 62	59,034 67	139,311 23	18 55	40,049 42	20,045 15
	643,638 10	185,040 86	353,583 26	411,602 65	353 25	98,878 49	72,093 65

No. 7 (A).—Agricultural Statistics, &c.—*Continued.*

No.	FOOD GRAINS—*Continued.*						
	Wheat.	Raggy.	Varagu.	Cumboo.	Dhall.	Châma.	Korra.
	13.	14.	15.	16.	17.	18.	19.
1.	...	3,782 88	...	663 17	3,414 97	1,200 13	160 89
	...	1,013 27	...	87 69	968 4	215 88	12 90
2.	...	...	...	...	90 ...	60 ..	40 ...
3.	...	...	...	...	...	...	...
	...	...	...	...	...	...	...
4.	...	...	...	...	...	...	...
5.	...	...	...	...	...	...	...
6.	18 ...	938 36	685 45	145 26	12,049 15	198 39	892 44
	6 ...	649 46	75 2	14 ...	8,486 90	720 12	531 33
7.	...	821 58	1,258 36	272 89	1,196 5	751 77	1,702 60
	3 38	422 61	270 99	8 84	1,508 96	988 34	2029 3
8.	...	3,122 71	47 13	280 43	1,845 54	1,105 91	218 79
	...	962 60	...	79 34	1,025 23	217 92	135 83
9.	...	265 42	130 6	65 4	10,037 47	250 58	725 11
	...	295 20	60 8	2 61	3,803 57	101 1	575 21
10.	...	243 ...	...	624 98	8,009 22	250 32	54 15
	...	30 5	...	151 98	698 27	33 36	18 17
11.	...	518 37	...	2,470 81	4,476 46	1,954 37	550 21
	...	60 79	...	332 92	3,212 32	225 54	345 38
12.	...	2,244 55	240 71	1,577 19	3,179 65	258 46	592 78
	...	496 72	64 37	363 36	834 95	279 79	369 15
13.	...	336 38	...	...	511 38	...	...
	...	80 76	...	...	159 20	...	...
14.	...	...	...	...	...	...	...
...	...	...	...	...	...	...	...
	18 ...	12,272 25	2,361 ...	7,099 ...	44,809 79	6,029 93	4,936 97
	9 38	4,011 46	470 ...	1,040 ...	22,797 44	2,781 96	4,017 ...
	27 38	16,283 71	2,832 17	8,140 ...	67,607 23	8,811 89	8,953 97

No. 7 (A).—Agricultural Statistics, &c.—*Continued.*

No.	FOOD GRAINS—*Continued.*				OTHER PRODUCTS.		
	Aruga. 20.	Maize. 21.	Other Food Grains. 22.	Total. 23.	Sugar-cane. 24.	Cotton. 25.	Indigo. 26.
1.	6,332 12	38 80	...	33,456 78	951 67	4,024 6	1,129 42
	1,763 65	8 51	...	11,048 78	423 90	1,608 46	254 5
2.	20 ...	...	...	1,431 ...	...	60 ...	...
3.	...	...	...	107 99	...	...	...
	...	...	...	52 37	...	...	...
4.	...	...	...	... 43	...	...	...
5.	...	...	...	20 92	...	...	...
6.	207 65	...	...	93,072 27	138 25	7,091 9	290 24
	734 24	...	...	63,123 39	17 69	4,674 94	139 16
7.	39 98	19 20	...	43,935 15	151 42	5 8	18 87
	2 60	9 20	...	39,796 69	50 96	46 73	49 33
8.	4,130 78	68 11	...	28,718 14	18 57	949 98	1,017 57
	1,267 16	5 71	...	13,719 35	... 6	354 84	196 47
9.	181 49	2 42	...	62,499 53	49 66	5,549 63	40 ...
	41 80	3 88	...	35,162 78	22 15	2,728 14	...
10.	341 75	786 46	584 8	62,541 34	...	229 66	...
	54 42	117 85	...	5,121 68	...	12 61	3 ...
11.	1,438 53	69 89	...	37,386 79	...	2,573 3	4 ...
	222 97	1 6	...	17,090 84	...	1,146 49	...
12.	693 24	...	879 3	60,147 9	467 89	74 29	31 84
	126 29	40 54	216 88	33,687 45	265 11	22 18	18 18
13.	...	...	...	53,618 21	...	...	...
	...	...	...	20,366 22	...	...	...
14.	...	...	...	...	...	...	...
...	...	...	...	...	...	...	...
	13,385 54	984 88	1,463 11	476,865 64	1,777 46	20,556 82	2,531 94
	4,213 13	186 75	216 88	239,169 55	779 87	10,594 39	660 19
	17,598 67	1,171 63	1,679 99	716,035 19	2,557 33	31,151 21	3,192 13

No. 7 (A).—Agricultural Statistics, &c.—*Continued.*

No.	OTHER PRODUCTS—*Continued.*							
	Oil Seeds, of various sorts.	Horse Gram.	Cocoa-nuts.	Areca-nuts.	Betel-nuts.	Cheyroot and other Dyeing Roots.	Chillies.	Turmeric.
	27.	28.	29.	30.	31.	32.	33.	34.
1.	8,347 86	2,876 62	5 63	...	...	...	208 95	20 15
	1,791 93	677 18	2 ...	...	...	...	65 86	9 50
2.	30 ...	20 ...	...	...	...	...	14 ...	...
3.	...	...	...	...	...	...	...	...
	...	...	...	...	...	...	...	...
4.	...	...	...	...	...	...	...	...
5.	...	...	...	...	...	...	...	...
6.	8,196 18	1,959 11	122 20	...	25 21	...	721 84	71 73
	4,021 99	1,058 96	40 64	...	10 91	...	472 72	32 13
7.	4,294 44	1,215 29	2,254 66	78 60	1 24	...	312 66	44 75
	3,936 41	1,160 3	8,092 10	324 74	... 50	...	128 88	33 10
8.	14,651 49	2,017 4	13 36	...	...	...	23 76	...
	5,863 54	931 16	...	...	...	...	65 64	...
9.	8,525 8	2,130 81	49 16	...	...	...	387 18	86 61
	4,441 97	827 75	26 14	...	...	...	228 1	17 15
10.	8,985 85	1,110 65	3 14	...	...	...	23 20	19 40
	966 95	297 91	9 1	...	16 44	...	12 80	6 66
11.	27,286 99	2,612 99	...	...	...	...	131 ...	...
	6,051 39	1,490 88	2 ...	...	...	...	52 69	...
12.	4,411 98	1,573 6	3,172 33	...	16 76	418 74	1,218 5	47 94
	1,766 3	599 10	2,612 90	9 8	5 80	113 67	216 96	18 65
13.	1,514 13	693 76	10 46	...	...	...	7 72	1 38
	213 19	138 88	3 42	...	...	...	5 14	...
14.	...	...	...	...	...	...	...	...
...	...	...	...	...	...	...	...	...
	86,244 ...	16,209 33	5,630 94	78 60	43 21	418 74	3,048 36	291 96
	29,053 40	7,143 85	10,788 31	334 54	33 65	113 67	1,248 70	117 19
	115,297 40	23,353 18	16,419 25	413 14	76 86	532 41	4,297 6	409 15

No. 7 (A).—Agricultural Statistics, &c.—*Continued.*

No.	Tobacco. 35.	Plantains. 36.	Flax. 37.	Hemp. 38.	Durada-kanda. 39.	The Châma-root Colo-casia. 40.	Yams. 41.	Tiyya-kanda. 42.	Brinjals. 43.
	OTHER PRODUCTS—*Continued.*								
1.	31 72	7 13	96 46	47 30	...	... 23	1 6	8 7	87 31
	2 99	9 75	51 70	11 12	...	... 52	... 11	... 23	23 89
2.	...	...	...	...	...	...	...	...	...
3.	...	...	...	...	...	...	...	...	...
	...	...	...	...	...	...	...	...	...
4.	...	...	...	...	...	...	...	...	...
5.	...	...	...	...	...	...	...	...	...
6.	2,074 97	115 80	7,261 61	70 64	208 59	...	118 56	31 2	163 88
	129 78	51 94	5,040 65	44 63	119 39	... 40	62 30	10 50	47 32
7.	2,888 10	990 17	667 46	1 24	24 32	2 84	... 16	15 41	29 21
	49 45	818 1	1,134 34	10 49	57 97	4 32	... 25	9 38	70 18
8.	248 42	... 10	54 1	5 12	...	...	...	2 90	50 30
	1 14	11 43	27 53	... 11	...	...	...	2 12	37 55
9.	489 53	297 86	3,188 ...	30 64	64 91	...	... 93	5 71	59 46
	137 38	250 59	1,793 25	12 19	54 5	...	... 61	9 90	28 92
10.	286 22	4 14	...	11 95	... 10	...	...	21 19	10 13
	10 3	...	...	22 50	...	...	...	15 7	18 44
11.	391 63	13 82	144 28	...	... 47	...	...	2 22	2 17
	91 72	18 22	116 10	... 5	... 50	...	...	3 6	2 ...
12.	773 11	867 68	267 19	...	67 74	21 73	20 ...	6 8	118 29
	4 ...	340 24	239 79	... 25	12 45	8 17	10 ...	1 62	91 69
13.	... 18	22 99	...	...	7 4	...	... 38	... 68	1 ...
	4 99	1 17	...	...	... 70	...	...	...	... 40
14.	...	...	...	...	...	...	...	...	...
...	...	...	...	...	...	...	...	...	...
	7,183 88	2,319 69	11,679 1	166 39	373 17	24 80	141 9	93 28	521 75
	431 48	1,501 35	8,403 36	101 34	245 4	13 41	73 27	51 88	320 39
	7,615 36	3,821 4	20,082 37	268 23	618 21	38 21	214 36	145 16	842 14

No. 7 (A).—Agricultural Statistics, &c.—*Continued.*

No.	OTHER PRODUCTS—*Continued.*									
	Jack Trees	Benda-káya.	Fenu-greek.	Coriander Seed.	Pumpkins.	Mangoes.	Goa Mangoes.	Mustard.	Bishop's Seed.	Onions
	44.	45.	46.	47.	48.	49.	50.	51.	52.	53.
1.	...	...	...	..	... 52	2 33	...	4 ...	...	..
	...	...	...	...	... 26	...	...	...	...	...
2.	...	...	...	...	...	...	...	...	...	...
3.	...	...	...	...	...	...	...	...	...	...
	...	...	...	...	...	...	...	...	...	...
4.	...	...	...	...	...	...	...	...	...	...
5.	...	...	...	...	...	...	...	...	...	...
6.	...	...	287 50	157 50	66 24	2,200 14	...	68 81	40 ...	295 35
	...	...	172 95	110 36	5 18	1,326 37	...	36 27	32 9	97 52
7.	...	... 35	4 46	114 54	37 91	9 77	...	2 ...	...	64 16
	2 3	11 93	10 86	75 58	10 64	76 66	...	...	...	37 16
8.	...	...	...	...	13 78	...	...	...	...	11 54
	...	...	...	...	... 25	...	...	...	...	8 13
9.	...	10 20	11 56	4 55	27 54	...	...	14 18	199 89	85 90
	...	8 ...	5 74	...	10 1	...	...	... 10	68 42	3 56
10.	...	1 50	...	...	... 40	...	...	...	...	133 42
	...	...	12 50	...	... 9	...	...	...	...	27 19
11.	...	...	...	... 4	13 12	...	...	...	...	5 94
	...	... 35	...	...	...	...	...	...	...	1 23
12.	...	...	127 10	20 ...	24 79	51 66	21 68	7 ...	13 55	366 77
	1 ...	...	65 85	10 ...	...	34 41	4 13	...	4 ...	120 76
13.	...	...	...	...	1 36	...	...	...	...	13 50
	...	...	...	...	...	...	...	...	...	2 19
14.	...	...	...	...	...	...	...	...	...	...
...	...	...	...	...	...	...	...	...	...	...
	...	12 5	430 62	296 63	185 66	2,263 90	21 68	95 99	253 44	976 58
	3 3	20 28	267 90	195 94	30 67	1,437 44	4 13	36 37	104 51	297 74
	3 3	32 33	698 52	492 57	216 33	3,701 34	25 81	132 36	357 95	1,274 32

No. 7 (A).—Agricultural Statistics, &c.—*Continued.*

No.	OTHER PRODUCTS—*Continued.*										
	Garlic. 54.	Limes. 55.	Pampelmoses. 56.	Cashu-nuts. 57.	Ginger. 58.	Bíra-káya. 59.	Tamarind Trees. 60.	Sweet Potatoes. 61.	Bottle-gourds. 62.	Cucumbers. 63.	Total. 64.
1.	6 20	...	...	...	...	...	...	...	...	...	17,856 69
	2 14	...	...	...	...	...	...	...	...	...	4,935 59
2.	...	...	...	...	...	...	...	...	...	...	124 ...
3.	...	...	...	...	...	...	...	...	...	...	...
	...	...	...	...	...	...	...	...	...	...	...
4.	...	...	...	...	...	...	...	...	...	...	...
5.	...	...	...	...	...	...	...	...	...	...	...
6.	279 38	...	...	...	...	...	...	...	...	...	32,055 84
	115 78	...	...	...	...	...	...	...	...	...	17,872 55
7.	3 ...	1 70	...	...	... 2	... 70	...	...	... 12	...	13,234 65
	...	...	...	...	...	3 9	4 24	...	...	...	16,209 36
8.	...	...	...	...	...	...	...	...	29 3	...	19,106 97
	...	...	...	...	...	...	...	...	11 74	...	7,511 71
9.	6 25	13 43	...	...	3 26	23 47	...	... 76	...	...	21,356 16
	22 48	6 7	...	...	... 97	11·22	...	1 14	...	...	10,716 1
10.	99 56	...	...	...	...	44 97	...	...	...	2 ...	10,987 48
	...	...	...	...	... 25	22 75	...	1 80	...	4 50	1,442 50
11.	...	...	...	...	...	...	...	...	...	...	33,181 70
	...	...	...	...	...	...	...	...	...	...	8,976 68
12.	195 6	23 50	47 91	142 46	... 20	...	...	...	...	...	14,616 38
	80 97	12 86	105 61	54 1	... 60	...	...	...	...	...	6,830 79
13.	...	...	...	...	...	...	...	...	...	...	2,274 58
	...	...	...	...	...	...	...	...	...	...	374 32
14.	...	...	...	...	...	...	...	...	...	...	...
...	...	...	...	...	...	...	...	...	...	...	...
	589 45	38 63	47 91	142 46	3 48	69 14	...	... 76	29 15	2 ...	164,794 45
	221 7	18 93	105 61	54 1	1 82	37 6	4 24	2 94	11 74	4 50	74,869 51
	810 82	57 56	153 52	196 47	5 30	106 20	4 24	3 70	40 89	6 50	239,663 96

No. 7 (B).—Agricultural Statistics, Acreage of Crops, &c., in Agraharams for Fasli 1284 (1874–75).

No.	Taluks.	Population, as per Census of 1871.	Arable Area in Acres.	Total Acres in Holding.	No. of Acres under Crop and Fallow. Whereof under Food Grains.	Other Products.	Fallow and Waste.
1.	2.	3.	4.	5.	6.	7.	8.
1.	Rámachandrapuram	2,106	1,010 88	1,010 88	743 86	30 6	236 96
2.	Amalápuram	7,705	4,945 54	4,945 54	2,291 97	1,691 45	962 12
3.	Nursapore	2,926	3,251 45	3,251 45	675 28	32 71	2,543 46
4.	Bhímavaram	2,062	1,782 50	1,782 50	1,395 86	25 45	361 19
5.	Tanuku	11,010	14,010 96	14,208 57	7,992 48	737 48	5,478 61
6.	Ellore	15,775	28,254 42	28,254 42	9,029 70	3,470 77	5,753 95
7.	Yarnagúdem	7,591	12,264 63	12,264 63	3,536 64	1,996 78	6,731 21
8.	Rajahmundry	2,699	3,983 23	3,827 25	830 25	544 65	2,452 35
9.	Peddapore	570	580 ...	580 ...	222 ...	40 ...	318 ...
10.	Bhadráchalam	...	...	...	...	...	...
		52,444	70,083 61	70,125 24	26,718 4	8,569 35	34,837 85

No. 7 (B).—Agricultural Statistics, &c.—*Continued.*

No.	FOOD GRAINS.											
	Rice.											
	One Crop Irrigated.	Second Crop do.	Unirrigated.	Cholum.	Baggy.	Varagu.	Cumboo.	Dhall.	Cháma.	Korra.	Aruga.	Maize.
	9.	10.	11.	12.	13.	14.	15.	16.	17.	18.	19.	20.
1.	620 20	...	102 10	...	...	...	...	18 40	...	3 16	...	...
2.	826 89	... 97	871 50	252 50	40 50	...	...	134 60	63 ...	102 1	...	...
3.	435 62	...	239 66	...	...	...	...	...	...	...	...	...
4.	1,217 78	...	169 77	...	8 31	...	...	...	...	...	...	...
5.	7,018 97	...	138 42	561 73	66 65	... 90	...	360 41	2 39	2 25	16 93	...
6.	1,294 87	...	248 88	6,008 61	103 22	...	448 41	1,256 2	213 14	28 ...	173 53	121 20
7.	886 65	...	178 ...	1,259 30	322 64	...	179 ...	572 50	75 ...	41 ...	245 50	...
8.	437 15	...	33 80	13 ...	157 ...	...	30 ...	101 80	41 ...	...	16 50	...
9.	64 ...	...	...	...	58 ...	...	...	4 ...	...	...	100 ...	...
10.	...	...	...	...	...	...	...	...	...	...	...	...
	12,802 13	... 97	1,982 13	8,095 12	756 32	... 90	657 41	2,447 73	394 53	176 12	552 46	121 20

No. 7 (B).—Agricultural Statistics, &c.—*Continued.*

No.	FOOD GRAINS—*Continued.*			OTHER PRODUCTS.											
	Other Food Grains.	Wheat.	Total.	Sugar-cane.	Cotton.	Indigo.	Oil Seeds, of various sorts.	Horse Gram.	Cocoa-nuts.	Areca-nuts.	Chillies.	Tur-meric.	Tobacco.	Plantains.
	21.	22.	23.	24.	25.	26.	27.	28.	29.	30.	31.	32.	33.	34.
1.	...	...	743 86	...	3 57	...	...	20 46	...	...	12 27	...	...	5 14
2.	41 ...	...	2,332 97	7 1	...	...	116 36	85 ...	917 67	462 70	...	5 60	...	65 22
3.	...	...	675 28	...	...	...	... 95	...	...	...	8 50	...	...	...
4.	...	...	1,395 86	...	...	...	13 65	4 ...	... 20	...	1 ...	...	...	... 60
5.	...	...	8,168 65	...	79 77	...	635 30	169 33	...	...	21 14	3 44	5 54	2 75
6.	...	...	9,895 88	...	34 2	...	2,418 75	836 35	6 4	...	2 71	...	167 90	...
7.	...	...	3,759 64	...	321 50	...	1,132 88	505 92	...	...	7 50	...	39 48	...
8.	...	...	830 25	...	...	...	352 15	187 50	...	...	... 50	...	...	4 0
9.	...	...	226 ...	...	...	...	10 ...	30 ...	...	...	...	...	..	...
10.	...	...	...	...	...	...	...	...	...	...	...	...	...	...
	41 ...	...	28,028 39	7 1	438 86	...	4,680 4	1,838 56	923 91	462 70	53 62	9 4	212 92	77 71

No. 7 (B).—AGRICULTURAL STATISTICS, &c.—*Continued.*

No.	OTHER PRODUCTS—*Continued.*															
	Flax.	Hemp.	Durada-kanda.	Yams.	Tiyya-kanda.	Brinjals.	Fenu-greek.	Coriander Seed.	Mangoes.	Bishop's Seed.	Onions.	Garlic.	Limes.	Bíra-káya.	Ginger.	TOTAL.
	35.	36.	37.	38.	39.	40.	41.	42.	43.	44.	45.	46.	47.	48.	49.	50.
1.	...	...	...	... 34	...	...	...	...	...	...	1 14	...	...	...	...	42 92
2.	...	...	5 ...	...	... 14	4 25	..	...	22 ...	...	... 50	...	...	...	...	1,691 45
3.	...	...	...	...	...	... 44	...	...	...	...	16 83	5 99	...	...	...	32 71
4.	...	...	...	...	...	6 ...	...	...	...	...	...	...	...	...	...	25 45
5.	7 67	3 81	4 16	...	... 48	6 45	...	4 ...	...	28 96	1 88	8 67	...	...	...	983 32
6.	...	...	...	...	2 ...	1 ...	...	...	...	...	...	...	...	2 ...	...	3,470 77
7.	9 ...	...	...	...	1 ...	28 ...	...	...	...	...	...	...	...	...	...	2,045 28
8.	...	...	...	...	...	... 50	...	...	...	...	...	...	...	...	...	544 65
9.	...	...	...	...	...	...	...	...	...	...	...	...	...	...	...	40 ...
10.	...	...	...	...	...	...	...	...	...	...	...	...	...	...	...	...
	16 67	3 81	9 16	... 34	3 62	46 64	...	4 ...	22 ...	28 96	20 32	14 66	...	2 ...	...	8,876 55

No. 8.—STATEMENT showing the Collections under the several heads of Revenue in the District of for a Series of Ten Years.

Faslis.	Official Years.	Land Revenue.	Forest Revenue.	Abkári.	Income and Licence Tax.	Sea Customs.	Land Customs.	Salt.	Stamps.	Total.
		Rupees.	Rupees.	Rupees.	Rupees.	Rupees.	Rupees.	Rupees.	Rupees.	Rupees.
1276	1866-67	35,12,825	...	1,66,105	* 55	47,799	401	4,09,473	1,39,798	42,76,456
1277	1867-68	38,67,333	...	1,93,194	† 40,427	78,333	986	4,21,328	1,67,947	47,69,553
1278	1868-69	34,87,702	...	1,97,648	† 48,535	98,781	1,950	4,74,699	1,85,999	44,95,314
1279	1869-70	41,38,043	...	1,79,749	† 1,225	1,10,799	682	5,08,100	2,06,934	52,28,985
1280	1870-71	38,87,095	...	1,54,524	† 5 *2,24,589	1,28,087	583	5,32,890	1,98,364	50,42,684
1281	1871-72	42,66,508	...	1,62,056	* 69,533	93,906	298	5,75,656	2,16,438	53,84,395
1282	1872-73	39,00,043	...	2,19,151	* 33,299	54,844	392	5,78,633	2,21,131	50,07,493
1283	1873-74	41,50,386	...	2,43,497	* 948	78,813	200	5,45,429	2,42,845	52,62,118
1284	1874-75	42,36,416	...	2,33,985	* 9	1,60,538	216	6,21,728	2,79,625	55,32,517
1285	1875-76	43,63,693	...	2,70,211	...	1,04,735	151	6,00,399	2,96,449	56,35,638

* Income Tax. † Licence Tax.

NOTE.—The above figures have been taken from the Madras Administration Reports, and confirmed by the Board of Revenue.

No. 9.—STATEMENT showing the Total Value of Trade for a Series of Ten Years.

Official Years.	Value of Imports.			Value of Exports.			Value of Re-exports.	Gross Duty.
	Merchandize.	Treasure.	Total.	Merchandize.	Treasure.	Total.		
	Rupees.	Rupees.	Rupees.	Rupees.	Rupees.	Rupees.		Rupees.
1865–66	11,67,625	46,67,855	58,35,480	88,74,321	8,66,376	97,40,697	...	43,832
1866–67	18,14,347	17,27,914	35,42,261	64,12,041	6,83,600	70,95,641	...	46,832
1867–68	14,45,878	14,34,531	28,80,409	48,24,603	8,46,800	56,71,403	...	78,151
1868–69	18,59,388	37,61,228	56,20,616	80,57,106	2,53,990	83,11,096	...	96,966
1869–70	20,70,487	34,93,797	55,64,284	89,56,078	17,91,409	107,47,487	...	1,10,342
1870–71	19,01,118	7,23,789	26,24,907	59,21,558	31,23,713	90,45,271	...	1,27,793
1871–72	15,62,392	16,75,555	32,37,947	86,66,326	7,14,300	93,80,626	...	93,665
1872–73	13,83,215	5,49,721	19,32,936	64,39,807	10,27,600	74,67,407	...	54,389
1873–74	16,20,870	13,52,885	29,73,755	67,19,136	17,99,666	85,18,802	...	78,472
1874–75	20,42,388	4,14,642	24,57,030	90,32,539	7,55,500	97,88,039	...	1,58,658

No. 10.—STATEMENT showing the Value of Export Trade, with particulars of Articles, for a Series of Ten Years.

Articles.	Official Years.									
	1865–66	1866–67	1867–68	1868–69	1869–70	1870–71	1871–72	1872–73	1873–74	1874–75
	Rupees.	Rupees.	Rupees.	Rupees.	Rupees.	Rupees.	Rupees.	Rupees.	Rupees.	Rupees.
Bones	502	...	1,627	847	299	1,047	2,660	2,633	1,338	1,603
Coffee	...	94	...	264	...	...	...	...	...	...
Cotton Wool	...	11,60,800	12,02,755	27,16,743	35,84,759	16,57,543	42,26,132	24,69,032	15,64,320	16,31,667
Cotton Goods	2,29,469	4,15,828	2,61,656	2,14,057	3,05,249	2,78,924	1,34,123	2,75,912	1,62,992	1,80,458
Gingelly	151	...	1,079	1,512	2,135	762	7,268	5,199	12,826	3,990
Drugs	2,702	1,643	531	108	1,807	...	565	3,741	587	252
Indigo	5,324	...	248	63,987	4,019	32,243	68,925	15,840	86,682	85,072
Dyes of Sorts	1,387	6,326	4,756	9,878	14,768	9,109	41,509	45,531	63,283	1,49,351
Emigrants' Stores	...	...	...	...	...	...	...	...	...	...
Feathers	300	...	...	...	...	...	255	...	...	...
Fish Maws	300	926	80	436	1,328	699	702	2,581	466	568
Fruits and Nuts	19,220	13,772	13,734	32,764	21,686	7,366	47,396	29,351	14,858	48,251
Paddy	2,64,184	5,57,889	2,24,298	9,89,048	6,78,912	2,86,581	1,28,169	95,189	1,77,214	1,56,621
Rice	4,83,304	14,35,659	5,00,805	7,94,354	2,39,431	7,99,205	6,33,933	1,04,639	6,33,165	13,64,511
Wheat	...	...	1,343	1,302	100	...	...	69	1,546	223
Grain of Sorts	4,13,194	8,99,382	4,30,543	3,97,868	77,253	34,690	1,81,032	1,94,743	1,65,199	7.22,304
Hides	27,165	55,568	1,25,352	1,44,219	92,899	1,92,180	2,17,131	3,33,584	3,27,505	2,29,682

Horns	33,220	20,749	75,799	36,412	68,348	68,217	53,126	1,05,645	50,578	43,308
Ivory and Ivoryware	105	...	...	...	...	...	...	...	...	...
Jewellery	...	2,000	2,000	6,000	...	530	560	6,350	10,060	9,472
Mats	10	20	4	4	636	615	964	1,471	733	336
Molasses	1,03,415	63,262	2,976	97,919	810	6,601	301	1,05,279	...	1,02,448
Coir and Coir Rope	10,959	5,374	1,687	5,945	19,473	8,638	3,569	4,434	8,747	14,149
Hemp	15,161	14,847	8,518	15,567	1,04,217	44,489	71,639	29,549	26,625	64,763
Naval Stores of Sorts	216	123	685	51	...	396	594	9,116	15,475	1,359
Oil	31,796	46,342	40,586	89,298	99,597	60,599	1,44,224	1,74,929	4,08,522	3,81,670
Perfumery	240	...	...	...	...	...	...	...	...	...
Precious Stones	...	...	...	...	...	...	...	...	...	...
Salt	7,501	24,368	4,968	5,898	810	...	...	...	...	4,800
Saltpetre	...	...	3,600	...	...	...	...	...	...	...
Seeds	6,68,586	2,04,612	12,60,964	13,42,273	23,87,758	13,09,595	18,01,309	10,87,614	16,29,469	22,90,830
Shawls, Cashmere	200	...	...	...	...	...	...	...	...	...
Silk Piece Goods	41	279	...	...	...	16	946	150	...	36
Spices	54,984	1,51,994	1,04,973	73,243	20,904	30,770	47,111	2,03,158	50,809	44,517
Spirits	20,009	4,212	600	613	2,935	8,521	360	420	3,865	1,200
Sugar	3,67,858	8,40,038	55,351	6,33,024	3,29,353	1,94,772	46,532	4,64,986	1,74,983	2,34,229
Timber and Wood	12,831	7,981	12,378	17,001	7,762	16,714	2,804	14,039	11,190	9,558
Tobacco	2,35,881	2,06,588	2,43,673	2,29,074	4,85,041	3,07,116	4,57,614	5,18,678	6,22,366	6,32,241
Wax and Wax Candles	12,318	3,308	459	2,937	1,620	496	5,569	7,745	1,892	11,895
Sundries	58,51,788	2,68,057	2,36,575	1,34,460	4,02,169	5,63,125	3,39,304	1,28,200	49,183	6,11,175
Total	88,74,321	64,12,041	48,24,603	80,57,106	89,56,078	59,21,558	86,66,326	64,39,807	67,13,196	90,32,539

No. 11.—STATEMENT showing the Value of Import Trade, with particulars of Articles, for a Series of Ten Years.

Articles.	Official Years.									
	1865–66	1866–67	1867–68	1868–69	1869–70	1870–71	1871–72	1872–73	1873–74	1874–75
	Rupees.	Rupees.	Rupees.	Rupees.	Rupees.	Rupees.	Rupees.	Rupees.	Rupees.	Rupees.
Millinery and Wearing Apparel	1,006	7,908	1,578	5,337	1,351	5,381	5,605	8,289	3,610	56,538
Gold and Silver Lace and Thread	57,564	62,930	70,535	94,449	98,204	83,100	1,35,685	1,18,915	82,974	80,306
Books and Stationery	4,461	7,653	11,415	1,08,424	1,04,809	1,722	12,765	16,327	16,600	31,667
Twist and Yarn	1,03,369	9,84,138	3,37,841	4,74,341	5,59,558	5,75,638	4,94,786	4,86,640	3,99,647	5,27,478
Piece Goods, Dyed	10,784	25,749	19,774	36,943	19,274	9,823	76,864	40,195	16,904	1,00,278
Do. Printed	173	20	11,160	47,470	52,631	...	2,788	4,182	38,719	4,352
Do. Plain	9,755	34,912	79,351	1,06,234	1,27,764	1,96,440	86,259	97,247	1,25,410	1,43,353
Drugs	1,089	2,893	2,590	7,886	9,853	8,992	9,094	10,912	14,477	609
Dyes	1,445	1,168	1,522	1,957	6,945	1,087	3,142	2,131	1,220	2,223
Betelnut, Boiled	146	2,080	14	65	66	...	...	834	1,284	5,840
Do. Raw	...	...	...	...	...	...	...	3	...	...
Glassware	3,253	2,718	3,780	4,294	4,705	5,496	2,228	2,646	5,253	5,373
Paddy	42,453	82,950	14,595	26,911	4,692	94,092	7,657	10,046	10,865	16,184
Rice	91,070	19,411	2,351	26,969	10,776	90,628	9,821	13,281	28,646	13,383
Grain of Sorts	31,982	14,856	16,935	9,299	4,608	11,875	12,026	10,524	7,819	...

Gunnies and Gunny Bags	35,355	1,00,680	70,366	1,34,224	1,91,773	1,47,581	1,45,349	1,12,186	1,32,015	3,31,355
Jewellery . . .	420	11,850	500	80	1,180	5,120	670	3,780	1,290	1,321
Machinery . . .	10,292	...	255	91,780	1,51,327	14,320	11,486	22,190	30,956	2,400
Malt Liquors . .	5,204	14,088	10,447	11,107	14,101	16,020	13,863	6,427	12,959	10,693
Metals	88,140	61,446	1,25,492	2,12,499	1,74,310	1,76,242	1,46,990	69,267	76,102	2,05,572
Naval Stores . .	29,856	17,886	12,623	29,866	20,957	18,551	11,314	21,652	21,353	29,581
Oilman's Stores . .	1,129	1,278	5,750	849	4,929	535	725	2,105	8,086	2,846
Porcelain and Earthernware	16,175	3,845	4,294	555	3,267	5,198	5,174	1,128	2,811	4,574
Pipe Staves and Casks .	1,729	1,927	2,623	1,534	2,904	1,262	560	2,651	298	11,480
Provisions . . .	3,415	4,444	3,638	3,739	3,758	8,796	8,256	11,429	5,415	63,281
Railway Stores . .	...	...	...	...	...	...	...	...	...	...
Seeds	29,825	7,950	31,017	13,841	21,179	3,509	20,512	22,548	11,492	13,710
Silk, Raw . . .	480	50	1,360	1,140	311	3,647	570	275	400	840
Silk, Piece Goods .	1,657	1,010	2,424	5,315	2,577	5,187	7,885	5,561	5,765	6,942
Spices	3,623	3,935	6,782	9,423	8,509	6,883	10,534	13,143	10,748	27,102
Spirits	18,695	21,915	28,376	31,922	16,913	37,054	54,323	34,031	42,449	31,061
Tea	294	333	652	1,156	1,070	718	808	586	521	946
Timber and Planks .	1,27,599	18,223	2,61,751	87,481	30,760	63,311	21,014	47,505	43,292	94,180
Wines	26,636	27,516	30,220	36,830	10,539	42,231	34,219	49,951	27,759	24,515
Woollens . . .	5,911	681	6,175	6,054	4,581	10,041	4,557	3,403	2,691	3,177
Wool	...	1,981	...	...	...	...	...	...	...	...
Sundries . . .	4,02,640	2,63,923	2,67,692	2,29,414	4,00,306	2,50,638	2,04,863	1,31,225	4,31,040	1,89,228
Total . .	11,67,625	18,14,347	14,45,878	18,59,388	20,70,487	19,01,118	15,62,392	13,83,215	16,20,870	20,42,388

No. 12.—**Statement** showing the Number and Tonnage of Vessels which arrived at, and departed from, the District for a Series of Ten Years.

Official Years.	Square Rigged.				Native Craft.		Total.	
	Steamers.		Ships.					
	Number.	Tonnage.	Number.	Tonnage.	Number.	Tonnage.	Number.	Tonnage.
	ARRIVALS.							
1865–66	84	55,902	83	45,015	428	47,875	595	148,792
1866–67	87	54,011	75	39,223	312	39,326	474	132,560
1867–68	73	47,273	78	43,426	414	51,162	565	141,861
1868–69	77	52,752	93	45,993	411	59,352	581	158,097
1869–70	81	62,827	99	49,223	412	55,048	592	167,098
1870–71	86	78,916	93	49,301	379	48,111	558	176,328
1871–72	85	75,461	64	38,857	199	27,407	348	141,725
1872–73	87	76,366	71	45,605	257	29,027	415	150,998
1873–74	104	99,512	70	36,241	323	32,175	497	167,928
1874–75	141	156,772	114	59,688	254	30,579	509	247,039
	DEPARTURES.							
1865–66	84	55,902	78	40,627	464	51,074	626	147,603
1866–67	87	54,011	84	45,132	331	42,556	502	141,699
1867–68	73	47,273	72	41,323	438	50,477	583	139,073
1868–69	77	52,880	92	45,950	392	60,187	561	159,017
1869–70	82	62,986	100	49,225	439	55,390	621	167,601
1870–71	86	78,916	90	48,354	369	45,397	545	172,667
1871–72	85	75,461	69	41,289	225	29,371	379	146,121
1872–73	87	76,366	70	44,957	276	29,795	433	151,118
1873–74	104	99,475	69	36,647	326	33,702	499	169,824
1874–75	139	154,690	109	56,213	233	28,375	481	239,278

No. 13.—STATEMENT showing the Number and Value of Suits disposed of in the Civil and Revenue Courts for a Series of Ten Years.

Years.	Number of Suits Disposed of in the Different Courts.													
	Ordinary Suits.								Small Causes.					
	Village Munsiffs.	Revenue Courts.	District Munsiffs.	Principal Sadr Amins.	Judges of Small Cause Courts as Principal Sadr Amins.	Civil Judges and Judicial Commissioners.	Total Number of Suits.	Total Value in Rupees.	District Munsiffs, Assistant Agents, and Assistant Commissioner.	Principal Sadr Amins.	Judges of Small Cause Courts.	Civil Judges and Judicial Commissioners.	Total Number of Small Causes.	Total Value in Rupees.
1.	2.	3.	4.	5.	6.	7.	8.	9.	10.	11.	12.	13.	14.	15.
								Rupees.						Rupees.
1865	408	...	3485	37	...	32	3962	...	4469	...	...	...	4469	...
1866	487	...	3531	63	...	340	4421	...	4721	...	...	...	4721	...
1867	458	...	3578	66	...	164	4266	...	4244	...	...	...	4244	...
1868	499	...	3466	62	...	30	4057	...	4988	...	...	...	4988	...
1869	607	...	3599	50	...	4	4260	8,35,048 2 7	4250	...	...	...	4250	1,14,968 3 7
1870	838	123	3671	59	...	18	4709	8,29,133 10 3	4718	...	...	...	4718	1,25,079 10 5
1871	992	97	4204	61	...	13	5367	9,03,397 12 4	6460	...	...	...	6460	1,41,689 6 5
1872	1104	79	4840	47	...	14	6084	12,40,738 6 9	5748	...	...	...	5748	1,23,893 9 0
1873	1647	175	3954	39	...	14	5829	10,35,718 8 6	6082	148	...	...	6230	1,91,770 12 3
1874	1605	401	4014	33	...	15	6068	9,43,376 14 11	5591	213	...	...	5804	1,76,994 13 7

NOTE.—The Value of Suits for a period of 4 Years, *i.e.*, from 1865 to 1868, is not given in the Civil Statements for those years.

No. 14.—STATEMENT of Persons Tried, Convicted, and Acquitted, and of Property Lost and Recovered.

Nature of Offences. 1.	Number of Persons tried during the Year. 2.	Acquitted or Discharged. 3.	Convicted. 4.	Remaining under Trial. 5.	Property. Stolen. 6.	Property. Recovered. 7.
1865.						
					Rupees.	Rupees.
1. Murder	32	29	3	...	...	...
2. Culpable homicide	2	2	...	...	...	...
3. Rape	3	3	...	...	...	...
4. Hurts and assaults	1328	787	541	...	...	...
5. Other offences against the person	25	18	7	...	...	...
6. Dacoity	66	56	10	...	2,672	195
7. Robbery	15	13	2	...	453	27
8. Housebreaking	151	89	62	...	7,373	1,332
9. Theft	555	220	335	...	14,345	2,357
10. Other offences against property	718	444	274	...	478	230
11. Other offences against the Penal Code	847	376	471	...	...	...
Total	3742	2037	1705	...	25,321	4,141
12. Special and Local Laws	2978	720	2258	...	104	73
Total	6720	2757	3963	...	25,425	4,214
1866.						
1. Murder	22	12	10	...	...	...
2. Culpable homicide	4	4	...	...	...	...
3. Rape	...	...	...	...	...	...
4. Hurts and assaults	1194	569	625	...	...	...
5. Other offences against the person	21	8	13	...	..	...
6. Dacoity	41	30	11	...	...	...
7. Robbery	14	5	9	...	528	153
8. Housebreaking	146	59	87	...	487	154
9. Theft	704	239	465	...	18,314	1,583
10. Other offences against property	567	348	219	...	14,109	3,921
11. Other offences against the Penal Code	607	235	372	...	905	1,165
Total	3320	1509	1811	...	34,343	6,976
12. Special and Local Laws	2631	351	2280	...	109	92
Total	5951	1860	4091	...	34,452	7,068

STATEMENT of Persons Tried, Convicted, &c.—*Continued.*

Nature of Offences. 1.	Number of Persons tried during the Year. 2.	Acquitted or Discharged. 3.	Convicted. 4.	Remaining under Trial. 5.	Property. Stolen. 6.	Property. Recovered. 7.
1867.					Rupees.	Rupees.
1. Murder	16	...	16	...	...	...
2. Culpable homicide	4	1	3	...	...	...
3. Rape	...	...	...	...	...	...
4. Hurts and assaults	1327	719	608	...	...	...
5. Other offences against the person	38	27	11	...	...	...
6. Dacoity	12	7	5	...	133	24
7. Robbery	6	6	...	...	597	3
8. Housebreaking	116	51	65	...	11,695	2,106
9. Theft	723	263	460	...	13,814	4,878
10. Other offences against property	571	359	212	...	1,013	680
11. Other offences against the Penal Code	949	338	611	...	...	...
Total	3762	1771	1991	...	27,252	7,691
12. Special and Local Laws	4279	408	3871	...	70	47
Total	8041	2179	5862	...	27,322	7,738
1868.						
1. Murder	29	17	12	...	...	...
2. Culpable homicide	2	1	1	...	...	...
3. Rape	6	4	2	...	...	...
4. Hurts and assaults	1718	985	733	...	..	...
5. Other offences against the person	29	13	16	...	...	...
6. Dacoity	22	5	17	...	3,163	501
7. Robbery	36	21	15	...	932	614
8. Housebreaking	130	39	91	...	18,942	4,471
9. Theft	885	290	595	...	13,627	5,219
10. Other offences against property	603	377	226	...	2,288	580
11. Other offences against the Penal Code	950	461	489	...	...	...
Total	4410	2213	2197	...	38,952	11,385
12. Special and Local Laws	3960	443	3517	...	96	74
Total	8370	2656	5714	...	39,048	11,459

STATEMENT of Persons, Tried, Convicted, &c.—*Continued.*

Nature of Offences. 1.	Number of Persons tried during the Year. 2.	Acquitted or Discharged. 3.	Convicted. 4.	Remaining under Trial. 5.	Property. Stolen. 6.	Property. Recovered. 7.
1869.						
					Rupees.	Rupees.
1. Murder	17	11	6	...	...	...
2. Culpable homicide	10	1	9	...	...	...
3. Rape	7	1	6	...	...	...
4. Hurts and assaults	1761	920	841	...	...	...
5. Other offences against the person	31	12	19	...	6	6
6. Dacoity	5	...	5	...	1,100	11
7. Robbery	20	8	12	...	401	117
8. Housebreaking	112	34	78	...	12,353	2,657
9. Theft	908	285	623	...	21,536	7,482
10. Other offences against property	554	239	315	...	1,933	519
11. Other offences against the Penal Code	1090	502	588	...	...	...
Total	4515	2013	2502	...	37,329	10,792
12. Special and Local Laws	4218	491	3727	...	99	85
Total	8733	2504	6229	...	37,428	10,877
1870.						
1. Murder	32	25	7	...	745	...
2. Culpable homicide	10	2	8	...	...	...
3. Rape	5	5	...	...	...	...
4. Hurts and assaults	1595	899	696	...	...	...
5. Other offences against the person	21	9	12	...	...	...
6. Dacoity	...	...	...	...	59	...
7. Robbery	21	9	12	...	184	106
8. Housebreaking	131	56	75	...	17,754	1,520
9. Theft	1037	337	700	...	15,028	7,182
10. Other offences against property	451	185	266	...	3,730	740
11. Other offences against the Penal Code	1512	453	1059	...	...	...
Total	4815	1980	2835	...	37,500	9,548
12. Special and Local Laws	4008	419	4480	...	103	83

STATEMENT of Persons Tried, Convicted, &c.—*Continued.*

Nature of Offences. 1.	Number of Persons tried during the Year. 2.	Acquitted or Discharged. 3.	Convicted. 4.	Remaining under Trial. 5.	Property. Stolen. 6.	Property. Recovered. 7.
1871.						
					Rupees.	Rupees.
1. Murder	24	15	9	...	196	183
2. Culpable homicide	8	4	4	...	...	...
3. Rape	3	2	1	...	...	...
4. Hurts and assaults	1847	1045	802	...	...	...
5. Other offences against the person	30	11	19	...	...	...
6. Dacoity	16	5	11	...	110	2
7. Robbery	10	6	4	...	461	146
8. Housebreaking	173	62	111	...	18,452	4,212
9. Theft	1067	510	557	...	18,339	4,780
10. Other offences against property	687	364	323	...	5,108	930
11. Other offences against the Penal Code	1579	576	1003	...	...	...
Total	5444	2600	2844	...	42,666	10,253
12. Special and Local Laws	4257	909	3348	...	101	82
Total	9701	3509	6192	...	42,767	10,335
1872.						
1. Murder	20	13	7	...	...	...
2. Culpable homicide	13	9	4	...	...	...
3. Rape	1	1	...	...	...	...
4. Hurts and assaults	2499	1716	783	...	...	...
5. Other offences against the person	188	143	45	...	75	...
6. Dacoity	20	18	2	...	1,806	1,022
7. Robbery	38	17	21	...	453	56
8. Housebreaking	206	92	114	...	20,897	4,002
9. Theft	1358	658	700	...	32,591	7,970
10. Other offences against property	1523	1159	364	...	16,974	6,424
11. Other offences against the Penal Code	1840	594	1246	...	...	...
Total	7706	4420	3286	...	72,796	19,474
12. Special and Local Laws	3401	651	2750	...	123	85
Total	11107	5071	6036	...	72,919	19,559

STATEMENT of Persons Tried, Convicted, &c.—*Continued.*

1873.

Nature of Offences. 1.	Number of Persons tried during the Year. 2.	Acquitted or Discharged. 3.	Convicted. 4.	Remaining under Trial. 5.	Property. Stolen. 6.	Property. Recovered. 7.
					Rupees.	Rupees.
1. Murder	33	20	13	...	68	8
2. Culpable homicide	17	11	6	...	...	...
3. Rape	5	3	2	...	...	...
4. Hurts and assaults	1683	874	809	...	...	...
5. Other offences against the person	92	50	42	...	16	1
6. Dacoity	38	37	1	...	1,106	802
7. Robbery	10	2	8	...	519	34
8. Housebreaking	174	33	141	...	35,704	4,057
9. Theft	767	199	568	...	25,835	11,639
10. Other offences against property	1131	765	366	...	6,108	1,701
11. Other offences against the Penal Code	1224	421	803	...	...	...
Total	5174	2415	2759	...	69,356	18,242
12. Special and Local Laws	3066	944	2122	...	92	62
Total	8240	3359	4881	...	69,448	18,304

1874.

Nature of Offences. 1.	Number of Persons tried during the Year. 2.	Acquitted or Discharged. 3.	Convicted. 4.	Remaining under Trial. 5.	Property. Stolen. 6.	Property. Recovered. 7.
1. Murder	14	2	12	...	...	...
2. Culpable homicide	25	23	2	...	...	...
3. Rape	1	1	...	...	...	...
4. Hurts and assaults	1722	992	730	...	66	...
5. Other offences against the person	92	48	44	...	...	...
6. Dacoity	15	15	...	...	954	76
7. Robbery	19	13	6	...	1,176	671
8. Housebreaking	219	44	175	...	53.578	3,441
9. Theft	775	136	639	...	14.739	3,887
10. Other offences against property	999	654	345	...	4,253	673
11. Other offences against the Penal Code	970	389	581	...	...	...
Total	4851	2317	2534	...	74.766	8,748
12. Special and Local Laws	[illegible]	[illegible]	[illegible]	[illegible]	[illegible]	[illegible]

No. 15.—STATEMENT showing the Expenditure on Public Works from Imperial and Provincial Funds for the Years 1870–71, 1871–72, 1872–73, 1873–74, and 1874–75.

Years.	Imperial.					Provincial.			
	Miscellaneous Public Improvements.	Communications.	Civil Buildings.	Agricultural.	Total.	Civil Buildings.	Communications.	Miscellaneous Public Improvements.	Total.
	Rupees.	Rupees.	Rupees.	Rupees.	Rupees.	Rupees.		Rupees.	Rupees.
New Works.									
1870–71	...	481	14,185	97,587	1,12,253	...	...	...	...
1871–72	...	...	13,738	1,64,965	1,78,703	7,269	...	...	7,269
1872–73	...	...	7,942	2,75,511	2,83,453	26,510	...	...	26,510
1873–74	637	..	6,010	2,65,418	2,72,065	34,705	...	...	34,705
1874–75	...	...	2,575	3,44,730	3,47,305	4,663	...	2,791	7,454
Repairs.									
1870–71	5,684	17,519	3,859	1,54,241	1,81,303	...	...	...	..
1871–72	...	...	...	1,58,300	1,58,300	5,110	...	1,544	6,654
1872–73	...	...	...	1,77,356	1,77,356	4,350	...	4,968	9,318
1873–74	...	...	...	1,86,121	1,86,121	5,669	...	7,423	13,092
1874–75	...	.	648	1,76,978	1,77,626	4,276	...	5,203	9,479

No. 16.—STATEMENT showing the Receipts and Expenditure

RECEIPTS.	1870-71	1871-72	1872-73	1873-74	1874-75
		Rupees.	Rupees.	Rupees.	Rupees.
1. Balance	Act IV. of 1871 was brought into operation after 1871-72, and consequently this column is left blank.	1,71,618	1,08,720	1,74,836	1,46,432
2. Provincial Grants for Roads		31,060	42,020	42,020	42,020
3. Provincial Grants for Schools		480	480	480	480
4. Provincial Grants for General Purposes		...	...	...	...
5. Surplus Pound Fund		12,653	12,059	5,954	7,618
6. Avenues		521	821	578	1,185
7. Grass Rents		14,595	18,381	10,006	654
8. Miscellaneous		827	410	204	43
9. Road-cess under Act III. of 1866		1,40,191	12,888	1,437	145
10. Land-cess under Act IV. of 1871		1,12,854	2,52,149	3,60,992	2,94,929
11. Tolls		...	...	...	...
12. House Tax		...	260	5,951	3,846
13. Cesses under Act VI. of 1863		2,403	8,918	...	...
14. Fees in Schools and Training Institutions		...	...	...	179
15. Contributions		20,000	10,100	100	80
16. Educational Receipts		...	...	...	146
17. Sale of Elementary Books		...	...	...	35
18. Choultry Receipts		...	2,936	4,576	4,475
19. Fees from Travellers' Bungalows		...	311	125	114
20. Balance of Bungalow Fund		...	667	...	...
21. Fines and Penalties		...	...	...	...
22. Sale of other Property		...	...	...	...
23. Public Works Receipts		940	23,937	1,778	5,465
24. Do. Refunds of Expenditure		...	...	29,122	66,025
25. Miscellaneous		...	3,731	17	1,575
26. Miscellaneous Debt Accounts		1,12,387	7,270	25	22
Carried forward		6,20,529	5,06,058	6,38,201	5,75,468

Local Funds under Act IV. of 1871 for Five Years.

Expenditure.		1870–71	1871–72	1872–73	1873–74	1874–75
		Act IV. of 1871 was brought into operation after 1871–72, and consequently this column is left blank.	Rupees.	Rupees.	Rupees.	Rupees.
New Works.						
1. Communications	By P. W. Dept.		3,15,867	1,24,569	2,57,360	2,05,673
	By Other Agency		...	10,161	1,515	...
2. Educational	By P. W. Dept.		...	...	...	...
	By Other Agency		...	...	...	...
3. Sanitary and Miscellaneous	By P. W. Dept.		574	5,377	5,710	12,351
	By Other Agency		734	...	...	...
Repairs.						
4. Communications	By P. W. Dept.		37,880	54,903	63,022	60,015
	By Other Agency		...	10	184	...
5. Educational	By P. W. Dept.		...	19	...	...
	By Other Agency		...	...	...	...
6. Sanitary and Miscellaneous	By P. W. Dept.		9,349	9,486	12,337	15,359
	By Other Agency		98	...	...	225
7. Public Works Department Supervision			79,046	46,276	81,484	59,737
8. Petty Establishment			4,140	5,898	11,758	1,200
9. Tolls and Ferries			707	330	400	562
10. Tools and Plant			2,685	2,469	6,237	1,510
11. Refunds of Fines			...	...	...	13
12. Contributions to other Circles			20,000	10,000	...	...
Total Grant I.			4,71,080	2,69,498	4,40,007	3,56,645
13. Payment for Inspection			2,933	4,536	5,037	1,688
14. Training Schools			280	1,040	2,380	185
15. Local Fund Schools			11,602	22,658	21,160	24,743
16. Purchase of Books, &c.			...	...	175	439
17. Salary Grants			312	307	155	60
18. Result Grants			3,378	4,295	4,708	3,255
Total Grant II.			18,505	32,836	33,615	30,370
19. Hospitals and Dispensaries			...	...	...	225
20. Vaccine Establishment			2,469	2,766	2,651	2,732
21. Sanitary Establishment, Cleansing of Tanks and Wells, &c.			16,150	10,071	3,543	8,783
22. Choultry Establishment			...	2,782	5,461	3,862
23. Travellers' Bungalow Establishment			...	509	431	422
24. Miscellaneous			1,070	1,824	1,690	4,350
Total Grant III.			19,689	17,952	13,776	20,374
25. Establishment at the Presidency and in the Collector's and Local Fund Board's Offices, and Contingencies			2,215	3,640	3,990	4,652
26. Refunds			6	16	321	326
27. Incorrect Credits of District Road Fund and Balances written back			...	...	28	...
Total Grant IV.			2,221	3,656	4,339	4,978
28. Miscellaneous Debt Accounts			314	7,280	32	20
Total Expenditure			5,11,809	3,31,222	4,91,769	4,12,387
29. Balance			1,08,720	1,74,836	1,46,432	1,63,081
Grand Total			6,20,529	5,06,058	6,38,201	5,75,468

No. 17.—STATEMENT showing Receipts and Expenditure for Special Funds for Five Years.

	1870-71.					1871-72.			1872-73.			1873-74.			1874-75.		
	Balance at the beginning of the Year.	Receipts during the Year.	Total.	Expenditure during the Year.	Balance at the end of the Year.	Receipts during the Year including Balance.	Expenditure during the Year.	Balance at the end of the Year.	Receipts during the Year including Balance.	Expenditure during the Year.	Balance at the end of the Year.	Receipts during the Year including Balance.	Expenditure during the Year.	Balance at the end of the Year.	Receipts during the Year including Balance.	Expenditure during the Year.	Balance at the end of the Year.
	Rupees.	Rupees.	Rupees.	Rupees.	Rupees.	Rupees.	Rupees.	Rupees.	Rupees.	Rupees.	Rupees.	Rupees.	Rupees.	Rupees.	Rupees.	Rupees.	Rupees.
1. Jungle Conservancy Fund	5,371	2,391	7,762	941	6,821	9,487	648	8,839	12,189	385	11,804	13,827	4,830	8,997	13,812	6,268	7,544
2. Nanal Grass Fund	...	...	...	...	...	...	...	...	...	...	...	...	...	...	...	...	...
3. Cattle Pound Fund	10,363	16,760	27,323	14,670	12,653	31,886	16,987	14,899	30,215	28,545	1,670	16,663	16,366	297	21,650	21,312	338
4. Public Bungalow Fund	656	804	1,460	615	845	1,636	620	1,016	1,189	1,189	...	...	...	...	...	...	...
5. Endowment Fund	8,900	3,523	12,423	3,169	9,254	14,717	3,236	11,481	12,321	1,356	10,965	10,965	...	10,965	10,965	...	10,965
6. Village Service Fund	2,357	62,091	64,448	12,216	52,232	2,62,273	81,005	1,81,268	3,25,460	1,70,186	1,55,274	5,06,674	2,38,004	2,68,670	5,66,344	3,32,946	2,33,400
7. Canal and Ferry Fund	...	...	...	...	...	13,134	215	12,919	28,053	1,391	26,662	45,437	2,701	42,736	61,330	1,006	60,324
8. Irrigation Cess Fund	...	...	...	...	...	...	...	...	...	...	...	...	...	...	...	...	...
Total	27,847	85,569	1,13,416	31,611	81,005	3,33,133	1,02,711	2,30,422	4,09,427	2,03,052	2,06,375	5,93,566	2,61,901	3,31,665	6,74,202	3,61,530	3,12,571

No. 18.—STATEMENT showing the Progress of Education for a Series of Ten Years.

Description of Schools.		1866-67. No. of Schools.	1866-67. No. of Pupils. Boys.	1866-67. Girls.	1867-68. No. of Schools.	1867-68. No. of Pupils. Boys.	1867-68. Girls.	1868-69. No. of Schools.	1868-69. No. of Pupils. Boys.	1868-69. Girls.	1869-70. No. of Schools.	1869-70. No. of Pupils. Boys.	1869-70. Girls.	1870-71. No. of Schools.	1870-71. No. of Pupils. Boys.	1870-71. Girls.
A. Government Schools— 1. Maintained from Imperial or Provincial Funds	Higher	1	196	...	1	201	...	1	202	...	1	196	...	1	198	...
	Middle	3	170	...	3	202	...	3	132	...	1	85	...	2	137	...
	Lower	...	...	...	...	...	...	...	...	...	...	...	...	...	...	...
2. Maintained from Local or Municipal Funds	Higher	...	...	...	...	...	...	...	...	...	...	...	...	...	...	...
	Middle	..	...	...	...	...	...	6	200	...	3	107	...	3	90	...
	Lower	2	51	...	68	978	...	...	...	...	55	862	...	45	787	...
Total		6	417	...	72	1381	...	10	534	...	60	1250	...	51	1212	...
B. Schools Aided— 1. By Salary Grants	Higher	...	...	...	...	...	...	1	43	...	3	434	...	3	450	...
	Middle	19	1095	...	41	1942	...	37	1798	...	30	1257	...	27	1088	...
	Lower	71	947	...	...	...	...	59	847	...	37	982	...	4	114	...
2. By Results Grants	Higher	...	...	...	..	...	...	...	...	...	...	...	...	...	...	...
	Middle	...	...	...	...	...	...	...	...	...	...	...	...	...	...	...
	Lower	...	...	...	...	...	...	...	...	...	...	...	...	72	1769	...
3. Combined Salaries and Results Grants	Higher	...	...	...	...	...	...	...	...	...	...	...	...	...	...	...
	Middle	...	...	...	...	...	...	...	...	...	.	...	...	...	...	...
	Lower	..	...	...	...	...	...	...	...	...	...	...	...	...	...	...
Total		90	2042	..	41	1942	...	97	2688	...	70	2673	...	106	3421	...
C. Schools under Inspection for Results Grants, but not aided	Higher	...	...	...	...	...	...	...	...	...	...	...	...	...	...	...
	Middle	...	...	...	...	...	...	...	...	...	...	...	...	...	...	...
	Lower	...	...	...	...	...	...	...	...	...	...	...	...	...	...	...
Total		...	...	...	...	...	...	...	...	...	...	...	...	...	...	...
Candidates passed the Uncovenanted Civil Service Examination			56			45			28			40			19	
Do. do. Special Tests			70			58			40			39			89	
Do. do. Matriculation			...			4			2			2			7	
Do. do. First Arts			...			1			2			...			...	
Total			126			108			72			81			115	

Description of Schools.		1871-72. No. of Schools.	1871-72. No. of Pupils. Boys.	1871-72. Girls.	1872-73. No. of Schools.	1872-73. No. of Pupils. Boys.	1872-73. Girls.	1873-74. No. of Schools.	1873-74. No. of Pupils. Boys.	1873-74. Girls.	1874-75. No. of Schools.	1874-75. No. of Pupils. Boys.	1874-75. Girls.	1875-76. No. of Schools.	1875-76. No. of Pupils. Boys.	1875-76. Girls.
A. Government Schools— 1. Maintained from Imperial or Provincial Funds	Higher	1	193	...	1	219	...	1	196	...	1	197	...	1	251	...
	Middle	2	123	...	3	160	...	2	92	...	2	99	...	2	105	...
	Lower	...	...	...	...	...	...	2	56	...	2	103	...	2	100	...
2. Maintained from Local or Municipal Funds	Higher	...	...	...	...	...	...	...	...	...	...	...	...	...	...	..
	Middle	3	150	..	3	121	...	3	150	...	3	105	...	...	...	...
	Lower	159	3264	...	168	3751	...	168	3507	...	207	4765	...	217	6093	...
Total		165	3730	...	175	4251	...	176	4001	...	215	5269	...	222	6549	...
B. Schools Aided— 1. By Salary Grants	Higher	3	442	...	3	413	...	3	257	...	2	273	...	3	432	...
	Middle	26	1007	...	16	567	...	14	705	...	13	707	...	10	641	...
	Lower	4	88	...	8	225	...	4	188	...	2	94	...	2	100	...
2. By Results Grants	Higher	...	...	...	...	...	...	...	...	...	...	...	...	...	...	...
	Middle	...	...	...	6	156	...	16	568	...	14	445	...	8	334	...
	Lower	83	1968	...	98	2371	...	108	2401	...	136	3141	...	196	4699	...
3. Combined Salaries and Results Grants	Higher	...	...	...	...	...	...	...	...	...	...	...	...	...	...	...
	Middle	...	...	...	...	...	...	...	...	...	...	...	...	...	...	...
	Lower	...	...	...	...	...	...	...	...	...	...	...	...	31	796	...
Total		116	3500	...	131	3732	...	145	4119	...	167	4660	...	250	7002	...
C. Schools under Inspection for Results Grants, but not aided	Higher	...	...	...	...	...	...	...	...	...	...	...	...	...	...	...
	Middle	...	...	...	...	...	...	...	...	...	...	...	...	...	...	...
	Lower	...	...	...	...	...	...	...	...	...	...	...	...	...	...	...
Total		...	...	...	...	...	...	...	...	...	...	...	...	...	...	...
Candidates passed the Uncovenanted Civil Service Examination			23			66			45			47			25	
Do. do. Special Tests			28			39			38			38			39	
Do. do. Matriculation			16			14			24			36			27	
Do. do. First Arts			...			...			...			3			7	
Total			67			119			107			124			98	

There are two Girls' Schools, one at Rajahmundry, supported by H.H. the Maha Rajah of Vizayanagaram, and the other at Cocanada, supported by the Rajah of Pittapore.

No. 19.—STATEMENT showing Receipts and Expenditure of the several Municipal Commissions for a Series of Five Years.

Years.	Municipal Towns.	Receipts.												Expenditure.							Balance.
		Rate on Houses and Lands.	Trade Tax.	Tolls.	Tax on Carriages and Animals.	Registration of Carts.	Licences.	Fines.	State Contribution.	Arrears including Balance.	Miscellaneous.	Other Receipts and Advances Recovered.	Total.	New Works.	Repairs.	Conservancy.	Police.	Establishment.	Miscellaneous.	Total.	
1870–71	Cocanada	Rs. 4,183	4,515	2,136	380	80	534	501	3,433	7,577	305	158	23,802	9,394	No Accounts were kept to show distinctly the amount spent on repairs.	2,677	4,005	1,461	2,755	20,292	3,510
	Rajahmundry	2,543	2,966	2,802	434	124	509	698	1,410	1,932	1,050	38	14,506	3,922		3,697	2,876	1,392	601	12,488	2,018
	Ellore	2,290	3,286	2,889	...	468	657	121	2,441	3,330	...	32	15,514	2,990		4,106	2,621	1,696	453	11,866	3,648
	Total	9,016	10,767	7,827	814	672	1,700	1,320	7,284	12,839	1,355	228	53,822	16,306		10,480	9,502	4,549	3,809	44,646	9,176
1871–72	Cocanada	6,066	6,740	3,734	347	126	556	554	440	3,510	329	21	22,423	11,530		3,853	663	1,469	3,441	20,956	1,467
	Rajahmundry	3,605	2,874	4,213	412	120	534	420	2,814	2,018	301	...	17,311	5,946		4,060	273	2,107	1,625	14,011	3,300
	Ellore	3,033	3,216	3,882	...	540	450	321	1,526	3,648	357	...	16,973	7,580		4,136	437	1,308	804	14,265	2,708
	Total	12,704	12,830	11,829	759	786	1,540	1,295	4,780	9,176	987	21	56,707	25,056		12,049	1,373	4,884	5,870	49,232	7,475
1872–73	Cocanada	5,754	5,955	3,483	689	178	659	1,746	3,238	1,467	1,043	2,455	26,667	10,063		7,284	...	2,437	5,409	25,793	1,474
	Rajahmundry	3,043	5,609	1,890	674	136	1,006	881	1,325	3,300	841	881	19,086	3,056		6,203	...	1,387	4,977	15,623	3,463
	Ellore	3,283	3,444	4,640	...	603	383	134	...	2,708	176	...	15,371	3,047		4,915	...	1,102	935	9,999	5,372
	Total	12,080	15,008	10,013	1,363	917	2,048	2,761	4,563	7,475	2,060	2,836	61,124	16,166		18,402	...	4,926	11,321	50,815	10,309
1873–74	Cocanada	5,494	5,372	3,800	698	162	876	473	5,402	1,474	1,302	83	25,136	7,012		3,921	...	3,044	7,562	21,539	3,597
	Rajahmundry	3,365	4,604	2,251	499	141	1,244	534	1,658	3,463	2,231	...	19,990	3,380		6,357	...	1,229	5,833	16,799	3,191
	Ellore	3,125	3,206	4,400	...	812	535	183	...	5,372	154	...	17,787	4,316		3,146	...	1,341	1,680	10,483	7,304
	Total	11,984	13,182	10,451	1,197	1,115	2,655	1,190	7,060	10,309	3,687	83	62,913	14,708		13,424	...	5,614	15,075	48,821	14,092
1874–75	Cocanada	8,449	414	4,582	...	259	822	1,189	1,847	3,597	3,246	1,523	25,928	8,493		4,080	...	2,110	9,120	23,803	2,125
	Rajahmundry	4,604	1,446	2,277	493	138	1,337	226	1,253	3,191	5,343	475	20,783	3,214		6,106	...	956	4,782	15,058	5,725
	Ellore	3,362	398	6,115	...	708	1,013	348	...	7,304	535	...	19,783	9,418		2,646	...	1,198	2,637	15,899	3,884
	Total	16,415	2,258	12,974	493	1,105	3,172	1,763	3,100	14,092	9,124	1,998	66,494	21,125		12,832	...	4,264	16,539	54,760	11,734

No. 20.—STATEMENT showing the Particulars of the several Tenures other than Ryotwary.

	Names of the Zemindaris and Inam Villages.	The entire Beriz of the Estate for Fasli 1284, or A.D. 1874-75.			Peshcush or Quit-Rent for Fasli 1284, or A.D. 1874-75.		
	1	2.			3.		
	ZEMINDARIS.	Rupees	A.	P.	Rupees	A.	P.
1	Végayyammapéta	17,196	2	2	8,464	4	7
2	Pánangipalli	2,975	6	6	737	12	8
3	Mukkámala	482	3	2	107	12	0
4	Vilasa	2,639	12	0	1,440	11	6
5	Jánupalli	242	10	6	218	6	8
6	Bantumilli	884	10	7	200	0	0
7	Sirasavilli Savaram	610	0	0	300	3	11
8	Nidadavólu and Baharzalli	3,22,102	12	1	1,19,468	5	4
9	Ambapéta	22,267	10	1	16,142	6	3
10	Tangalamúdi	17,155	5	1	5,203	4	5
11	Singanagúdem	501	14	3	46	0	0
12	Telikicherla	...			962	8	0
13	Gundópalli	1,719	3	3	962	8	0
14	Jálimúdi	745	4	0	277	0	11
15	Undéshwarapuram	1,272	7	6	630	0	4
16	Pittápuram	5,51,231	3	10	2,50,160	7	6
17	Kottám	82,995	0	0	26,429	3	9
18	Bhadráchalam and Rékapalli	26,495	3	7	16,797	0	0
	Total	10,91,516	12	7	4,48,547	15	10
	MUTTAS.						
1	Vella	4,704	14	2	1,240	2	6
2	Kapiléshwarapuram	19,255	0	0	8,778	0	6
3	Viravallipálem	13,793	14	3	3,536	10	5
4	Nadavapalli	6,252	11	0	3,129	3	4
5	Késhanakurru	18,430	12	2	11,577	14	5
6	Krípa	4,306	15	7	2,385	13	9
7	Anatavaram	2,196	0	5	1,764	0	9
8	Surasani Yánám	629	8	0	529	4	3
9	Magam	2,850	8	5	1,746	13	4
10	Potukurru	1,774	11	0	910	13	5
11	Mungandapálem	2,152	5	5	545	8	0
12	Guttinadivi	6,209	11	0	776	12	0
13	Gópálapuram	60,917	3	2	18,540	3	2
14	Palivela	42,294	13	2	19,240	12	0
15	Yelamanchili	11,891	11	4	8,824	10	1
16	Chinchináda	2,312	4	4	1,651	10	5
17	Chinna Manidipalli	348	4	0	255	2	7
18	Nérédumilli	699	0	0	445	4	5
19	Varidhanam	605	12	0	546	9	4
20	Konitiváda	4,928	1	2	2,004	5	3
21	Náráyanapuram	6,921	12	8	2,966	0	0
22	Duddipúdi	495	14	2	378	0	0
23	Vasantaváda	25,165	12	11	7,353	14	9
24	Malakacherla	2,821	7	0	1,495	0	0
25	Timmannagúdem	122	7	11	64	8	9
26	Vadlapatlanútanam	162	9	6	86	11	9
27	Anumunilanka	1,582	4	3	611	0	0
28	Jangáreddigúdem	789	8	0	499	10	0
	Carry forward	2,44,615	13	0	1,01,884	7	2

STATEMENT of Tenures—*continued.*

	Names of the Zemindaris and Inam Villages. 1.	The entire Beria of the Estate for Fasli 1284, or A.D. 1874–75. 2.			Peshcush or Quit-Rent for Fasli 1284, or A.D. 1874–75. 3.		
		Rupees	A.	P.	Rupees	A.	P.
	Brought forward	2,44,615	13	0	1,01,884	7	2
29	Bayyanagúdem . . .	1,724	12	0	1,008	12	4
30	Billumilli	2,293	6	9	1,619	13	6
31	Lakkavaram . . .	3,825	13	9	2,643	9	9
32	Borrampálem . . .	3,917	15	3	1,938	15	7
33	Végavaram	1,070	5	9	787	15	5
34	Kondagúdem . . .	2,371	12	0	753	8	8
35	Yernagúdem . . .	4,307	14	7	1,725	9	3
36	Yadavólu	7,460	15	11	2,161	15	5
37	Gauravaram . . .	588	2	0	145	2	3
38	Jagannádhapuram . .	341	0	0	117	15	3
39	Kalavalapilli . . .	3,379	1	9	1,346	13	8
40	Vonakaramilli . . .	2,035	10	9	1,630	8	7
41	Tyájampúdi . . .	9,500	0	0	2,791	4	6
42	Kurukúru				1,482	9	10
43	Gauripatnam . . .	4,098	10	9	1,853	14	4
44	Dhumantinagúdem . .	335	0	0	142	7	8
45	Bhimólu	7,911	3	7	3,031	0	0
46	Chidipi	2,312	11	9	1,676	12	6
47	Gútála	16,334	11	5	6,749	5	3
48	Annadévarapéta . . .	10,869	2	9	3,895	8	0
49	Prakkilanka . . .	19,954	8	4	1,822	12	3
50	Malakapalli . . .	5,398	6	10	2,282	0	0
51	Nallamillipádu . . .	554	5	0	203	4	11
52	Nandigúdem . . .	3,375	5	0	380	6	10
53	Gangólu	3,734	7	4	1,264	13	10
54	Payidemetta . . .	738	10	6	110	1	8
55	Peddéham	5,515	12	3	2,628	11	0
56	Dharmavaram . . .	5,539	11	5	2,402	15	11
57	Tirugudumetta . . .	3,876	14	0	1,856	10	8
58	Pólavaram	18,920	8	7	6,727	13	0
59	Patesham	12,538	2	3	5,249	3	0
60	Marumonda . . .	3,884	14	0	1,850	2	0
61	Buchempóta . . .	1,857	10	2	738	10	0
62	Hukumpóta . . .	1,902	4	0	1,401	15	0
63	Katavasam . . .	3,527	8	6	2,135	0	0
64	Bommúru	1,279	9	0	833	6	2
65	Vangalapúdi . . .	14,770	6	0	3,817	10	0
66	Dundangi	2,911	5	0	551	12	4
67	Víravaram	4,182	6	7	554	10	7
68	Pettamutta . . .	2,611	2	0	583	3	9
69	Dontamúru . . .	11,037	4	1	3,248	0	0
70	Ráyavaram	8,085	1	2	1,998	8	0
71	Jaggampóta . . .	70,759	5	8	33,072	10	0
72	Víravaram	95,054	9	5	26,876	8	0
73	Kírlampúdi . . .	65,892	1	8	23,306	8	0
74	Gollaprólu	34,073	12	3	11,673	7	2
75	Kólanka	48,374	12	4	14,352	8	10
76	Uppáda and Aminabáda .	2,359	14	0	673	0	7
77	Mallavaram	7,504	15	2	947	4	11
	Carry forward	7,89,509	12	3	2,92,931	11	4

STATEMENT of Tenures—*continued.*

	Names of the Zemindaris and Inam Villages. 1.	The entire Beriz of the Estate for Fasli 1284, or A.D. 1874-75. 2			Peshcush or Quit-Rent for Fasli 1284, or A.D. 1874-75. 3.		
		Rupees	A.	P.	Rupees	A.	P.
	Brought forward	7,89,509	12	3	2,92,931	11	4
78	Patavala and Gurajanapalli .	5,462	13	4	1,471	8	0
79	Nílapalli	1,151	6	0	481	4	0
80	Injaram	12,824	0	9	3,222	0	9
	Total	8,08,948	0	4	2,98,106	8	1
	Polliams.						
	Tótapalli	46,462	0	0	6,310	0	0
	Total Zemindaris, Muttas, and Polliams . . .	19,46,926	12	11	7,52,964	7	11
	SHRÓTRIAM VILLAGES.						
1	Ambikapalli	190	0	0	108	6	0
2	Yédarapalli	1,665	7	5	342	8	6
3	Sattipalli	814	12	6	30	6	0
4	Khandrika	678	0	0	82	8	0
5	Vakkalanka	2,219	7	2	470	2	0
6	Mungonda	4,651	3	1	1,711	14	6
7	Sakurru	1,618	2	0	386	4	0
8	Nadupúdi	2,008	8	0	990	11	1
9	Valivéla	...			747	0	0
10	Minumanchilipádu . .	...			221	0	0
11	Vaddiparru	...			921	8	0
12	Utada	...			200	0	0
13	Narasingarázapuram . .	1,169	10	10	294	9	9
14	Pennáda	3,975	1	8	1,095	13	2
15	Véndra	510	11	2	324	8	9
16	Itempúdi	879	4	10	110	4	8
17	Bhattamugutúru . .	5,692	9	4	680	10	2
18	Bódapádu	1,203	13	5	210	8	0
19	Chébrólu Khandrika . .	470	1	1	141	12	0
20	Chintapalli	2,901	4	10	302	2	0
21	Dévaracheruvu Khandrika .	379	5	9	30	0	0
22	Dontavaram	784	4	5	111	14	0
23	Yélátipádu	2,099	8	3	550	0	0
24	Jattipálem	4,552	2	3	1,276	6	0
25	Kórumilli	1,697	9	1	547	12	3
26	Kottapalli	3,274	2	11	745	1	8
27	Narasimha Apparowpuram .	544	2	3	41	8	0
28	Paddala	2,092	4	4	738 (28 and 29)	0	0
29	Gópinádhapatnam . . .	708	15	3			
30	Tállapuram	524	6	5	141	8	0
31	Tammaráda	1,289	2	9	277	0	0
32	Umamahéswaram . . .	917	1	11	183	12	0
33	Vallúrupalli	1,905	13	2	193	5	3
34	Venkatádri Apparowpuram .	2,227	10	3	144	6	5
35	Vipparti Khandrika . .	261	4	9	55	0	0
36	Yagarlapalli	661	0	6	211	14	0
37	Yellamilli	1,645	4	0	858	4	0
	Carry forward	56,212	3	7	15,478	4	2

STATEMENT of Tenures—*continued.*

	Names of the Zemindaris and Inam Villages. 1.	The entire Beriz of the Estate for Fasli 1284, or A.D. 1874-75. 2.			Peshcush or Quit-Rent for Fasli 1284, or A.D. 1874-75. 3.		
		Rupees	A.	P.	Rupees	A.	P.
	Brought forward	56,212	3	7	15,478	4	2
38	Kúnavaram . . .	1,051	6	0	488	12	0
39	Chendrempálem Agraháram	162	10	3	32	0	0
40	Chipuragúdem . . .	286	13	9	201	0	0
41	Dadavilli	73	13	10	30	0	0
42	Dorasánipádu . . .	830	11	3	109	0	0
43	Yadavalli of Gundugólu Pargana . . .	346	0	0	311	4	0
44	Yadavalli of Chintalapúdi .	433	12	4	86	6	0
45	Gauravaram . . .	464	12	0	68	8	0
46	Gadigunta	1,082	10	3	264	0	0
47	Havalilingapálem . .	...			60	2	0
48	Venkatakrishnápuram .	491	10	0	...		
49	Idulagunta . . .	101	5	6	23	0	0
50	Jagannádhapuram . .	374	0	0	226	2	0
51	Kommara (Northern portion)	274	15	3	177	0	0
52	Lakshminarasimhápuram .	22	0	0	42	0	0
53	Lingagúdem . . .	50	0	0	35	4	0
54	Lingaravapálem . . .	40	12	0	17	8	0
55	Malasánigunta . . .	180	0	0	75	0	0
56	Malléshwaram Mokhása .	53	0	0	45	0	0
57	Malléshwaram Agraháram .	84	4	4	27	4	0
58	Múlajalampádu . . .	305	0	0	287	8	0
59	Nágulapalli	519	15	0	304	2	0
60	Palasigúdem . . .	85	0	0	22	6	0
61	Pattayagúdem . . .	102	0	0	87	2	0
62	Ponukumadu . . .	100	0	0	88	4	0
63	Rállagunta	153	9	8	126	0	0
64	Rámannapálem . . .	375	13	3	140	4	0
65	Ravulagunta . . .	300	0	0	27	8	0
66	Rácherla	443	8	0	77	14	0
67	Sattanagúdem . . .	152	0	2	83	0	0
68	Sattala	160	1	6	24	0	0
69	Sitánagaram . . .	100	0	0	36	2	0
70	Talarapalli	66	0	0	57	0	0
71	Tedlam	...			272	8	0
72	Asanagúdem . . .	390	0	0	...		
73	Venkampálem . . .	350	0	0	122	2	0
74	Puppalavárigúdem . .	315	12	0	211	6	0
75	Jógulagunta . . .	150	10	0	77	0	0
76	Kamavarapukóta . .	1,801	14	0	1,430	8	0
77	Timmápuram . . .	512	15	0	211	12	0
78	Médipalli Agraháram . .	326	2	6	162	12	0
79	Isukapalli	1,554	0	0	771	15	6
80	Jagannapéta . . .	503	0	0	264	6	0
81	Kadakatla	1,681	13	9	992	2	0
82	Kondaprólu . . .	1,552	5	0	723	12	0
83	Kunchanapalli . . .	905	10	0	919	14	0
84	Prattipádu. . . .	810	0	0	1,039	6	6
85	Jadepalligúdem . . .	1,560	15	9	153	12	2
	Carry forward	77,894	13	11	26,511	12	4

STATEMENT of Tenures—*continued.*

	Names of the Zemindaris and Inam Villages. 1.	The entire Beriz of the Estate for Fasli 1284, or A.D 1874-75. 2.			Peshcush or Quit-Rent for Fasli 1284, or A.D. 1874-75. 3.		
		Rupees	A.	P.	Rupees	A.	P.
	Brought forward	77,894	13	11	26,511	12	4
86	Venkatrámannagúdem	268	12	0	180	0	0
87	Arulla	1,125	0	0	644	3	3
88	Krishnápuram	420	3	0	155	8	0
89	Shríniváspuram Agrahâram	186	8	0	25	0	0
	Total	79,895	4	11	27,516	7	7
	INAM VILLAGES.						
1	Puttakonda	720	0	0	78	0	0
2	Husanbáda	1,337	8	0	1	12	0
3	Mernipádu	899	11	0	22	14	0
4	Gunnepalli	3,770	1	0	45	10	0
5	Korumillipádu	439	9	3	16	0	0
6	Chivatapúdi	4,618	1	2	181	12	0
7	Túrpulanka	4,463	4	4	274	0	0
8	Machapuripálem	...			38	8	0
9	Pentapádu	2,138	15	1	177	6	0
10	Podalada	748	11	0	32	4	0
11	Tállamudunaripádu	1,039	15	1	32	8	0
12	Venkatrámapuram	885	12	10	45	14	0
13	Narasimhápuram	350	0	0	105	0	0
14	Jagannádhapuram	243	15	4	22	0	0
15	Morampúdi	1,359	2	3	102	6	0
16	Yillapalli	...			72	0	0
17	Rálla Khandrika	...			36	0	0
18	Ámudála Chilaka	19	8	0	4	0	0
19	Guruvubotlagúdem	38	0	0	8	10	0
20	Gudipádu, a hamlet of Chintalapúdi	5	0	0	2	8	0
21	Gudipádu, a hamlet of Yerraguntapalli	43	8	0	2	0	0
22	Kottúru	1,920	13	6	187	0	0
23	Potunúru	464	13	6	87	12	0
24	Rangapuram Khandrika	20	0	0	5	0	0
25	Senechakrapuram	74	8	0	3	4	0
26	Sayannarávupálem	90	0	0	5	0	0
27	Sómavaram	24	0	0	4	0	0
28	Venkatráyapuram	24	0	0	5	2	0
29	Mankanapalli	157	0	6	24	0	0
30	Shrirámavaram	104	6	0	10	6	0
31	Sarapuram	217	12	0	0	12	0
32	Ayyavváripólavaram	411	0	0	10	8	0
33	Kanavaram	100	0	0	12	0	0
34	Pallepúdi	301	4	0	37	0	0
35	Tógammi	2,728	0	0	1,042	4	0
36	Venkatráyapuram	279	8	5	62	6	0
	Total	30,027	12	3	2,797	6	0
	Total Shrótriam and Inam Villages	1,08,873	9	2	30,313	13	7

No. 21.—Statement showing the Actual Collections under all Items of Revenue from the Year 1820.

Year.	Fasli.	Collector.	Revenue.	Remarks.
		Rajahmundy District.	Rupees.	
1820–21	1230	Mr. Robertson.	21,45,863	Ordinary year.
1821–22	1231	" "	22,84,322	" "
1822–23	1232	" "	22,44,885	Sir T. Munro visited district. Exports and extra sources high.
1823–24	1233	" "	21,84,747	Famine.
1824–25	1234	Mr. Kindersley.	25,74,936	Good year. Crops abundant.
1825–26	1235	Mr. Hanbury.	23,41,727	Ordinary year. Prices still very high.
1826–27	1236	Messrs. Gardiner, Bayard, and Anstey.	25,04,382	Produce abundant.
1827–28	1237	Mr. Anstey.	23,64,114	Ordinary year. Large balance of Peshkush.
1828–29	1238	" "	24,88,739	Factories abolished, on which the annual expenditure was eight lacs.
1829–30	1239	Messrs. Anstey and Crawley.	23,42,254	Insufficient rain.
1830–31	1240	Mr. Crawley.	23,60,094	Favourable year. Produce large.
1831–32	1241	" "	20,78,769	Abundant rain. Hurricane.
1832–33	1242	" "	19,11,466	Famine. High floods and storm.
1833–34	1243	" "	26,91,719	Continued dearth. Prices enormous. Revenue realised by the Asara system. Largest annual revenue ever collected before the construction of the anicut.
1834–35	1244	" "	26,43,534	Ordinary year.
1835–36	1245	Messrs. Lewin and Grant.	19,61,855	Insufficient rain.
1836–37	1246	Mr. Grant.	21,56,484	Unseasonable rain.
1837–38	1247	Mr. G. A. Smith.	21,42,002	
1838–39	1248	" "	17,28,112	Hurricane and inundation of the sea. Extreme distress.
1839–40	1249	" "	17,44,087	Extreme distress.
1840–41	1250	" "	17,36,105	Scanty rain.
1841–42	1251	" "	20,99,136	Seasonable weather. Abundant crops, but large imports of rice from Arracan.
1842–43	1252	" "	19,63,190	Ordinary year.
1843–44	1253	Mr. Smith, Sir H. C. Montgomery, and Mr. Prendergast.	17,25,841	Sayer abolished. Great destruction from floods.

STATEMENT of Revenue—*continued.*

Year.	Fasli.	Collector.	Revenue.	Remarks.
			Rupees.	
1844–45	1254	Mr. C. J. Bird (Acting).	23,30,507	Favourable year.
1845–46	1255	Mr. Prendergast.	19,95,639	Scanty rain. Several estates bought in.
1846–47	1256	,, ,,	24,27,498	Abundant produce. Joint rent. Export of rice. Annicut commenced.
1847–48	1257	,, ,,	24,96,649	Bikkavole and Kápavaram receive water.
1848–49	1258	,, ,,	23,33,071	Indifferent.
1849–50	1259	,, ,,	22,45,468	Heavy floods and inundation. Considerable loss.
1850–51	1260	,, ,,	24,19,756	High floods. Rice crop abundant.
1851–52	1261	,, ,,	24,50,406	Ordinary year. Rain abundant.
1852–53	1262	,, ,,	25,01,963	Very high floods. Inconsiderable damage.
1853–54	1263	,, ,,	24,45,199	Drought and consequent high prices.
1854–55	1264	Mr. Purvis.	25,49,163	Tolerably favourable season.
1855–56	1265	,, ,,	25,65,371	
1856–57	1266	,, ,,	26,82,468	
1857–58	1267	,, ,,	26,46,380	Unfavourable season.
1858–59	1268	,, ,,	30,23,701	Favourable season.
		GODAVERY DISTRICT.		
1859–60	1269	Mr. Purvis.	32,17,044	Rearrangement of the district.
1860–61	1270	,, ,,	41,41,739	Commencement of the Income Tax.
1861–62	1271	,, ,,	39,22,148	Unfavourable season.
1862–63	1272	,, ,,	40,98,076	New Settlement introduced into the Western Delta.
1863–64	1273	Mr. H. Morris (Acting), Mr. Newill.	41,65,308	
1864–65	1274	Mr. Fraser.	43,47,997	
1865–66	1275	,, ,,	49,16,951	New Settlement introduced into the Eastern and Central Deltas.
1866–67	1276	,, ,,	42,76,456	Income Tax abolished.
1867–68	1277	Mr. Fraser, Mr. J. H. Master (Acting).	47,69,553	Licence Tax imposed.
1868–69	1278	,, ,,	44,95,314	
1869–70	1279	,, ,,	52,28,985	
1870–71	1280	Mr. H. E. Sullivan (Acting)	50,42,684	Income Tax reimposed.
1871–72	1281	,, ,,	53,84,395	
1872–73	1282	Mr. W. S. Foster.	50,07,493	
1873–74	1283	,, ,,	52,62,118	Income Tax abolished.
1874–75	1284	,, ,,	55,32,517	Favourable season.
1875–76	1285	Mr. J. Hope (Acting).	56,35,638	,, ,,

No. 22.—STATEMENT showing the Length of the Canals in the Godavery District, and the Number of Miles they are Navigable.

Length of Canals.	No. of Miles Navigable.	Remarks.
Miles.	Miles.	EASTERN DELTA.
29½	29½	Main channel, or Cocanada canal, navigable from Annicut to Covoor Lock.
37¼	23½	Bank canal, not navigable from 23½ to 38th mile.
22½	22¼	Coringa canal, navigable from head to Manjair lock.
10	10	Injeram canal, navigable from 22d mile on Coringa canal to 32d mile.
32¾	32¾	Samulcotta canal, navigable from 4th mile on Main canal to Samulcotta and Cocanada.
13½	13½	Mundapetta canal, navigable from 6½ miles on Main canal to 20th mile (into Coringa canal).
145½	131½	+ 14½ miles, the unnavigable portion of the Bank canal = 146 miles.
		CENTRAL DELTA.
8	8	Main duct, navigable from head to 8th mile.
32	27	Ralli main canal or Amalapur canal. Proposed to extend navigation to Sallapilly, 5 miles.
14	2	Bendamurlunka canal, navigable to Indupilly weir. Proposed to extend it to Bendamurlunka, 12 miles.
44	28	Gannaram or West Bank canal, navigable to Razole, or 36th mile. Proposed to extend it to Goundee, or 52d mile.
...	2½	Manepilly branch canal, navigable 2½ miles.
41	35	East Bank canal to Mogaltippa, navigable between June and December.
4	4	Billakurru canal, navigable. Junction canal to East Bank canal and Amalapoor canal.
7	7	Vilsa canal, navigable. This is seldom used owing to a rough stone regulating dam at its head.
7	1	Kaddalli channel } Minor irrigation branches in Nagaram Island.
2½	2½	Manepilly channel } Minor irrigation branches in Nagaram Island.
159½	114½	

STATEMENT of Canals—*continued.*

Length of Canals.	No. of Miles Navigable.	Remarks.
Miles.	Miles.	WESTERN DELTA.
6·5	6·5	Main canal, navigable from Annicut to Chettipett Calingulah.
40·27	40·27	Ellore canal, navigable from Chettipett Calingulah to Ellore.
22·29	22·29	Weyeru canal, navigable from Perimella lock to Yelurpad tidal lock.
20·80	14·73	Undi canal, navigable from Venkiah canal to Undi. There are 5 miles 7 chains of unnavigable canal below Undi.
15·75	15·75	Attili canal, navigable from Ellore canal to Attili.
40·0	40·0	Kakarapurru canal, navigable from Chettipett to Peravelli and Nursapur canal from Peravelli to Mogultur (tidal lock) *via* Nursapur.
28·35	28·35	Gostanaddi and Velpur canal, navigable from 1 mile 30 chains from head of Kakaraparru canal to Basavaroo Kodu drain.
25·40	25·40	Bank canal, navigable from 8 miles 65 chains from head of Kakarapurru canal to Godavery river near Latchmeswaram.
10·29	10·29	Kakarapurru canal, navigable from Chettipett Calingula to Peravilli.
2·32	2·32	Mukkamala canal, navigable from Bank canal to Mukkamala lock.
3·43	3·43	Junction canal, navigable from Ellore canal to near Duvva.
7·45	7·45	Venkiah canal, navigable from end of Junction canal to Perimella lock.
223·40	217·33	
528·40	463·33	Grand Total.

J. BEATTY, R.E.
District Engineer.

No. 23.—LIST of the Products mentioned in the Agricultural Statistics commencing p. 340.

English.	Telugu.	Botanical Name.
Rice	Vari	Oryza sativa.
Cholum (Millet)	Jonna	Sorghum vulgare.
Raggy	Rági	Eleusine corocana.
Varagu	Varigelu	Panicum pilosum.
Cumboo (Spiked millet)	Sazza / Gante	Penicillaria spicata.
Dhall	Anumulu	Dolichos lablab.
Cháma (Small millet, Somolina)	Tsámulu	Panicum frumentaceum.
Korra (Italian millet)	Korra	Setaria Italica.
Aruga (Common millet)	Aruga	Paspalum frumentaceum.
Indian corn	Mokka jonna	Zea mays.
Sugar cane	Cheruku	Saccharum officinarum.
Cotton	Patti	Gossypium herbaceum.
Indigo	Nili	Indigofera tinctoria.
Horse gram	Ulavulu	Dolichos uniflorus.
Cocoa-nut	Tenkáya	Cocos nucifera.
Areca-nut	Vakkalu	
Betel-nut	Tamalapáku	Chavica betel.
Chey root	Chiru-véru	Oldenlandia umbellata.
Chillies	Mirapa-káyalu	Capsicum frutescens.
Turmeric	Pasupu	Curcuma longa.
Tobacco	Pógáku	Nicotiana tabacum.
Plantains	Ariti-káyalu	Musa paradisiaca.
Flax	Gógu-nára	Hibiscus cannabinus.
Hemp	Zanumu	Crotalaria juncea.
Indian root	Durada-kanda	Arum campanulatum.
Cháma	Cháma-gadda	Colocasia antiquorum.
Yams	Pendalam	Dioscorea alata.
Edible root	Tiyya kanda	Arum campanulatum.
Brinjals (Egg plant)	Van-káyalu	Solanum melongena.
Jack fruit	Panasa-káyalu	Artocarpus integrifolia.
Benda	Benda-káyalu	Abelmoschus esculentus.
Fenugreek	Menti	Trigonella fœnum Græcum.
Coriander seed	Dhaniyam	Coriandrum sativum.
Pumpkins	Gummadi-káyalu	Cucurbita maxima.
Mangoes	Mámidi-káyalu	Mangifera Indica.
Mustard	'Aválu	Sinapis ramosa.
Bishop's weed	'Omamu	Ptychotis ajowan.
Onions	Vulli-gaddalu	Allium cepa.
Garlic	Tella gaddalu	Allium sativum.
Limes	Nimma-káyalu	Citrus bergamia.
Pamplemoses	Pamparamása-káyalu	Citrus decumana.
Cashu nuts	Jidimámidi-káyalu	Anacardium occidentale.
Ginger	Allam	Zingiber officinale.
Béra	Bira-káyalu	Loffa acutangula.
Tamarinds	Chinta-káyalu	Tamarindus Indica.
Sweet potatoes	Genusu-gaddalu	Batatas edulis.
Bottle gourds	'Anapa-káyalu	Cucurbita lagenaris.
Cucumbers	Dósa-káyalu	Cucumis utilissimus.

INDEX.

THE END.